Historics

In the increasingly busy and crowded knowledge-based economy, history dominates. Through 24/7 news bulletins; in the press; in fashion; on TV in films, docu-dramas, and documentaries; in novels, biographies and monographs; through local history associations, membership of the National Trust or English Heritage; at family visits to museums and theme parks; through local and national remembrance ceremonies, 'sites of memory' and rituals of commemoration, history shapes the fabric of experience at every turn.

In this highly original, fascinating and engaging study, Martin L. Davies examines the consequences of living in such a historicized world and offers a critique of our obsession with historical knowledge, revealing how history informs and underpins narratives central to our understanding of identity and society. The concept of historics, Davies argues, reveals how history has become an empty category – a repository of promiscuous meanings – and how it has become embedded in matrices of power and governance.

Martin L. Davies is Reader in History at the University of Leicester. He is author of *Identity or History?* (1995).

Historics
Why History Dominates
Contemporary Society

Martin L. Davies

Routledge
Taylor & Francis Group

LONDON AND NEW YORK

First published 2006
by Routledge
2 Park Square, Milton Park, Abingdon, Oxon OX14 4RN

Simultaneously published in the USA and Canada
by Routledge
270 Madison Ave, New York, NY 10016

Routledge is an imprint of the Taylor & Francis Group

Transferred to Digital Printing 2005

© 2006 Martin L. Davies

Typeset in Sabon by Keyword Group

British Library Cataloguing in Publication Data
A catalogue record for this book is available
from the British Library

Library of Congress Cataloging in Publication Data

Davies, Martin L.
Historics/Martin L. Davies.
p.cm.
Includes bibliographical references and index.
1. History—Philosophy.
2. History—Psychological aspects. I. Title
D16.9.D29   2005
901—dc22
2005002653

ISBN10: 0-415-26166-X (pbk)
ISBN10: 0-415-26165-1 (hbk)

ISBN13: 9-78-0-415-26166-1 (pbk)
ISBN13: 9-78-0-415-26165-4 (hbk)

Contents

Preface

Historics is cultural criticism. It presents a critique of historicized culture. It focusses on the contemporary historicizing mentality. In going into what this prevailing obsession with history means, it attempts to outline the scope of the present "sense" of history. It is part of a larger project to discover what's behind the humanities disciplines, how they conceal real knowledge deficits, what their knowledge claims in practice amount to. It comes out of an interest in the history of ideas, which leads one inevitably into thinking about how knowledge is produced, which, in turn, raises the question of how historical knowledge is fabricated – a dialectical thought-process that overcomes the historical interest it started with.

Historics sets out to question both academic and public confidence in historical knowledge as a foundational discipline in the humanities. That's why it focusses on the question of history's "sense". That's also why it gives relatively little attention to two key issues in the academic theory of history: historical narrative and social memory. It merely alludes to the question of narrative, because a vast literature on it already exists (e.g. Ankersmit 2001; Berkhofer 1997; Munslow 2003; Ricœur 1983/1985; White 1985, to name but very, very few) the deconstructionist critique it often comes with is too narrow to challenge the legitimacy of historical knowledge, and it would have distorted the central discussion of history's characteristic illusionism. (In any case, Sande Cohen's *Historical Culture* (1988) already offers a radical critique of historical writing that *Historics* could not improve on.) *Historics* also has relatively little to say on the issue of memory. That's because, according to its underlying conceptual structure, memory is an aesthetic issue (– unless it is understood purely technically, as the electronic storage and management of data).

That's because the counterpart to a *Historics* concerned with how ordinary, personal experience, memory included, is sequestrated by the history technology for politically affirmative reasons, would be an *Aesthetics* that would reassert the ever actual, material imperatives of personal social existence.

I would like to thank Marsha Meskimmon for her encouraging comments on the typescript at quite an advanced stage.

Sarah Beal, Matthew Bull, Victoria Mannering, and Jessica Shanks took time after their summer exams to sample parts of the typescript and make helpful comments, for which I am grateful.

I must also thank the readers consulted by Routledge who first approved the project and those who evaluated the final typescript. In particular, I must say how indebted I am to Alan Munslow and Beverley Southgate for their comments and criticisms: they helped in strengthening the argument, though perhaps not as they intended.

I must say how grateful I am to Vicky Peters for taking this project on. I must thank her, Liz Gooster, and Philippa Grand at Routledge for their encouragement and helpful advice during the process of writing.

Finally, this book is for Rasida – for reminding me what the real issues are.

Acknowledgements

The extract from Ludmilla Jordanova, *History in Practice* (Arnold, 2000) is © Ludmilla Jordanova. Reproduced by permission of Edward Arnold.

The value of a thought can be measured by the distance which keeps it from being continuous with what is known already. It declines tangibly as this distance decreases; the closer it gets to the pre-determined standard, the more its antithetical function diminishes, and only this, its declared relationship to its opposite, not its isolated presence, justifies the claim it makes.

– Theodor W. Adorno, *Minima Moralia*

...
So in the world: 'tis furnished well with men,
And men are flesh and blood, and apprehensive;
...

– William Shakespeare, *Julius Caesar*

Introduction
Getting at What is Behind History: the Concept of *Historics*

The already historicized world

The already historicized world is a world not just dominated by history, but dominated by history as knowledge already known, as the same old thing – as the dominant idea of our time. 'There is no telling what history will encompass next', says Nietzsche in *The Joyful Science*, surely ironically: it was always clear what the development of history as a human science would mean (Nietzsche 1988: III, 404, §34). The historicizing mentality would absorb everything. Everything would go down in history: everything would be historicized, everything acquire a historical finish. The fabric of experience would dissolve into history, the particular textures of ordinary days irretrievable without it.

History does dominate the public mind: its hold over the social imagination is total. History is a 'mass activity' that 'has possibly never had more followers than it does today, when the spectacle of the past excites the kind of attention earlier epochs attached to the new' (Samuel 1994: 25). Virtually anyone can contribute to historical consciousness – philologists and musicologists, bibliographers and archivists, librarians and collectors, popular illustrators and cartoon animators, stand-up comics and the impresarios of open-air museums, do-it-yourself enthusiasts and the directors of television costume-dramas, so 'history . . . is rather, a social form of knowledge; the work, in any given instance, of a thousand different hands' (Samuel 1994: 8).

Professional, academic historians, however, have doubts about this public interest. Certainly, when humanities disciplines need to prove their social value, they gladly affirm history's popular resonance. They can talk of making history "relevant", of aligning academic and social interests. But they are also sceptical about the depth of public knowledge. They can point to public ignorance of dates, incidents, or personalities in national history, to the mass media distorting history by going for dramatic, photogenic, or human interest appeal, or to the political manipulation of social memory. In terms of content, these deficiencies in public knowledge simply indicate that, on a routine level, history is not a distinctive value, but one value amongst many others. But precisely for that reason, their prevalence only reinforces history professionals' expertise as indispensably corrective, as the vital guarantee of society's self-knowledge.

However, the historicization of social interests creates a blind spot. Once "historical" and such associated epithets as "traditional", "period", and "heritage" are applied to *anything* (e.g. from monographs and ruins, homes and interior design, recipes and fashions, ancient woodlands and Victorian warehouses, latrines for Roman soldiers and National Trust properties) by *anyone* (e.g. from radical nationalists to unreconstructed communists, New Age ecologists and corporate public-relations managers, wealthy land-owners and redundant coal-miners, property-developers and countryside preservationists), "history" itself actually means specifically *nothing* (cf. Samuel 1994: 205ff., 259ff.). In an already historicized world, the qualitative distinction between academic and public historical interests collapses. They're just different versions of the same generalized historical consciousness.

Dominating the public mind, dominating public institutions, history also has a total hold over knowledge. Particularly in the university, in the human sciences, it is synonymous with the *research mentality*. Professional history can encompass a wide range of different knowledge practices (e.g. learning "dead" languages, other alphabets, palaeography, statistics, econometrics, etc.). A wide range of professional knowledge practices, based on sources and evidence (e.g. genetics, archaeology, medicine, biology, zoology, climatology, astronomy, etc.), feed into history (cf. Pomian 1999: 392–3). No wonder it is consecrated as the pre-eminent university discipline. No wonder either that it can claim to be the 'ultimate humanistic discipline' (Southgate 1996: 137). Structuralism tried to challenge it, but from that struggle it emerged victorious and extended its empire over the natural sciences (with, e.g., cosmology becoming a history of the universe, geology a history of the earth, etc.). The twentieth century will surely have been even more significant for history than the nineteenth (Pomian 1999: 9–10).

But here too it's easy to miss the trick. Professional historians celebrate history's manifold "varieties", its comprehensive "pluralism". But they're just euphemisms for history's 'incurable heterogeneity' (Pomian 1999: 404). Certainly, it may be explained by the inevitable 'historicity of history' – by history as a discipline having evolved in history through various historiographical practices and functions. But this explanation only compounds the problem: history must be heterogeneous because history's history was heterogeneous. It exemplifies the identitary thinking, the "tautological redundancy", that typifies historians' disciplinary self-reflection. Consequently, the call for a 'history of history' intended to link 'the history of knowledge with the different purposes it serves' is the ultimate conceit (cf. Pomian 1999: 159). The intention is unexceptionable, because its result would be heterogeneous. History is so much the case, there's no case it could ever exclude.

'History is the way in which we conceive the world *sub specie praeteritorum* ... the attempt to organize the whole world of experience in the shape of past events.' (Collingwood 1978: 152). This is the dominant feature of an already historicized world: experience cannot be conceived *except* in the shape of past events – except as knowledge already known, as the same old thing. *Historics* confronts both this social domination of historical heterogeneity and the mentality that legitimizes it. *It attacks the arrogance of a social practice that not only organizes the world in the shape of past events, but imposes its practice as the sole, exclusive way of organizing it.* It rejects the claim, typical of history in an already historicized world, that history "naturally" organizes human reality. Instead, *Historics* starts with the realization that, containing everything, history can be anything, hence its organizational capacity is fundamentally spurious. It recognizes it has no special cognitive virtue. Or rather it perceives that history's special virtue is precisely its lack of virtue: that being heterogeneous, it is a repository of promiscuous meanings.

Consequently, *Historics* treats the public predisposition towards history as symptomatic of a world already historicized. The already historicized world is made by the past. It is also made by all the historical knowledge of that past and by all the historians working in, and now still working on, it. Hence, all knowledge reverts to being historical knowledge. Being known in the past or in relation to the past, all historical knowledge is knowledge already known. The public, therefore, can't help being disposed towards history. It has no option: history dominates. History comes at it 24/7 in news bulletins, in the press, in fashion, on TV in films, docu-dramas, and documentaries, let alone in novels, biographies, and erudite monographs. It fosters sociability through local history associations, membership of the National Trust or English Heritage, or family outings to living museums. It crops up in a host of local and national "sites of memory". It imposes its rituals of commemoration: e.g., a few months ago the bi-centenary of the death of Immanuel Kant, more recently the tenth anniversary of the Rwandan genocide, last week the fifteenth anniversary of the Tiananmen Square massacre, just now the sixtieth anniversary of D-Day.

Further, in the already historicized world knowledge is already known because it ensures the continuance of the same old thing. Talk to any historian, he or she always comes up with an antecedent to show that this *latest thing* is actually the same as the *same old thing*. In history the latest knowledge is by definition old knowledge, because it comes from and concerns the past (i.e. what was already, or could have been, known then). The already historicized world, imperious with inherent historical precedence, inevitably engulfs the latest thing. (The modern motor-car with safety air-bags, electronic engine-management, satellite navigation-system still only does now relatively what the Model T Ford did then. Both only constitute in their own time the *latest thing* in the history of transport.) In an already historicized world, historical self-consciousness thus creates affirma-tive, diachronic identities. The latest thing, superseded by a still later thing, is transformed into the same old thing. The terrorist train-bombing in Madrid (March 2004), referred to as "Europe's 9/11", thus becomes the "same thing" as the attack on the World Trade Center (September 2001), and creates a historical ideal-type known as "9/11s" that will now always recur in the same old way. The recent (2003) violent régime change in Iraq turns out to be the same as all the other violent régime changes since the time of Nebuchadnezzer. Iraq's cultural identity will apparently ensure that 'to define the wished-for future', the new interim government will 'turn ... to historical precedent'. In such a culture where the same old thing evidently keeps recurring 'the distant past still wields such power' (MacGregor 2004: 18).

Because the latest thing always turns out to be the same as the same old thing, a historically self-conscious world will comprise both the archaic and the actual, the pre-modern and the postmodern. In a historically self-conscious world they do co-exist and reinforce each other. That also makes history heterogeneous.

The concept of *historics*

Historics is the theory of history for an already historicized world. Unlike the proliferating theory of history produced within the discipline by professional historians and history theorists, it does not primarily attempt to say what history *is* (cf. Carr 1968). Certainly, it recognizes that it's possible to ask rhetorically: 'what ... the significance [is] of the carefully "constructed" accounts of the past which historians produce, if they cannot be regarded as largely true descriptions of what happened' (McCullagh 1998: 57). But then it still wants to ask what the social function of those 'true descriptions' actually comes down to. Starting with an already historicized world, a world in which history is *the* socially dominant idea, *Historics* examines what history *does*.

It takes a cool look. Its cue is the word "domination": the idea that history dominates, that history is a dominant, even "victorious" idea (cf. Pomian 1999: 9). This idea arouses suspicion – that 'the dominant ideas of a time were always only the ideas of the dominant classes' (Marx 1968: 546). *The German Ideology* (1845/1846) elucidates this inference from *The Communist Party Manifesto* (1848). The class that is the dominant economic power in society is also its dominant intellectual power. The class that controls the means of material production thereby controls the means of intellectual production: it thus dominates the thinking of those who don't. This means, therefore, that 'the dominant ideas are nothing other than the ideal expression of the dominant material conditions, the dominant material conditions formulated in thought [i.e. in intellectual form]'. They are 'the conditions that enable a class to dominate, the thoughts [i.e. the intellectual form] of their domination' (Marx 1968: 373–4). Furthermore, bourgeois society is the material product of a material production process, the production process history itself is. The capitalist system it depends on is also a material production process: it turns living labour into a steadily accumulating mass of dead commodities. The result is that 'in bourgeois society the past thereby dominates the present' (Marx 1968: 541). The world of bourgeois material and intellectual domination is, therefore, an already historicized world. That clinches it: that's where *Historics* starts. It intends to challenge the attitudes "naturally" instilled by history in an already historicized world: the expectation of the same old thing, resignation towards how things are.

Historics takes it as axiomatic that history, the socially dominant idea of an already historicized world, is the intellectual instrument of dominant socio-economic interests. What history is, comes from what history does; what history does, affirms dominant material interests.

It does so in two ways. *First*, history promotes "affirmative culture": i.e. that use of culture by dominant socio-economic interests to dispense in an ideal, intellectual form the personal fulfilment they withhold in material, social terms (Marcuse 1973: 66). This is where all the guff about history as "rich heritage", as "enduring legacy", as "long tradition", as "inalienable identity" comes from. This is why the discipline dolls itself up in moral idealism such as 'providing an awareness of the development of differing values, systems and societies and the inculcation of critical yet tolerant personal attitudes' (Quality Assurance Agency 2000: 2). That's what makes 'historical knowledge ... a precious source of wisdom essential to the efficient formulation of social, economic, political and military policy' (McCullagh 2004: 8).

Second, history represents dominant socio-economic interests in their ideal, intellectual form. The significations it employs 'support capitalist culture by perpetuating its elementary cultural categories – exchange, loss, acquisition, pseudo-communion'; its academic functions 'can be suggestively compared with contemporary monetary relations' (Cohen 1988: 36–7, 40). This is where the axiom needs refining and why *Historics* must get at what's behind history. Certainly, in terms of content, historical truth does correct social memories, empirical historical research does offset public opinion, historical evidence does dispel unfounded allegation. Outside the former Communist states, Marxist history itself could hardly have been called affirmative. For *Historics*, however, neither historical content nor this content's ideology is the issue. Both were always heterogeneous: Marxist history (in particular) was always only one type of history amongst a variety of types. Instead, *Historics* focusses on what is essentially a form of catachresis: why historical truth is ultimately various, historical objectivity heterogeneous. Who benefits when 'cultural relativism is compatible with historical truth' (McCullagh 1998: 171)? Who or what needs "truth" as "heterogeneous variety"?

This has to be a formal issue, a question of the intellectual principle behind it. That's why the argument involves historics, not historiography. *Historics* 'is the *organon* of the discipline, its theory of knowledge'. Its purpose is to make its practitioners and readers aware of what goes into, what justifies historical thinking and research (Droysen 1977: 44). But Droysen's *Historik* (1857/1882) promoted an affirmative view of history. Its systematic defence of the autonomy of historical thought was a cultural strategy to 'engender a certain kind of reading subject who will identify with the moral universe incarnated in the "Law" of a society organized politically as a nation-state and economically as a part of an international system of production and exchange'. It was a way of '"fixing" the subject within a given system of social praxis' (White 1987: 86, 89). *Historics* operates as an anti-Droysen. In getting at what's behind history, it exposes its affirmative character, it exposes its otherwise unconscious ideological effects. That history represents dominant socio-economic interests in an ideal, intellectual form, comes out of a formal analysis of historical knowledge.

Ostensibly history begins and ends with comprehension: it must be comprehensive – no matter that, in terms of content, how it comprehends, how it can be comprehensive, provokes interminable debate. Comprehension reconciles *the* one and only (objective, fact-based) truth with history's variety, heterogeneity, and promiscuity. Being comprehensive constitutes history's special cognitive virtue: the virtue of having no special virtue because it includes everything and so means anything. It also has its own objectivizing effect. Formally, the comprehensive view detaches the historian from the diachronic dimension both historian and historical object share. It allows the historian an ideal, transcendental perspective on the historical object, which turns the object into something *spectacular*, to be observed, to be contemplated (*illusio*; cf. Appendix: Table 1). To work convincingly the spectacle has to be technically reliable, thoroughly rehearsed. Whether factual or fictional: it is always *virtual*. The more technically accomplished – the more fact and evidence substantiate it – the more accurate, convincing, realistic, truthful, etc., it becomes. After all, 'accurate', 'convincing', 'realistic', 'truthful', are judgements about virtuality not reality.

Conversely, the premiss of the formal analysis of historical knowledge is material, even visceral – *apprehension*. For *Historics* it is axiomatic that what history does, has to do with apprehension. Being apprehensive, it fixes on what both comprehensive, academic history and the historical theory concocted by historians and history theorists conventionally excludes: the social and psychological conditions that produce it, it works in, and it affirms. These are as follows:

First, history results from coercion, violence, conflict, terror, both symbolic and physical. As narrated in a historical text-book, they may not primarily induce apprehension. But that just shows history affirming violence as historically normal. In an already historicized world, this means it is also socially and politically affirmed as normal. Historical affirmation thus affirms other social representations of dominant force. So recently British TV viewers could watch on Channel 4 News Israeli or US helicopter gunships "in action", while on Channel 5 a historian verbally caressed the 'Weapons and Heroes of World War II' ('to show ... victory could depend on a perfect match between people and machines').[1] Identifying with what was, history ultimately enforces public acquiescence in what is. It functions as a social anaesthetic.

Second, in an already historicized world, historians – ironically – can neither say what history really is, nor what they themselves really do. As *Historics* shows, their explanations – buoyed up by moral aspiration or oneiric wishfulness – blow out in tautology or catachresis. That's where apprehension arises. History, an academic discipline capable of "organizing the world" yet unable to account for itself; historians, convinced that history naturally needn't account for itself, since their "unaccountable" research speaks for itself: they make ideal, compliant and pliable instruments for socially dominant interests.

Third, the historicized world history produces, explains, justifies, and administers, is suffused with a morbid psychopathology. It evinces now 'a planet-wide phenomenon, a pandemic of social evil which is more than merely an aggregation of the dysfunctioning of subordinate societies. The globalizing of social systems is also a globalizing of social morbidity' (Allott 2002: 138–9). History has no remedy for this global disease. How could it have? As an agency integral to this historicized world, it is completely implicated in this morbid world-system. Certainly, history would buy us off with the past's "rich legacy", but that's only because it trades with death. By definition, legacies come from the dead. In a historicized world, thanks to history, the past dominates the present – morbid curiosity for a morbid world: 'The pathology of a society may include a morbid relationship to its own past' (Allott 2002: 336).

Fourth, history is embedded as an academic discipline in public institutions that replicate the political and social system (cf. Munslow 2003: 192). The university proves to be the socio-economic governance-system in its ideal form – 'a bureaucratically organized and relatively autonomous consumer oriented corporation' (Readings 1997: 11; cf. Allott 2002: 174). If it no longer embodies humanist values, it also abandons any personally enriching vocation. Instead, in the very social space where knowledge could be critically reflexive, it promotes the total domination of bureaucratic regulation and market values. In this structure, whatever they think they are doing, scholar-teachers become 'academic bureaucrats', technical 'resource managers'

---

[1] From the factsheet description on http://five.tv/factsheets/war/ (14 April 2004).

(Allott 2002: 274; Heidegger 1967a: 26). In the corporate university, history is the ideal discipline, historical knowledge the ideal corporate product. Being both heterogeneous and objectively true, history mirrors a social reality in which consumer choice is the dominant politico-economic principle. And this 'one-dimensional world', the 'stuff of total administration', is the already historicized world – a world totally historicized because totally administered by historians, the ideal 'academic bureaucrats' (Marcuse 1986: 169; Cohen 1988: 67, 80; Niethammer 1989: 40ff.).

Historics argues that apprehension is the only reflex now left to alert human beings to the insecurities of the historicized world they inhabit. It insists that historical comprehension, rationalizing and normalizing the pathological convulsions of a globally dysfunctional system, effectively anaesthetizes this last pang of intellectual and ethical consciousness. That's why *Historics* is apprehensive about history.

Historical illusions; aesthetic situations

Historics dispenses with the "subjective-objective" opposition (cf. Appendix: Table 1). This binary conception is misleading anyway, as neurophysiological and cognitive psychological factors in the process of knowing suggest. The objectivity issue is the sterile, key issue of the sterile discussion about what history *is*. It has little significance for a theory about what history *does* in a world already historicized. Certainly, it persists in academic discourse about history. Why it persists? The affirmative function of history, let alone of the "humanities", would otherwise collapse.

Historics instead derives knowledge from human *situatedness* in the world and the *practices*, social and cultural, that arise therefrom. To be situated, is to exist as a particular, gendered body, at a particular time, in a particular place, in particular circumstances. Situatedness necessitates adaptability. These conditions are contingent: the body ages, times and places change, circumstances alter. In ourselves, as between ourselves and the world, there is continuous interaction between comprehension and apprehension, acceptance and resistance. Social and cultural practices, involving (e.g.) work, ideas, projects, beliefs, duties, choices, regrets, fears, both derive from and produce the situation that currently happens to envelop us.

Further, situated knowledge has to be vital knowledge since it has a bearing on our current existence. The only knowledge that can be vital is existentially situated knowledge. After all, we are now in the world and the world is now in us: the mind maps the world and the world is mapped onto the mind (cf. Southgate 1996: 59ff.). Knowledge comes from how we now "sense" the world and how the world now "senses" us [*aesthesis*]; that means it also comes from the conceptions that shape how we "sense" the world and how the "sense" we get of the world shapes our conceptions of it [*illusio*]. Thus, ideally, "sensing" and "conceptualizing", *aesthesis* and *illusio*, work together, respond to each other. *Aesthesis* derives from its Platonic context, meaning "perception", "knowledge" (Cornford 1970: 30; *Theaetetus*, 150E). *Illusio*, from the Latin "ludere", "to play", means "illusion" or "deceit".[2] In Bourdieu's theory of knowledge it functions in the social process of knowledge production as a mental map of the discipline's "game" and the rules and strategies required for playing it (Bourdieu 1997: 135). Hence, *aesthesis* (as existential knowledge) produces illusions that are meant to be illusory in order to bring us to our senses. *Illusio* (as disciplinary knowledge) produces illusions our senses are meant to take for reality.

The snag is, sense and conception don't often match. That they don't is the dilemma of human consciousness. As we routinely know from our own projects, imagined intention and actual realization, physical reaction and moral consequence, inevitably diverge. So too with the knowledge process. A scientific consensus may adequately explain a syndrome, until, based on different data, an apparently better one emerges, now invalidating it. At any given moment, the prevailing scientific order reveals its antecedents as so many 'previous illusions' (cf. Weber 1988: 598).

History proves illusory in both action and knowledge (cf. Appendix: Table 2).[3] Contrasting the reality with the appearance of the British diplomatic system, Allott remarks: 'British diplomacy had for centuries played a leading part in making a world-system whose peculiar rationality could be seen as a form of madness'. It derived from the 'pathological behaviour' of politicians and diplomats who 'were privileged inhabitants of a world of unreality, an unreality which was life-threatening on a grand scale, a world which nevertheless seemed to

---

[2] For a more detailed exploration of these terms, see 'On Two Types of Knowledge in the Human Sciences' (Davies 2004).

[3] "History" refers to both "what happened" in the past, *res gestae*, and "knowledge about what happened", *cognitio rerum gestarum*. *Historics* designates this difference as "history [*rg*]" and "history [*crg*]" respectively (cf. Appendix: Table 2).

its inhabitants, in characteristic paranoid fashion, to be perfectly real and natural and inevitable and right' (Allott 2001: xlii). Historical knowledge, in its academic self-sufficiency, reveals its own oneiric character: 'History ... represents neither an aesthetic enjoyment, nor a "scientific" recognition, nor a practical understanding. Like these it is a dream; but it is a dream of another sort'. That is to say, it is something entirely self-referential, 'a coherence in a group of contingencies of similar magnitudes' (Oakeshott 1991: 182–3).

History is beguiled by the illusions inevitably involved in action and knowledge. However, in an already historicized world it generates illusions of its own. In claiming to reveal the "real reality", how things really, objectively were, it becomes absorbed in its own self-reflection. After all, in an already historicized world, with historical thinking as 'an original and fundamental activity of the human mind', there obviously won't be anything for the human mind that isn't *already* historical (Collingwood 1978: 247). Further, though the documentary record of the past may be unclear or fragmentary, the principle of comprehensivity, enhanced by narrative presentation, ensures the historian produces a coherent, self-referential account. For their part, 'readers expect an illusion of seamlessness, and they will try to project one onto even the most static and disorganized text. Once the illusion locks in, they credit the historian with having brought the past to life' (Menand 2003: x). History can thus produce not just a 'sense of "reality" that is "more comprehensible" than [one's] present social existence', but a 'sense of the "real" that can be used as a criterion for determining what shall count as realistic in [one's] own present' (White 1987: 89). So, in an already historicized world, the sense of history [*illusio*] occludes what immediate situatedness makes us sense [*aesthesis*].

This is how history works anaesthetically, why it causes apprehension. This 'more coherent reality' it projects, is formally speaking a purely affirmative reality. That's because, in an already historicized world, writing history, 'inventing the past in the present-here-and-now ... is itself a form of behaviour ... which is not different in kind from the rest of the willing and acting which is the present here and now of society'. It's affirmative, because it's illusory: the kind of events it deals with are 'epiphenomena, the appearances of appearances'. It distracts from the immediate challenges confronting situated human existence, simply because 'it would not be possible to determine the future on the basis of such a description of the past' (Allott 2001: 187). Instead you get a public sphere with people mesmerized by an 'artificial hallucination of the past' (Nora 1984: XXXII).

The logic of "sense": the dynamics of the present argument

Whoever thinks, knows that thinking works with texts and signs. It arranges them into patterns of issues; these patterns renew its vital energy. In academic disciplines these patterns, like the thinking, come off the peg: the decisive concepts are there ready, waiting to identify the research data. So, though *Historics* reflects on history as a dominant academic discipline, its primary aim is not to address disciplinary debates. Rather than "engage" with the latest technical academic issues for technical academic purposes, it takes issue with the dominant obsession with history in contemporary society. It's a sustained critique of a social illusion promoted by history theorists and practitioners: the total naturalness of history and historicized consciousness. It offers philosophical arguments that bring out the implications of living in such an already historicized world. Whether or not the conceptions of history it deals with are "dated" or not is, therefore, immaterial (cf. Southgate 2003: 49). What does matter, is their enduring preponderance in the social imagination. After all, it's a typically academic conceit for theorists taking issue with other academics' theories to believe that knowledge is "advancing" just because they are up with the "latest thing", while whole enclaves of the social imagination get by on naïve positivism. In disciplinary terms, *Historics* is, therefore, deliberately an "unseasonal meditation". Disregarding the esoteric conventions of disciplinary disputation, it elaborates its own "untimely" [*unzeitgemäß*] attitudes through a classically eclectic procedure – extracting 'good things' from the reflective writings that helped to formulate it (cf. Xenophon 1979: 74–5; I.vi.14; cf. Davies 2003: 25–6).

For this reason, *Historics* takes the (always latest) postmodernist position in history theory as read. What the theorists keep laboriously expounding, that our representations of the world are projections of grammar and rhetorical figures, it regards as self-evident. Rather it wonders why, despite their best efforts, history still persists in its same old "traditional", "modernist", "constructionist" forms (however these rather arbitrary categories go) (cf. Southgate 1996: 13). One reason is: postmodernism is simply 'the modernist project without its foundational matrix' (Gray 1995: 147). It shows that academic priorities are set not by purely academic considerations, but by material, institutional considerations no theory will shift, certainly not postmodern theory.

That proves to be just another way of affirming the same socially affirmative interests that sustain history's academic conventions. In any case, on its own self-definition, postmodernist historical theory works in the same *illusory* mode as other history (cf. Appendix: Table 1). This comes out each time it stresses its essentially "playful" (i.e. ludic) character. Postmodernism in principle insists that 'criticism should learn about playful continuity and become less than the sum of its parts'. After all, 'play is the vice and joy of postmodernism; play is fatuousness but also fantasy' (Hassan 1984: 25, 83). Implicit here is the idea that writing [*écriture*] is itself a self-referential play [*jeu*] of signs and meanings (cf. Derrida 1967: 16). Given that 'for us, the post-modern condition of fractured perspectives and groundless practices is an *historical fate*, which we are wise to make the best of', postmodern playfulness is integral to an already historicized world that insists on its historicized historical consciousness (Gray 1995: 146 (my italics)).

Clearly, postmodern playfulness [*illusio*] wouldn't be possible if the world were not already totally historicized, if everything had not 'become contemporary, with the remarkable correlate ... that everything has become history', if history were 'no longer the reconstruction of what has happened to us in the various phases of our lives, but a continuous *playing* with the memory of this' (Ankersmit 1989: 151, 152 (my italics)). So the notion that the 'endless play of unstable becoming at the levels of the personal-political ... gives a radical disobedient and thus counter-hegemonic (counter-dominant) politics a chance', just won't wash (Jenkins 2003: 4). The ludic potential of postmodern history is inherently part of the *illusion* history in *any* form generates. It's part of its "sheer amusement value", "naturally", "inevitably" generated by "the game of historical construction", that, e.g., dresses Pyrrho (*c.*360–*c.*270 BC) up as a "true proto-postmodernist", thanks to the same old identitary thinking that will always exchange the latest thing (i.e. postmodernism) for the same old thing (i.e. Classical Greek scepticism) (Southgate 1996: 29; Southgate 2003: 61–3). A historicized world does nothing but play around like this with its history (as, e.g., in living-museums, theme parks, the 'Oxford Experience', TV docu-dramas, etc.). Postmodernism is what a historicized world will come up with *because* of the illusion history is, *because* of its ludic potential.

Historics isn't, therefore, yet one more postmodernist theory of history. Certainly, it goes with the premisses of the postmodern position (e.g. the textual character of reality, the figurative fabric of texts, scepticism towards the natural reality of true facts, etc., etc.) – not because they are the current campus *chic*, but because these issues have always preoccupied the theory of knowledge. Moreover, though Derrida's deconstructionism (i.e. the critique of logocentrism) is radical, it provides a too narrow basis for getting at what's behind the historicizing mentality. It still leaves history *essentially* intact: it just transposes it into a different, self-conscious mode. Conversely, *Historics* aims to demonstrate that the illusions historicizing methods and attitudes generate, result from a much wider range of social-psychological factors. So it distinguishes itself from postmodern versions of history in the following ways:

First, it cannot endorse the postmodernist conviction that history is still a legitimate academic discipline, so long as it is somehow post-modernized, e.g. as in the notion of 'problematizing postmodernism in the area of social history' (Jenkins 1997: 314). *Historics* dissociates itself from this unquestioning conviction of a self-evident, irreducible 'area of history' that necessarily underlies the postmodernist debate, that was always already there for postmodernists to problematize and play around with and still remains there after it has been problematized and played around with.[4] In effect, what the post-modern, deconstructive approach offers is more historicization. After all, it itself moves towards 'new historicizations' (Berkhofer 1997: 263ff.). Already an 'essentially historicist conception', postmodernism augments the historicizing of an already historicized world – what with its 'new approaches and new kinds of history ... on the agenda', what with proposing, after having deconstructed it, a 'new

---

[4] A personal note: *Identity or History? Marcus Herz and the End of the Enlightenment* (Davies 1995) is one example of what is now called 'new history' (cf. Munslow 2003). This exercise in the 'historiography of unrecognized persons', of a German-Jewish intellectual in the late eighteenth century, is multi-perspectival, involves asynchronicities, and foregrounds its own discursive practice by drawing attention to the ironic mode that lends it its form and the dominant trope, preterition (*paralipsis*), that forms its narrative structure (Davies 1995: 1ff., 15; cf. Berkhofer 1997: 263ff.; Munslow 2003: 193–4; Southgate 2003: 163–4). This biographical study basically denies history's capacity to generate identities. Still, one's thinking moves on: after all, even experimental antiquarianism is still antiquarian; even a "new" take on the late eighteenth century still involves the same old eighteenth century. Ultimately, as *Identity or History?* implies, it's history itself as an identitary construct and a specialized, disciplinary, social institution that gets in the way of knowledge and is intellectually obstructive (Davies 1995: 15–18). So, after further thought, one ends up wondering what's behind it. Something has to be ...

history' (cf. Zagorin 1990: 264; Joyce 1997a: 248; Munslow 2003). Once it emerges that 'all histories always have been and always will be aesthetic, figurative discourses', that 'all histories are thus of the aesthetic type postmodernists raise to consciousness. ... so that in coming to the end of epistemological histories we have ... come home to ourselves', the 'new', postmodern history boils down to the same old history (Jenkins 2003: 70). Stressing its ludic character, postmodernist history only massively reinforces the historian's traditional position of being 'deliriously self-encoded as a cultural operator incapable of being transcended / overthrown by other discursive systems' (Cohen 1988: 227). Conversely, *Historics* has it in for this relentless, totalitarian historicization of human experience, for the colonization of the social imagination by historians and historical theorists, let alone for the armoury of various, co-existent, heterogeneous varieties, types, modes, concepts, representations, constructions, schools, and houses of history at their disposal. Postmodernist history theory only makes the same old historical world even older, and older, traditional academic history even older and more traditionally academic – just what the morbid social psychopathology of this self-styled, late, historicized world desires. That's why *Historics* discounts any idea that history, let alone its postmodernist variant, has a 'potentially subversive' effect (cf. Southgate 1996: 57). It's never going to undermine the social conditions to which it owes its very existence.

Second, *Historics* distances itself from postmodernism, because, from a sociological perspective, postmodernist history operates with the same old disciplinary model, with its typical thought-styles and coercions, as any other conventional, academic discipline. Of course, it claims not to. It pretends to adopt a 'cantankerous, contentious, difficult, disobedient' attitude to historical orthodoxy (Jenkins 2003: 68). But, in the same old academic fashion, it discounts its own social context as an institutionalized, academic practice. This 'cantankerousness' is easily assimilated by the corporate university for its own, affirmative, socio-economic ends. Postmodernist academic history thus works like its more traditional academic counterpart. It is just as consensual – it's just a more self-styled radical consensus. Still, like the radical poses of cultural studies in general, this recalcitrance and disobedience 'come across not as daringly counter-hegemonic but as the most egregious sort of apologia for existing economic arrangements' (Frank 2002: 36). Rebellious attitudes are perfectly compatible with a sophisticated, corporate managerial culture attuned to group-identities in a highly segmented consumer-market (cf. Frank

1998: 4–5, 25). The fragmentation, the anti-foundationalism of the postmodern, simply endorses radical capitalism as well as a 'corporate right' politics out to sweep away all traditional constraints and values (cf. Frank 2002: 18, 51–2).

This postmodern 'disobedience' (particularly in a pedagogically orientated 'set-text') is just a pose (cf. Jenkins 2003: 7). It may be playful, its historical reconstruction just games: still, postmodern games are played by postmodern rules, anything else is not tolerated: disciplinary convention makes sure of that. So it's no use asserting that 'historians are not by nature herd animals. Most of the time we are loners only persuaded by the data in the archive and not our colleagues' assertions/interpretations' – most certainly not when discussing leading historians and theorists, citing journals and edited volumes, the collective disciplinary organs and structures, the very *collective* existence of which blatantly contradicts the initial assertion (Munslow 2003: 93)! Here, as with other works by postmodern theorists (e.g. Ankersmit, Jenkins, Joyce), the main purpose seems less to evangelize (i.e. extend the field) than to commune with itself (i.e. keep the field nicely irrigated). In this self-referential game, scoring against each other's books, categorizing, classifying, and approving types of historical practice, the postmodern theorist still fulfils the same old technical, academic function as a professional resources manager [*Besteller des Bestandes*] (cf. Munslow 1997: 17ff.; Jenkins 2003: 1ff.).

Third, *Historics* also dissociates itself from postmodernism because postmodernist history is just as academic as traditional or modernist history: i.e. it still includes the possibility of a transcendental perspective from which it discounts itself. Postmodernism still consecrates the technical expertise of the academic professional as the dominant mode of knowledge in a society managed by technical expertise, by the 'cognitariat' (cf. Jencks 1989: 44). Be it postmodern or traditional, historical knowledge still affirms the managerial ethos that affirms the dominant social reality. That's why, in its critique of history as academic knowledge, *Historics* analyzes how academic consensus is fabricated. Its strategy is not to debate the byzantine subtleties of postmodern theory for other subtle theorists to debate, but to examine typical forms of history's dominance. It brings out the illusory nature of all certainties because of the oneiric nature of technical expertise and managerial governance, the dominant knowledge practices, the intellectual aroma of this apprehensive society. The historicized humanities, generating oneiric figments [*illusio*] of the prevailing social imagination, have proved to be a defenceless province of the public mind for technical expertise and professional governance to colonize, reify, and instrumentalize.[5]

Fourth, what further differentiates *Historics* from postmodernist history is its critique of identitary thinking. *Historics* focusses on the identitary logic, the mimetic discourse, that keeps reproducing history and keeps history reproducing. Its chief criterion of truth is tautology: history tells how the past was what it was, how what the past was, is its historical identity. All postmodernism does is offer a different mimetic code. It also makes the past nothing but the mimetic code used to identify it. It helps the past to proliferate in the social imagination through constantly re-jigging the code that identifies it. But it's predicated on the same old tautology, as in the view that 'postmodernism [is] the continuing attempt to formulate a theoretical explanation for the situation ... that we're all in – the situation of postmodernity' (Southgate 2003: ix). This is as much a historicizing judgement as the apparently opposing view that 'historians no longer have much to say to a culture that seems too late to be modern and which is arguably so ahistorical in its practices such that modernist ways of doing history ... may well be coming to a close' (Jenkins 2003: 2).

---

[5] See the affirmative thinking promoted by the UK Arts and Humanities Research Board that sponsors the production of knowledge in the humanities in UK higher education institutions. Its impending move to achieving 'full research council status' will provide 'more financial support for research ... and greater emphasis on the development of partnerships between higher education, business, and the wider community'. Consequently, 'the establishment of the AHRC will ... provide leadership ... which encourages researchers to engage with projects that have the potential not just [!] to inform and illuminate, but also to enrich the UK's society, economy and culture'. Hence, 'the AHRC will face an exciting and welcome challenge ... to explore the increasing ways in which the arts and humanities ... can engage constructively with the needs of our rapidly changing society' (AHRB 2004: 2–3). Here a quasi-governmental organization 'based on a clear understanding of what motivates researchers' intends the seamless and total integration of individual psychology with social purposes through the economic exploitability of knowledge. Conversely, this exploitability ensures individual psychology complies with social purposes. The concepts of excellence and quality cover both. Here, as with all organizations in the culture and heritage industries managing the social production of knowledge, the "objectively" intrinsic qualities they commend in the knowledge products they sponsor, derive in reality from social criteria (cf. "needs") they have pre-emptively insinuated into them. Conversely, inevitably recognizing only what it already knows, their identitary logic binds knowledge production to immediate social demands, thereby excluding the more urgent thought: whether knowledge, in its *own* interests, need be socially productive at all. The arts and humanities thus abandon their vitally reflective vocation, 'with its resistance to the way things are currently run [*gegen die heute gängige Übung*] and what they serve, to the justification of things being as they now are' (Adorno 2003: 460–1).

However, both assertions simply demonstrate that, in an already historicized world, adopting postmodernist, a-historical perspectives is itself just another historicizing reflex (cf. 'coming to a close'; 'the closing decades of the twentieth century' (Southgate 2003: 10)). By contrast, *Historics* argues that history, in whatever form, will always give off the intellectual aroma of 'late capitalism' so long as this social structure and its consciousness persist. In any case, the notion of 'lateness' that apparently justifies envisioning the end of history, indicates a mentality so historicized that, even in its critique of history, it cannot but think in historical terms. After all, if there were no 'latest things', there would never be any old, historical things (cf. Davies 1999: 251). *Historics*, therefore, presents the obsession with history as a psycho-pathological malaise of contemporary society. It implies that therapy is required to cure it of this morbid self-interest. It perhaps offers a glimpse of another way of treating history. If universities were really places for critical intellectual reflection (and did not manage the training facility franchise for the so-called 'knowledge-based economy'), there might be, here or there, "Departments of Historics", not Departments of History. Since, just as economics appraises commercial trends, politics the tendencies of governments, and literary criticism the output of creative writers, historics would, indispensably, unmask the affirmative force of historical knowledge in its many public guises.

Historics will have worked, therefore, if it makes its readers start to question why the social imagination is constantly having to ingest a stale, nostalgic brew called history. It doesn't attempt, as academic monographs do, to provide a perfect, comprehensive picture. Instead, it offers a way of seeing. It doesn't presuppose its readers' agreement. It rather reckons with their disagreement. It asks them merely to go along with it for the while, knowing they'll always draw their own conclusions. To get at what's behind history, hence to prevent itself succumbing to the historicizing reflex, to being seduced by what is ever the same, it offers *philosophical* arguments that explore the *sense* of history. *Philosophical* arguments, because philosophy alone has the capacity to mediate between specialized technical discourses; and because, unlike technical academic expertise, it is an intellectual potential inherent in everyone's innate thinking capacity in relation to their own experience in the world they ordinarily live in [*Lebenswelt*] (Habermas 1988: 46). *Sense*, because this concept covers a wide range of ordinary, innate dimensions of experience, including "sensation", "consciousness", "meaning", and "purpose".

The concept of "sense", particularly "sense of history", is the argument's focal point. It asserts *Historics*' aesthetic intention (cf. Appendix: Table 1). Its premiss is that, in a historicized world, history is immediately experienced (as something disruptive, disorientating, unpredictable, uncontrollable, destructive) – not primarily contemplated in a detached, "objective", academic manner (to keep it at a safe distance). *Historics* thus reflects on history (and the historical disciplines) from the standpoint of situated experience, personal sense, *not* at the behest of detached expertise. It has a reductive intention, which is how it gets behind the concept of history as society's "natural" self-representation (cf. Levinas 1991: 99–100).

In other words, *Historics* is concerned with how history is "sensed". It recognizes that in a historicized world the sense of history, as the sense everyone has in common, has become commonsense. Still, the concept of "sense" articulates the reductive approach to history's heterogeneity. The senses themselves receive heterogeneous signals (e.g. a baby's cry; a bird singing); but they also consist of a unified, structured system of functions (e.g. the differing auditory signals are interpreted by one and the same complex neurophysiological system centred on the brain). "Sense" thus implies an intelligible system operating behind history's heterogeneity.

Historics explores this "sense system" dynamically, *aesthetically* (cf. *aesthesis*, cf. Appendix: Table 1), as with a musical theme and its variations.[6] This both permits systematic analysis of the dimensions of historical sense and displays their multi-faceted character. It unfolds a "phenomenology" of history's "sense" that reveals the implications of living in a historicized world. Each variation, therefore, lifts the concept, "sense", to a higher and wider level of significance, each with a different, but related resonance.

— The **Theme**, Nietzsche's view of *history as the 'sixth sense' of modern Europeans*, establishes history's heterogeneity and dominance. What actually makes it socially dominant, comes out in the subsequent variations on it:
— **Variation 1** explores *the material, organic basis of the sense of history*. It deals with history and sentience: with both how history interacts with human sentience and sentience reacts to history. It comes in on Marx's idea that 'sense perception ... must be the basis for all knowledge [*Wissenschaft*]' (Marx 1981: 604).

---

[6] Think, e.g., of Mozart's Sonata in A, K331/300i; or Schubert's Impromptu, D 935 no. 3 in B flat major, Opus 142.

— **Variation 2** develops *the psychological aspect of historical sense*, since comprehension and apprehension are also mental attitudes. Its key-note comes from Henry Miller's observation from 1946: 'We have been thinking in terms of the past for several thousand years. Now, at one stroke, that whole mysterious past has been obliterated. There is only the future staring us in the face. It yawns like a gulf. It is terrifying, everyone concedes, even to begin to think what the future holds in store for us' (Miller 1962: 40).

— **Variation 3** presents history as a self-affirming *technology of technologies* – both extending human capacities and compensating for human catastrophes. The tone here is set by Freud's view of mankind as a 'prosthesis god', given that 'with every tool they have, human beings keep on refining their organs, both motor and sensory – or removing limitations on what they can achieve' (Freud 1977: 86–7).

— **Variation 4** ventures into the *psychopathology of historicized life*. Examples from historicism, Judaism, 'commodity thinking', and psycho-analysis show how history reinforces itself and the historicized world by producing *symbolic formations* that constitute history as a reality, as "naturally" objective and compelling. It echoes Lacan's insight that human beings are constituted by symbolic and figurative realities (Lacan 1966: 46, 96).

— Finally, the **Coda** makes explicit what *Historics'* critique of the historicizing mentality implies all along: that thinking would be impossible, could it not be untimely.

A Sense of History
Variations on a Theme from Nietzsche

Theme
A Sixth Sense – A Sense *for* History

Does history have a sense? Can there be a sense in history? What can the word "sense" mean for history? These are the questions *Historics* explores.

Nietzsche offers a place to start. In *Beyond Good and Evil* (1886), he defines history in terms of the contemporary attitudes and forms of behaviour behind it. The context is a scathing criticism of the values of his age, of those Europeans of the 'day after tomorrow', the 'first-comers to the twentieth century' (Nietzsche 1988: V, 151, §214). He is confronting the heterogeneity of values and theorizing in contemporary culture. What comes out, is a cultural malaise: historical interests produce existential disorientation.

The 'sense of history' is the 'sixth sense' of 'good Europeans' – fairly adaptable, democratic, intellectually mediocre people, susceptible still in this 'age of the masses' to atavistic bouts of nationalism (Nietzsche 1988: V, 157ff., 180, 182, §§224, 241, 242). It's a sensory aptitude conditioned by prevailing social and cultural values. The vast output of nineteenth-century historical scholarship has made the sense of history an extension of the human cognitive capacity. As a sixth sense, it suggests something uncanny, almost telepathic – a 'divinatory instinct' (as Nietzsche calls it). It's a quick and easy way of apprehending the scale of value-systems societies and individuals have lived by, how they relate to each other, and how the authority of these values relates to the authority of the forces at work in society. Though it's the pride of the 'good European', Nietzsche is ironically reserved. The sense of history is nothing to boast about. It's only an effect of the 'semi-barbarity' that has befallen Europe as a democratic melting-pot of different social orders and ethnicities.

History and indiscriminate interests

Nietzsche argues that a sense of history has thrown the modern psyche into total confusion. 'We are ourselves a sort of chaos,' he says. The heterogeneous character of modern life has left 'our modern souls' utterly exposed to the past. They are swamped by the antecedents of every form and way of life, by the heritage of cultures that once would have existed closely side-by-side, or with one dominating the other. Nowadays our instincts connect with a past that lies undifferentiated all around us. The mind, however, turns this confusion to its advantage. The 'semi-barbarity in body and desire' of modern Europeans gives them everywhere a privileged means of access more noble ages never enjoyed. In particular, it opens up to them 'the labyrinth of unfinished cultures and each and every moment of semi-barbarity there has ever been on earth'. This is, however, a highly dubious privilege. The greatest part of human culture up to now has been nothing but semi-barbaric. Consequently (Nietzsche continues), the sense of history amounts just to a sense or instinct for anything and everything, a taste and a palate for anything and everything. A sense of history is neither distinguished nor discriminating (Nietzsche 1988: V, 158, §224).

Two examples show what he means. He wonders what seventeenth-century French Classicists might have made of Homer and how Classical Greek tragedians would have reacted to Shakespeare. We can enjoy Homer (he says), and that, fortunately enough, gives us an advantage over the self-regarding French culture of the seventeenth century that, apparently, could not. This culture knew what it liked and disliked; it had a sure palate, and so easily felt disgusted. Anything unfamiliar it met with reserve; a lively curiosity it treated warily because it regarded it as tasteless. Being self-sufficient, it only reluctantly admitted to desiring something new, to being dissatisfied with what it had, and to admiring something other than itself. For these reasons Classical French culture disdained anything it could not regard or exploit as its own. In fact, Nietzsche insists, no sense could be more incomprehensible to the French Classicists than the historical sense and its 'subservient plebeian curiosity'. Taking the comparison of historical 'sense' and taste a step further, Nietzsche asserts that Shakespeare, 'this surprising Spanish-Moorish-Saxon synthesis of taste', would have reduced the ancient Athenians, fond as they were of Aeschylus, to uncontrollable laughter or irritation. Shakespeare's exuberant colourfulness, the way he combines the utmost delicacy, vulgarity and artistry, appeals to us now as something warm and familiar. Far from being put off by the revolting vapours from, and close proximity to, the common people of Elizabethan England Shakespeare's art and taste are rooted in, we savour it all as a refined aesthetic experience reserved especially for us (Nietzsche 1988: V, 158–9, §224).

The 'sense of history' is typical of all the other virtues modern Europeans possess. We are (says Nietzsche) undemanding, selfless, modest, brave, full of will-power, full of devotion, very grateful, very patient, very obliging – except we have no taste. A sense of history we may have; we have no way of grasping what makes for perfection and ultimate maturity in culture and art. We have no empathy for the inherent quality in works and individuals that lends them distinction. All our feeling for 'their moment of calm sea and halcyonic self-sufficiency, the golden cold lustre evinced by all things that have reached perfection', has gone. So the 'historical sense', our greatest virtue, is necessarily opposed to good taste. In particular, it has difficulty grasping the experience of the sublime. It has to force itself to appreciate 'precisely those brief, fleeting moments of extreme happiness or of transfiguration that suddenly flare up now and then.' As moments of true greatness, 'supra-historical' numinous – aesthetic or religious – experiences, they are essentially a-historical (Nietzsche 1988: V, 159–60, §224; cf. Nietzsche 1988: I, 330).

With his pun on 'sense', by treating the 'sense of history' as a form of sensation like touch, smell, hearing, sight, and in terms of taste, Nietzsche attacks the academic discipline. He is out to sabotage the historical methodologies that prop up the vast, tottering edifice of the humanities. Whatever the historical sciences as forms of knowledge achieve, relies on a 'sense' of history. Seen as a mode of sense-perception [*aesthesis*], it adds to human sensibility. Its scope and intentionality play their own particular part in cognitive processes. Nietzsche thus rejects historical knowledge as "ultimate knowledge", because he knows it derives from underlying social-psychological habits. Calling the 'sense' of history a sixth sense, makes nineteenth-century historical awareness already naturalized and innate, like the five senses themselves. The 'sense' of history, therefore, signals an ethological mutation in the human species.

The cultural politics of distinction

A sense of history, Nietzsche implies, indicates a pathological tendency: historical interests are symptomatic of decadence – the trouble is, this argument sounds unsafe, the vocabulary dated.

It comes from ethnology and vitalism, rather dubious nineteenth-century notions. But to dismiss his argument for that reason, ignores the legitimate issue being addressed. Nietzsche needs an incendiary vocabulary to get at a subversive issue: the crisis in the politics of distinction. How does a mass society – heterogenous in its cultural make-up, pluralistic, if not secular, in its value-systems, permeated by all kinds of social traditions and elements – make distinctions? How does a modern, let alone postmodern, society reach its value-judgements (cf. Sloterdijk 2000: 84)? Society, as a human collective, produces the distinctions it needs to run itself – e.g. gradations of status, degrees of wealth, habits of consumption, patterns of behaviour. But the politics of distinction also encompasses those that emerge from the social collective through its better self-awareness, that are transgressive or excessive, that scandalize or enrapture, that society may not initially recognize (cf. Durkheim 1996: 96). Coming from scientific or artistic endeavour, these distinctions produce the 'great thought' that alone 'lends greatness to deeds and things', but may not register with popular opinion (Nietzsche 1988: V, 181–2, §241). Art, in particular, is 'something immortal achieved by mortal hands ... become tangibly present', a form of human fabrication that in its durability both transfigures the world and 'legitimizes the conviction ... that a man's products may be more and essentially greater than himself' (cf. Arendt 1974: 168–9, 210). No wonder Nietzsche is apprehensive: the 'sense' of history either relativizes or patronizes. Its heterogeneity deflates the creative motivation of self-transcendence; it saps the effort required to invent the new values around which the world revolves (Nietzsche 1988: IV, 65).

We 'first-comers to the twenty-first century', living now in Nietzsche's tomorrow, have a sociological discourse to speak of 'mass indifference to difference' and identify 'the intellectual-political agenda to liquidate the elite of naturally talented individuals' which gives the crisis in the politics of distinction a new twist (Sloterdijk 2000: 83, 86–7). Forsaking Nietzsche's concept of 'slave morality', we can see contemporary society 'as a society of laborers ... about to be liberated from the fetters of labor', but no longer knowing 'of those other higher and more meaningful activities for the sake of which this freedom would deserve to be won'. This means that within this egalitarian society, 'there is no class left ... of either a political or spiritual nature from which a restoration of the other capacities of man could start anew'. Everyone, whatever their social position, thinks of what they do solely in economic terms, i.e. 'in terms of a job necessary for the life of society', 'in terms of making a living'. Consequently, 'nothing could be worse' than 'the prospect of a society of laborers without labor, that is, without the only activity left to them' (Arendt 1974: 5). Or we can speak of the 'Americanization' of culture and the anti-élitism of populist and popular values. Heterogeneity characterizes an undiscriminating historical culture; it drives a populist culture in which making money 'is ... the most interesting thing to do' (Steiner 1997a: 288).

Moreover, given that the populist money-interest 'Americanization' symbolizes, runs counter to a distinctive European value, 'the notion that artistic-intellectual creation is the crown of a city or of a nation', the overall value of civilization becomes questionable (Steiner 1997a: 288). 'Americanization' designates 'the frank and sometimes sophisticated articulation of a fundamentally, of an ontologically *immanent* economy of human purpose' – i.e. the likelihood that a 'ravenous appetite for material reward is inherent in the vast majority of the human species; that we are a poor beast compounded of banality and greed; that it is not the spiky fruits of the spirit but creature comforts we lunge for'. But, forsaking the Nietzschean rhetoric of contempt, Steiner concedes America might have just been 'more truthful about human nature than any previous society'. In that case, 'the high places and moments of civilization' will have been made possible by the 'evasion of such truth', by the 'imposition of arbitrary dreams and ideals from above' – in short, by a "life-lie" (Steiner 1997a: 290).

Demographic and sociological factors reinforce this 'despotism of the ordinary'. The populist consensus, represented by the '*profanum vulgus* numerically enormous and committed to self-flattering passivity in the face of excellence', is inevitably persuasive (Steiner 1997a: 294, 302). Those who create new cultural values will be marginal: their creative obsessions leave them no other option. It's self-deception to believe that cultural creation concerns more than a minority: 'the number of men and women capable of painting a major canvas, of composing a lasting symphony, of postulating and proving a fundamental theorem, of presenting a metaphysical system or of writing a classic poem, is, even on a millennial scale very restricted indeed' (Steiner 1997a: 290–1). Further, the generation of distinction, particularly in a mass society, is unpredictable. Genetic or environmental reasons don't fully account for the scarcity of natural talent, nor do the dissemination and reception of the creative, classic works themselves: 'no amount of democratization will multiply creative genius or the incidence of truly great thought' (Steiner 1997a: 291–2). Steiner concludes by affirming 'those autistic absolutes of possession and *self-possession* which produce an Archimedean theorem or a Rembrandt canvas' (Steiner 1997a: 301 (my italics)). There is probably no direct correlation, perhaps even conflict, 'between classic literacy and political justice, between the civic institutionalization of intellectual excellence and the general tenor of social decency'. There is nothing to prevent culture collapsing into meaningless heterogeneity, evinced by the 'mass of cultural fellow-travellers' and the 'pseudo-values instilled in them by a totally superficial and mendacious populist ideal of general education' (Steiner 1997a: 294, 296).

To make distinctions is to see significances. The politics of distinction is, therefore, central to any discussion of historical sense. If history is 'a method devoid of any corresponding object' and so, by definition heterogeneous, how can it recognize anything historically distinctive (Lévi-Strauss 1985: 312)? How can it make sense of anything (e.g. a work of art, a formula, or a belief-system) that reaches out above and beyond history? It's hardly coincidental that history, as the identical reality of all realities, is the ideal, formal identity of a world in which money, 'a stable signifier, appropriate, in its very form, for academic denotations', decides the real-value identity of each and every thing (Droysen 1977: 70, Certeau 1987: 74; Cohen 1988: 304; Simmel 1989: 64, Sohn-Rethel 1985: 105). History, like the US dollar, has global currency.

Historics: beyond history and the humanities

Historics makes distinctions. It splits historical methodologies, along with the shoddy "humanities", away from aesthetic reflection on human existence. And the reason? Because history – like the humanities in general – is now, socially and politically, a compromised form of knowledge. It makes claims it cannot substantiate. This is why it's designated as *illusio*. What characterizes history is its claim to be comprehensive, hence total, hence autonomous – to offer a common, basic, inescapable identity: to reproduce 'a culture of common language, common society, or common reality in the face of uncommon language ... class society, and uncommon realities ...' (Cohen 1988: 16). This claim assumes that historicity is the 'ultimate refuge of a transcendental humanism' (Lévi-Strauss 1985: 312). 'To see all the human race, from the beginning of time, pass, as it were, in review before us, appearing in their true colours, without any of their disguises which, during their lifetime, so much perplexed the judgement of the beholders:' this *circa* 1740 was for David Hume the fascination of historical study (Hume 1971: 560). So it remains today: 'we really can ... find out how it [the past] happened and reach some tenable though always less than final conclusions about what it *all* meant' (Evans 1997: 253; (my italics)). A 'comprehensive definition of history,' says Elton is 'concerned with all those human sayings, thoughts, deeds and sufferings which occurred in the past and have left their present deposit'. This means that: 'Since no other treatment of man's experience answers to this definition, the autonomy of history ... is established' (Elton 1969: 24). The modern study of history involves 'total history', i.e. not just primarily political or military history. It's a 'science of structures', whereby a structure is an 'organic totality which groups facts together but in a form and in a light – hence according to an aesthetic – appropriate for them at a given moment in time and at a given location' (Ariès 1986: 234–5).

This claim seems compelling. But then history itself does block any attempt to get at what's behind it. History is engineered to promote an 'imaginary obligation' to itself: the historical text works to 'prevent disengagement from its own sentence forms or it ceases to be readable' (Cohen 1988: 61, 104). Even so, it just takes a change of perspective, e.g. towards sociology, to get round it: 'societies differ in respect of whether or not understanding them requires direct references to "historical factors". The historical nature of a given society in a given period may be such that "the historical past" is only indirectly relevant to its understanding' (Mills 1970: 172). The conventional view of the past of societies offered by history is a perspective from a 'low level of synthesis'. It deals usually in short-term patterns of coherence, while social change itself operates over a much longer term, spanning even centuries (Elias 1992: 8). Historical explanation has a "blind spot". In making sense of events over a span of time, it cannot know over what time-span events make sense: it cannot assess its own relevance. In any case, its truth-claim betrays itself. Comprehensiveness may well justify both the autonomy of history and its transcendental humanism. But the humanistic sense history ascribes to itself doesn't mesh with artistic-metaphysical conjectures on the sense of human existence. History's abstract humanism pales beside the immediate force of aesthetic experience [*aesthesis*]. That's why 'literature and the arts are the perceptible witness to that freedom of coming into being of which history can give us no account' (Steiner 1989: 182). That's why the 'equivalence between the notion of history and the notion of humanity' has to go (cf. Lévi-Strauss 1985: 312).

The aesthetic diverges from the historical sense for another reason. Boredom [*ennui*] with the historicized world, as much as creativity, enjoins the poet to head for 'the ends of the unknown to find something new'.[1] Conversely, the comprehensive scholarship that manages history, takes the historian back always to the same old thing. In confirming how things were, history implicitly affirms how things are. In its 'validation of how things have always been', it's the bedrock of traditional legitimation: even its innovations present themselves as what was already known, as what was always how it was (Weber 1988: 580). After all, historical knowledge is by definition 'old knowledge', knowledge that is already known. Consequently, however fascinating it may be, 'we learn very little from history in the way of fresh general principles which we have not already acquired as part of our cultural inheritance' (Danto 1985: 243).

As both the totality and the comprehension of the past, history by definition contains knowledge people already know about. A historian studying a past age studies what people already knew then about themselves and their times. There may well be 'cognitive asymmetry' between current knowledge about the past and the past's own knowledge about itself (cf. Danto 1985: 351ff.). Still, historical knowledge is thus already known. Its basic form is the archive, e.g., the eighteenth-century Parisian police archives Arlette Farge describes. In their folios everyday misdemeanours are organized into a cognitive structure both for forensic purposes and for public surveillance. The historian only discovers them and their "historical reality" because they are already organized in the cognitive form the archive represents (Farge 1997: 14, 18). To capture this real reality at its source, the historian copies what she finds: she re-writes what has already been written. In constructing thematic contexts to make this already known reality historically intelligible, she carefully seeks out similarities: she always selects the 'same thing' (Farge: 1997: 24–5; 81).[2] Generally, each time a historian claims to be writing the first 'full-length historical monograph', e.g. of a political figure or public agency, it is usually received in terms of what it adds to, and how it reappraises, what is already known. That's because 'historians work within collective traditions of inquiry which set certain parameters and puzzles for which they seek solutions. They do not start ... with a blank sheet of paper, looking at a selection of historical "débris" and wondering how to "emplot" this into a coherent story'. Instead, 'they pose questions about problematic aspects of the past within pre-existing frameworks of assumed knowledge ... . Historians

---

[1] cf. Charles Baudelaire, 'Le Voyage'.
[2] 'Quel que soit le but, la recherche ... s'effectue à partir du même.'

frequently work ... within the context of collective "controversies"' (Fulbrook 2002: 67). But this means only that the same old conceptual schemes underpinning the same old things pre-figure what thinking sets out to grasp (cf. Adorno 1975: 17). Producing knowledge already known makes the historical sense heterogeneous: any new thing it uncovers, it assimilates to the same old thing. This particularly makes histories of music, art, or literature unsatisfactory: their psychologistic "traditions", "influences", and "precedents" neutralize the new.

In other words, the truth-claim of history obscures a cognitive deficit. The first-comers to the twenty-first century, let alone to the twentieth, are so historicized, they've all become "backward looking clairvoyants".[3] The sense of history pretends to be the sense of the world, to ensure continuity between the past and the unfolding future [*illusio*]. But history only makes sense because it offers familiarity in a familiar form. It's the ever-reliable "default-setting" of the social mind: the knowledge that is or ought to be already known. By contrast, immediate experience [*aesthesis*] shows the world being unrecognizably transformed. From Berlin to Beijing vast urban spaces are being drastically remodelled by the tremendous force of global capitalism. These changes may well be thrilling, they leave an after-taste of apprehension. Immediate experience feels this new thing cannot be the same as the same old thing, that already known historical knowledge won't explain it, that thinking itself needs new distinctions – and new ways of making distinctions.

Historics aims to start to address these deficits. It finds that a postmodern, mass-society has to be historicized. A world of heterogeneous values needs a heterogeneous form of knowledge as its dominant, legitimating idea. History will flourish while a global capitalism bulldozes any obstructive past relic. Historical awareness will increase through catastrophic economic growth and its self-renewing dynamic (cf. Benjamin 1977: 255, §IX). This is why history causes apprehension. Historical self-consciousness is not actually blind to cultural distinction. It just adds it to the pile of symbolic and material values it has already inherited, treats it as one more value amongst other different values. In doing so, however, it denies itself any distinctive, self-justifying value. History, as the ultimate reality of a world in which money is the ultimate value, actually turns out to

---

[3] cf. Schlegel's description of historians as 'prophets turned backwards' in *Athenäums-Fragmente* (1798) (Schlegel 1972: 33).

have no sense of reality or value. History encompasses all values, any values indiscriminately, thereby subverting the humanistic value it justifies itself with. Lacking discrimination, the sense of history cannot make any distinct sense of human existence – nor, for that matter, of itself.

Variation 1
History and the Senses

History and sentience

Historical sentience colours immediate experience. Historical aware-ness suffuses everyday life. The popular interest in local history brings this out. Unsurprisingly, it proves to be a heterogenous mix of mental representations:

> The old cotton mill, the humped back bridge across the canal, the cobbled narrow street between the terraced houses and the site of the coal mine: all are *evocative* to me. Not a *Hovis advertisement*, but my *impression* of some Cheshire outskirts of Manchester where my grandparents grew up and worked between the 1880s and the Great War. This location has a *fascination* and even *mystery* denied to other places, including the seemingly mundane area in which I was born. Its *magic* is in my mind linked to a past I can never know at first hand; but it is part of a past I can try to retrieve while some still have *memories* of it from a few years later or by searching such *records* as have survived.
>
> (Wrigley 1994: 2 (my italics))

Historical sentience comprises oneiric fancies (cf. 'evocative', 'impression', 'fascination', 'mystery', 'magic'); daily work-habits and the technologies moulding them ('cotton-mill', 'canal', 'coal mine'); the experience of personal loss or destitution, hence the need for salvage (cf. mundane place of birth, experiential impoverishment, retrieval of memory); the fusion of family memory, the periodicity of organic life-time, and world-time (cf. 'grandparents', '1880s and the Great War'); the current practice of historical study (cf. 'searching records'); and anachronistic reference to commodity fetishism (cf. '*Hovis* advertisement') – a significant allusion to the underlying socio-economic system that trades on historical heritage (i.e. what the past has produced) and in "traditional values". The historicizing mentality is evidently 'chaotic' – sincerely chaotic: what other discipline turns sentiment into science?

The world is sensed through history. Each person may well be an 'anthology of attachments' and the range of his or her interests 'a source of continuing hesitations and uncertainties' (Gay 1985: 114). Being the result of subconscious conflicts and compromises within the family group, social milieu, or cultural context, these attachments, hesitations, and uncertainties are essentially historical. Personal interests generally evince historical sentience: e.g. a taste for Baroque music or for 1930s Chicago Blues. Collective memory often sustains a melancholy sense of history, registering what changes, be it in the local community or in the nation, over a life-time's span, yet unable to reconcile 'the internal experience of time passing and the movement of external things' (cf. Starobinski 1989: 61–4). Historical awareness has, therefore, distinctly aesthetic aspects: moments of epiphany – as when, absorbed in the golden lights of evening traffic on the Parisian *boulevard périphérique*, Peter Handke realizes that even a universal man such as Goethe, himself the author of a treatise on colours, would envy him for living at the end of the twentieth century (Handke 1980: 87); shudders of apprehension – induced, e.g. by film-images of the Romanian Revolution, student protests in Tiananmen Square, or ethnic cleansing in, e.g. East Timor, Rwanda, or the former Yugoslavia.

Apparently, historical sentience proves to be a mode of consciousness, an experience like other ordinary experiences. It thus furnishes "professional" historical study with objective "truthfulness". That's because academic historical explanation is normally psychologistic: the kinds of explanation and the data it employs hardly differ from those used in everyday life (cf. Veyne 1996: 126, 211). Historical sentience seems, then, to function most effectively at a latent, unconscious level, in a neurophysiological way. A sense of history seems inherent in the cognitive processes that interpret the world around us. This implies also that memories come not from the "objective" past itself, as it was, 'living on in the present'. Rather, they 'imitate our present predicaments when our present feelings approach them and incorporate themselves in them'. The past as a reality memory brings to life, is an illusion; memories are produced through an ongoing present process of reflection. A sense of history projects present psychological dispositions (Halbwachs 1994: 26–8).

In this ethological form the "lessons of history" are far more effective, far more enduring, than the fabrications of historical scholarship. These come from the instrumentalization of historical interests, e.g.: 'The historian who equates his craft with story-telling is as one-sided a practitioner as the historian impatient with what he calls *l'histoire événementielle.*' These interests, these fabrications, actually mask the ethological dimension: 'the agitated currents of change cover, sometimes to invisibility, the slow moving depths of persistent human wishes, gratifications, and frustrations' (Gay 1985: 86). Beyond the events of history, there seems to exist 'an unconscious ... or rather a more or less conscious history that, for the most part, its clear-sighted agents, the perpetrators or their victims, fail to see: they make history, but history carries them along with it' (Braudel 1984: 103). It's on this ethological level that history generates apprehension. The sense of history is, therefore, (a) an ethological phenomenon with (b) ethological consequences.

(a.) Historical sentience as an ethological phenomenon. 'The *formation* of our five senses is a product of the work of the whole of previous world history': like Nietzsche, Marx too sees historical sentience in ethological terms (Marx 1981: I, 601). Human sensation and cognition are historical, constantly being shaped and re-shaped by phylogenetic factors. History thus impacts directly, even subconsciously, on the body: it affects body-tissue. Its lessons are learned neurophysiologically by 'the immense faculty of reason that the body itself is', especially since (as Nietzsche remarks) 'there is more reason in the body than in the best wisdom' (Nietzsche 1988: IV, 39, 40). From behind history there seems to emerge – alarmingly enough! – more history: the natural history of human sentience.

But historical sentience [*aesthesis*] hardly coincides with historical knowledge [*illusio*]. The ethological impact of historical events is not the past the technics of historical research discloses. Historical sentience reveals, beyond historical comprehension [*illusio*], wider patterns of ethological significance: 'Human nature has its own history,' Peter Gay asserts; 'change is a set of subtle variations that the world plays on persistent, often elusive themes' (Gay 1985: 88). (Historical studies of "natural" features of the human species would include, e.g. Ariès' history of the family or of death, or Foucault's history of sexuality.) The Freudian and Marxist views converge: 'History itself is a *real* part of *natural history*, of the development of nature in relation to human beings' (Marx 1981: I, 604). Past forms of political, economic, social, and cultural life inflect the underlying natural history of humanity: 'the *whole of so-called world history* is nothing other than the production of the human being through human work' (Marx 1981: I, 607).

History thus belongs to the natural history of human self-reproduction: ethological development happens through human work and the evolving technologies that define it. Just as implements, workshops, machines, and factories signify a historically dominant socio-economic system, so the history of human industry is an 'open book of the forces human beings have at their disposal' (Marx 1981: I, 602). Further, sentience is always being historically conditioned. Hence, a distinction arises between what human beings actually – historically – produce and what, as nature, they really are or, under different conditions of social production, might yet become: 'In *usual material industry* ... we have before us in the form of *sensory, foreign, useful objects*, in the form of alienation, the *objectified forces* of human beings' (Marx 1981: I, 603). The historical process operates dialectically. It is a natural process of human self-production, but it works – as in this, its capitalist phase – through alienation and its overcoming [*illusio*]. Marx's historicist theory was meant to make historical processes comply with the real material needs of human beings [*aesthesis*]. This prognosis fades; the analysis lasts. What people under given historical conditions create, may not materialize as they thought [cf. *illusio*]. Inherited historical meaning does not oblige human intention; the sense of history the past objectifies, conflicts with the immediate sense of human existence in a historicized world.

(b.) The ethological consequences of historical sentience. The reflexive potential historical knowledge offers a historicized culture is its only redeeming feature. Late in the day it might just realize, *tout ceci nous vise au cerveau*: all this is targetted on our brain (Valéry 1957 / 1960: II, 969). It might just wonder how historical sentience affects mind and behaviour – i.e. human self-production, social identity. The issue is not: what can we do with all this history? (i.e. *Why History?*, *Why bother with History?*), but rather: what can all this history do to us?

A sense of history in a historicized world ultimately generates apprehension. It arises not just from the social crises or political incidents the historicized world itself produces, but also from possible ethological modifications or body-tissue changes ensuing from them. The apprehension is, in other words, generic. Valéry's cultural criticism echoes late nineteenth-century, conservative pessimism and its fear of degeneration. He regards *homo sapiens* as a 'zoological species that voluntarily tends to modify the domain in which it exists'. European culture, therefore, has proven historically to be 'a vast factory; a factory in the literal sense, a machine for producing transformations, but still an incomparable intellectual factory'. The resulting intensity of sensory stimulation in the city-street, at work, and at home, turns contemporary culture into a gigantic experimental laboratory and human beings into experimental guinea-pigs – except that there is no chief-scientist, no laboratory assistant, to manage the dosage of stimulants, and so no way of anticipating their ultimate ethological effects (Valéry 1957 / 1960: I, 1003, 1006; II, 1061–2). But the Marxist view is no different. History may well be the accumulated product of human work and its supporting technologies, a means of human self-reproduction. It's still a vast laboratory, its flasks and alchemical apparatus continually refining the forms of future work-disciplines and the ethological adaptations they impose (Negt & Kluge 1993: 25). Moreover, these technological metaphors are now stark reality. The socio-economic production-system and its technological management actually generate risks to human health and safety as a corporate, commercial strategy. In a historically unprecedented way, society has become a place for experimenting on human beings, since neither the industries them-selves nor their expert scientific advisors care what damage they cause to human life. Increasingly, it's the apprehensive, suffering public, the 'laboratory animals' themselves, who alert sceptical experts to the poisoning they experience (Beck 1986: 92).

In a directly visceral sense, it is impossible to know what specific permutation of the same old thing awaits the human species in history. Even so, as Nietzsche suspected, ethological mutation is surely happening now, and all the more drastically for being imperceptible because its time-scale is indeterminate and sentience mutates with it.

The organic conception of history

There is, then, something essentially organic about history. 'Cultures are organisms,' says Spengler: they share a common morphology with human beings, animals, trees, and flowers. As constituted collectively by customs, myth, technics, and art, as well as the peoples who incorporate them, high culture, in particular, is 'the consciousness of a single, gigantic organism [*eines einzigen ungeheuren Organismus*]' (Spengler 1977: 140, 596). This conception mixes Romantic philosophy of nature and 'Hegelian panlogism'. The customary expressions of a social or an ethnic group, conceptualized as social anthropology, get contextualized within a global, temporal panorama of human cultural activity. Local, unselfconscious practice, contributes to a pan-rationalistic, historical structure of human development (Weber 1988: 142–4). It also reflects the idea of process that underpins natural science and history, 'the two entirely new sciences of the modern age' (Arendt 1974: 232). With Galileo, Newton, and Vico, processes, not things, became objects of knowledge: the object of science was 'no longer nature or the universe, but history, the story of the coming into being, of nature or life or the universe'. Even before the formation of modern historical consciousness, the natural sciences had already become historical disciplines: 'Nature ... became a process. And all particular natural things derived their significance and meaning solely from their functions in the over-all process' (Arendt 1974: 296). Consequently, human nature too would reveal itself through the historical process it initiates: 'the process which ... invaded natural sciences through the experiment, through the attempt to imitate under artificial conditions the process of "making" by which a natural thing comes into existence, serves as well or even better as the principle of doing in the realm of human affairs' (Arendt 1974: 299).

The organic conception of history has thus a distinct, pragmatic force. It underpins a self-authenticating, holistic view of history 'as everything', as when Mill argues that 'states of society are like ... different ages in the physical frame; they are conditions not in one or a few organs or functions, but of *the whole organism*' (Popper 1974: 72–3). The 'close connection between historicism and the so-called *biological or organic theory* of social structures', therefore, makes history an indispensable, prosthetic element of human existence (Popper 1974: 19). It would make a sense of history both comprehensive and exclusive of any other sense – as Raphael Samuel demonstrates in *Theatres of Memory*, where he explores history as 'an organic form of knowledge'. Its sources (he says) are 'promiscuous, drawing not only on real-life experience but also memory and myth, fantasy and desire, not only the chronological past of the documentary record but also the timeless one of "tradition"' (Samuel 1994: x).

'Organic' certainly is the operative word for the 'promiscuous' 'sense' of history – and for two main reasons. The sense of history is a part of human consciousness: it shares its neurophysiology; it uses the same organic infrastructure (cf. 'experience', 'memory', 'fantasy', 'desire'). But then history has made *homo sapiens* into the socialized creature it has become, because it also sustains the cultural environment, the 'second nature'(i.e. 'real life', 'myth', 'the chronological past', 'tradition'), it organically needs (cf. Hegel 1961: 87).

But suppose human beings organically produced a historical situation that actually jeopardized their 'organic' being? Suppose 'we changed and denaturalized nature for our own worldly ends, so that the human world or artifice on one hand and nature on the other remained two distinctly separate entities' (Arendt 1974: 148)? Would history still be integral to the history of human nature? Could identity still be defined by cultural tradition? Would history even be 'organic' any more? Then historical imperatives would surely prove to be illusory. Only an aesthetic view of the human predicament would be left. Precisely this situation, human historical production turning against human life, characterizes the current predicament. In the 'risk society' the economic system is not just degrading the socio-biological habitat, but also, in the developed countries, delivering a general rise in consumption and opportunity that is destroying traditional forms of life and identity (Beck 1986: 7ff., 115ff.). Risk-production on this species-threatening scale provides ample reasons for being apprehensive. History becomes a trap: however the concept of 'organic' is configured, it offers no way out. The populistic celebration of the 'organic' wealth of the British social memory in, e.g. *Theatres of Memory* distracts from a starker reality. Especially in its organic conception, history proves to be a dangerous place. If, by contrast, Beck is right, it would be impossible to live there. But then it always was.

The 'organic' conception of history is, then, the most comprehensive, coercive version of a comprehensive, coercive form of knowledge. It explains why history perpetuates 'the same old thing', is regarded as society's 'default knowledge', and inevitably affirmative. It also explains why history is essentially conservative, why it activates archaic, regressive tendencies. Though it imposes itself metaphorically, e.g. as (a) 'an everlasting animal' or as an 'inexorable chain', history [*crg*] proves to be (b) secondary to the immediate sense of personal purpose or self-possession [*aesthesis*, *Eigensinn*], and (c) a subordinate genre of aesthetic representation.

(a.) 'An everlasting animal'. The organic sense of history is beguiling –
as George Orwell's essay, 'England your England' (1941), shows: 'In
whatever shape England emerges from the war ... England will still be
England, *an everlasting animal stretching into the future and the past*,
and *like all living things*, having the power to *change* out of all
recognition and *remain the same*' (Orwell 2001: 89–90 (my italics)).
Organic continuity (cf. 'everlasting animal') and identity (cf. 'remain
the same') offer a reassuring vision, both comprehensive and heterogeneous. Each individual is totally assimilated, yet utterly particular.
No wonder Orwell affirms: 'And above all, it is *your* civilization,
it is *you*' (Orwell 2001: 64). History is thus truly a prosthetic
aid to cultural identity: in the 1940s it was surely indispensable.
English civilization (says Orwell) '... is continuous ... there is
something in it that persists, as in a *living creature*. What can
England of 1940 have in common with the England of 1840? But
then, what have you in common with the child of five whose
photograph your mother keeps on the mantelpiece? Nothing,
except that you happen to be the *same person*' (Orwell 2001: 64
(my italics)).

The organic conception sanctions a fundamental, historicizing
conviction: that any new thing is "really" the same as the same old
thing. But because the distinction between change and continuity is
arbitrary, it leads to false claims based on fallacious images [*illusio*].
Regarding just the growth of technology after the 1890s, 'even the
most resolute upholder of the theory of historical continuity cannot
fail to be struck by the extent of the differences between the world
in 1870 and the world in 1900' (Barraclough 1974: 43) – not to
mention the differences between 1840 and 1940! The notion of the
'same' covers a multitude of discontinuities, disruptions, and traumas.
And the comparison between a century of English history and
individual self-development works only because the common organic
morphology it would demonstrate underpins it to start with. But the
organic sense of history is most misleading when it vindicates
the conceits of particularism, since it thus derogates from 'species-
essential interests' (Heller 1984: x–xi, 20–1; Heller 1987: 124, 155).
Orwell sees 'English civilisation' as essentially different from the
German, Russian, or Spanish he mentions. But it clearly cannot be
differently organic. At the same time, the Nazis were also using an
organic sense of history (cf. *Volk*, *Lebensraum*, aryan ethnological
research) to stress Germanic uniqueness.

Apparently open, tolerant, and comprehensive, the organic
conception of history, therefore, soon becomes closed, dogmatic,

and exclusive. Its ambivalence is not mysterious. If history is a vital organic resource, existence *ipso facto* is impossible without it. As with any technological prosthetic, the helpful support becomes an indispensable aid. Even as it serves, it enslaves.

(a.i) History as human nature. The organic conception of history claims to be total and absolute. Its benefits seem material; essentially it's an abstraction. History, in reality, is nothing organic: it's "just" an idea (e.g. the alleged continuity in English life). It boils down to an artful epithet (cf. *'everlasting* animal'). But that's precisely where its power comes from. It's this image [*illusio*] of organicism that carries conviction – as when Ortega y Gasset observes: '*Man, in a word, has no nature; what he has is ... history. ...* Man ... finds that he has no nature other than what he has himself done' (Ortega y Gasset 1962: 217).

This version of the organic conception, reinforced by identitary thinking, is extremely persuasive. Human beings create human nature through human history. 'History is the reality of man ...', he says: 'Through history he has made himself such as he is' (Ortega y Gasset 1962: 62–3). However, for this historical process to work, the human individual must always be more than just what he or she has been or even currently is. Human beings have no option but to progress; that is the only way 'to accumulate being, to store up reality'. They actually have to be mutable: that is their 'ontological privilege' (Ortega y Gasset 1962: 219). If they were not, history would lapse into the immutable consistency of the natural world (Ortega y Gasset 1962: 184). The past, therefore, has a crucial function: it offers both 'the same old thing' and something different. On the one hand, 'the past is man's moment of identity ... nothing besides is inexorable and fatal' (Ortega y Gasset 1962: 213). It represents 'only one fixed, pre-established given line' that guides history and, with it, the human nature it has yet to make. But it limits the available historical possibilities: 'the experiments already made with life narrow man's future. If we do not know what he is going to be, we know what he is not going to be. Man lives in view of the past' (Ortega y Gasset 1962: 217). On the other, the 'absolute presence' of human life is sustained by the past (Ortega y Gasset 1962: 213–14). The past is an existential resource: it 'forms part of our present, of what we are in the form of having been ...'. It confirms historical sentience as something truly organic: 'If, then, *there is* a past, it must be as something present, something active in us *now* ...' (Ortega y Gasset 1962: 212–13). But for being persuasive, this organic conception is no less ambivalent. The dynamic for change is driven by archaic motive, which ensures a sense of history that is totally coercive: 'History is ... the system of human experiences linked in a *single, inexorable chain*' (Ortega y Gasset 1962: 221 (my italics)).

Still, this organic conception of history is persuasive. It vindicates historical comprehension, and not just for the usual reason: 'we can only throw light on yesterday by invoking the day before yesterday; and so with all yesterdays' (Ortega y Gasset 1962: 221). History can legitimately claim to be the 'master discipline' because it aspires to make human knowledge congruent with human action. This aspiration itself is history's most powerful dynamic: 'this systematism of *res gestae* becomes reoperative and potent in history as *cognitio rerum gestarum*. Every historical term whatsoever, to have exactness must be determined as a function of all history' (Ortega y Gasset 1962: 221). Its corollary is that: 'to comprehend anything human, be it personal or collective, one must tell its history. ... Life only takes on a measure of transparency in the light of *historical reason*' (Ortega y Gasset 1962: 214). Ortega y Gasset aims 'to discover in history itself its original, autochthonous reason', by which he means 'literally, *a substantive reason constituted by what has happened to man*'. Historical comprehension offers uniquely 'the revelation of a reality transcending man's theories and which is himself, the self underlying his theories' (Ortega y Gasset 1962: 231). This is the fulcrum of contemporary historical interests, the crux of professional historical scholarship. Rooted in it is the notion of the past as a living cultural heritage, a notion that indiscriminately embraces state papers and Orwell's suet puddings, national treasures and family keepsakes. In this classic formulation, history defines itself as the principle of all knowledge already known. It alone discloses the "real" reality of all things. In other words: history makes total sense.

What started out as a simple epithet, has turned substantial. It seems to defy analysis: what does it leave of history to get behind? So why, then, does Ortega y Gasset insist in *The Revolt of the Masses* that 'we have need of history in its entirety, not to fall back into it, but to see if we can escape from it' (Ortega y Gasset 1964: 96). There is, apparently, nothing behind this idea: its substantiveness is the illusion. The organic conception of history folds when confronted with an actual historical situation, hence a type of human nature, essentially indifferent to it. This is the situation *The Revolt of the Masses* confronts.

(a.ii) Escaping from history through history. Ortega y Gasset blames nineteenth century history for creating a 'mass-man' and a

mass-society that subvert the very historical civilization that created them (Ortega y Gasset 1964: 52). The threat comes from the character of mass-society itself; but also, ironically, from the organic, historical dynamic that produced it. A mass-society is no longer orientated by historical consciousness but by technical expertise (cf. Ortega y Gasset 1964: 108–9). With its apparently unlimited capacities, modern technology obscures the historical dynamic of human self-realization. Technological accomplishment, produced as an enhancement to human life by historical effort, now turns into its exacting, necessary condition (Ortega y Gasset 1962: 150–3). Why should the 'mass-man', therefore, even need a sense of history if technology can realize all his aspirations? The answer is, the promise of technology is the most illusory of all historical illusions: 'Just because of its promise of unlimited possibilities technology is an empty form like the most formalistic logic and is unable to determine the content of life.' The modern and ongoing technological revolution is absolutely inimical to the sense of history: 'That is why our time, being the most intensely technical, is also the emptiest in all human history' (Ortega y Gasset 1962: 151).

Ironically, this predicament is an "organic product" of history itself. History is the 'mega-machine' that turns the historicized world into a technological world, as Ortega y Gasset, using a familiar image, concedes: 'The *whole of history* stands out as a gigantic *laboratory* in which all possible *experiments* have been made to obtain a formula of public life most favourable to the *plant* "man".' History is where ethological experimentation happens: 'we find ourselves face to face with the fact that, by submitting the *seed* of humanity to the treatment of two principles, liberal democracy and technical knowledge, in a single century the species in Europe has been triplicated' (Ortega y Gasset 1964: 52 (my italics)).

If the organic conception of history is absolute and total (cf. 'the whole of history'), Ortega y Gasset must accept what it produces, even when it works against the human interest. The philosopher of history himself is coerced by his own coercive historical design. He cannot deny the 'astonishing fact' that 'the teeming fertility of Europe ... means that heap after heap of human beings have been dumped onto the historic scene at such an accelerated rate, that it has been difficult to saturate them with traditional culture'. He must accept that 'the average type of European ... leaves the impression of a primitive man suddenly risen in the midst of a very old civilisation'. He has to recognize that the masses have 'no feeling for their great historic duties' but are still 'getting ready to take command of the world as if the world were a paradise without trace of former footsteps, without traditional and highly complex problems' (Ortega y Gasset 1964: 50–1). That's why he demands more history in order to escape from it. He could hardly demand less without contradicting himself.

History as a System, published in 1941, after *The Revolt of the Masses* in 1930, sets out the "more history" he apparently requires. Alienation from the masses here modulates into existential self-assertion by affirming historical consciousness – as though this alone sufficed to 'rise up against the XIXth century', as the origin of the masses' threat 'to send our continent back to barbarism' (Ortega y Gasset 1964: 52). "More history" may well make it possible to be "other", but only ever within the conceptual totality of the same old thing. But, organically, all history ever wants is more of the same. No wonder the entire historical process is 'full of illusions' (Ortega y Gasset 1962: 215). Clearly, Nietzsche's critique of mass-society was sharper. He knew not just that history had advantages and disadvantages, but that its disadvantages outweighed the advantages. Where Ortega y Gasset criticizes the nineteenth century for having 'let loose upon the area of history the great multitudes', Nietzsche saw that the 'great multitudes' were all too susceptible to the nostalgias, affinities, and resentments history inspired. The response to a historically induced social-psychopathology [*illusio*] could never be "more history", more of the same, but the ideal of the 'Overman' [*Übermensch*], a transhistorical mutation towards a better, fully human life.

Ultimately, the organic conception of history is deceptive. It's not actually tenable. Identifying human history with human nature ignores the fact that 'human existence is conditioned existence' (Arendt 1974: 9). This distinction between human nature and the conditions of its existence is crucial. Certainly, as Arendt explains: 'In addition to the conditions under which life is given to man on earth ... men constantly create their own self-made conditions, which ... possess the same conditioning power as natural things.' However, she insists: 'the human condition is not the same as human nature, and the sum total of human activities and capabilities which correspond to the human condition does not constitute anything like human nature' (Arendt 1974: 9). Both the condition of natality that offers the 'capacity of beginning something new', and the inherent unanswerability of the 'anthropological question' about what human nature really is elude historical comprehension (cf. Arendt 1974: 9–10).

(b.) Historical conditions and personal purposes. History can be organic – and not metaphorically. As Marx confirms, in order to make history, human beings must first be capable of living. Organically speaking, to survive they immediately need food and drink, clothing and shelter. So the very first historical act is to produce the means to meet these basic needs. The production of the material basis of life is thus a constant 'basic condition of all history', now, as thousands of years ago (Marx 1968: 354). This fact reveals two key symptoms of a historicized world. First, work constitutes history as a production-system: the products of human work continually react on the work-process itself. This process also vindicates an 'autochthonous reason' in history and its claim to be the 'real reality': history is the production-system of production-systems, a technology of technologies. Second, work itself has become a distinctive historical phenomenon, given that 'the significance work has acquired in industrial society is historically without parallel' (Beck 1986: 220). And a specific type of work has become historically significant, absorbing all other serious activities. Labour, securing the necessities of life for the individual or society, has become the 'common denominator' of all human activities, so that anything socially "unnecessary" (e.g. cultural or artistic activity) is 'subsumed under playfulness' (cf. Arendt 1974: 127ff.).[1] History [rg] has produced work as its dominant form.

(b.i) History and human needs. History conditions the way in which people make their living. This materialist organic conception of history is as ambivalent as the liberal-humanist (cf. Aron, Orwell, Ortega y Gasset), but differently ambivalent. The liberal-humanist conception apparently gives you more than you ever knew you had (cf. 'it is *your* civilization, it is *you*'). It bestows on you, if not the entire cultural heritage itself, at least the idea of it. No wonder historical knowledge seems absolutely vital: 'History is the systematic science of that radical reality, my life. It is, therefore, a science of the present in the most rigorous and actual sense of the word. ... The past is I – by which I mean my life' (Ortega y Gasset 1962: 223). The *real* cultural heritage is, of course, kept by museums, galleries, libraries, colleges, etc. as symbolic capital. Access to it is managed by curators, producers, publishers, directors, teachers, academics, etc.

---

[1] Arendt starts from a distinction between 'labour' – the reproduction of life's necessities, 'work' – the making of tools and artefacts, and 'action' – the creation of political institutions (cf. Arendt 1974: 7). Arendt represents modernity as the ultimate vindication of existence as labour (Arendt 1974: 230–2, 313f.).

Conversely, human beings work because existence is inherently, organically necessitous. The materialist conception reveals that history offers less than you thought would be vitally indispensable. Worse still, through the changing work ethic, it shows that history discredits what you already have. In the "old" capitalism, you were deprived of the total value of your labour and a work-related illness (e.g. silicosis, asbestosis) might blight your life; but you had an occupational identity (e.g. as a miner in a mining community; as a mill-worker). The "new" capitalism diminishes the personality: 'The conflict between *family* and work poses some questions about adult experience itself. How can long-term purposes be pursued in a short-term society? ... How can a *human being* develop a narrative of *identity* and *life history* in a society composed of episodes and fragments?' (Sennett 1999: 26 (my italics)). No wonder historical reality generates apprehension and alienation. That people still resort to history, to the same old thing, for compensation, is an ironic symptom of social disorientation, lack of public enlightenment, and the absence of a democratic will to defy the dominant ideology of economic liberalism. That heterogeneous historicizing practices – e.g. indulging the nostalgic appeal of heritage, tracing one's family tree, renovating steam-locomotives, collecting antiques – are popular, proves history's anaesthetizing effect. Numbing even the sense of alienation itself, these ludic, aestheticized forms of history bind their practitioners ever tighter to the social production process their alienation comes from.

Work, then, connects heterogeneous working individuals with the historical processes manipulating them. But it also generates conflict between these individuals' personal attitude, their own sense of purpose, and these processes. Hence, its ambivalence. The world of work underpins both conceptions of history, the liberal-humanist and the materialist. Both react to this unresolvable split between prevailing historical conditions [*Geschichte*] and innate sense of self [*Eigensinn*], expressed in the obduracy of self-possession. However, the liberal-humanist conception would close it by assimilating human nature and personal identity to historical processes, the materialist widen it by offsetting personal purposes against changing historical conditions.

(b.ii) Alienation. The effects of the 'new capitalism', history's latest thing, are a major cause of apprehension: 'the culture of the new order profoundly disturbs self-organization' (Sennett 1999: 117). The technologically driven, flexible political economy is to blame, given that 'time ... has no trajectory in a continually re-engineered, routine-hating, short-term political economy. People feel the lack of sustained

human relations and durable purposes' (Sennett 1999: 98). In this situation, the postmodern apprehension that sustained narratives are impossible because their coherence is socially implausible, is met by history as a heterogeneous, indiscriminate form of discourse that will after all, thanks to its comprehensive, identitary logic, come up with sense that makes sense [*illusio*].

But the dilemmas of personal character in the global economy are only the latest version of the same old syndrome, alienation: the individual inhabiting an '"iron cage" of economic necessity' in its current, historical [*rg*] incarnation, while longing anachronistically (via history [*crg*]) to turn it into 'a *castle* of romantic dreams' (Campbell 1989: 227 (my italics)). The normal experience of work has always involved 'instability', 'conflicting tensions', as individuals struggle 'to cope with the necessity of making trade-offs between need and pleasure', i.e. between what they have to do and the way they would like to be (Sennett 1999: 31; Campbell 1989: 227). In fact, alienation seems indispensable: the 'cultural logic of modernity', in fact the very 'dynamism of the West', relies on the tension generated between 'rationality as the activities of calculation and experiment' and 'passion, ... the creative dreaming born of longing' (Campbell 1989: 227). Being both rational and nostalgic, both instrumental and fanciful, history exacerbates alienation as it vindicates itself. Fuelled by both work and desire, history and capitalism drive a powerful production-process.

Alienation, therefore, challenges the liberal-humanist conception that identifies history with human nature and endows historical study with a humanistic purpose. Indeed, in imposing itself as an absolute, ideal form, the humanist conception simply affirms the prevailing conditions of work and production. Thankfully, history does not and cannot condition you, your identity, or your nature totally. Rather it displaces them with its own synthetic nostalgias, its own ludic conceits (cf. Wrigley 1994: 2; Jenkins 2003: 4–5). However exacting the claims of history [*Geschichte*], personal purposes based on obdurate self-possession [*Eigensinn*] persist. The material, organic substance history would totally organize and manage, the human body, is inevitably recalcitrant.

Where there's alienation, there is also imagination. In the ordinary world people live in [*Lebenswelt*], shaped by a human sense of things [*aesthesis*], imagination has a crucial, material rôle. Through 'symbolic conversion' it gives social expression to private, often painful need (cf. Freud & Breuer 1975: 147–8). Certainly, history, in the guise of labour, will make imagination seem unrealistic, playful.

But it is a necessary supplement to real life. Unlike the anaesthetic effect of history and the "normality" of labour, it vitally enables human beings to recognize, even overcome, their destitution. The reason is: 'imagining is ... the ground of last resort. That is, should it happen that the world fails to provide an object, the imagination is there, almost on an emergency stand-by basis, as a last resource for the generation of objects.' Certainly, made-up objects 'may sometimes be inferior to naturally occurring objects', but 'they will always be superior to naturally occurring objectlessness' (Scarry 1985: 170). Where history shows only how the world 'got to be the way it is', imagination reveals how the world could or should be – how necessitous, alienated individuals need it to be (cf. Cannadine 1999: 8). It demonstrates that the labour that, by organic necessity, binds human beings to the same old historical process, could make the world more responsive to human needs: 'work and its "work" (or work and its object, its artefact)' describe 'the phenomena of pain and the imagination as they begin to move from being a self–contained loop within the body to becoming the equivalent loop now projected into the external world'. Imagination works with and through the obdurate body, as something material, neurophysio-logical: 'It is through this movement out into the world that the extreme privacy of the occurrence (both pain and imagining are invisible to anyone outside the boundaries of a person's body) begins to be sharable, that *sentience* becomes social and thus acquires its distinctly human form (Scarry 1985: 170 (my italics)).

History, though the dominant, is not the only way to make the world. Against the world's indifference, imagination can make it more knowledgeable about human discomfort. Imagination ensures 'the eclipse of the given'. The artefacts, institutions, the material forms of culture it generates instead, effectively alter the world in line with human needs. Though these artefacts cannot feel pain, they objectify the awareness of pain; though they are not sentient, their design incorporates 'the *structure of a perception*' (Scarry 1985: 171, 288–9). Work, then, in itself would not be alienating, had this organic activity not been monopolized by history, the mega-machine for producing reproduction-processes.

(b.iii) The anti-realism of the senses. This obdurate sense of self [*Eigensinn*] derives from the fact that everyone can be 'the impartial spectator of his own conduct', particularly in moments of extreme distress (cf. Smith 1982: 148). It doesn't fall for history's claim to reveal the 'real reality' of ordinary life, to provide the 'unofficial knowledge' of society. It won't swallow the proposition that historical

knowledge is a prerequisite of citizenship either. It isn't taken in by the view that history [*crg*] is indispensable to ethics, to a social sense. It just doesn't buy the coercive idea that history has already decided not just how society is, but how you yourself are or even should be. It's the hypocrisy that puts it off: history actually has no ethical value, given that it admits indiscriminately saints and sinners, philanthropists and tyrants. Actually it subverts ethical principles, hence moral action, for the sake of social conformity.

Historically, the most coercive society is totalitarian. Here social life is lived on the plane of historical destiny: it eliminates whoever refuses its ideological vision. The memorial sites that stretch across central Europe, from *Le Struthof* to *Auschwitz-Birkenau*, testify to a historical rationale dominating the world of everyday life. They confirm the impossibility of living in a totally historicized world, specifically the world as re-configured historically by Nazi ideologists in the 1930s and 1940s. Here historical knowledge loses meaning: the imperative for survival depends not on knowledge but personal judgement, not on social conformity but personal attitude. Drawing on his experiences in the Dachau and Buchenwald concentration camps, Bettelheim explains that those who conformed to their social stereotype became socialized into the camps, dependent on their guards, or simply abandoned themselves, stood little chance of surviving. Instead, 'what permitted the prisoner to remain a human being' in a situation of total historical coercion was the imperative of 'keeping informed and aware of one's actions ... this minimal distance from one's own behaviour, and the freedom to feel differently about it depending on its character'. In situations that expose the individual to the fatal forces of history, Bettelheim insists on the aesthetics of self-possession [*Eigensinn*] : 'Those prisoners who blocked out neither heart nor reason, neither feelings nor perception, but kept informed of their inner attitudes, even when they could hardly ever afford to act on them, those prisoners survived and came to understand the conditions they lived under'. When confronting coercive historical reality, a totally historicized world, a world infiltrated with all kinds of fatalism, hanging on to 'the last, if not the greatest, of the human freedoms', is the sole response. This comes down to the right 'to *choose* one's own attitude' (Bettelheim 1986: 158) .

The "sense" of history is, therefore, secondary to the human cognitive system that immediately constitutes the sense of self, one's own individuality [*Eigensinn*]. Certainly, individuality is produced by the totality of society. But the individual can still oppose it, since the individual's opposition comes from society's own better understanding of itself. That's because, in investing the individual with knowledge that is better than that available socially and, therefore, historically, society works towards its own moral improvement (Durkheim 1996: 95ff.; Adorno 1982: 56). This perspective refutes not only the claim that history is the "real reality", but also its organic, physiological justification – e.g. the notion that history is 'as natural as breathing', that historical understanding is 'an intrinsic element of the condition of being human, in the same way as the physical functions of eating, sleeping and reproduction' (Lerner 1997: 199; Fulbrook 2002: 193). Quite the contrary: the personal sense of self always takes precedence. Clearly, 'had the range of sensitivities of the sensory system experienced even a slightly different evolution, the brain and the entire intellectual history of humankind would be radically different'. Only a 'subtle shift' would enable humans 'to see some forms of heat, much like the pit viper ... but be blind to some deep violets': 'the impact on our cognitive world would be tremendous' (Solso 1994: 45).

Generally, the human cognitive system, the 'reason of the body', in itself knows immeasurably more about the temporal existence of humanity than all of recorded history that, on the applicable time-scale, appears inadequate and brief. The fact is: '... the human sensory system and brain, which evolved over millions and millions of years, have remained structurally unchanged for hundreds of thousands' (Solso 1994: 47; cf. Nietzsche 1988: IV, 39, 40). It governs human existence immediately, not mediately as history does. It orientates and motivates; but it also warns and preserves. It's always ready and makes itself felt in the least flicker of apprehension – and for this reason: 'We see and interpret our modern world ... with the same old Pleistocene sensory system and brain whose primordial functions included seeing moving prey ... , making tools, surviving ...' (Solso 1994: 47).

A complex dialectic between the demands of history (i.e. of politics, culture, society, and economics) and the demands of personal life sustains the phenomenology of labour forces set out in *Geschichte und Eigensinn*. Ultimately personal attitudes can never be assimilated to the sense of history because the neurophysiological system always works in its own way. However much it is influenced by social conditions, it always regulates itself (Negt & Kluge 1993: 41). Further, in regulating itself, the sensory system shapes the individual's personal attitude. In establishing patterns of coherence, it also practices 'a vital criticism of conformity and coercive force' (Negt & Kluge 1993: 65; cf. Hegel 1979: 155, §IV.A).

In general, consciousness functions as a network of relationships between specific internal systems of self-regulation and external social processes, history included. Human autonomy is nothing other than the interconnectedness of these self-regulating systems (Negt & Kluge 1993: 397, 1091). Still, in this structure, the anti-realism of the senses is decisive, since this generates the self-confidence to defy the unflinching reality-principle in a society antagonistic to human interests. This anti-realism is a social effect generated by collective work experiences. Institutionalized social norms and controls produce in response deep-seated psychological structures as individuals renounce their desires or postpone their life-goals as a self-preservation tactic in coercive circumstances. No mutual understanding occurs between social institutions and personal psychological structures: the socio-economic process just reinforces their antagonism (Negt & Kluge 1993: 109, 1046).

For reasons of this sort, there is no real connection between the individual person and history. History is an inadequate guide not just to the present but also to how the individual observer relates to history as a whole. The individual is just one person, history a vast, diffuse production created by thousands of millions of people. He or she may well be versed in the history of the medieval Holy Roman Emperors or the Prussian state, but this kind of interest has nothing to do with a real relationship to history that far exceeds such a partial, selective interest (Negt & Kluge 1993: 598–9).

Particularly in the case of history, it is important to take into account 'the vast psychological implications of operating [i.e. now, in the twenty-first century] with a brain born and bred over a million years ago' (Solso 1994: 48). This basic asynchronicity in human reality surely provokes the atavistic regression that occurs in an "advanced" society. But it also provides that 'invincible piece of nature' that stands in the way of total assimilation by all forms of social domination (Freud 1977: 83). That's why self-possession, a sense of personal purpose [*Eigensinn*], is necessarily essential to this life-affirming reservation: that, where history is concerned, whatever is, is not quite right.

(c.) Historical veracities [illusio] *and human truth* [aesthesis]. Traditionally, history is a form of knowledge that seeks the truth of contingent realities. Apparently, it works pragmatically, accounting for sequences of events, sets of circumstances, political structures (e.g. *The Age of Extremes. The Short Twentieth Century 1914–1991*;

'The eastern empires from the challenge of Napoleon to the Restoration, c.1806–1830'). But how much sense historical accounts claim to make is problematic. To underpin the veracity of any specific analysis, history [*crg*] need not represent the total sense of the world. But the specific meaning of any particular account does imply a wider sense of history than it itself contains (e.g. it also requires already knowing what 'capitalism', 'imperialism', 'Europe', 'Napoleon', 'the Restoration', '1806' all signify). All historical explanation, therefore, involves a "weak form" of historicism. The contingent aspect of contingent realities history sets out to explain, gets removed by the explanation. The truth behind them, what really happened, reveals the "real" necessity that binds them.

History was always concerned with contingent realities, as Aristotle remarks: 'poetry is something more philosophical and more worthy of serious attention than history; for while poetry is concerned with universal truths, history treats of particular facts' (Aristotle 1965: 43–4). That the historically particular, not the poetically universal, has become a common value, does reveal an ethological mutation in human interests (cf. Nietzsche 1988: I, 34ff., §3). The production of cultural technologies for human self-assertion apparently dispels mythic fatality (cf. Horkheimer & Adorno 1973; Blumenberg 1974). The 'particular facts' of history, as the "default knowledge" of the social mind, set the universal standard of truth. The 'universal truths' of poetry have come to signify merely a cultivated taste. So where the tragic sense (e.g. with Aristotle) apprehends 'some great error' in the human condition and tracks its fateful consequences, the historical sense (e.g. with Hegel) sees reason as the content, substance, force, and truth of history and therefrom reconstructs the redemptive logic of world events (Hegel 1961: 48ff.). The tragic sense exposes the fatal eccentricity of human consciousness. The historical sense vindicates human intention (i.e. in terms of its successes or failures, culpabilities or mitigations, legacies or heritages, progressions or regressions). Tragedy represents a world haunted by dark, mythical necessity, lit only by reflective reason (as in Pascal's poignant image of the 'thinking reed' that captures the dignity of human vulnerability (Pascal 1963: 528)). History represents a world made meaningful by human beings taking responsibility for it and managing it for their own sake according to their own precedents, possibilities and truths (Blumenberg 1974: 69ff., 87ff., 247ff.).

But still the question of cognitive priority remains. Both poetry and history have a direct sensory basis [*aesthesis*]; both express human nature; both offer convincing forms of meaning in the versions of the world they project (cf. Goodman 1988a: 4–5). Moreover, both open up spheres of knowledge this side of the abstractions of rationalism. As Meinecke argues, 'after Locke's empiricism had discredited innate ideas, the credibility of the absolute character of rational truth dissolved, thus awakening a sober and open-minded interest in human phenomena and, at the same time, in their historical transformations' (Meinecke 1936: I, 14). On this positivistic basis, both aesthetics and history deal in the diversity of human experience. With its interest in its classical, modern, and national variations (e.g. in the work of Boileau, Muratori and Dubos) and their relative values, the discussion of taste as a specifically aesthetic concept, reveals historical change and social, cultural, and regional particularity: 'art, the language of individuality, makes modern civilized peoples aware of their individuality as a nation. It is easy to see that this way of thinking about national individuality was capable of influencing the formation of historical self-consciousness' (Baeumler 1981: 54–5).

What splits human sentience [*aesthesis*] from historical representation [*illusio*] is their respective ways of dealing with contingent realities – as Alexander Gottlieb Baumgarten (1714–1762) argues in his aesthetic theory. Rationalist logic is not the sole measure of truth in the life of the mind. As the norm of infinite, divine understanding, it transcends purely human ideals. Because human beings *ipso facto* have a limited understanding, filling human consciousness with conceptual clarity, though beneficial to logic, is detrimental to humanity (Cassirer 1961: 77). Baumgarten (like Marx much later) thus reduces knowledge to its material (i.e. physical and physiological) situation: he stresses its corporeality. For this reason he also re-evaluates the essentially human ethos of contingency: he proposes the idea of an inherently contingent, intellectual culture.

The new science of aesthetics derives from these two premises. Significantly, Baumgarten reaffirms aesthetics in its Platonic meaning as 'sensory cognition' [*aesthesis*] (Baumgarten 1988: 3–4, §1).[2] He thus insists on the latent truth-potential of the immanent sense of a purely human world. He conceives of the human body as a

---

[2] In his *Aesthetica* (1750/1758) Baumgarten defines aesthetics as 'scientia cognitionis sensitivae'. In *Theaetetus* Plato explores the view that 'perception is knowledge'. 'Perception' translates the Greek *aisthesis* which 'has a wide range of meanings, including 'sensation', our awareness of outer objects or of facts, feelings, emotions, etc.' (Cornford 1970: 30).

natural organism with a cognitive function dictated not by empirical philosophy but by its material situation. Physiological location determines the relative clarity or obscurity, the plenitude or partiality of what the soul perceives (Baumgarten 1983a: 4–5, §§509, 513). The customary preoccupation with reason, logic, and understanding overlooks the fact that many more mental faculties (e.g. imagination, memory) are involved in cognition (Baumgarten 1983a: 69). The routine, material operations that constitute the truth of everyday life, therefore, have real cognitive value.[3] The sensations thus produced are 'the truest in the whole world' (Baumgarten 1983a: 23, §546).

Baumgarten thus crucially defines a sphere of 'aestheticological truth' patterned not on abstract generalities, but on a plethora of particulars, tangible specifics, exemplary instances, and symbolic attributions. Still obeying the principles of contradiction, causality, and sufficient reason (like formal logic), it alone establishes a formal coherence for the phenomena produced by sensory cognition (Baumgarten 1988: 55–7, §§426–8; 69–71, §§440–1). Baumgarten's 'aestheticological truth' is thus a form of scepticism that recognizes the temporal and spatial limitations of the human mind, is content with knowing only an infinitely small part of the highest, logical truth, yet revels in the immeasurable plenitude, the chaos and material quality of ordinary human sentience (Baumgarten 1988: pp. 141, 147, 149; §§557, 561, 564).

Here, though, distinctions are necessary: Baumgarten, metaphysician as he is, discriminates. The human sense he defines, looks like the sense of history. His arguments for aestheticological truths sound like current historians' arguments for partial truths where, for various reasons, the "whole truth" about the past is unattainable.[4] But, like Aristotle, Baumgarten still isolates historical truth. He distinguishes between philosophical truth [*veritas*] and the verisimilitude attained by aesthetic cognition [*aesthesis*]. He also distinguishes between these two contrasting forms of truth [*veritas*; *aesthesis*] and the relative, partial verities of the historian, the experimental scientist, and politician [*illusio*]. The historian (says Baumgarten) needs to draw

---

[3] 'The aesthetic, then, is simply the name given to that hybrid form of cognition which can clarify the raw stuff of perception and historical practice, disclosing the inner structure of the concrete' (Eagleton 1990: 16). Totally erroneous, Eagleton's observation disregards the scope of Baumgarten's thinking.

[4] e.g. Arnold 2000: 77,116–7; Evans 1997: 249; Fulbrook 2002: 185ff.

much more on logical and critical understanding when managing the past and evaluating the sheer weight and diversity of material evidence, before constructing a final account (Baumgarten 1988: 169–75, §§583–8).[5]

These distinctions articulate a still fundamental typology of knowledge. *Veritas* is the mode of truth derived from knowledge of 'primary causes' or from 'Being *qua* Being'. Its sphere is metaphysics, specifically ontology: it operates with logically clear and distinct ideas (Aristotle 1996: 17ff., 147ff. (I.iii.1–2; IV.i, ii); Leibniz 1992: 29–30, 34). *Aesthesis* is the mode of truth derived from human experience. Its aim is to represent experiential reality as a reality for audiences or observers to experience for themselves. It deliberately creates illusions in imitation of real experiences. That's why poetry is 'sensuous speech'; that's why tragedy provokes 'pity and fear' (Baumgarten 1983b: 11ff, §§VIIff.; Aristotle 1965: 39). *Illusio* is the mode of truth of history, politics, and empirical science because they deal in issues that, being contingent and unclear, have to be demonstrated or proved. As Aristotle argues: 'there is no science of the accidental – because all scientific knowledge is of that which is always or usually so' (Aristotle 1996: 305 (VI.ii.12)). Science deals with what is necessarily always the case, i.e. first causes, Being, matter. History, being 'devoid of any object', belongs properly to the realm of rhetoric, since this is a science that, not dealing with 'any one definite class of objects', is 'merely a faculty for furnishing arguments'. Moreover, since history and politics also have an instrumental, managerial intention, their aim is rhetorical: they are concerned 'to discover the real and apparent means of persuasion' (Aristotle 1994: 13; 19 (I.i.12–14; I.ii.7–8); cf. Lévi-Strauss 1985: 312).

Since history, then, deals with accidental facts, i.e. 'antecedent possibilities', 'examples', it proceeds by means of 'enthymemes', i.e. by 'rhetorical syllogism' or 'rhetorical induction', that require a lesser standard of proof than logic offers (Aristotle 1994: 19, 271, 275, 295 (I.ii.7–8; II.xix.19–25 to xx.3–4; II.xxii.13ff.)). What it demonstrates, relies on likelihood, on general principles – particularly on knowledge that is already well-known (cf. Ginzburg 1999: 40). This type of accidental knowledge, this persuasive way of proceeding is, says

---

[5] That 'poetic discourse and history are clearly aesthetic discourses', and that 'poetic discourse is the larger concept by which historical discourse is determined', is just not the case (Gasché 1990: 150). That comes from relying solely on Baumgarten's *Reflections on Poetry* (1735).

Aristotle, particularly pertinent in forensic rhetoric dealing with the past as something 'already known', 'because the past, by reason of its obscurity, above all lends itself to the investigation of proof' (Aristotle 1994: 105, 455 (I.xi.40; III.xvii.10); Ginzburg 1999: 40, 42, 50). If history does now see itself as a science, it's because these procedures and proofs have been institutionalized and codified by the logic inherent in disciplinary practices, these 'thought-collectives' and their attendant, coercive, reality-generating 'thought-styles' (Fleck 1999: 85, 130, 134; 1983: 114). But that transformation has metaphysical consequences. In making the accidental into science, history promotes the accidental to a necessary 'first cause'. By comprehensively embracing both the heterogeneity and the "real reality" of all things, history makes itself uniquely persuasive as the science of "necessary accidents".[6]

Both aesthetics and the sense of history involve contingent realities. But the sense of history, being obligated to prove what it maintains, is still more limited and limiting (as when historians accuse filmmakers of distorting historical truth for the sake of intensifying aesthetic experience, if the experience did not actually happen in that way). Baumgarten's distinctions confirm history as a human sense, as an integral, but still partial, aspect of cognition (Croce 1984: 33). But they also reveal that the human sense of reality [*aesthesis*] will not be resolved into the accidental necessities [*illusio*] that make history make sense.

'The common denominator of all our sensibilities'

Except in the immediate, aesthetic response, the sense of history and the human sense of the world do not coincide. It's surprising

---

[6] The *locus classicus* for the transformation of the particular, contingent truths of history into the eternal truths of science is Vico's *The New Science* (3rd ed. 1774). Vico elaborates both 'a mental language common to all nations, which uniformly grasps the substance of things feasible in human social life and expresses it with as many diverse modifications as these same things may have diverse aspects'; and propositions 'which give us the foundations of the true, [and which] will serve for considering this world of nations in its eternal idea, by that property of every science, noted by Aristotle, that science has to do with what is universal and eternal'. He wants the reader to 'experience in his mortal body a divine pleasure as he contemplates in the divine ideas this world of nations in all the extent of its places, times and varieties' (Vico 1984: 67, §§161, 163; 103, §345). Vico thus constructs the principle that allegedly enables *all* history [*crg*] to be both heterogeneous and true, i.e. both comprehensive in scope while immune to all criticism of its epistemological basis.

historians (e.g. Gerda Lerner) insist they do: 'All human beings are practicing historians. As we go through life we present ourselves to others through our life story'. Following Dilthey, she affirms personal, existential reflection as the 'foundation of historical vision' – i.e. 'We stress different events as having been decisive at different times in our life history and, as we do so, we give those events new meanings.' She adds: 'People do not think of this as "doing history"; they engage in it often without special awareness.' Here, too, a sense of history becomes an organic component of cognition, a physiological reflex: 'We live our lives; we tell our stories. It is as natural as breathing' (Lerner 1997: 199).

Being both coercive and illusory, this view of history is evidently untenable. It's also worth remembering that "telling stories" is a euphemism for "fiction", for "telling lies": 'Life does not tell stories. Life is chaotic, fluid, random; it leaves myriads of ends untied, untidily. Writers can extract a story from life only by strict close selection and this must mean falsification. Telling stories really is telling lies' (Johnson 1973: 13, 14). 'Telling stories', therefore, makes historical truth less truthful than aesthetic truth. Further, history does not just 'tell stories'. The 'stories we tell as we live our lives' (e.g. oral history narratives) are distinct from historical accounts. On the one hand, there are those stories which, even if not lies, can be random, untidy, and selectively edited, depending on whom they are told to, e.g. a friend, a chance acquaintance, a historical researcher. On the other, there is the rhetorical figure of *narratio*, an ordered statement of the facts of a case, i.e. as one discourse component following the introduction and followed by division, proof, refutation, and conclusion ([Cicero] 1968: 8–9). *Narratio* is itself defined by the spin the discourse has – by its type (i.e. either epideictic, deliberative, or judicial (i.e. forensic)), by its various qualities (i.e. its clarity, brevity, or plausibility), and by the forms it takes (i.e. legendary, historical, or realistic) ([Cicero] 1968: 4–5, 23–7).

The existential motive, in particular, is spurious: 'nobody is the author or producer of his own life-story' (Arendt 1974: 184). Self-disclosure through speech happens within an existing web of human relationships and actions. This produces both stories and actions: it makes the narrator an agent not an author. Conversely, the fact that 'an individual life between birth and death can eventually be told as a story is the prepolitical and prehistorical condition of history, the great story without beginning and end'. The sense of history is constructed analogously to the *post mortem* sense that can be made of human life (except that history does not have a natural life-span and so sense-structures have to be constructed by historians, e.g. in terms of "periods" or "ages"). History becomes 'the story-book of mankind, with many actors and speakers and yet without tangible authors' because, just like the individual life story, it too is 'the outcome of action'. Even so, the subject of history, mankind, being 'an abstraction which can never become a social agent', remains *ipso facto* 'the great unknown in history' (Arendt 1974: 184 (cf. Cohen 1988: 13)).

In "telling stories", history accesses but a part of human reality. Why then do historians still see history as natural – as (a) a common social sense and (b) a socially particular sensibility? Going into that, reveals the affirmative nature of historical knowledge – both the legitimation it guarantees for traditional reasons and its ideological endorsement of whatever is, the same old thing.

(a.) History as society's "common sense". Historical knowledge is not just the work of the professional scholar, but 'a social form of knowledge; the work, in any given instance, of a thousand hands' (Samuel 1994: 8). That's why it's considered to be the 'general knowledge' of society, the lack of which is alarming and amusing when schoolchildren fail to identify, e.g. Sir Winston Churchill or Adolf Hitler. It functions as a performance-indicator of social intelligence. It expresses the widely held assumption that history is knowledge 'degree zero': i.e. the default form of knowledge, the knowledge everyone should know, even if they know nothing else. Hence, those who defer to a 'commonsense' theory of historical truth – i.e. those who argue that 'the meaning of commonsense events is normally given by their commonsense, every day context' or that 'an historian must use a commonsense theory of mind, relating ... attitudes and intentions to actions' – propose tautology (McCullagh 2004: 139, 153). In a totally historicized world, commonsense, the sense everyone has in common, *is nothing but* the sense of history.

If history is legitimately the 'unofficial knowledge' of society, then (as Nietzsche recognized) it will be heterogeneous and undiscrim-inating (Samuel 1994: 3ff.). And so it is. Those wanting "history for all" gladly affirm that 'any account of history as a social form of knowledge would need to admit, and rejoice in, the motley character of its following' (Samuel 1994: 23). History is essentially 'promiscuous': 'History has always been a hybrid form of knowledge, syncretizing past and present, memory and myth, the written record and the spoken word' (Samuel 1994: 443). It treats distinction as anathema. Society's historical interest consists of 'unstructured eclecticism': 'our tradition is no longer an organized historical corpus but a pot-pourri of everything that ever happened, in which a 1930s cinema attracts the same degree and type of interest as the Parthenon' (Lowenthal 1993: 383). Including anything but explaining nothing, promiscuity, hybridity, syncretism are the hallmarks of history as affirmative knowledge. The social hegemony of indiscriminate historical values and interests is the ideological endorsement of whatever is, the same old thing.

However, a paradoxical consequence ensues. Where history is natural and naturalized, it no longer seems distinctive to itself. Historical interests, therefore, seek always more history, if only to make it more distinctive for itself (but then, history, the same old thing, always hankers after more of the same: more is always more). The general public, naturally unconscious of their historicized environment, might well fail to identify figures from the nation's past or key historical events. What better justification for accumulating even more historical knowledge? – As though that, in a historicized society, would ever make any historical difference.

Take the following two examples. On American campuses, allegedly, history is a 'disadvantaged discipline' because it loses out to disciplines (e.g. psychology) that 'can examine in depth the behavior of living subjects' (Wilson 1999: xi–xii). But how, then, to argue for history being placed 'at the apex of intellectual pursuit'? Obviously because knowledge exists within a 'historical context ... history subsumes all other disciplines'. But this surely implies not only that history seeks 'Archimedean points from which to make value-judgements about the past', but also that history, as a discipline must, by its *own* definition, subsume itself under history, and then subsume that historically subsumed knowledge under history – and so on *ad infinitum*. Perhaps then 'we need ambitious and passionate historians ... willing to create new questions and answers'. What they would show is that, as 'change is the only constant', the 'otherness of the past' is the product of change. What they would offer is a 'perspective of this otherness' that 'cures us of our provincialism by revealing the uncanniness of our own world' (Wilson 1999: 4, 139). This argument only takes us back again to the usual indefinable quantities ('provincialism') and oneiric qualities ('uncanniness'). Nothing so indiscriminate belongs at any intellectual apex.

In fact, historical awareness seems to be inherently problematic for American culture as the symbol of social indifference to cultural distinction – as Christopher Hitchens argues:

> According to statistics compiled by the National Center for Education Standards, fewer than 19 percent of high-school and middle-school social-studies teachers in 1994 had majored (or minored) in history. That same year, when Alan Bennett's wonderful play *The Madness of George III* was released as a motion picture, its title was given as *The Madness of King George*. Hollywood's publicity people worried that audiences might think they had missed parts I and II.
>
> (Hitchens 1998: 40)

Here, too, the heterogeneous historical values already circulating in society offset the demand for distinctive historical knowledge – as in Hitchens' remark that 'there is still an unmet need, an unanswered yearning, for an intelligible past. It finds its expression in surrogate forms'. Including Hollywood film versions of Shakespeare's plays, TV documentaries on topics from the American Civil War to the Normandy landings, and Mel Gibson's *Braveheart* and its possible links to the revival of Scottish nationalism, these forms show how heterogeneous the social sense of history is (Hitchens 1998: 38). The article blames incompetent history teachers and the political correctness or the ideological (i.e. chauvinistic) tendencies of their aims and objectives for the public ignorance of American history. It explores the dangers of historical ignorance, coming out with the standard, clichéd stuff, the same old thing: public amnesia benefits totalitarian régimes and makes democratic governments less accountable; those who forget the past are bound to repeat it; the erasure of history is symptomatic of a wider loss of social reality and impoverishment of personal experience. It suggests as a remedy 'the idea of trying to teach the whole story, not just "warts and all" but as an *inquiry* or argument'; the conviction that 'history must become a field of ardent contestation and not another patch of arid middle ground', and that 'if properly joined, this battle would also and of itself lead to more confident and thoughtful citizens' (Hitchens 1998: 46, 47).

But this historical apprehension typifies the sense of history: a society indifferent to history allegedly thereby forsakes its common sense. The argument assumes at the start what it would prove: history providing the comprehensive reality of society; history (what else?)

defining the social "default knowledge". The predicament Hitchens describes is the same as Ortega y Gasset's: how to deal with indifference to history as a historical development, i.e. as a historical problem for contemporary society. The idea of overcoming it by more history, by more of the same, is bound historically to fail. A world of heterogeneous historical values inevitably denies any distinctive value, especially history as a 'field of ardent contestation', its distinctiveness. The economic interests that see the past as a value need 'surrogate forms' to make it sell. They are themselves powerful historical agents promoting heterogeneous products.[7] In any case, the real issue is always how to lead a meaningful life in the present rather than pacifying a meaningless life with "meaning substitutes", however contestable, from the past. As history's 'surrogate forms' particularly show, the world is always "ready made" by the accumulated "dead weight" of the past, compelled by the gathering momentum of all the energy ever invested in it, compelling us especially when we least suspect it (cf. Durkheim 1997: 104). It rarely responds to our own sense of what would meet our own needs and facilitate our own self-fulfilment – particularly if that sense finds a distinctive interest in history appealing.

(b.) Particular historical sensibilities. The promiscuity of historical interests and complaints about the ignorance of history are, therefore, two sides of the same coin. It surely reflects (as Nietzsche suggests) the emergence of multicultural interests and the plurality of social values, particularly in the liberal societies of the USA and Europe. The 'exemplars of the liberal form of life are always particular *common* cultures ... highly internally complex, embodying subtle adjustments among a variety of traditions and styles of life'. This means that 'there is no impartial or universal standpoint from which the claims of all particular cultures can be rationally assessed'. Consequently, 'any standpoint we adopt is that of a particular form of life and of the historic practices which constitute it'. Contrary to 'the philosophical anthropology of the Enlightenment', Gray insists, 'human identities

---

[7] e.g. the Hollywood film industry; *The History Channel*, run by A&E Television Networks, a joint venture of the Hearst Corporation, ABC, Inc., and NBC with over 125 million subscribers worldwide (http://www.aetv.com/global/corporate/index.jsp? NetwCode=AEN(16.02.2004)); UKTV which, besides *UK History*, runs entertainment channels, including *UK Style* and *UK Food*. The past produces a wide range of profitable things, from crude oil to facsimiles (cf. the *Past Times* shopping catalogue).

are always local affairs, precipitates of particular forms of *common* life, never tokens of the universal type of generic humanity' (Gray 1995: 79 (my italics)).

The dominant liberal pluralism makes historical sense hetero-geneous, both by vindicating academics' indiscriminate, specialized interests and by creating a multifarious social need for multifarious historical identities. Academic specialization, the study of increasingly localized issues or of the traditions of particular, common cultures, helps sharpen particular historical sensibilities (be they, e.g., of Ugandan migrants to Britain in the 1970s or of experts on the architecture of medieval cloisters). The historical interest in a liberal, multi-cultural society operates, therefore, as an 'exasperated form of defence against gigantic and anonymous History', the generic structure of universal humanity (Ariès 1986: 58). Historical research needs to focus on particular issues, and local interests, because history, the grand narrative of a transcendent humanity, often ignores them.

However, the recognition micro-history offers is illusory: particu-larized, specialized history is still history, part of an implied, larger, grand design. By definition a comprehensive discipline, history provides a total context for all realities (i.e. all sensibilities, all identities), however particular they may be. Particular historical practices may identify particular cultures, but their own sense depends on them being 'determined as a function of all history' (according to Ortega y Gasset) – hence, on implied generic structures, even though they need not involve the philosophical anthropology of the Enlight-enment. We live in an 'expanding historical culture': history has become the only means for all kinds of social, cultural, common particularities to be recognized (Samuel 1994: 25). Hence Ariès' observation, that the increasing popularisation of historical interests in the course of the twentieth century is 'an important socio-logical fact': history has become 'the common denominator of all our sensibilities' (Ariès 1986: 49, 58).

Consequently, in ignoring generic events in history as specifically generic events, even though their particular sense derives ultimately from a generic structure, post-liberal, postmodern multi-culturalism has a clear, ideological intention. It breaks the "natural" link between historical specialization (i.e. the cultivation of particular historical sensibilities) and the humanistic, species-essential signifi-cance of history (cf. Ortega y Gasset, Aron), always cited as the ultimate, ethical justification of studying history. It represents the deliberate rejection of any human sense, the eradication of human solidarity, the repudiation of human species-essential values (Heller 1984: 15). It uses history as the most widely available, hence most effective means, to propagate its chaotic, pessimistic vision. 'Particularity is the subject of alienated life': the historical culture of local particularities and common sensibilities is essentially anti-human, a derogation from species-essential interests and aspirations conducive to the solidarity of humankind itself – as conflicts, e.g. in Northern Ireland, the former Yugoslavia, and in Israel have shown (cf. Heller 1984: 20; Heller 1987: 124–5, 154–5).

This ideological tendency clearly comes out in Ariès' own work. Its preoccupation with the traditions of privacy and the rituals of death surely reflects the influence of the *Action française*, the French fascist movement, on Ariès' formation as a historian (Boutang 1999: 433). His interest in the French population, in 'its real territories and families', and 'lived traditions at the heart of local communities', confirms his own view that the 'veritable historian' would be the 'veritable adept' of its most prominent publicist, Charles Maurras (1868–1952). In this way (as Roger Chartier remarks), '"History seen from below", entirely occupying itself with the study of specific mentalities and unconscious determinations, converges with the political, but even more existential, adherence to perpetuated particularities and cultivated differences' (Ariès 1986: 19, 253).

The most decisive argument for common sensibilities and perpetuated particularities comes, then, from a political philosophy intended to repudiate humanity as a socializing value, hence to affirm the dominant "what sells, goes" attitude of the free-market social and economic ideology (cf. Davies 2002a: 32–4). Clearly, then, the ingrained specialization of historical study that both responds to, and cultivates particular historical sensibilities, has no necessary connection with human species-essential values. It doesn't so much undermine the ethical, humanistic value of history as a humanities discipline, as reveal that this value was always a cosmetic touch, a final gloss. Precisely in affirming multi-cultural diversity, the flourishing heterogeneity of historical interests and identities is effectively nihilistic.

History presents itself as total sense, because it claims to be organic, naturally innate. In pretending to make sense of everything and anything, it produces a historical culture that is both heterogeneous and indiscriminate. It encompasses indifferently the universal and the particular, the global and the local, self-incrimination and nostalgia, traditional sensibilities and the latest things. But the result is a meaninglessness that negates first and foremost the species-essential values actually inherent in human diversity. By its very nature, history can't make any specific human sense of the world: it remains mesmerized by its own illusions [*illusio*]. In persuading society that senseless heterogeneity makes sense, history is really only affirming what it always affirms: whatever is, the same old thing. History, as *illusio*, effectively isolates itself from human experience and human reality, from sentience as such that, being archaic, immediate, and 'anti-realist' is all the more obdurately reliable [*aesthesis*; *Eigensinn*]. Like all ideology, 'emancipated from the reality that we perceive with our five senses', history – here too a 'sixth sense' – 'insists on a "truer" reality concealed behind all perceptible things, dominating them from this place of concealment' (Arendt 1986: 470–1). That whatever is, is not just the "real", but the only reality, is what it affirms ideologically – unlike our own sense.

Variation 2
History as Apprehension

'The anguish secreted by human infirmity'

Braudel's inaugural lecture at the Collège de France in 1950 links anxiety and history. History (it says) depends on material social conditions. It is the "child of its time": if it produces anxiety [*inquiétude*], it's 'the very anxiety which weighs on our own hearts and minds'. Braudel is reflecting on a century already 'too rich in catastrophes', that has both invalidated and transformed the traditional methods and aims of history. The events of the previous four decades have been particularly cruel, hurtling us towards the common destiny of human beings, hence towards the crucial problems of history. If only to remain alert, historians 'had constantly to draw on the suffering and flagrant insecurity of human beings'. History is no longer a calm, reassuring enterprise. It leaves us uncertain about how to define its scope. The idea of the 'solid ground of history', to which both Ranke and Goethe subscribed, seems utterly alien. After all, Braudel asks: 'why should the fragile art of writing history escape the general crisis of our epoch?' (Braudel 1984: 15–17, 19).

However, Braudel doesn't see apprehension as endemic in history. It can be remedied: the scope of hitherto traditional history just needs broadening. The alarming complexity of human experience is better managed by extending historical interests to include economics, institutions, social architecture, civilizations, and the various different locations and time-scales they imply (Braudel 1984: 23ff.). But the remedy defeats itself. Enlarging the scope of history only further historicizes an already historicized world. It makes it more apprehensive.[1]

Historical discourse articulates apprehension. Tragedy reveals fatal flaws in the human condition, produces pity and fear, and resolves them by catharsis. Comedy exposes human obsessions, focusses on their absurdity, and alleviates them through laughter. History is predisposed towards apprehension. It details the repetitive-compulsive tendencies to self-incrimination in human beings. However, it offers no resolution or happy ending, let alone redemption. It provokes Aristotelian 'pity and fear' but withholds catharsis. That's because the sense of history is melancholic.

That things change, both stimulates historical knowledge and induces melancholy. Underlying both reflexes is apprehension. Melancholy arises when there is 'no correspondence between the internal experience of time passing and the movement of external things' (Starobinski 1989: 61–4). Melancholy, like history, dwells on the vanity, transience, and ruination of the world. The problem of meaning is as acute for the historian as it is for the melancholic – as Dürer's engraving, *Melencolia I* (1514), suggests. The angel of melancholy, surrounded by the signs and symbols of all human knowledge, confronts the sheer heterogeneity of all mortal things: the primordial situation of historical consciousness. Hers is a world bereft of a theological armature, for once a truly human world: whatever meaning can be gleaned from it, must be constructed from this heterogeneity. But it is psychologically problematic, existentially arduous: humanity inevitably takes the rap for the outcome (cf. Böhme 1989: 71–3).

'Imagine the terror of living in a world without any idea of the causal processes at work in it' (McCullagh 1998: 302): the historical condition is constituted by a quest for a sense in human activity, the fear that it is undiscoverable, and the depressing conclusion that 'partial truths', 'fair descriptions', and heterogeneous arrangements will have to do. That's because history is what is wrong with the world. It's symptomatic of a human situation that is inherently terrifying and depressing – not just because (a) apprehension is endemic in the human situation, but also because (b) history, as human action, does nothing but generate apprehension, while (c), as knowledge, denying it.

---

[1] As is shown by Sande Cohen's devastating semiotic critique of Braudel's mentality (Cohen 1988: 233ff.).

(a.) Apprehension is endemic in the human situation. In *The Natural History of Religion* (1757), Hume explains why: 'We hang in perpetual suspense between life and death, health and sickness, plenty and want, ' he says. We do not have 'either sufficient wisdom to foresee, or power to prevent those ills, with which we are constantly threatened.' They are 'distributed amongst the human species by secret and unknown causes, whose operation is oft unexpected, and always unaccountable.' So 'these *unknown causes*' themselves become 'the constant object of our hope and fear'. Because we cannot comprehend what immediately affects us most, 'the passions are kept in perpetual alarm by an anxious expectation of events' and 'the imagination is equally employed in forming ideas of those powers, on which we have so entire a dependence'.

In response, Hume advocates the use of 'intelligible philosophy'. If that were used to 'anatomize nature', 'men ... would find, that these causes are nothing but the particular fabric and structure of the minute parts of their own bodies and of external objects; and that, by a regular and constant machinery, all the events are produced, about which they are so much concerned'. But 'intelligible philosophy', is the one thing that 'exceeds the comprehension of the ignorant multitude, who can only conceive the *unknown causes* in a general and confused manner' (Wollheim 1966: 40). They explain their fearful lives by recourse to anthropomorphic identifications. To create transcendent meaning in the midst of absurdity, they resort to 'identitary logic' (cf. Castoriadis 1975: 284–5, 311). It is (says Hume) a 'universal tendency of mankind to conceive all beings like themselves, and to transfer to every object, those qualities, with which they are familiarly acquainted'. What spurs mankind immediately to 'acknowledge a dependence on invisible powers, possessed of sentiment and intelligence thinking', is their 'absolute ignorance of causes', and their 'being at the same time so anxious concerning their future fortune'. Anxiety, as a psychological state, makes us respond psychologistically, ascribing to these 'unknown causes' 'thought and reason and passion, and sometimes even the limbs and figures of men, in order to bring them nearer to a resemblance with ourselves'. But because they cannot be unmasked or seen differently without 'intelligible philosophy', they appear 'always in the same aspect', hence 'are all apprehended to be of the same kind or species' (Wollheim 1966: 41). The identitary logic of society just reinforces knowledge already known, the 'same old thing': it automatically substantiates itself.

Hume's comments on the psychology of religious belief apply to historical knowledge. Historical comprehension and religious belief do converge: both are sacrosanct. Like religion, history has a reassuring function: 'as moral mediators between past and present, historians ... appear as saviours' (Southgate 2000: 91–2). History allegedly constructs order from the remains of the past, justifies what happens, stabilizes the contingent experiences of everyday life, and gives shape and purpose to the world. It could become even a religion-substitute, the 'faith of fallen Jews' (Yerushalmi 1996: 86). History also offers something like a final judgement. History (as Hegel remarked) becomes effectively the ultimate judicial authority of the world (Hegel 1967: 288, §340). And sooner or later, villains and victims, the great and the insignificant, the powerful and the powerless, the achievers and the failures, all appeal to it to claim retribution, redemption or vindication. Moreover, historians themselves defer only to God. Aron insists that the human world can never know the full truth of a person's biography: 'The historical interpreter composes just an image [cf. *illusio*]. Only God would grasp the unity of an ultimate intention' (Aron 1986: 137). Going in for long-term observations where, 'far from our personal lives and our ordinary misfortunes, history writes itself', Braudel finds refuge in the position of God the Father (Braudel 1994: 15). Historians bestow on themselves a charismatic aura that derives from the divinatory skills that disclose exclusively to them the "real reality" of the "real past" that once "really" existed, and so raise them up above the centuries' ebb and flow to survey their transcendental intention. This only confirms Montesquieu's view, that 'historians are stern examiners of the actions of those who have walked upon the earth, and they resemble those magistrates in Ancient Egypt who summoned to judgement the souls of all the dead' (Montesquieu 1949: 1133).

History and religion have a common root in apprehension. They feed off the endemic apprehensiveness of the human situation. They are governed by the same illusory intention, i.e. to put a transcendental gloss on ordinary life. Both affirm that 'to be within history is at the same time to be capable of a transcending grasp of it'; that 'history is itself inseparable from transcendence' (Fackenheim 1994: 160). As teleology, providence, or theodicy, history always endorses an essentially religious world-view. According to, e.g. Bossuet's *Discourse on Universal History* (1681), God's will permeates everything. What appears as chance or irregularity, is the fault of the purely human, essentially limited perspective on things. In particular, the Divine will is revealed in the political realm, specifically through the apprehensiveness it generates: 'From the pinnacle of heaven, God holds in his hands the reins of all the kingdoms ... and from there he stirs up all the human race. If he wishes to create conquerors, he sends out terror [*l'épouvante*] to precede them ...' (Bossuet 1961: 1025).

(b.) History, then, does nothing but generate apprehension. History has always generated apprehension. As Hegel observed, 'world history is not the ground of happiness'. Periods of happiness (he explains) are 'blank pages' in history. 'They are periods of harmony': they lack any internal principle of opposition to produce the conflict that actually drives history (Hegel 1961: 70–1).

Actually being in history is a source of apprehension. CNN's "landmark documentary" [*sic*], *The Cold War* (1998–1999), provokes apprehension when I learn fuller details about the tense confrontation of the USA and the Soviet Union during the Cuban missile crisis in 1961. In *my* life-time (for heaven's sake!) there was nearly nuclear war which would have put paid to *my* life! When the same documentary tells me about the nuclear-arms race, I feel apprehensive that leadership élites seriously pursued a lunatic policy called "mutual assured destruction". That this policy allegedly "worked" does not reduce the risk of inadvertent hostility through human error or technical malfunction. I watch a documentary about the treatment of deaf children in Britain in the 1920s with mounting apprehension as each new interviewee retails from their personal childhood stories of abandonment, institutionalized brutality, and bureaucratically induced desperation. I watch on the television in my Berlin hotel room archive footage of halcyon days in late 1920s Berlin, with the breezy melody of '*Wochenend' und Sonnenschein*' ['Happy Days are Here Again'] as its theme tune, only to be alarmed at its near-sighted insouciance. These and similar instances we apprehend, actually are physically arresting. We are, in our turn, *apprehended* – seized by them personally, physically. The historical scale may be the macro-political: all the more reason why our own (insignificant) lives are collectively targeted. It may be the micro-social: but the individual narratives of personal misery coalesce into the spectre of a bureaucratic, perversely managed society that owns us all. But, then, being in history has always been a source of apprehension. 'Who can read of the cruelties and oppressions of Verres without horror and astonishment?' Hume exclaims (Hume 1971: 18). Rousseau's vision of the innocence of human origins, expressing alienation from the present, is a reflex reaction to a history so decadent that it promises an even more alienating future. This regressive sentiment (says Rousseau) will, therefore, be a 'source of apprehension [*effroi*]' for an unenviable posterity (Rousseau 1959: 133).

Apprehension, then, comes into its own in history – for several reasons:

(b.i) Human beings are by nature apprehensive. Apprehension is a response to human vulnerability. In *The Birth of Tragedy* (1872), Nietzsche observes that the Ancient Greeks knew all about the terrors of life: that was why they invented tragedy. As the myths of Prometheus, Oedipus, or Orestes show, they lived in constant apprehension of what remorseless fate had in store for them (Nietzsche 1988: I, 35, §3). In his *Pensées* (1670), Pascal expresses the sheer terror induced by the cosmic isolation of a human species that, compared to the gaping void which is the universe, amounts to nothing and everything: 'the everlasting silence of this infinite space terrifies me' (Pascal 1963: 526, 528). Reduced to its own terms, the human condition is nothing but 'inconstancy, boredom [i.e. melancholic *acedia*], and apprehension [*inquiétude*]' (Pascal 1963: 503). Freud sees the individual subject (the ego), beset by all the various pressures of life, as the 'veritable site of anxiety' [*die eigentliche Angststätte*] (Freud 1982: 206; Freud 1986:10). No wonder, then, that apprehension is endemic in the experience of living in an already historicized world, taken hostage by its prevailing technologies and mired in all kinds of interlocking crises: political (the future of Western democracy), economic (the unprecedented demands of globalization), social (the global distribution of health, prosperity, opportunity); ecological (industrial pollution, the destruction of the rain forests). Humanity is driven to seek redemption from all this through what Edgar Morin calls the 'anguish incessantly secreted by the infirmity of the human condition'. 'We have to live in anguish,' he says, 'and recognize at the frontiers (or at the heart?) of hope the nagging presence of despair' (Morin 1999: 60). The basic human disposition towards being-in-the-world [*In-der-Welt-sein*; *Dasein*] is apprehension [*Angst*]: 'Human finitude, *qua* human, manifests itself as anxiety-about-being-in-the-world-as-a-whole' (Fackenheim 1994: 159–60).

(b.ii) Apprehension is the estranged consciousness *of historical consciousness.* Being aware of what happened before, apprehension grows keener. In a historicized world, it becomes acute. Knowing what

happened, it dreads what is possible in history, what history makes possible. And for this reason, the past has already decided how the world should be. The clock cannot be turned back: neither the destruction of the great library of Alexandria, nor of the World Trade Center can be undone. The historical outcome of the ever-extending past has already decided for us. It has already taken many crucial decisions out of our hands. Hence, we become apprehensive of similar determining events we suspect are already, even now, in preparation.[2] Life in an already historicized world is truly that described by Kierkegaard. Who would not gladly claim their freedom with all the risks it involves? But hasn't history already got there first? History's management of the world has already implicated us, incriminated us. History already makes us apprehensive. We have reached 'that *consequence* of the historical situation' (as Kierkegaard argues) where 'the individual in dread of sin produces sin'. History has fostered its own climate of risk. Our historical situation has already fatally compromised us: 'The individual in dread, not of becoming guilty, but of being regarded as guilty, becomes guilty' (Kierkegaard 1967: 67 (my italics)). History nurtures apprehensiveness.

So apprehension must resist being persuaded by history. Remarkably enough, it bears its own remedy within it. Apprehension is by definition an *always actual* sense: after all, 'it is in the immediate present that the cognitive subject actually lives' (Varela 1999: 45). It has in itself the capacity to distanciate the apprehensive subject; it gives it an immediately reflective sense of self-possession [*Eigensinn*]. As it kicks in, apprehension smashes the conventions that give the world its normal meanings, which include the rationales of historical explanation (in other words, it makes dissent from any knowledge already known imperative).

Apprehension sees that 'history is pathology in the process of self-realization', a process of human self-incrimination (Morin 1999: 28). It, therefore, enables the anguished human being to adopt a diagnostic stance towards the precarious world that frames his or her existence. This is because, though mindful of what happened before, it is more urgently directed forward, orientated towards what is to come, by the actual present. Apprehension thus makes human beings the sentient and moral creatures they are capable of being. It's the precondition of a humane, but not a historicized, culture.

---

[2] The first drafts of this section were written a few weeks before 9/11.

*(c.) **History denies the apprehension it causes.*** Historical under-standing is split between comprehension and apprehension. Compre-hension is an academic procedure; apprehension, an existential experience: 'apprehension is created in a climate emphasizing constant risk, and apprehension increases when past experience seems no guide to the present' (Sennett 1999: 97). The one comes up with the precious constructs of the 'actually quite narrow' current 'professional expertise amongst historians' (Black & MacRaild 2000: 5). The other comes from our "incorporation" into the world of history, most directly through prevailing social and economic practices: 'What's peculiar about uncertainty today is that it exists without any looming historical disaster; instead it is woven into the everyday practices of vigorous capitalism. Instability is meant to be normal' (Sennett 1999: 31). It reproduces the polarity between the 'predatory embrace' of history (i.e. the technological macro-structures that produce it [*Geschichte*; *illusio*]) and the redemptive recalcitrance of personal behaviour [*Eigensinn*; *aesthesis*] (cf. Sontag 1991: 74). Split thus between comprehension and apprehension, historical knowledge is always already compromised.

(c.i) Historical understanding needs both comprehension and apprehension. It is both a technical, academic operation and, as a means of self-orientation, a cognitive imperative (cf. Appendix: Table 3). Historical understanding, being extrapolated from this imperative, shares its basic features. History begins with the apprehension of certain data and ends with general inferences drawn from them within a comprehensive framework (e.g. the historical period, substantive event, etc.) supplied by knowledge already known – as Dilthey suggests.

What differentiates the hermeneutic process of understanding [*Verstehen*] from the technical, academic process of comprehension, 'the abstract intention to know what happened' [*das abstrakte Wissenwollen*], is apprehension (Dilthey 1959: 140). Apprehension immerses historians in the otherness of past life, because it draws on the historian's immediate life-experience [*Erlebnis*], the aesthetic substratum [*aesthesis*] of his or her behaviour and thinking (Dilthey 1959: 80). The problem of representing past experience in all its vital complexity cannot but generate 'concern' [*Sorge*] and 'stress' [*Leiden*] (Dilthey 1959: 139). But this is where comprehension comes in. It resorts to common identitary forms [*Gemeinsamkeiten*] that derive from the hegemony of the same: the structures of state, society, culture, and religion, both immanent in, and transcending experience. Behind these lies the supreme identitary concept, 'common humanity', that ensures history continues to disclose human self-knowledge through reflection on the cultural forms human life has created. Consequently, the past is not a 'remote object', but an active nexus of already historicized experience (Dilthey 1959: 140).

In the process of establishing historical knowledge comprehension eclipses apprehension. The reason is:

(c.ii) Historical understanding becomes comprehensive by denying apprehension. This denial affects the way historical discourse is organized and received. The discipline conventionally differentiates 'serious' historical monographs, text-books, and specialized articles from other works that just reflect on what history means and what it means to be a historian (cf. Marwick 2001: 273). That history splits like this, exposes a fault in the knowledge it produces. That this disciplinary distaste for self-reflection is professionally sanctioned, also explains why history [*crg*] causes apprehension.

This fault can be regarded in two ways. It shows that the conditions for producing knowledge differ from those for reflecting on it; but also that both standpoints are 'required for assessing knowledge as a whole in terms both of the motives which drive it forwards and the enduring logical conditions through which it exists' (Cassirer 1994: 279). Or it reproduces the duplicity inherent in idealist theories of knowledge: the distinction between the absolute ego (the – comprehending – pure knowing subject) and the empirical self (the situated – apprehensive – social individual). This split divides knowledge and existence or, more precisely, knowledge about knowledge from knowledge about existence. Knowledge about knowledge produces (e.g.) those philosophies of cognition represented by Kantian and post-Kantian philosophy. They are *transcendental* constructions of reality that drive a metaphysics of human historical purpose. The practical problem is how to create these structures in ordinary life. Fichte expounds the infinite capacity of the absolute ego to fashion its own world: but the desperate empirical self first needs courage to defy convention and claim its freedom. Hegel elaborates the epic process of the world moving towards complete self-knowledge: any particular individual is humiliated by the parochial part he or she plays in it. But the converse of this idealism is more disturbing. If the empirical self takes itself for the absolute ego, the parochial claim has absolute force: contingent preference becomes absolute truth. For this reason, those who criticized idealism (e.g. Kierkegaard, Marx, and Nietzsche) based knowledge on the apprehensive experience of everyday life.

Academic practice is the last refuge of crude idealism – 'designed for maximum distance from reality and intimate appropriateness to reality' (Cohen 1988: 6). The 'working historian', with his vast documentation and comprehensive knowledge, comes close to Fichte's absolute ego, 'the absolute totality of reality' (Fichte 1970: 59, §4). History's very claim to comprehend the "real reality" of the world relies on a cognitive abstraction (cf. Oakeshott 1999: 28). This is because historical meaning and intention are essentially problematic. The outcomes of historical events are often unintended by the agents involved. However, historical comprehension always presents them retrospectively in a coherent and meaningful pattern. That's because its ideal transcendent perspective is meant 'to make unthinkable the negation of that "which ties one to reality" and holds one in place'; it 'emphasizes the inseparability of historical discourse from the things discoursed about' (Cohen 1988: 46, 200). It employs a logic that is neither subjective (i.e. of the agents themselves) nor objective (e.g. as in natural processes), but inherently historical – i.e. an autochthonous rationale that transcends, but still governs the particular historical situation under analysis (cf. Castoriadis 1975: 62, 70). History thus locates itself 'in a place that one can do nothing about, but which affords history the power to enact its overall accumulative functions' (Cohen 1988: 28). This ideal, transcendent nature of historical reality explains why the "lessons of history" can never be learned, let alone applied. The expectation that they should be, arises from the inability to discriminate between the logical, comprehensive plane on which history looks coherent and the sphere of ordinary life in which particular agents have only a partial perspective on the events that involve them. Apprehensive these agents might well be: they look in vain for support to historical understanding that, once it had repressed apprehension, had already eliminated any possible present or future relevance.

(c.iii) Apprehension, once repressed, returns to spook the rationality of historical comprehension. Historical comprehension is, apparently, objective, unbiased, and impartial. Disciplinary correctness [*Denkzwang*] demands absolute reticence towards all those apprehensive matters (i.e. political, economic, social, cultural, psychological) that exceed the technics of comprehension. With these matters repressed, the "objective" analysis becomes suspect, the "unbiased" interpretation dubious, and the "impartial" account unreliable (cf. Davies 2002b: 55). Remnants of the repressed apprehension show up in a preface, or in a sentimental phrase, an anachronistic aside, or a personal comment. David Cannadine concludes his inaugural lecture

as Director of the Institute of Historical Research in 1999 by endorsing G. M. Trevelyan's conclusion to his inaugural lecture at Cambridge in 1927. Historical comprehension establishes continuities and identities like this, by implementing what Castoriadis calls a 'totalizing identity logic' [*logique ensembliste-identitaire*] that ensures social conformity with prevailing social interests (cf. Castoriadis 1975: 284–5, 311). But the resulting poverty of historical analysis exudes a typically academic complacency. Apparently, what compels the historian is 'the *ardour* of his own curiosity to know what really happened in that *land of mystery* we call the past'. The '*burning desire* that consumes ... him all his life', is 'to peer into that *magic mirror* and see fresh figures there every day' (Cannadine 1999: 28; Trevelyan 1941: 195 (my italics)). Here comprehension dissolves into sentimentality. A rigorous discipline is but a puff of mystery. Historical scholarship rides on a fancy.

Repressing apprehension, history [*crg*] can never account completely for the process of understanding that produces it. Comprehensive historical knowledge claims to disclose the reality of reality. It would be tempting to say that its repressiveness disqualifies this claim. In fact, conversely, *because* it denies the apprehension behind it, history [*crg*] must see itself as the real reality. Evans typically separates history from present reality by insisting that 'present reality can be felt and experienced by our senses; but the past no longer exists, it is not real in the same sense as the world around us in the present is real' (Evans 1997: 96). But this bars something in-between: the actual apprehension of the past-in-the-present – a warm July day with motley tourists wandering sombrely between the barracks of Theresienstadt concentration camp; early autumn near the Harz mountains with their stark relics of GDR frontier controls and villages where time seemed to have stopped for fifty years.

History always finds a reason to drape apprehension [*aesthesis*] in its synthetic garb. Its comprehensive objectivity works for *other reasons* it doesn't admit to. History is no autonomous discipline, but – apprehensively enough – crystallizes in ideal form *other* comprehensive social tendencies, the rationality that is socially dominant: the alliance of instrumental thinking, the comprehensive organization of society, and its total administration.

Ultimately, as their modes of operation show, apprehension and comprehension aren't complementary (cf. Appendix: Table 3). Both constitute the *intellectual basis* of historical understanding, given that comprehension, like apprehension, signifies 'the faculty of grasping with the mind, power of receiving and containing ideas,

mental grasp'.[3] Comprehension denotes 'the mental state of comprehending (often viewed as a property which one may have); an
adequate notion'; apprehension, 'the product of grasping with the
mind; a conception or idea; *also* the abiding result of such conception;
a view ... entertained upon any subject'.

However, the way in which knowledge is grasped, depends on
the relative inputs of comprehension and apprehension. *Synthetic
modes* of making sense rely on comprehension, because it ensures
"inclusiveness". It conduces to 'a comprehensive arrangement,
summation, summary of any matter'; 'the sum of attributes
comprehended in a notion or concept ... '. *Analytical modes* rely on
apprehension. Deriving from sensation [*aesthesis*] rather than from
rationalization, it is essentially positivistic. It brings us to our senses
and our senses to us. It returns us to the sense we attempt to make of
the world. Hence, its adjectival form, "apprehensive" refers to the
'laying hold of sensuous or mental impressions', hence to 'mental
faculties and their operations'. It implies 'being ... discerning'. It is
synonymous with 'realizing', with being 'conscious, sensible'.

The *temporal mode* too reveals a similar split. Does objectivity mean
discounting the present to see the past as it was? What temporal
parameters appropriately define a historical problem? However, this
issue does not need resolving, because comprehension, being abstract
and ideal, is always temporally transcendent. Conversely, as a means
of self-orientation, apprehension is always present – especially when,
in its own interest, it enquires into what happened before. It, therefore,
takes on a pathos unknown to comprehension. Being apprehensive
means being 'anticipative of something adverse'. Apprehension
connotes 'fear as to what may happen; dread'. It alone, therefore,
reacts to the historicization that makes everyday life pall. It alone
negotiates the 'risk society' the historicized world has become.
It alone copes with its dire historical consciousness brooding
always on the past, a hazardous waste awkward and potent like
any other.

Comprehension and apprehension ensue from the primary cognitive
distinction between *illusio* and *aesthesis* (cf. Davies 2004: 2–5).
Despite a common basis in intellection, they represent divergent
conceptualizations of history. Historical understanding breaks up.
The academic practice of history is, by professional deformation,

---

[3] cf. *Oxford English Dictionary* (Compact Ed., 2 vols, London: Book Club Associates,
1979).

blind to the desolation of human existence in the totally administered, totally historicized world it sustains. Reason enough for being apprehensive towards history: it unconsciously produces a culture of apprehensiveness. Only it takes apprehension to see how deceptive historical comprehension is.

Comprehension and history

Comprehension constitutes the value of history: 'For historical identity the regulative idea of comprehensiveness [*Ganzheit*] remains a guiding idea and a constitutive ideal' (Angehrn 1985: 296). History needs to be comprehensive: it organizes and manages the diversity of human life in time. Comprehension implies that, beyond all the specialized monographs professional expertise produces, a 'general frame of history' exists that embraces this heterogeneity in order to respect the 'unity of history which itself is the unity of life' (Braudel 1984: 30). History depends on comprehension. Being a historian entails a 'fundamental commitment' 'to the comprehensiveness and exhaustiveness of the historical endeavour in principle' (Fulbrook 2002: 187). The trouble is, the principle is illusory. Coming from the holistic theory of historicism, 'the intuitive view of a *history of mankind* as a vast and comprehensive stream of development ... cannot be written'. The reason? 'Every written history is a history of a certain narrow aspect of this "total" development, and is anyhow a very incomplete history of even the particular incomplete aspect chosen' (Popper 1974: 81). No single knowledge-system can encompass the real world. To claim it ever could, '*is the great scientific lie*' (Neurath 1994: 376; cf. Weber 1988: 92; Fleck 1983: 128). This basic fault makes historical knowledge illusory. Comprehension thus (a) derives from the fantasy that there could be such a thing as 'a paradigmatic form of knowledge'; (b) retails knowledge already known, the 'same old thing', given that paradigms always ensure fundamental identities; and (c) proposes a 'crippling ideal', an apt allusion to history's prosthetic functions.

(a.) 'The paradigmatic form of knowledge'. At least, that's the theory. In the human sciences, the historian comprehends entities that are objectifications of human minds, of intellectual and moral values (whereas in the natural sciences the object of enquiry is distinct from the mind investigating it). The historian aims to comprehend this

intellectual quality in the objects being investigated, but is also deeply implicated in them, linked to them in an evolving, vital relationship. They share a common intention: they work with common aesthetic and moral value-systems, common presumptions of intelligibility. The historian embraces both his own lived experience and these intellectual objectifications from the past. These representational resources at the historian's disposal are in turn substantiated by his wider involvement in the social exchange of experiences and ideas. Similarly the concepts, inferences, and theories on which the historian draws, are not hypothetical constructions, but rather generated by these vital processes of experience and comprehension. So just as the totality of the life of the historian is present in his or her experience and comprehension, so the plenitude of life still echoes in even the most abstract propositions of the human sciences from the past (Dilthey 1959: 117–18). Comprehension, therefore, counts on the *a priori* adequacy of the mind now to respond to the socially objectified forms created by other minds in the past. Between understanding (of the past and its remaining residues of experience) and current experience (enlarged by the understanding of past cultural forms), there is a reciprocal relationship of comprehension: 'Life and life-experience are the ever freshly flowing sources of the understanding of the social-historical world; from life itself understanding penetrates into ever new depths; only when they react upon life and society do the human sciences attain their greatest meaningfulness, and this meaningfulness is bound to increase' (Dilthey 1959: 138).

That is the theory, and it does sound fine. But in rooting history in life, Dilthey tries to dispel the melancholy historical conscious-ness generates. All history has to show for itself is a desolate heterogeneity – an 'immeasurable expanse strewn with the ruins of religious traditions, metaphysical assertions, and articulated systems ... each excluding or refuting the other, but unable to vindicate itself'. It simply exposes 'the relativity of every historical form of life' and causes the 'absolute validity of any particular form of life, constitution, religion or philosophy to disappear' (Dilthey 1962: 76, 77).

What made history a 'substratum to almost every type of cultural activity', 'the paradigmatic form of knowledge to which all others aspired', was the historical consciousness of the Romantic period, when 'the whole range of our contemporary concerns with the past first became accessible to representation' (Bann 1995: 4–6). Dioramas and their 'illusory experiences', Bentham's *panopticon* as a total surveillance prison-structure, are symptomatic of the nineteenth century's 'extraordinary appetite for commanding vision' (Bann 1984: 61). In the panoptically sounding *Observations on World History* (written in 1868), Burckhardt claims nineteenth-century European culture had a special aptitude for evaluating greatness in history and so displayed a high degree of comprehensivity (Burckhardt 1969: 212). But "comprehensivity" here translates Burckhardt's term *Allempfänglichkeit*. Literally it means: 'receptivity for everything'; it suggests the lack of discrimination in historical taste Nietzsche, Burckhardt's sometime colleague in Basle, rejected.

Comprehension is thus inherently ambiguous. It denotes intellectual capacity and worthless heterogeneity alike. It justifies the totalizing view (e.g. the *longue durée*, epochal surveys, e.g. *Migration in Irish History 1600–2000; European Economic Integration, 1815–1970*). Without it, some "historical entities" might not even be visible (e.g. *A People Apart. The Jews in Europe, 1789–1939; The Common People, 1746–1946*). So it reliably produces more history: for history [*crg*], more is always more. Burckhardt's view still prevails: history is 'genuinely all-encompassing, without qualification' (Fernández-Armesto 2002: 152). Conversely, comprehension 'without qualification' also makes it heterogeneous, so much 'mixed rubbish': 'The work of professional historians has never been as multifarious'; but, 'the results have been *mixed*'. 'Inevitably, the growth of output means the growth of *rubbish*. But it means increased availability of good work too' (Fernández-Armesto 2002: 149–50 (my italics)). To tell what is what, the reader is left to pick-and-mix.

Usually contradiction and ambiguity put paid to a concept – but not to comprehension. These are its convenient virtues. Thanks to them, historians can be rigorous and exhaustive while being selective, scientific and systematic while indulging oneiric fancy, objective and value-free while transmitting the corporate ideology. Deriving from an allegedly paradigmatic form of knowledge, a substratum to whatever happens, comprehension – conveniently enough – always delivers sense, for anyone, in any way. It starts with the sense it sets out to find. As Dilthey argues, based on a common substratum of life-experience, the mind is always *a priori* attuned to what other minds in the past have generated. As Aron points out, given that historical reality is equivocal and inexhaustible, the historical fact is never given, but produced by thought (Aron 1986: 147). 'The past itself is ... as chaotic, uncoordinated, and complex as life', so 'history is about making sense of that mess, finding or creating patterns and meanings and stories from the maelstrom' (Arnold 2000: 13). Only a comprehensive attitude could equate 'finding' with 'creating' or make 'mess' and 'meaning' synonymous. But that's how it makes history meaningful. It starts with the idea that, however chaotic history [*rg*] seems, a pattern of intelligibility (as in a Rorschach test) inheres in it (except that in the Rorschach test there really is an embedded pattern). But how do you find the focal distance that resolves chaos into coherence? That's where it gets illusory. Comprehension cannot verify whether or not the focal distance it decides to adopt produces adequate understanding, i.e. detects a valid pattern. (How *longue* does the *longue durée* have to be? How much specialization constitutes historical specialization? How much more is more?) A change in perspective or focal-length produces a comprehension that always only seems better.

Comprehension, being thus indeterminate, explains why the sense of history cannot be determined (cf. Veyne 1996: 216). That's why comprehension turns into a 'retrospective illusion' (Veyne 1996: 239). History largely involves "retrodiction" (i.e. the converse of prediction). In and around the documentary traces history leaves, there are numerous gaps and omissions that, for the sake of narrative coherence, the historian must somehow fill (Veyne 1996: 194, 207). The need to produce a comprehensive synthesis compels the historian to resort to hypothetical causes and motivations, based on his or her own sense of the past. History is always the historian's representation of what happened in the past: its verisimilitude, like the comprehension it derives from is always illusory. Its claim to be paradigmatic, congruent with life itself, the "real reality", to take a deeper or longer view, to 'seek refuge in the position of God, the Father', is empty (Braudel 1994: 15). Comprehension makes history [*crg*] a pastiche of real knowledge – i.e. of knowledge that illuminates the here and now, where ordinary people ordinarily live.

Comprehension might seem like a cognitive reflex – as if the mind would go for any likely explanation. But it means to be anything but arbitrary. By definition, it wants to be right; its conclusions need to be justified by *all* the evidence available, by the *whole* truth. This intention dictates its characteristic behaviour-pattern. Comprehension takes its cue from knowledge already known, the paradigmatic 'same thing' (e.g. Braudel's 'general frame' of history). It vindicates itself by defining its relevance in terms of prevailing knowledge conventions, of what is already known. This ensures that, from the start, it endorses the dominant trends in the historical disciplines and the knowledge institutions that manage them. That's why, in this historically hyper-conscious era, it creates the severe, inertial drag the humanities exert on thinking. That's how – whatever the subject and however it deals with it – it affirms affirmative social attitudes.

(b.) The same old thing: knowledge already known. Comprehension produces more of the same. It always does. As a 'paradigmatic form of knowledge', it is bound to. Paradigms ensure basic patterns keep replicating themselves. Comprehension, in other words, creates identities. It does so in two complementary ways. *First*, it affirms socially affirmative attitudes. These ensure that, however much it changes, society remains the same. As a technology for managing social reality, it constructs the continuities, periodizations, traditions, ideal types, concepts, that perpetuate the same old thing: 'the past is perpetually returned (recalled, made repeatable), not only as omni-temporal and quasi-universal but also ... as a formal institutiona-lization of obligative-thought' (Cohen 1988: 176). *Second*, comprehension affirms history's own indispensable, paradigmatic status: the technology always backs itself up. If history is to affirm affirmative attitudes, comprehension must always affirm itself. It remains identical to itself by reiterating knowledge already known. To that end, it employs concepts that are essentially ambiguous, i.e. both absolute and contingent. History's "natural bias" to affirm its own paradigmatic status makes it look objective and true.

(b.i) The recurrence of the same. 'Historical explanation consists of rediscovering in history a mode of explanation that, in some way or other, we have "always known": that is why it can be defined as comprehension, that is why history is familiar to us, and we are everywhere at home in it' (Veyne 1996: 148). History was always set up to ensure human identity, to recognize what was already known (cf. Cohen 1988: 85). So, e.g. 'history establishes the iden-tity of social groups, institutions and nations'; 'it identifies trends at work that can enhance or diminish [present society's] quality of life'; it 'can foster a sense of corporate identity, an ability to see one's life as part of that of a greater social whole' (McCullagh 2004: 193–4). Comprehension is sustained by the 'logic of identity

production' [*logique ensembliste identitaire*] that drives society's self-reproduction.[4]

That the same old thing recurs, that 'the human race or at least each epoch repeats itself somewhat', makes the retrospective construction of historical patterns, (what Veyne calls 'retrodiction') possible (Veyne 1996: 205). In order to exist, society needs essentially imitative social behaviour, the reproduction of the same. So too does history, as both a comprehensive account of social behaviour and an imitative social practice. 'History,' says de Tarde, 'consists of the most successful things, the most imitated initiatives'. Hence, history is about 'what happens to imitations [*le destin des imitations*]', i.e. how the same old things rise or decline, interact or evolve (Tarde 1993: 151). Ultimately, as Nietzsche argues, '"reality" itself lies in the constant

---

[4] Castoriadis' concept, 'logique ensembliste identitaire' translates as 'set-theoretical identity logic' (cf. Castoriadis 1984: 208ff.). It refers to seeing reality in terms of classifications, 'i.e. the possession of a property defines a class and being a member of a class defines a property'. That also implies: 'one must always be able to "form a collective whole" ... and also ... to decompose a given "whole" into "wholes" of a different order or into distinct and defined "elements"' (cf. Castoriadis 1984: 208ff.). It means reality is managed by identitary logic that defines which classes are identified by which identical properties of their constituent elements. It comes from a key premise of Western thought since Parmenides, the identity of being and thought (e.g. Descartes' maxim: 'I think therefore I am'): 'this logic tells us, that "what is – what can be thought" is capable of ... being fully and distinctly defined, composable and decomposable into totalities defined by universal properties and comprising parts defined by particular properties' (cf. Castoriadis 1984: 210). From this, it is clear that the characteristics of identitary logic supply the infrastructure of historical comprehension. This also comprises whole classes (e.g. the Victorian Age) defining and definable by their constituent elements (e.g. 'Victorian values', Neo-Gothic architecture, the Great Exhibition). However, identitary logic is open to radical criticism. The logical empiricists, following Nietzsche, point out that all logic is identitary logic: all truths, as the product of language-rules, are tautological and *have nothing to do with reality* (cf. von Mises 1990: 191ff.). As *Beyond Good and Evil* and his own unpublished notes from the 1880s show, Nietzsche sets out to destroy identitary logic, because it is deceptive. It just creates fictions [*illusio*] society receives as reality. Nietzsche sees such classes as 'subject' (i.e. the thinking 'I') and 'object', 'cause' and 'effect', as pure inventions, features read into the world to make it intelligible. Nietzsche's scepticism has been endorsed by developments in the philosophy of language, semiotics, psychology, anthropology and sociology (e.g. by Wittgenstein, von Mises, Freud, Marx and Adorno). Nietzsche's and Castoriadis' perspectives do coincide: identitary logic enables society to create the affirmative, imaginary structures and principles that enable it to function. And they would include history itself. History proves to be the last refuge of identitary thinking. That's why the humanities, based essentially on historical methodologies, are deceptive – claiming to produce objective knowledge while endorsing whatever goes politically or socially.

recurrence of the same, familiar, and related things, in their logicized character, in the conviction that here we can calculate and quantify' (Nietzsche 1956: III, 534). That is because 'our needs have narrowed down our senses to such an extent, that the same "world of phenomena" keeps on recurring, thereby acquiring the appearance of reality' (Nietzsche 1956: III, 526).[5] Certainly, identitary thinking, this attempt to manage the world in terms of 'identical cases', is an illusion, even if it does create a world that is simplified, manageable, regulatable (even if only in belated retrospect) (cf. Wellmer 1985: 148). That the world is systematically manageable, is the illusion. It represses the apprehension that the world of phenomena conceals not the 'real world', but the 'formless-unformulatable world of sensation-chaos – another kind of phenomenal world, one which is for us "unknowable"' (Nietzsche 1956: III, 534). Worse, it suppresses the idea that truth is, by definition, oppositional, contradictory – something different (cf. Adorno 1982: 17).

History is, therefore, already persuasive, because it is an imitative practice based on identitary logic. History can provide comprehensive meaning because the world itself has none. 'It is only because there is no instrinsic significance in the world that human beings have had to, and been able to, invest it with this extraordinary variety of heterogeneous meanings,' Castoriadis argues: 'It is because there is no voice sounding out from behind the clouds, and no language of Being, that history has been possible' (Castoriadis 1990, 263–4). Society creates comprehensive meanings through the logic of identity formation. Some identity structures are predicated on the natural situation of human life. The concept of time, mathematics, geometry mirror patterns already identifiable in the cosmos: with its production of 'recurrent equivalences', nature provides a model for the stability of human institutions. Others have no natural analogy: the social imagination creates them (e.g. contrast Christian and Buddhist conceptions of time). They mirror the fact that, mysteriously enough, the world seems to operate through its own identitary dimension (e.g. each living species only ever reproduces itself)

---

[5] Current cognitive theory backs Nietzsche up: 'Prototypes are abstractions of stimuli against which similar patterns are judged. Even with the billions of cortical neurons working in parallel, it is impossible to store *all* the sights and sounds (and other sensations) of this teeming world. It is possible, and far more economical, to store impressions that embody the most frequently experienced features of a class of objects' (Solso 1994: 251).

(Castoriadis 1990, 263). The social imagination follows suit: it creates institutions, organized frameworks for imitative practices that similarly enable society to keep on reproducing itself. Knowledge plays a crucial rôle in cloning the symbolic, fiduciary structures that underpin the reproduction of social identities, both personal and institutional. And history's is decisive. Apprehension is stimulated by a sense of mortality, the fear of our own personal destruction, let alone the destruction of any meaningful reality in which people live. So 'heteronomous societies undertake the creation of a sense, for everyone, and impose on everyone the internalization of this sense,' observes Castoriadis. 'They institute real or symbolic representatives of a perennial sense and of an imaginary immortality in which everyone, in various ways, can participate.' These institutions can be mythical and religious; they can also be political and historical: the monarch, the state, the nation, the party (Castoriadis 1990: 153). Behind the comprehensive structures (e.g. traditions, continuities, identities, etc.) history generates, lies the identitary logic of the social imagination. That's why history constitutes the substratum of all human activity. The 'real reality' it claims to comprehend, ensures the perpetual social reproduction of 'the same old thing'. It thus anaesthetizes apprehension and opposition alike.

(b.ii) History affirms itself through knowledge already known. 'Thinking means identifying. Satisfied with itself, conceptual order moves ahead of what thinking intends to grasp' (Adorno 1982: 17). That, *in nuce*, is how historical comprehension operates. It generates knowledge already known by working with what it already recognizes: 'Historical continuity ... implies a specific form of self-constitution in history, "a becoming what it is" [*ein 'Sich-selbst-Werden'*], whereby its "remaining identical with itself" [*'Identischbleiben-mit-sich'*] is not only the presupposition but also the outcome' (Angehrn 1985: 316). Its identitary character comes out in tautology – as when Hobsbawm, writing about the twentieth century, asserts that his 'object is to understand and explain *why* things turned out as they did' (Hobsbawm 1995: 3); or Cannadine claims that 'history ... helps us understand how our world got to be the way it is' (Cannadine 1999: 8); or Oakeshott, that: 'Historical events are ... circumstantial convergencies of antecedent historical events; what they are is how they came to be woven' (Oakeshott 1999: 73); or McCullagh, that 'to make the past intelligible, historians spend a lot of time explaining why events happened as they did' (McCullagh 1998: 9, cf. 304–5). Tautology is an illusory, 'self-referential definition' (Steiner 1997a: 351). It 'reveals nothing about reality, and results from arbitrarily

determined language rules' (von Mises 1990: 192–3). It is generated through satisfying pre-conceived 'identifiable truth conditions' (cf. McCullagh 1998: 16, 64). Precisely through being formal, it affirms already instituted meanings and currently prevailing realities (cf. Davies 2002a: 20). Primarily, though, history's identitary thinking affirms history itself. Its aim to be identical with itself justifies its claim to truth: 'The objectivity which we are committed to seeking ... lies at the sum total of all possible subjectivities ... That is why historical enquiry should always shift perspective. By changing perspective, we compile multiple perspectives and approach the objectivity which lies at the sum of them' (Fernández-Armesto 2002: 155). But this too is just word-play [*illusio*]. Multiple specialized perspectives can never be anything but multiple. If they did 'approach' objectivity and you knew how 'close' they got, that would mean you already knew what you were looking for, i.e. that 'perspectives' and 'objectivity' were *a priori* identical.

Comprehension is, therefore, in essence a paralogism, a surreptitious substitution of words for things. 'An historically understood past ... is a past that has not itself survived. Indeed, it is a past which could not have survived because ... it was never itself present. It can neither be ... dug up, nor retrieved, nor recollected, but only inferred ... ; it is to be found nowhere but in a history book' (Oakeshott 1999: 36). Oakeshott's distinction between a 'practical past' and a 'historical past' is a classic instance of 'scholastic epistemocentrism', this 'systematic principle of error' (Bourdieu 1997: 63, 67). This produces an 'unreal anthropology'. It imputes to the agents and their practice the historian is studying something alien to them the historian's perspective conceals from itself: its 'interest derived from pure knowledge and pure comprehension', i.e. its 'essentially scholastic connection with the world' (Bourdieu 1997: 67). Only if 'the rationale [*logique*] detected by a retrospective, totalizing and detemporalizing interpretation by the *lector* [i.e. historian] had actually, from the outset, shaped the creative action by the *auctor* [i.e. historical agent]', would comprehension provide objectivity (Bourdieu 1997: 68). Otherwise, its claim to identify the 'real reality'of the past remains illusory. The identitary, paralogical constructs it produces instead can be put to any ideological use.

Certainly, the historian is at best 'in an unfortunate predicament because historical knowledge involves concrete issues that involve process and interaction, but it is in need of concepts; however being and identity exist only through abstraction' (Veyne 1996: 185, 189). Cognitive asymmetry between the past and the conceptual classifications that organize it, is unavoidable. Or it would be, if comprehension didn't come with a discourse that is, paradoxically, both self-identical (i.e. tautological, self-referential) and heterogeneous: 'the connection with identity formation is a guiding-interest of historical knowledge' (Angehrn 1985: 230).

Explaining historical change needs continuous identities, in order to reveal what changed: '*History*, i.e. the description of change, and *essence*, i.e. that which remains unchanged during change, appear here as correlative concepts' (Popper 1974: 33). This correlation perpetuates the 'same old thing' in different ways. 'Unit ideas', teleological processes, or organic evolution, each involving both change and essential identity, can be traced in the course of history [*rg*] (Oakeshott 1999: 109, 110, 117). These are historicist principles; but all particular causal explanations arguably imply some general historicist pattern (Popper 1974: 146). Academic history claims to rise above this determinism. However, fixated on its own, formal criteria of truth and objectivity, it deludes itself with a more dire form of determinism, elicited this time from history [*crg*]: the automatic recourse to identitary thinking. 'What unites an assemblage of historical differences, gives it an identity and makes it recognizable as a passage of change cannot be something imposed upon it from the outside,' says Oakeshott. Instead, 'we must seek it in some intrinsic quality of the assemblage itself, or else confess that an historical past is no more than a tissue of fortuitous conjunctions.' Hence his conclusion that 'this identity may be found in its own coherence' (Oakeshott 1999: 123–4). The 'historical situation' is, therefore, a 'coherent structure of ... conceptually related occurrences', a 'situational identity' abstracted from all that may have been going on then and there (Oakeshott 1999: 59, 62). The resulting knowledge will, of course, be "true" and "objective", but only because its basis is tautological: identity = coherence; coherence = identity.

Knowledge, then, does progress through increasing abstraction. This goes for natural science: 'the more it extends its jurisdiction, the more it is forced to rely on conceptual structures that have no longer any analogue in the realm of concrete sensation' (Cassirer 1994: 303). It also goes for history, 'a monolith where the distinction of causes, purposes, and contingencies is an abstraction' (Veyne 1996: 135). But there is a difference. In science, less is more. Scientific explanation looks for laws and patterns. It proceeds by "conceptual parsimony": it aims to account for the maximum number of phenomena with the minimum number of causes. For history, more is always more. Historical explanation focusses on specific cases, it identifies individual cases (Angehrn 1985: 51ff., 244ff.). Historians aim 'to talk about what happened on particular occasions in all its variety'. To do so, they need a conceptual apparatus that permits heterogeneity and abstraction. So they resort to 'accommodating terms, able to cover a vast number of events falling within an indefinitely prescribed range'. The generalizations they permit, 'must *inevitably* be vague, open to a multitude of exceptions and saving clauses, because of the looseness of the terms they employ'. They are not meant to be scientifically precise, but to 'function ... as *guides to understanding*' (Gardiner 1968: 60–1, 93). This "indeterminate" conceptual organization makes history both self-identical and heterogeneous, both "objective" and arbitrary.

The heterogeneity of history mirrors the heterogeneity of its conceptual schemes: their ultimate aim is to ensure 'functional connectivity', the self-identical coherence that constitutes the historical event (cf. Simmel 1999: 165). On the one hand, the explanation of historical change seems to require essentialism; on the other, the conceptual apparatus that organizes history seems to require nominalism. The ambivalence is structural: historical concepts appear realist (essentialist) in relation to history [*crg*] and nominalist in relation to history [*rg*], i.e. in constructing identical or typical cases. Realism (essentialism), the assumption that knowledge is identical to reality, that words represent intrinsic properties in things, not only correlates identity and difference. It is also evinced (e.g.) when literary description is used to evoke a particular sense of historical place or character; or when comprehension "naturally" identifies, and identifies with, "ready-made" historical structures, by definition already organized to make sense – e.g. the police archive; collections of state papers; a fiscal or legalsystem; an institution such as a state, a business, university, or religious organization (cf. Popper 1974: 30; Hessen 1909: 27, 29; cf. Cassirer 1994: 303).[6]

Nominalism generates heterogeneity. It confirms that the comprehensive arrangements produced by identitary thinking are synthetic, owing more to explanatory paradigms and current disciplinary trends, than to the past as it actually was – as the identitary logic that drives the formation of ideal-types – and similar colligatory patterns, or 'narrative substances' – clearly shows. Colligation, e.g. produces intelligible patterns of events, rational frameworks for 'common set[s]

---

[6] However, non-historical concepts that can be tested by experiment, are inevitably much closer to reality than historical concepts (Hessen 1909: 27).

of ideas' (McCullagh 2004: 126–7). Narrative substance, e.g. 'is not *found* but *made* in and by [the historian's] text' (cf. Ankersmit 2001: 135ff.; Jenkins 2003: 53). So concepts such as 'capitalist culture', 'individualism', 'feudalism', 'mercantilism', though inherently vague, can be defined by abstracting their specific characteristics from existing examples. The resulting ideal-type can then be used to identify other social formations. Weber stresses that, being purely classificatory concepts, ideal-types never occur in reality. As 'intellectual constructs', the product of 'fantasy disciplined and guided by reality', they are heuristic devices, used to manage the otherwise inchoate flood of historical events (Weber 1988: 194–5, 198–9).[7] So, in analyzing, e.g. the causes of revolution in 1848, historians can survey a range of social, economic and political evidence. But the guiding idea, "revolution", makes sense only through an ideal-type – the conceptual identity of the 'same old things' – that also includes 1688, 1789, 1830, 1871, 1917, 1968, 1989. In any case, the social sciences do characteristically 'make up' their objects of enquiry, hence construct new concepts and categories for historically organizing them (Hacking 2002: 40, 106). As the theory of knowledge shows, structures of meaning, criteria of evidence, are never stable: 'Once a colligatory word or phrase has been accepted historians often disagree as to what it really refers to' (McCullagh 2004: 129). History [*crg*] chronicles what happens to them in history [*rg*], so affirming itself. New varieties of history, underpinned by new ideal-types, new forms of colligation, new narrative substances, are always being fabricated (e.g. gender history; post-colonial history, history of sexuality, etc.). Historians have only to manufacture new concepts, identify their constituent features, and they create more history, new history (but of the same old thing, in the same old way). Ultimately, what their heterogeneous conceptualizations produce, is a phantom – a comprehension, based on fabricated identities, no agents at the time could have had (or used, if they'd had it) (cf. Veyne 1996: 62). Always nominalistically identifying the latest thing as the same old thing, only a historian would perversely describe the elephants the Romans brought with

---

[7] Ankersmit's distinction between historical truths *de re* and *de dictu*, i.e. between statements about (past) reality and statements about language, between 'things we can unproblematically identify without taking their history into account' and 'things where identification depends on the ... historical representations we have of these things', puts a cognitive-linguistic spin on Weber's theory of ideal-types (Ankersmit 2001: 33–5, 82ff.).

them to invade Britain as 'weapons of mass destruction' or enthuse over the Roman *ballista* as the 'cruise missile' of its day.[8]

(c.) 'A crippling ideal'. Comprehension legitimizes history as a human science: 'one word ... dominates and illuminates our studies: "comprehend [*comprendre*]"'. We always rush to judgement, we are suspicious of others who differ from us: i.e. 'we never comprehend enough'. History is there to cure us of being judgemental, since it is 'a vast experience of human variety, one long series of encounters between human beings. Life, like knowledge itself, has everything to gain from these encounters being fraternal' (Bloch 1974: 121). Comprehension, therefore, constructs a total, transcendent context for humanity's self-knowledge. That raises the stakes, scientifically speaking: 'ideally the student should never consider less than the total historical material which may be conceivably relevant to his enquiry'; 'historical research ... consists of an exhaustive, and exhausting, review of everything that may conceivably be germane to a given investigation' (Elton 1969: 87–8). It also generates hetero-geneity. Embracing human variety, comprehension needs a 'plurality of systems of interpretation', a 'plurality of perspectives', hence a 'plurality of modes of consideration' (cf. Aron 1986: 107ff., 149ff., 394ff.). Its typically academic, transcendent stance ensures it gives rise to 'the multiplication of nonconnecting contexts' (Cohen 1988: 4). Furthermore, if the human condition is inherently historical, it is inevitably aleatory. 'History is free because it is not written down in advance, nor determined like nature or fatality, but unpredictable, like human beings themselves' (Aron 1986: 404). It is always as much as it wants to be.

So comprehension is still a phantom experience. Always having to cope with more – more material, more interpretations, more values, comprehensiveness turns out to be a 'chimera', 'a crippling ideal'

---

[8] Presenting *The Seven Ages of Britain* (Channel 4), Bettany Hughes observes: 'An elephant was part exotic novelty, part weapon of mass destruction. By choosing to make his entrance on one Claudius was driving home his message. Oppose us and we will crush you, join us and we will show you a whole new world.' (I must thank Philip Clarke, of Wildfire TV, for confirming this comment.) See also *What the Romans Did For Us* (BBC 2). Curiously enough, these analogies don't appear in the books accompanying these series (cf. Pollard 2003: 74; Wilkinson 2000: 30–1). Claudius and George W. say the same old thing; but something is seriously wrong if a historian identifies elephants as anthrax.

(Jordanova 2000: 102, 103). One solution is to treat it not as content but as a 'thought style': 'the goal of reading and working comprehensively' thus implies 'a seriousness of purpose that helps to raise the quality of historical knowledge' (Jordanova 2000: 103). After all, history is a technology designed always to deliver comprehension, however substantive (or not) any particular monograph or article actually is. Set up as the 'substratum of human activity', a 'paradigmatic form of knowledge', sustained by the identitary logic already operating in society, history always provides society's "default knowledge". Comprehension, be it as style or as substance, is thus a "natural" academic habitus, a necessary convention, however compromised. And compromised it certainly is, to judge by the contradictions and circular arguments it produces – as when both Elton and Jordanova try to explain how to achieve it through 'controlled selection', its very antithesis. Jordanova asserts: 'The only ways forward are through careful selection, through being thoughtful and open about the criteria of selection, and through traditional forms of evaluation. ... They rest on making one's sources and procedures open to the scrutiny of others, and drawing upon other work of proven quality.' But she can't even persuade herself: 'the quality of historical knowledge cannot be judged by absolute criteria, but must be evaluated in terms of the goals, selections and so on operative in any given piece of writing' (Jordanova 2000: 103; cf. Elton 1969: 92ff.). Clearly, it's not just postmodernist critics who can turn history into a 'reflexive, ... *refractive* discursive experiment without foundations': it's academic historians, all by themselves (cf. Jenkins 2003: 68).

If comprehension collapses, the humanistic claims it supposedly supports, collapse too. That just leaves historians studying the past 'in its own right, for its own sake, and on its own terms' (Elton 1969: 86; Fernández-Armesto 2002: 154). This is also where the logic gets fuzzy. Ultimately, the reasons for studying history are those 'for studying anything: to enhance life and prepare for death'. What claim could be more comprehensive – or less heterogenous? But it's pure phantom – no sooner glimpsed than gone. Now it's here: history enhances life 'because it conjures in the mind a vivid context for ... appreciation and understanding'. Next, it 'prepares you for death by cultivating "imaginative understanding"'. Next, the very peak of fancy: 'By broadening the mind, by exercising the ability to understand the other, history has a moral effect on the person that studies it. It can make you a better person.' Then it's vanished: 'But other disciplines can also have effects of these sorts. Our best peculiar justification for history is to say that it needs no justification. Because it is everything, it is inescapable' (Fernández-Armesto 2002: 154). Comprehension makes history totally coercive (cf. 'inescapable') but completely meaningless. Worse, it makes professional arrogance look respectable. That's because it comes from a type of social practice – the academic – that, blind to its own conventions, comprehends everything except itself.

Apprehension and history

Far from reducing apprehension, comprehension makes it worse. Behind the tatty humanist frills, the fancy-stuff of "rigorous methods", a comprehensive sense of the past leaves you in reality as destitute and apprehensive as ever – as Braudel, no less, confirms. 'Let us not judge this present by the scale of our individual lifetimes, like these daily segments, so thin, insignificant, and transparent, our personal existences represent,' he admonishes: 'The scale of civilisations, and even of any collective construction, requires the use of other measures to comprehend or grasp them' (Braudel 1984: 309). It's the historian's illusory self-abstraction from ordinary life, as an academic, "pure knowing subject", that generates apprehension. If only we did have a *longue durée*, dwell *sub specie aeternitatis*, "objectively", beyond life and death, 'pure and uninvolved and purposeless' (cf. Blanning 2002: 181; Southgate 2000: 10–11). In this oneiric state, history would not be 'inescapable' at all: it would be sheer spectacle, affording Vico's contemplative 'divine pleasure' (Vico 1984: 103, §345). On us – as academic spectators, "absolute egos" – it would have absolutely nothing.

In reality, academic self-abstraction suffers from misapprehension. What makes history 'everything' and 'inescapable', is not history, but being embodied. In reality, what claims us, is not history, but 'the particular fabric and structure of our own bodies' (Wollheim 1966: 40). Our own bodies hold us hostage in a specific place, at a specific time, for a specific time. Personal experience of temporality and comprehensive knowledge of historicity are incommensurable. From the existential standpoint, human beings cannot know the ultimate significance of the age they live in or of their own lives: 'one's own situation simply cannot be defined in world-historical terms' (Schmidt-Biggemann 1991: 80–1). Consequently, 'nobody can write about his or her lifetime as one can (and must) write about a period known only from outside, at second or third-hand, from sources of the period or the works of later historians' (Hobsbawm 1995: ix). Conversely, historical comprehension

[*Geschichte*] diverging from our own sense of things [*Eigensinn*], is symptomatic of broader, abstract rationalizing tendencies in culture. Its self-abstraction 'articulates man's incapacity to live in the body, which is also his incapacity to die', i.e. his inability to find either cathartic release of his apprehension or existential affirmation of his mortal condition in aesthetic (mythological or tragic) form (Brown 1970: 264–5).

History, perpetuating itself, perpetuates the same old apprehension. It needs humanity kept apprehensive so that it can keep perpetuating itself. However, apprehension is a reflex that won't be abused. It stresses it has (a) its own, different conception of knowledge. This reveals (b) the terrorizing intention of historical processes, and (c) the sophistical basis of historical comprehension.

(a.) Apprehension has a different conception of knowledge. 'The self, from foot to toe, unto the very marrow of its bones, is vulnerable': knowledge comes from nowhere but our vulnerable, physical presence in the world (Levinas 1972: 104). 'Intelligible philosophy' starts with embodied existence: the 'truest knowledge comes from the deepest wounding action': the 'living spirit of understanding' only arises from the 'susceptibility to being wounded': 'the human being is human because it is a wounded creature' (Jaspers 1958: 193; cf. Jaspers 1948: 67). The body, vulnerable to being traumatically injured, has to take the world around it seriously, since 'in varying unequal degrees,' it is 'exposed, put into play and into danger in the world, runs the risk of emotion, injury, suffering, sometimes death'. After all, 'nothing is more serious than the emotion that touches the very depths of our organic resources' (Bourdieu 1997: 168). Apprehension is a neurophysiological survival reflex, rooted in the deep time evolution of the species. It instinctively knows far more about us than historical comprehension does. It should do: it has had several million years or so more to find out in – since before the Pleistocene era when the immediate predecessors of *homo sapiens* with recognizably human brains emerged, and needing to protect themselves from powerful predators (cf. Ardrey 1970: 251).[9] After all, 'what is "remembered" in

---

[9] Anthropologists now see *homo sapiens* emerging from clusters of hominids, not just *australopithecus*, that emerged over a period of some six million years (cf. Lemonick & Dorfman 2002: 46–53).

the body, is well remembered' (Scarry 1985: 109). That's why apprehension mutates least: it's the real, visceral "historical heritage" of human existence.

Apprehension derives from the body's capacity to acquire 'dispositions which themselves are an opening onto the world, that is to say: onto the very structures of the world of which they [i.e. the dispositions] themselves are the incorporated form' (Bourdieu 1997: 168). That means: 'The architecture of the brain allows us to process information by means of massive parallelism, in which basic visual patterns engage countless millions of neurons simultaneously.' The brain tends 'to organize information in terms of categories, prototypes, and schemata'. In other words, 'lurking in the brain of all normal humans is a collective image or prototype of people, objects, things, ideas and the like. We see the world through a thousand hypotheses' (Solso 1994: 187, 250). This neurophysiological reality underpins theories of knowledge based on categories of understanding (e.g. Aristotle, Kant) or on symbolic forms (e.g. Cassirer). Being thus vitally vigilant, apprehension provides the stimulus to cultural action: 'The wise man ... is *ever on the watch* to prevent the occurrence of anything unforeseen, anything unexpected ... He also directs *so searching a glance in all directions* with the constant aim of finding an assured retreat for life free from vexation and worry ...' (Cicero 1996: 366–9, IV.XVII. 37–8 (my italics)).

(a.i) Apprehension fosters an aesthetic rather than a historical culture. Apprehension [*aesthesis*] is definitely not "subjectivity" by another name. The immediate experience of the world involves nothing if not unidentifiable, unconceptualized, basic, aesthetic qualities: colours, sounds, smells, textures (cf. Schlick 1986: 19; cf. Fleck 1983: 64). These qualities are objective in a very elementary sense: 'basic experiences are not first person experiences' (Schlick 1986: 288). Rather, *aesthesis* is a 'universal species experience' (cf. Dissanayake 1995: 185). That is to say: it is nothing abstract or transcendental, but absolutely material, neurophysiological. Generated within the body, it is 'the very stuff of which our life-in-the-world is composed and through which our thought is mediated' (Dissanayake 1995: 185). The aesthetic, apprehensive form of cognition is, by this very fact, 'species essential': 'Our perceptual apparatus ... originally evolved to help us survive, so that the sensory elements artists use and to which we respond arose in life-serving ... contexts.' Consequently, 'to make something special [i.e. to make art] is ... intentionally to draw attention to its empathetic properties, to engage and to accentuate its

emotion-rich associations. Seen in this way, the arts are extensions of what we have evolved to do naturally in order to survive' (Dissanayake 1995: 185–6). For these aesthetic reasons, apprehension fosters human solidarity (as the social response to the aftermath of violent and disruptive historical events shows). It is an antidote to divisive and particularistic political ideologies. The artwork inspires in its observers a 'mute rapprochement' that implies their common human being (Rosenzweig 1996: 88–9). The occasion art provides for 'analyzing the faculty that corresponds to "our pleasures and displeasures"', offers 'a way of embracing human freedom and of seeing it as bearable for natal and mortal beings like ourselves' (Arendt 1982: 93).

Certainly, the senses can be deceived: apprehension is susceptible to *illusio*. But where comprehension, as *illusio*, already produces more of the same, more *illusio*, apprehension, as *aesthesis*, returns to real sensations: it needs to know practically, immediately, how things feel. Apprehension brings us to our senses. It comes to its senses: 'current neurophysiological findings … suggest that the work of art writes itself on the perceiver's body: electrochemically in the signaling patterns of activity that comprise the brain's cortical maps, which may in turn have concomitant physiological and kinesthetic effects'. Apprehension connects immediately with 'real realities': 'the sensation (in bones and muscles, in the being) … – of union or communion between viewer and object, listener and musical work, reader and poem – is real, not illusory or only metaphorical' (Dissanayake 1995: 185).

Apprehension demonstrates, therefore, that aesthetics offers real cognitive advantages. The aesthetic dimension brings people to their senses by focussing on their own intentions [*Eigensinn*], even as history overwhelms them. It provides the optic to go behind history, into the existential situations of historical agents to reveal what drives them, as in Classical tragedy (e.g. Sophocles, Shakespeare, and Racine).

Further, with its vital interests, apprehension needs always to test knowledge, to assure itself it is sure. It approaches it from this everyday sense of things. It focusses on knowledge practices, on what knowledge does. That is why it is enhanced by objectivity. Take the information about the battle-site of Verdun in the Michelin *Guide de Tourisme*. It is understated, even euphemistic, when it describes it as an 'exemplary place for humanity' [*haut lieu de l'humanité*]. It is not partisan. Here are maps and diagrams, dates and statistics. The apprehension is in the plain statement: that the *Ossuaire*

(137 metres long) was constructed in memory of 400,000 French casualties and to hold their unidentifiable, scattered remains collected from the field of battle. It is in the legend: 'ⵔDouaumant' designates 'village totally destroyed and not reconstructed'. It is in the solecism of the conclusion's sub-title: 'the balance-statement of the hecatomb'.[10] Apprehension registers facts and figures; it registers too the shredded human tissue they signify. That, too, is why it has a positivistic base. Given that, as *aesthesis*, 'basic experiences are not first person experiences', any interpretation placed on them invokes a 'thought style', i.e. a knowledge-system and its structural and logical rules. Just formulating verbally an immediate sense impression requires reflective judgement, hence both a psychological and a collective social dimension (cf. Schlick 1986: 53, 66–7, 101; Fleck 1983: 157, 161, 168). Apprehension (as *aesthesis*) operates vitally, reflectively, in between the immediate sense and the knowledge structure already known. It would ensure that sense determines knowledge, rather than knowledge sense. Further, with this radical cognitive function, apprehension (as *aesthesis*) stops historical thinking both monopolizing reality itself and reiterating the same old thing. Each new work of art (e.g.) reorganizes history around it through the influences it creates for itself: Pre-Raphaelitism reconceives Medieval art, German Expressionism the art of the German Reformation, Surrealism the Baroque. That's why histories of art, literature, or music are redundant: they misrepresent the way in which art engenders itself; they deny *aesthesis* its own cognitive priorities.

(a.ii) Apprehension is thus rooted in an ecological conception of knowledge. It embeds the human body in its social, cultural, and natural environments. Human thinking constitutes with them a vital, dynamic set of communication-loops (cf. Bateson 2000: 316ff., 464–5). This ecology of mind involves a materialistic theory of perception predicated on the 'idea of organic thinking through which the connection between the "psychic" and the "physiological" would be conceivable' (Merleau-Ponty 1995: 92). The resulting 'organic consciousness' [*pensée organique*] provides the means for 'communicating internally with the world', an 'initial openness towards things without which objective thinking would be impossible' (Merleau-Ponty 1995: 113). At the moment of apprehension [*perception*], we think neither about the object nor about ourselves thinking but rather 'we are with the object and become one with

---

[10] *Guide de Tourisme Alsace et Lorraine. Vosges*: 174–9.

our body which knows more than we do about the world and the reasons and means for producing its synthesis' (Merleau-Ponty 1995: 275–6).

Ecologically speaking, human existence is always already implicated in the world – materially, physiologically, as well as morally: 'the cognitive system cannot live without this constant coupling with and constantly emerging regularities provided by its environment: without the possibility of coupled activity the system would become a mere solipsistic ghost' (Varela 1999: 56). That's why it has this 'organic consciousness'; that's also why it is apprehensive. This means that 'the reference point for understanding perception is no longer a pre-given, perceiver independent world'. Everyone is differently implicated in the world, everyone has a different situation to deal with. What shapes apprehension and action, is the 'sensorimotor structure of the cognitive agent, the way in which the nervous system links sensory and motor surfaces ... and not some pre-given world'. Apprehension thus breaks with the 'received view that perception is fundamentally the truthful reconstruction of a portion of the physical world through a registering of existing environmental information'. Because the apprehensive subject is already implicated and by definition, therefore, in an enactive situation, 'reality is not a given: it is perceiver dependent, not because the perceiver "constructs" it as he or she pleases, but because what *counts* as a relevant world is inseparable from the structure of the perceiver' (Varela 1999: 12–13).

This ecological conception of knowledge breaks with the naïve subjective-objective structure "disembodied", academic comprehension offers. And for this reason: 'A situated cognitive entity isn't related to its environment "objectively," independently of the system's location, heading, attitudes, and history' (Varela, 1999: 55). The issue is not about universal truth, but about what someone in a given situation would recognize as real (cf. Merleau-Ponty 1996: 52). Our apprehensive implication in the world always comes first. That is to say: it [*perception*] takes priority since 'it places us in the presence of the moment when things, truths and values are constituted for us, it provides us with a *logos* in its nascent state, it undogmatically teaches us the true conditions of objectivity itself, and reminds us of what knowledge and action must do' (Merleau-Ponty 1996: 67). Apprehension thus makes us question how knowledge, including historical knowledge, is constituted, how it logically works. Each human being is a situated agent and, as such, his or her perspective on the total world-system is 'established by the constantly emerging properties of the agent itself [e.g. the growing awareness he or she has of being already implicated] and in terms of the role such running redefinition plays in the coherence of the entire system' (Varela, 1999: 55).

Human consciousness evolves in relation to its environment. It needs to understand itself ecologically, both for this environment and for itself. The world 'out there' is already mapped, and continues through experience and reflection to map itself, onto the human mind. Conversely, the world makes sense through the cognitive map the mind projects onto it. Long after a limb has been amputated because of traumatic injury, the patient keeps receiving real sensations in the phantom limb from the still intact receptors in the brain (cf. Merleau-Ponty 1990: 38–9). As Bourdieu remarks, 'The body is in the social world but the social world is in the body ... The very structures of the world are present in the structures (or rather cognitive schemes) which agents put to work to understand them'. The world the human mind sets out to know is also already known, since 'by being an object of knowledge for those who are involved in it, the social world is ... the product, be it reified, be it incorporated, of all the different (and concurrent) acts of knowledge of which it is the object' (Bourdieu 1997: 218).

Stressing the function of knowledge as a means of self-orientation, apprehension breaks with the professional (i.e. technocratic) interest in recognized historical problems (i.e. the knowledge already known – the 'thought-style', 'thinking-habits' that fix the 'thought-constraints' of historians as a social collective) (cf. Appendix: Table 1; cf. Fleck 1999: 56–7, 85). At the same time, it explains why historical discourse is so powerful, why history perpetuates itself as the same old thing: for 'when the same history drives both the habitus and the habitat, dispositions and position, king and court, entrepreneur and enterprise, bishop and diocese, history in some ways communicates with itself, reflects itself in itself' (Bourdieu 1997: 180). What for a self-styled historical agent (or historian) counts as a historical environment, will turn through habit and identitary thinking into a historical aspect of the world.

(b.) The terrorizing intention of historical processes. Apprehension is the experience of being implicated in history. The sublime prospect of history as a total, overwhelming system, triggers it. The limited scope for action it offers already implicated individuals in their embodied cognitive situation, causes alarm. No wonder, the comprehensive

breadth of historical knowledge dispensed by 'practising historians' only enhances the destitution of ordinary people in ordinary existential predicaments. Historical knowledge, having nothing to say about this human-all-too-human reality, is merely interference.

Historical and cultural processes operate on human tissue, conditioning its behaviour, re-programming its sense. Cultural refinement comes from a savage historical process of human self-punishment (Nietzsche 1988: V, 294–7; Pt.II, §3; Kafka 1983: 147–55). Natural obduracy is corrected by violent, state intervention (Negt & Kluge 1993: 453, 760ff.; Foucault 1975: 133). Cultural achievement and barbaric practice are two sides of the same coin (Benjamin 1977: 254, §VII).

History cuts into our most immediate reality, our material being, our bodies, because it does, because it must. What gives history its feel, is its human fabric: its very texture is a product of human tissue. (Though grotesquely unique, the artefacts made from human "material" recycled from the Nazi death-factories are, therefore, characteristically historical.) That's what keeps apprehension alert: history cuts for cutting's sake. It has it in for life itself, for that 'critical mass of genetic material and diversity' that keeps a civilization 'energized'. Taking (e.g.) the 'enormous, … cruelly selective casualties of the First World War', Steiner argues 'that the butcheries of Passchendaele and the Somme gutted a generation of English moral and intellectual talent, that they eliminated many of the best from the European future'. Moreover, he links the subsequent crises of Western culture (e.g. the rise of totalitarianism) to Europe after 1918 being 'damaged in its centres of life'. By that he means: 'Decisive reserves of intelligence, nervous resilience, of political talent had been annihilated. … An aggregate of mental and physical potentiality, of new hybrids and variants, too manifold for us to measure, was lost to the preservation and further evolution of Western man and of his institutions.' As a result, 'already in a biological sense we are looking now at a diminished or "post-culture"'(Steiner 1971: 33).

History [*crg*] that comprehends so much, cuts out human tissue. (The genre normally requires casualty-figures to be kept to footnotes in military history.) The world historians *sub specie aeternitatis* transmute into polished conceptions in polished monographs is in reality mutilated and traumatized – mutilated and traumatized by history. But then, as something academic, history does coat its objects in a nice gloss. It can't help it. On the one hand, to disembodied comprehension embodied apprehension is, technically, anathema: what produces apprehension – e.g. suicide bombers, frenzies of ethnic cleansing – is, in reality, absurd, "incomprehensible". On the other, once the apprehensive moment has wrought its havoc, damaged human tissue itself is purposeless. Wounds themselves are 'empty of reference' and the hurt body is 'referentially unstable' (Scarry 1985: 118, 121).

Injuring, though, does have a purpose. The apprehension history causes, flows from the *illusio* that guides its comprehensive projects. Wars happen because inflicting injury uniquely makes the abstract, historical issues in dispute – e.g. ideology, sovereignty, territoriality – real. The process of conferring meaning on suffering, the process of conceptualization, turns the 'incontestable reality of the physical body' into 'an attribute of an issue which has no independent reality of its own' (Scarry 1985: 125). War, then, is the quintessential historical experience, because it is the 'ultimate source of substantiation'. It extracts 'the physical basis of reality from its dark hiding place in the body out into the light of day ... making available ... the precious ore of confirmation, the interior content of human bodies, lungs, arteries, blood, brains'. This is 'the mother lode that will eventually be reconnected to the winning issue, to which it will lend its radical substance, its compelling, heartsickening reality, until benign forms of substantiation come into being' (Scarry 1985: 137). Injuring thus not only 'determines which ... set of disputed beliefs will be the winner', but also 'substantiates whatever outcome is produced' as a result of afflicting or sustaining injury in the first place. 'Injuries-as-signs' have, therefore, two functions: a 'memorialization function', making 'perpetually visible an activity that is past'; and a 'fiction-generating' or 'reality-conferring function', acting 'as a source of apparent reality for what would otherwise be a tenuous outcome, holding it firmly in place until the postwar world rebuilds that world according to the blueprint sketchily specified by the war's locus of victory'. For the reality-conferring historical narratives written after the event, this means that the injuries as contents can be discounted: 'the eventual transfer of the attributes of injuries to a victorious national fiction requires as a prelude the severing of those attributes from their original source, an act of severing and disowning that has a wide, perhaps collective, authorship' (Scarry 1985: 120–1, 136). History [*rg*] involves 'tissue alteration', producing apprehension history [*crg*] subsequently denies.

As an illustration of historical apprehension, the Jewish experience is paradigmatic. If history is the story of human self-incrimination as a result of a primal transgression, the verdict condemning mankind can be known only through its inscription on the human body. Mankind finds itself in the position of the condemned prisoner in Kafka's story, *In the Penal Colony* (1919). The incriminated victim discovers his guilt only once he has been strapped naked to the punishment machine, a needle-tipped, glass harrow, suspended above a vibrating, padded bed designed to hold him still, prevent him screaming, and absorb his blood. Only as the harrow cuts it into his flesh in a highly ornamented, almost illegible script, does he discover in his hours of agony what the verdict on him is (Kafka 1983: 102, 104, 107). Kafka's impulse to write comes from apprehension with being in the world. It is not surprising that the excruciatingly decorous script the harrow tattoos its victim with – literally – pinpoints the keen, aesthetic link between historical experience and apprehension.

For Kafka, it is a metaphor; for Fackenheim, a catastrophic reality: what law was inscribed on Jewish bodies in Auschwitz? His question is insistent: how to survive afterwards with the absolute rupture of all previous religious and philosophical assumptions (Fackenheim 1994: 193, 200, 320)? This includes the concept of historical continuity itself: 'Historical continuity is shattered because "at Auschwitz not only man died, but also the idea of man"; because our "estrangement from God" has become so "cruel" that, even if He were to speak to us, we have no way of understanding how to "recognize" Him. ... because the Holocaust ... is a total rupture' (Fackenheim 1994: 250). Far from naturally assuming a disembodied, academic stance *sub specie aeternitatis*, Fackenheim – as a Jew implicated in the aftermath of the Holocaust – wonders if transcendence is still possible. His apprehensive meditation consequently exemplifies historical reflection as *aesthesis* (cf. Appendix: Tables 1 and 3). What drives it, is 'ever-new, ever-again-surprised outrage' (Fackenheim 1994: 28). In fact, the metaphysical magnitude of the topic exceeds comprehension: 'the better a Holocaust historian succeeds in explaining the event, the closer he comes to suspecting the inevitability of ultimate failure,' says Fackenheim. And he continues: 'we confront in the Holocaust world a *whole of horror*. We cannot comprehend it but only comprehend its incomprehensibility' (Fackenheim 1994: 230, 238).

This is not just another instance of 'unknown causes' at the root of human apprehension. Rather, historical comprehension, the "normality" of historical continuity, of historical explanation, diminishes the numinous significance of Auschwitz. According to Fackenheim, post-Holocaust Jewish solidarity would erode less by forgetfulness (as the atrocity recedes into the past), than by historical universalization, by theological 'flattening', by the way the Holocaust is 'tamed, as it were', for 'an academic curriculum', and by what he calls 'the abortive nineteenth-century positivistic search for an illusory "objectivity"' – i.e. by various technical forms of "anaesthetization" (Fackenheim 1994: xii–xiv, 257, 280, 292). Instead, he advocates resistance in thought while insisting on the 'flesh and blood history of a flesh-and-blood people' (Fackenheim 1994: 18, 33). He urges Jews to remember in their 'very guts and bones the martyrs of the Holocaust, lest their memory perish' (Fackenheim 1978: 23–4). This means embracing historical existence knowing that they, as an 'accidental remnant', are 'obliged to consider [themselves] as heirs to the *whole* murdered people' (Fackenheim 1994: 308). *Aesthesis*, mindful of the past, thus inculcates vital vigilance. The lasting, eloquent memorials, haunted by both apprehension and melancholy, are created by art and artists. (*Illusio*, being purely technical, pleases *itself* when its 'cautious rationality' and 'reasoned conclusions' triumph (Evans 2002: 114, 272).)

In the end, though, comprehension [*illusio*] usually does triumph: pain and trauma, as immediate sensation [*aesthesis*], are incommunicable. World War I survivors came home from the trenches mute and experientially destitute (Benjamin 1977: 386). In-depth treatment of World War II aerial-bombing of German cities hardly figures in post-war German literature. W.G. Sebald remarks that 'it is impossible to plumb the depths of traumatization in the souls of those who fled from the epicentres of the catastrophe'. He recognizes their 'inviolable right' to silence (Sebald 2002: 75–6, 95). By contrast historians' chatter about causes and results, diplomatic manoeuvrings, military strategies and technology, casualty statistics, sounds like a way of filling what would otherwise have been a mortified silence, if we really had known (i.e. first-hand) how it had really been. Thus the mind excuses itself. Through the reflex of displacement, it subconsciously substitutes for the object it cannot face more amenable – in this case more rational, more explicable, more understandable – ones it can (cf. Laplanche & Pontalis 1990: 117–20). It needs history to generate a 'reality effect', a 'referential illusion' (cf. Barthes 1984: 174). Thus, historical explanation, along with its "truth-objective", acquires an indelible oneiric quality [*illusio*].

(c.) The sophistical basis of historical comprehension. In revealing the vulnerability of human existence, history causes apprehension: historical events cut right into human tissue. The question is still: how

does historical knowledge deal with the anxiety they generate? How does it react to what happens in its own name? Normally, historical comprehension projects the image [*illusio*] of an explainable past to reassure a perplexing present. It works as "an-*aesthesis*": it anaesthetizes, or de-sensitizes – particularly when it evokes virtual realities, oneiric fancies, or nostalgic cravings. Ultimately, though, its narcotic effect generates a more acute anxiety of its own, thus enhancing the apprehension history [*rg*] causes (cf. Appendix: Table 2). It reveals that history, the knowledge-practice that would represent "real" reality, has no real grasp of its own reality. Not only is it too heterogeneous to define itself, but also, 'a method devoid of a correspondingly distinct object', a 'hybrid discipline which defies simple pigeon-holing', it 'has neither turf nor principles of its own' (cf. Lévi-Strauss 1985: 312; Schorske 1999: 219; Tosh 1999: 131). Basically, it is indefinable. Its practitioners cannot say what they are really doing when they are doing history, nor what history actually does. The perpetuation of knowledge becomes so routine, so "natural", that its underlying rationale recedes from consciousness (cf. Fleck 1999: 114). Its claim to know and be everything, while not knowing itself, makes historical knowledge the cause of apprehension.

To see this, involves examining the 'thought habits' and 'thought constraints', that constitute history as a form of knowledge (cf. Fleck 1999: 58f., 165ff.). It means analyzing the discourse of disciplinary self-reflection. As the following example shows, the apprehension historical apologetics typically causes is its unintended, unconscious consequence:

(a) 'So I want now, finally, to turn to the question of how the discipline of history **may be** distinctive.'

– 'None of the skills I have described define the discipline of history'
– 'If we put them all together, and **think of them as** closely related to substance, we **may get** closer.'
– 'There can be no firm boundaries around "history."'
– 'There are no watertight definitions for any humanities or social science discipline.'

(b) 'It is **possible** to **think of the discipline as** a capacious umbrella –'

– 'People choose to come under it and call what they do "history", and others can agree or not as the case **may be**.'

- '"History" has never been and cannot be a stable category.'
- 'Those who shelter there ... construct a professional identity around the label.'

(c) 'It **may be** possible to get <u>slightly closer</u> to what is distinctive about "history" if we *think about* the *assemblage* of skills involved.'

(d) 'It is **not** possible to define history simply as the study of the past, because other disciplines do that too.'

- 'For the most part history is concerned with a past for which there are extensive written records and with accounting for continuities as well as changes.'

(e) 'It **is** possible to be <u>a little more specific</u>. For example, we can say what history is *not*.'

- 'History does not involve one specific category of human activity or production.'
- 'Historians study human nature in operation ... but mediated through sources.'
- 'They want to make statements of a fairly high level of generality about the past.'
- 'History involves intricate dialogues between the specific and the general.'
- 'Any given text, image, activity or experience is set in contexts ... such contexts involve structural elements, that is, the systems through which society functions.'
- 'A correspondingly wide range of historical explanations results.'

(f) 'So it **would be** possible to say that history is simply what historians do.'

- It **would follow** that skills were anything people who call themselves historians deploy in their work.'
- 'Yet this is too bland.'

(g) 'The rather abstract account I have just given of what **may be** distinctive about the discipline indicates some of its habits of mind.'

(h) 'We can be <u>a bit more precise</u> by examining some of the ways in which history is *unlike* related disciplines.'

- 'There is no single concept around which the discipline of history is organized in the way that sociology is predicated upon the concept "society".'
- 'There is no set of master theories.'

Summary of propositions (a) – (h):

- 'In other words, history is inherently <u>an eclectic discipline</u> and the skills it requires are <u>correspondingly diverse</u>. And therein lie its strengths. Eclecticism ... sounds <u>untidy</u> – just so: if historians treat the past in <u>too tidy</u> a manner <u>they lose a great deal</u>.'

Concluding inferences drawn from propositions (a)–(h):

(i) 'Hence the discipline is rightly <u>pragmatic</u>, including in its methods and the <u>skills</u> these demand.'

(ii) 'It is precisely the ability to <u>embrace complexities</u> while <u>making sense</u> of them, and to <u>think flexibly</u> about diverse phenomena at <u>distinct analytical levels</u>, that characterizes historians' purchase upon the past.'

(Jordanova 2000: 196–8)[11]

(1.) Its tentative nature (cf. the repeated 'possible', 'may') makes this argument striking: what the professional historian does daily, what her 'mental habits' are, she cannot say. She seems to know, since she gets 'slightly closer', 'a little more specific', and 'a bit more precise'; but, (like Fernández-Armesto earlier) unless she states exactly what it is, the reader can't tell how much 'closer', 'more specific' or 'more precise' she actually gets. This evasiveness prompts again the question: why academic historians reject postmodernism when they do it so well themselves? Here a 'practitioner' finds it acceptable to view history and its methods as a non-foundational 'coping practice', i.e. not as what they essentially are or do, but as what they can be thought of as being or as doing, as how they can be 'positioned and repositioned' (cf. Jenkins 2003: 60). (2.) The argument is characterized – predictably – by tautology (cf. *(b)*: people call what they do 'history'; *(f)* 'history = what historians do'; *Summary*: an 'eclectic' discipline is by definition 'diverse'; *Concluding inference*: a 'pragmatic' discipline by definition involves 'skills', since "skill" means "the capacity to do something"

---

[11] All marks of emphasis, except for non-bold italics, are my own.

and so implies utility). (3.) The argument proceeds by negation, thereby inevitably defeating itself. Defining anything as what it is not, is just another version of tautology. Obviously, anything distinctive will not be 'like' anything else (whatever 'like' means here); but that still does not specify what something (e.g. history) essentially is. But negation also produces its own contradictions. It's not true that the human sciences resist definition like history (as Jordanova alleges): think of linguistics, semiotics, psychology, English literature, etc. In any case, she subsequently concurs with Lévi-Strauss that, unlike sociology, history does not have a specific object after all. (4.) Even the definite propositions are contradictory. The idea that history deals with 'human nature in operation' implies what the historical process, be it represented by Ortega y Gasset, by Aron, or by Marx, precludes: a non-historicized human nature that at any given historical moment is "outside" or "above" history itself. Where there is such a thing (e.g. anatomy, physiology), you don't need history to study it. (5.) Consequently, mention of the 'contexts' in which the historian 'sets' historical activity (i.e. the institutional and administrative systems that manage society), affirms the normative control exerted by the identitary thinking that manages these systems, thereby ensuring history reiterates the same old thing, the knowledge already known. (6.) Finally, that the *summary* and the *concluding inference* (ii) sound hollow, is not surprising. The argument, by culminating in self-contradiction, fails. *What* exactly is an '"eclectic" discipline', given that 'eclectic' and 'discipline' refer to two distinct ecologies of knowledge (cf. Davies 2003: 25–6)? *Who* exactly defines what is 'untidy' or 'too tidy', i.e. what would make these metaphors precisely intelligible? So how do you 'make sense' of complexities by 'embracing' them? What does this metaphor actually mean? How does the reader 'think flexibly' while performing a 'distinct analysis' of 'diverse phenomena'? Isn't thinking already 'flexible', except when it is being evasive or dogmatic? But these claims are in any case groundless. Based on catachresis, they fall apart.

The obvious counter-argument is that the history a historian writes, matters much more than their reflections on 'historical epistemology' (Marwick 2001: 273). However, it only accentuates the apprehensiveness the historicizing mentality generates. First, dubiously enough, it assumes that the end justifies the means, that action, justifying itself, can dispense with reflecting on its motives. But it begs the further question: what does the monograph the historian writes reveal about the discipline his or her reflections on it cannot say? Rather, historical practice and historical reflection are in reality two variants of the same illusory objective (cf. Appendix: Tables 1 and 2). Second, this objection reveals a 'blind spot' in historical knowledge itself. Why else should historians who by profession account psychologistically for what others have done, prove to be diffident about accounting for what they themselves do? Used to thinking comprehensively, they do not see that comprehension can neither grasp their own existential situatedness, nor their contingent knowledge practices. As academics, they fall victim to the incommensurability of knowledge and existence their practice itself produces. That's why history can be "objectively true", yet inherently tautological and illusory [*illusio*]. That also leaves it wide-open to heteronomous influences. Lacking its own principles, it can only affirm others'.

All this is reason enough to be apprehensive of history. But there is more, and more alarming still. Truth claims or academic precedent alone cannot guarantee the integrity of knowledge. Knowledge tends to develop by criticism and falsification. In any case, no knowledge-system is exempt from sceptical re-examination. Nor can knowledge depend on how it may be categorized (i.e. "history as science" or "history as art"): there can be highly dubious sciences (e.g. astrology, ethnology); and art accommodates a wide range of practices. Least of all can the integrity of knowledge derive from its use or purpose, since it may be re-functioned in ways unintended by its author. Instead, it relies solely on the self-conscious clarity that reveals to the scholar or scientist the scope, responsibilities, and objectives of his or her intellectual practice. Left to themselves, understanding and systematic enquiry [*Wissenschaft*] run wild, turn promiscuous, and sell out to whatever interest happens to come along. 'Reflection and self-consciousness' are the only remedy (Jaspers 1958: 251). The very least that can be demanded from the scholar or scientist is 'intellectual honesty', 'remorseless clarity', about what properly constitutes his or her intellectual activity (Weber 1988: 490–1). Each and every academic expert must be able to 'account to him- or herself for the ultimate sense and meaning of what he or she does' (Weber 1988: 608).

Consequently, no amount of 'serious research', no quantity of polished erudite monographs can by itself justify history – as Cannadine admits with the remark that 'much of this vast public output is read by so small an audience that it is tempting to wonder what is the point of writing it and publishing it in the first place' (Cannadine 1999: 10; cf. Marwick 2001: 273). Rather, it is the reverse. Since 'so much history is now being written that very few scholars can keep up with more than a tiny fraction of what is being published', since 'all of us know more and more about less and less' (cf. Cannadine 2002: xi), self-conscious clarity about this production process becomes indispensable. It needs to be a basic requirement of a discipline that is not just 'flourishing', but in reality has "bolted" – is going to seed. The volume production of specialized works makes historical meaning gratuitous. Sheer quantity makes it look persuasive; in reality, it ceases to be 'binding' (cf. von Mises 1990: 141). The discipline produces knowledge without knowing how it knows what it knows. The historical precedents, traditions, or interests, rationales that make history make sense, can't be validated. As a source of human truth and guidance, history is void. Human action in all its forms – social, political, economic and cultural – projecting into the future, is like sleepwalking: humanity flying blind . . .

Historical knowledge: deep time apprehensions

Mesmerized by its own scholastic priorities, history inevitably produces apprehensiveness, e.g. '. . . history is flourishing in Britain as never before, and so, too, are its principal – and abiding – justifications. For history is above all a *humane* subject, providing the quintessential "liberal education"' (Cannadine 1999: 7). The scholastic conceit is blind to its own duplicity. History's "humaneness" is an academic abstraction that negates the time of our own lives. History may well 'make plain the . . . range and variety of human experience', and 'enable us to know about other centuries and other cultures', but only because 'it provides . . . the best antidote to the temporal parochialism which assumes that the only time is *now*, and the geographical parochialism which assumes that the only place is *here*. There is not only here and now; there is there; and there is then' (Cannadine 1999: 8).

Clearly, the existential situatedness of the real life of real people doesn't count, historically speaking. If you have been made redundant, if you are dying of a fatal illness, if you are a refugee, if your life seems to be going nowhere, if only there were a 'there' and a 'then': there is only here and now – for you – and to you it has nothing 'parochial' about it. Cleansed of such 'ultimate situations' [*Grenzsituationen*], historically abstracted life fits the more easily into history's self-authenticating structures, the identitary thinking that perpetuates the 'same old thing': 'the best guide to there and then, and thus also the best guide to here and now, is history: in part because it helps us understand how our world got to be the way it is; in part because it

helps us understand how other worlds got to be the way they were –
and the way they are' (Cannadine 1999: 8; cf. Jaspers 1967: 20).
What generates apprehensiveness, is that these apparently edifying
claims come from the history technology rather than reality. Because
it identifies with itself, blocks any disengagement from itself, the very
technology that explains 'how our world got to be the way it is',
causes the world to become increasingly like itself, i.e. increasingly
historicized (cf. Cohen 1988: 104, 200). 'The fact that there is . . .
only one word to designate history as we live it and the intellectual
operation that makes it intelligible . . . here delivers its profound truth:
the movement that carries us along with it, is of the same nature that
represents it to us' (Nora 1984: XVIII–XIX). However, history [*crg*]
discounts its own ecological effects. History is a technology, a 'mega-
machine' for studying the world; but the world is also transforming
itself through technology – most obviously through the technology
that history itself is. The point is: 'A new technology does not add or
substract something. It changes everything. In the year 1500, fifty
years after the printing press was invented, we did not have old Europe
plus the printing press. We had a different Europe' (Postman 1993:
18). So, the more history is produced, the more history there is to
know about. But the more historical study proliferates, the more it
changes the historical world being studied. This in turn produces
a dilemma for historical comprehension. Apprehensively enough, the
object it would grasp is constantly receding from it. History may well
be 'everything'; but 'everything does not mean very much in this case;
for with every new gain in knowledge at least one further new problem
emerges: the re-examination of the knowledge already known. Thus
the number of problems to be solved becomes infinite and the
designation "everything" meaningless' (Fleck 1999: 70).

The academic perspective habitually discounts from its objects its
own relation to them. If history is comprehensive, it should be truly
comprehensive. If history comprehends the world, it should confront
the tautology its comprehension implies. Certainly, it can determine
that producing historically 'fair explanations' means comprehending
such influential factors as an individual's habits, beliefs, emotions,
convictions, biological needs, personal interests, unconscious dispositions, cultural norms and social sanctions (McCullagh 1998: 213ff.).
But that means realizing that these factors also influence academic
historians when they write history, since writing history is itself, quite
literally, a historical act. So, if historians don't keep historicizing
themselves, they compromise the very 'fairness' of the explanation
they, as individual historical actors, intend to achieve. Historians have

to see that the world history would grasp totally already includes history, already is a historical artefact, an already-made product of historical action and knowledge. The relationship between history and the world in reality comes down to the relationship between history and this world where history 'matters a great deal', where history is 'more vital and vigorous than it ever has been' (Cannadine 1999: 5, 7). In reality, it comes down to the relationship between history and history itself – the dead end of the inevitably self-referential historicizing mentality and its identitary logic.

However, it is possible to get behind this fundamental tautology in historical thinking. This means: (a) seeing the world history studies not just as already made by history, but as history, i.e. as a historical text. From this, it follows (b) that history dehumanizes the world in which, as a 'humane subject', it 'flourishes as never before'; and (c) its 'vigour and vitality' are symptoms of wastage and death.

(a.) The world is itself a historical text, the final account. 'We have inadvertently sent down through history a crucial deep time message: the world itself as we have made it. Our planet, the background for our great dramas, is itself a mixed message from antiquity, shaping all our unconscious assumptions' (Benford 2000: 171). To see this, it takes not a historian, but a physicist. Gregory Benford does so by inverting the historical situation. Instead of focussing on how we now understand the past, he confronts the problem of how we get the future (i.e. a future present) to understand us now (i.e. that future's past). His motive is ethical and ecological. It concerns a project set up by the US House of Representatives in 1989 that aimed to warn posterity about the location of deadly nuclear-waste disposal-sites that could be active for 10,000 years or more (Benford 2000: 33, 46). Leave aside such intractable issues as the question of the survival of nation states as we now know them, whether moral responsibility can extend to 10,000 years, the huge financial cost of any proposed warning-system, whether the human race would still be intact (i.e. without some Cro-Magnon variant appearing), and problems of natural erosion that would obliterate the sites: focus on the basic issue of signs (Benford 2000: 43, 45, 53, 64). The most obvious solution, written warnings, would not work. Questions of the durability of the medium apart, no language lasts for more than 5000 years and 'basic vocabularies change about twenty per cent in a thousand years'. However, symbols and images might convey meaning 10,000 years hence: the oldest ones, Spanish Levantine rock art, date back 11,500

years (Benford 2000: 75–6). Instead, the project would have to rely on massive, imposing, architectural edifices, akin to Stonehenge, the Great Pyramid, or Neolithic earthworks, that can survive for thousands of years. Proposals included: a Plain of Thorns that would 'sprout eighty-foot-high basalt spikes erupting from the ground'; a Black Hole, 'a black basalt slab, unbearably hot from accumulated solar heat'; a Rubble Landscape, 'local stone, dynamited and bulldozed into a crude square pile covering the project, . . . a place destroyed, not made' (Benford 2000: 67–9). And what would be their purpose? Not comprehension; but apprehension – as both the necessary response to a lasting historical legacy and the crucial cognitive survival reflex. They intend to 'frighten the future': what mutates least, is apprehensiveness (cf. Benford 2000: 55).

In effect, Benford challenges the historical format of human knowledge, particularly its identitary logic. Progress in physics, biology, and biotechnology discloses a 'more general truth': 'the most difficult realization about the future is that it can be qualitatively different than the present and past.' This means that 'an irreducible unknown in all our estimates arises from our very world-view itself, which is inevitably ethnocentric and timebound' (Benford 2000: 47). He stresses that 'seemingly minor acts today can amplify through millennia, leaving legacies we do not consciously intend'. In other words, 'deep-time has become ever present in our age' (Benford 2000: 49). He acknowledges, conversely, that 'our modern attention span is quite short', e.g.: 'Most industrial societies have an increasingly bottom-line attitude. Stocks had better show a good quarterly statement, and long range research is uncommon in industry.' He also points out that 'in this century many countries have failed to outlive their citizens', that 'most people consider their own grand-children the furthest time horizon worth worrying about' (Benford 2000: 5). Further, he argues that current historical attitudes evince real deficits in species-essential knowledge, the humane knowledge, needed to ensure the meaningful survival of *homo sapiens*. (So there is a 'there' and a 'then', after all, but not selfishly for us – as *our* past – but for someone else – i.e. brought about by what we as *their* past will have done to them – and historical thinking will not take us to it.) Where humane values are concerned, history clearly is not 'everything'. Its identifications prove inadequate, because urgent deep-time issues operate minimally at their extreme limit: 'ten thousand years is the upper limit of consciousness, planned deep-time communication', because 'not coincidentally, this is roughly the age of civilization' (Benford 2000: 4, 6). That means, 'the past . . . can tell us little about the deep future beyond a thousand years': we have only to look back, e.g. at Europe or the USA as they were a thousand years ago to see that. Consequently, 'the probability of radical shifts in worldview and politics means that we cannot anticipate ... future generations based on an understanding of the past, even when we anticipate the use of modern information storage capabilities' (Benford 2000: 38).

The world history studies is, therefore, out of sync. On the one hand, 'we have leisure and inclination to study the past as never before', with high culture increasingly reaching 'backward in time ... almost as if we seek our identity in distant ancestors'. On the other, 'our current concern for the past may not be itself long-lasting', due to a 'recent ... quite modern condition' – our growing awareness of being implicated in deep-time perspectives for which we have only 'inadequate theoretical tools'. That's because 'advances in radioactive dating and astronomical science have left us standing, as a species, on a vast plain, perspectives of time stretching from our murky origins to the universe's cosmological destiny' (Benford 2000: 3, 6, 184). *Homo sapiens* thus confronts an unprecedented historical situation beyond history itself: 'Whipsawed by incessant, accelerating change, the modern mind lives in a fundamental anxiety about the passing of all referents, the loss of meaning' (Benford 2000: 3).

(b.) History, a 'humane subject', dehumanizes the world in which it 'flourishes as never before'. History [*crg*] comprehends and humanizes what history [*rg*] keeps making incomprehensible (cf. Appendix: Table 2). It acts as a sweet anaesthetic or a soothing narcotic. It would restore to the world the meaning global agencies (e.g. nation states, corporate business), having the political and economic potential not just to make history, but to make the history they want, keep expropriating.[12]

To see what history does means consulting the testimony of exiles, dislocated refugees, disorientated asylum-seekers, those who 'change countries more often than they changed their shoes' (cf. Brecht's historically self-conscious poem, *An die Nachgeborenen* [*To Posterity*] (Brecht 1966a: 58)). With history etched into their bodies, into their souls, they are most perceptive about history and its 'humane' effects;

---

[12] e.g. 'The Republicans' victory in the mid-term elections last November was secured with the help of $60m from America's big drug firms' (Monbiot 2003: 19).

their writings convey the inhumanity history itself causes: (e.g.) Walther Rathenau's *Zur Kritik der Zeit* [*A Critique of the Age*] (1912), Theodor Lessing's *Geschichte als Sinngebung des Sinnlosen* [*History: the Attribution of Meaning to Meaninglessness*] (1919), Ernst Bloch's *Erbschaft dieser Zeit* [*The Heritage of this Age*] (1935) or his *Politische Messungen, Pestzeit, Vormärz* [*Political Soundings, Age of Pestilence, Pre-March*] (1970), Stefan Zweig's *Die Welt von Gestern* [*The World of Yesterday*] (1944), Heinrich Mann's *Ein Zeitalter wird besichtigt* [*An Age Reviewed*] (1946), Siegfried Kracauer's *History. The Last Things Before The Last* (1969) or Max Horkheimer's *Notizen* [*Notes and Jottings*] (1974). History [*Geschichte*] engulfs them totally: still these witnesses of their time would salvage from the wreckage some meaning of their own [*Eigensinn*]. To them history comes as dislocating asynchronicity and unprecedented rupture (Rathenau, Bloch, Mann, Kracauer and Horkheimer), as arbitrary and meaningless force (Lessing), but even so as not the 'last thing' (Kracauer). That makes its flesh cuts only more vicious: Rathenau being assassinated in 1922 and Lessing in 1933, Zweig committing suicide in exile in Brazil in 1942. Through the threadbare fabric of historical sense, these texts illuminate the underlying, desolate, apprehensive reality. The (historical) world of technological progress, says Rathenau, 'bears death in its heart', for 'in the depths of its consciousness this world is terrified of itself' (Rathenau 1918: 135).

Hardly gratifyingly humane, historical consciousness is an estranged, traumatized consciousness. The pleasure-principle enjoins one to live: the death-drive manifest in history, destroys the world one lives in. So being conscious of what history really does, is an impoverishing, melancholic experience. Basically, it reveals the unhappiness of living in time, the poignant recognition that human beings have only the time of their own life-time [*Lebenszeit*], the world's time [*Weltzeit*] – i.e. both historical time and cosmic 'deep time' – transcends and nullifies (cf. Blumenberg 1986a: 100). History, therefore, is no surrogate immortality. Here tragedy [*aesthesis*] sees better. It voices the unhappiness historical consciousness induces: the fact that the situation foisted now on the tragic hero arises from a precursor's transgressions, turning a previous contingent circumstance into ineluctable destiny, a force that is always obligating, a past they have not consented to (cf. Durkheim 1997: 104). In reality, if not in history, the time always is 'out of joint' (*Hamlet*, I, v); 'the weight of this sad time' must always be obeyed (*King Lear*, V, iii).

The estranged consciousness that is historical consciousness is an apprehension generated by the age itself. The consciousness of being always historically conscious, of always having had a history, hence of being ever historical, elicits melancholy and depression. Its main symptom is the conviction that 'we have arrived too late': everything has already happened, and we must cope on our own 'in necessitous times' in a disenchanted world (cf. Hölderlin's elegy *Brod und Wein* ['Bread and Wine'] (Hölderlin 1946: II, 93)). Historical consciousness thus induces an apprehension of what Steiner calls 'coretiredness' in 'the climate of spirit': 'the inward cliometry, the contracts with time which so largely determine our consciousness, point to late afternoon in ways that are ontological – this is to say, of the essence of the fabric of being. We are, or feel ourselves to be, latecomers' (Steiner 2001: 2). The world that is historically conscious, in which 'history matters', has always come after. Here, it is always 'the night-time of the world', a world on which night is always falling (Heidegger 1972: 248; Péguy 1961: 244), a world immersed in the 'melancholy of everything that has been finished', the 'everlasting, tiresome "Too late!"' (Nietzsche 1988: V, 229, §277). In these circumstances, the human creature, 'projected into existence' (as Heidegger says), becomes self-conscious through being (historically) conscious of the traces left by the world's previous inhabitants. It is always having to see itself as being 'additional after the event' [*nachträglich*], and to reposition itself in the light of subsequent remembrances, or deferred reconstructions, of past events (cf. Davies 1999: 247–8; Laplanche & Pontalis 1990: 33–6). But then, for being late, late-comers always have had to excuse or vindicate themselves – to explain how, as late-comers, they got to be late, i.e. how they got to be how they are. Their indentitary thinking is, therefore, both indispensable and symptomatic.

The past as a rich, humane, historical legacy, therefore, only heaves into panoramic view in a 'post culture', an era of 'post-history', a 'post intellectual age', an age in which *homo sapiens* has ensured its own antiquatedness and obsolescence (cf. Steiner 1975, 2002; Seidenberg 1950; Anders 1985, 1986; Niethammer 1989; Wood 1996). A post-historical culture is a pessimistic, conservative inversion of the nineteenth-century ideology of progress (cf. Niethammer 1989: 164–5). 'Postmodernism' represents this historical legacy as this estranged, 'post-historical' apprehension perceives it. Its cultural practices result from the coincidence of various circumstances – as a conservative historicist reaction to modernism (e.g. to the functionalist architecture of Adolph Loos or Walter Gropius); a left-wing subversion of dominant forms of culture; the commodified reconfiguration of knowledge in a knowledge economy driven by information technology and the virtual realities it generates (Niethammer 1989: 35ff.). Why 'working' historians should take issue with it is a mystery. That they do, reveals a typically academic misapprehension: a large and disparate social interest-group (i.e. historians themselves) perpetuating knowledge already known, but unaware that, in reality, their 'flourishing' activity in all its manifold 'varieties' is what produces the (postmodern) fragmentation, the ludic rootlessness of issues, they deprecate.

Moreover, as an apprehension, the sense of lateness implied by a postmodern post-culture cannot just be regarded as the latest in a sequence of historical epochs – as the current historical illusion. Apprehension (as *aesthesis*) is sustained by archaic patterns of consciousness and behaviour that prompt especially the latest thought and action (Davies 2002b: 68; 2003: 26, 28). Knowledge, let alone historical knowledge, knowledge of what 'really happened', can only ever come after. Reflection and meaning have an in-built time-lapse: philosophy 'comes in any case always far too late' (Hegel 1967: 17). Consequently, the desolation that characterizes post-culture, is in itself archaic. It was already there, at the beginning. 'Thereafter, would that I were not among the men of the fifth generation, but either had died before or been born afterwards. For now truly is a race of iron, and men never rest from labour and sorrow by day, and from perishing by night' – thus Hesiod's nostalgic lament for a long distant golden age. Now, by contrast, in a world bereft of the gods, of Aidôs and Nemesis, 'bitter sorrows will be left for mortal men, and there will be no help against evil' (Hesiod 1995: 15–17). As Nietzsche argues, this late, technocratic, theoretical, Alexandrine culture encloses reality in the finest webbing, made of all kinds of concepts, rationalizations, explanatory patterns, causes, effects, in its attempt to comprehend it (Nietzsche 1988: I, 100–101, 116, §§15, 18). It's never straightened out in time, it doesn't reach everywhere, it's full of holes, however much technicians keep renewing the same old thing so no-one knows the difference. Still, and this is what causes apprehension, it's just that – webbing.

Delayed melancholic insights and a 'flourishing' historical culture inviting 'new approaches and new kinds of history' as well as 'new accounts of process and structure' radically reinforce each other (Joyce 1997a: 248; 1997b: 361). Their combination is methodologically indispensable – as historians themselves confirm: 'we ... act ... in the knowledge or perception of what we think has gone before and in the light of what we think of it. We inhabit human worlds which are intrinsically suffused with a sense of history and a placement within webs of historical significance' (Fulbrook 2002: 189; cf. Southgate 2003: 135). Webs: the historical world is a musty world, wreathed in webs: cobwebs spun in dark, ancient, undisturbed nooks and crannies – webs of antiquarian erudition, webs of knowledge already known, webs information technology fabricates, veils of virtual reality [*illusio*]. History produces meaningless webs of words both to veil its meaninglessness and make up for the meaning it lacks. To be meaningful, history requires 'supra-paradigmatic guidelines or ground rules' that would endorse a rationale 'for accepting, rejecting, or amending different perspectives in more detail', as well as 'for determining whether in some areas at least a relatively broad scholarly community can collectively engage in closer approximations to adequacy in accounts of the past in the present, while certain issues will prove to be insurmountable stumbling blocks'. 'Some grand synthesis might be possible', apparently – at least in principle, thanks to the notion of 'perspectival paradigms', even if it is invalidated by the 'mutual incompatibility of certain approaches under the headings of both implicit paradigms and paradigms proper' (Fulbrook 2002: 187). This rationalizing is meant to produce 'some more theoretically sophisticated notion of history' (ibid.). All it does, is put a thin, scholastic gloss on the sole certainties of historical knowledge: its heterogeneity (of subject-matter), its arbitrariness (of scope and focus), its conjecturality (of meaning). It's like making intricate patterns in shifting sand ...

(c.) History's 'vigour and vitality' are symptoms of wastage and death. The vitality of history spells a world in ruins. A culture with a 'vigorous' interest in history is in reality mesmerizing itself with its 'excremental vision', obsessed with its own waste, minutely cataloguing its own débris (cf. Brown 1970: 256). It goes with the contemporary 'vigorous' production of ruin and débris in the wars, genocides, environmental catastrophes, industrial accidents of this time, the political and economic investment in the research, manufacture, and maintenance of the technology of death. It's an index of the ever-increasing capacity of a historicized culture to produce death, to 'construct death in life for the body' (cf. Brown 1970: 256). It reproduces itself by its self-perpetuation as the same old thing – by the destruction it causes, by the apprehension it generates, by its repetitive-compulsive self-incrimination. 'During the twentieth century,' Zbigniew Brzezinski reckons, 'no less than 167,000,000 lives

– and quite probably in excess of 175,000,000 – were deliberately extinguished through politically motivated carnage'. This figure represents 'more than the total killed in *all* previous wars, civil conflicts, and religious persecutions throughout human history' (Brzezinski 1995: 17). And it is not just the numerical estimate of human, genetic loss: 'it is impossible to account for the churches or temples blown up, for the monuments torn down, for the library collections robbed or burned, for the artworks stolen, ... to say nothing of the denigration of the human spirit' (Brzezinski 1995: 8, 18). The scale of the wastage is 'so unprecedented that it becomes incomprehensible' (Brzezinski 1995: 8).

The historicized world is *ipso facto* endangered and desolate. Caring about the past may well be 'an essential element in public consciousness, cultural enrichment and civilised living' (Cannadine 1999: 21): the history 'mega-machine' that fabricates it, creates in reality a brutalizing present. Everyday consciousness diminishes to a reflex for coping with the stresses and strains of living. In a historicized world, oppressive, chaotic, claustrophobic, repetitive, routinely frustrating, life itself objectively appears the way it would look to someone consumed by melancholy or severe depression (Bodinat 1996/1999: II, 50–1). The historicized world jeopardizes itself, as the concept of the 'risk society' indicates. It distresses itself through the inequalities of life-chances, the uneven distribution of resources and opportunities, inherent in the investment strategies that manage the material and cultural capital of Western civilisation (cf. Bourdieu 1993). It is a world of self-induced obsolescence: 'the celebrated modern "economy" is in reality the fantastic squandering of a capital accumulated by the biosphere over three thousand million years, and this squandering increases exponentially with every day that passes' (Castoriadis 1990: 170). History, as the story of human development (represented physically by an ever increasing world population), correlates with ecological degradation: 'The coming wave of extinctions, then, may be our most lasting, important heritage, far surpassing our gilded monuments or abstract plaques on spacecraft, for the vast loss will be felt throughout humanity in a world truncated and diminished, perhaps irretrievably.' Inscribed in the historical text the world itself is, 'this message ... will be an unconscious message, unnoticed, for most species shall die by being crowded out while we are about our busy business; but it shall be no less effective' (Benford 2000: 138).

History, a 'humane subject', does anything but humanize the world. Far from opening up a 'breadth of view' (Cannadine 1999: 8), it forecloses on both the human future and the hope it symbolizes. Braudel's *longue durée*, transcending the human life-span, could not be more mendacious: in reality, 'the world grows older and more tired faster than the sand runs out in the hour-glass of our own physiological time-span'(Bodinat 1996 / 1999: I, 16). History [*crg*] conspires in the dehumanization: 'the historian is a functionary of the negative who promotes the "value" of deriving positivity from negation, and who ceaselessly promotes the sense of suffering as a necessity arising from the innermost core of the world' (Cohen 1988: 227). It would have us deprecate the sense of our own life, persuade us that melancholy and ruination were perfectly "normal", by affirming that what is, is what had to be – by helping us 'understand how the world got to be the way it is' (Cannadine 1999: 8). In disregarding embodied existence here and now, being engrossed in 'there and then', history [*crg*] creates a late, historical culture in which death has 'dominion over life'. That is to say: 'mankind's diversion from the actuality of living-and-dying, which is always in the present, is attained by the reactivation in fantasy of the past and regressive attachment to fantasy of the past, ultimately the womb from which life came' (Brown 1970: 249). But a culture in which 'the past seems more vital and vigorous than it has ever been' (Cannadine 1999: 7), is a culture incapable of accepting death. Its 'war against death ... turns the death instinct into its distinctively human and distinctively morbid form' (Brown 1970: 249). This suggests that 'at the deepest level the morbid human death instinct is at the back of the human sense of time' (Brown 1970: 249). Hence, historical comprehension acts as an anaesthetic, deadening in reality the desolate present, denying the apprehension history actually causes.

However, 'tempocentric notions of "the human condition" do not survive'. They can be misleading and superficial:

> Confronted with one of our current skyscraper monoliths of glass and steel, what would a citizen of the year 5000 B.C. think? No doubt these soaring towers would provoke awe. On the other hand, what perspective would a person of the year A.D. 5000 bring? That ours was a great era, perhaps – or merely that for some reason, possibly without noticing, we made our grandest buildings in the same shape as our gravestones?
>
> (Benford 2000: 6)

To see the morbid character of historical interests, it takes non-identitary thinking, an anthropological perspective 'outside our civilisation and our own moment of history' (Éliade 1968: 233). Given that 'in the sphere of culture there is no primary process and certainly no primary form of the signifier', Western society is distinctive in 'privileging its culture by historicizing it' (Cohen 1988: 18). What's more, this interest in history proves to be psycho-pathological. Both 'the desire for an ever more complete and more exact knowledge of the past of humanity' and 'the tendency to define man as above all a historical being conditioned, and in the end created, by History', are 'almost abnormal' (Éliade 1968: 234). They confirm an archaic, mythological truth: that 'upon the screen of memory the dying man once more reviews his past'. By analogy, therefore, 'the passion for historiography in modern culture' would be a portent of 'imminent death': 'Our Western civilisation, before it foundered, would be for the last time remembering all its past, from protohistory until the total wars. The historiographical consciousness of Europe ... would in fact be the supreme moment which precedes and announces death' (Éliade 1968: 235–6). That historical interest appears natural, that it 'arouses no presentiments of disaster', is its fatal attraction. It's an effect of the illusion it creates: 'depth-psychology has taught us to ascribe more importance to the active presence of a symbol than to the conscious experience which manipulates and evaluates it'. The symbolic recollection of the life of the departed is institutionalized in funerary ritual. It helps the mourners to deal with the fact of death. It's also where the sense of history comes from: 'the anxiety of modern man is obscurely linked to the awareness of historicity, and this, in its turn, discloses the anxiety of confronting Death and Non-being'. This 'anguish before Nothingness and Death seems to be a specifically modern phenomenon', an apprehension only a historicized world could produce (Éliade 1968: 236).

History is no longer, therefore, what happens when, in the fullness of time, things change. Rather it follows on relentlessly from the interests of economic and political power. The hectic pursuit of the 'latest thing' junks everything in its wake, setting off a sequence of catastrophes, an ever accumulating pile of ruins (cf. Benjamin 1977: 255, §IX). The global economic power-complexes make history as and whenever they like, just by trashing whatever obstructs them – by making even the latest thing dated and obsolete. For this reason, says Baudrillard, talk about consigning old ideologies, régimes or values to the dustbin of history is futile: 'history has itself become a dustbin' (Baudrillard 1992: 45). That's why, in the end, history doesn't affirm human existence. History is a symptom of what's wrong with the world: it is the ever imminent catastrophe. Historical knowledge causes apprehension because it doesn't help. It anaesthetizes: it normalizes; it stabilizes; it perpetuates the same old thing. If human beings survive, it will be despite history. Finally they will have acknowledged the apprehension it causes. Finally they will have found a cathartic, life-enhancing way of resolving it. 'How we present ourselves in these ancient sepulchres may be our longest-lasting legacy', says Gregory Benford in reference to the radio-active land-fill sites meant to last 10,000 years or more. 'It is sobering to reflect that distant eras may know us mostly by our waste – and by our foresight' (Benford 2000: 85).

Variation 3
History as Prosthesis

The 'prosthesis god'

In producing the tools, artefacts, and structures their life depends on, human beings create not only their living conditions, but also themselves. This is 'the primary act of history'. Because the technics for human self-determination require intelligence, history forms a 'spiritual link' between individuals (Aron 1986: 44). Aron's thinking is essentialist and psychologistic: 'By his very essence man creates documents since he extends the action of his body by means of instruments and all his creations reveal immediately the activity of a mind' (Aron 1986: 37). But stressing this aptitude of human beings to make things, hence to make themselves, also makes history [*rg*] a form of *techne*. This in turn makes historical scholarship [*crg*] a *technasma*, an artful device, for comprehending what human beings both have made and have made of themselves. This is the basis of historical sense and meaning. It makes history both the "official knowledge" of the academic world and technocratic élites, and society's "unofficial knowledge" of itself. Hence, 'historical knowledge is a technique of the first order to preserve and continue a civilisation already advanced.' History is a 'perfected means' of solving the problems that get increasingly complex as 'life gets gradually better'. It has 'a great deal of the past at its back, a great deal of experience' and is 'most plainly attached to the advance of a civilisation' (Ortega y Gasset 1964: 91). From this perspective, history [*crg*] is a technology that enables humanity to communicate with itself, to inform itself about itself (cf. Schnädelbach 2000: 137). History, connecting (subjective) human motivation and its (objective) effects, the psychologistic and the technical, is thus the cleverest technological invention. It's a technology of technologies.

A technology of technologies: this explains history's hold on consciousness. Its reliance on fact, its quest for objectivity, its claim to truth do not solely vindicate its claim to be the "real reality". It needs also (a) technical efficacy, (b) metaphysical necessity, and (c) organizational competence.

(a.) Technical efficacy. With any technological contrivance, efficacy sustains reliability: so too with historical comprehension. History proves to be a 'mega-machine driven by a mega-technology', highly effective at generating technical development (Negt & Kluge 1993: 296). It produces, as Freud remarks in *Civilization and its Discontents* (1930), the marvellous auxiliary powers that augment human sentience. The human creature has at its disposal (amongst other things) motors that lend its muscles enormous strength; spectacles, telescopes, and microscopes that improve, extend and enhance its natural sight; the camera, capturing fleeting visions that, like the gramophone record, retaining transient aural sensations, extends its memory; the telephone that augments its sense of hearing (Freud 1977: 86). Invested with this fabulous potential, the human creature becomes a 'prosthesis god', a description still prescient now in the age of the cyborg and genetic cloning (Freud 1977: 87; cf. Gray et al. 1995; cf. Beck 1986: 333ff., 345).

History is the ultimate prosthetic, the technological appliance that applies to everything. It regulates a world that has become a 'macro-appliance' [*Makrogerät*; *Ge-stell*], the sum of all the prosthetic machines and tools people use in their daily lives (Anders 1985: 2; Heidegger 1967a: 20). It gives human beings a god-like vocation, though as much from metaphysical desperation as from mortal aspiration. What counts is not its jurisdiction over the past alone, but its cognitive techniques that disclose meaningful patterns of human activity. History is persuasive because it is an information technology designed to produce a world that has meaning. As Kant argues, human beings are creatures naturally configured to ascribe aims and purposes to themselves, since they and their moral development are the ultimate purpose of nature (Kant 1968: 305, §84). The highest natural purpose humanity can establish for itself is culture. Technologically speaking, this is the most 'noble tool' [*das vornehmste Werkzeug*] it has for bringing order and harmony to the unreasoning nature it lives in (Kant 1968: 300, §83). To do this, mankind needs civil society, governed by constitutional freedoms guaranteed by law, to offset the anarchy that naturally occurs with conflicting human interests. What brings out the talents needed to drive this cultural purpose forward, is the interaction of these societies, politically organized into states (Kant 1968: 301–2, §83). Hence, history is this ever-unfolding, apprehensive cultural project that reveals humanity to itself. This sense of ultimate immanent purpose, found in all the various historical disciplines, bestows on a shallow, historicized present the patina of reality.

(b.) Metaphysical necessity. Like all prosthetics, history is meant to compensate for loss, for the tendency in human experience to deplete itself. It thus meets a metaphysical need. Adrift from the agenda of divine salvation that made it make sense, the world looks to history as a substitute supreme intelligence, to banish absurdity. History must exculpate God for the evils of this world. Since the time of St Augustine (Blumenberg remarks), the meaning of the concept of evil has continued to shift: 'the evils of the world appear ever less clearly as physical defects in nature and ever more distinctly as the result of human actions, on account of their being technically amplified' (Blumenberg 1974: 68). In detailing humanity's own responsibility for the world, history releases God from any liability for its degenerate state. It relieves Him of the task of redemption – not that it arrives anyway, as the world's evils constantly mount up. History has to be a *prosthetic faith*.

'Secularization' is the term for this historical syndrome. The process of secularization makes the sense of history critical. By enabling mankind to take responsibility for the world, history (i.e. what human beings do), let alone the philosophy of history (i.e. the idea of an autochthonous reason in what human beings do), lets God off a moral and metaphysical hook – and for the sake of God Himself. This is a desperate, defensive measure. Humanity continues inevitably to incriminate itself in history. The idea of God watching this happen and not intervening, would make Him no better than a cruel tyrant. Humanity might, therefore, lose faith, perhaps even turn to atheism (cf. Leibniz 1962: 109, 110, §§4, 6). Having a self-incriminating history is bad enough; but to lose sight of the idea of God as well would make it even worse. Fortunately, humanity knows that God has his excuses – and this is where the idea of theodicy comes in. As Leibniz points out, God has made several worlds: mankind should not be so conceited as to believe this one has His sole attention (cf. Leibniz 1962: 119–20, §19). In any case, a moment's thought reveals that, with a just balance of good and evil to prevent both moral complacency and total degeneration, it is still designed to be the best possible for promoting mankind's moral improvement (cf. Leibniz 1962: 123–4, §§25, 26). The drawback with theodicy is that it verges on the idea of the 'hidden God' [*deus absconditus*], even agnosticism. Descartes ventures one plausible inference from it: he wonders how anyone could even tell if God were playing mischievous tricks on humanity, thus making everything in the world illusory (Descartes 1970: 31, 34, 38; I, §§9, 12; II, §4). Reassuring theodicy may be, reality is still deceptive: humanity has to produce truth by its own efforts (Blumenberg 1974: 87).

In the aftermath of genocide – particularly that of God's chosen people – Leibnizian theodicy shows its callous streak. But the strain falls on history. The critical question of its sense gapes open: under human management, could history ever mean anything? Incontrovertibly, therefore, the sense humanity finds in history always amounts to less than what God's grace would have afforded. After all, the natural world is already made and mankind a part of it. So human beings create the world they need by exploring the possibilities already latent in themselves. By implication, they cannot produce anything new; i.e. it is always the 'same old thing' (Blumenberg 1976: 93). But 'theory' which, as *theoria*, once meant eudaemonistic contemplation of the divine perfections of the cosmos, now refers to instrumentalized cognitive schemes, expressions of a technical, scientific, but human-all-too-human arrangement. The 'artificiality' [*Künstlichkeit*] of scientific inferences about the natural world falls far short of those available even to Aristotelian or Scholastic reflection. Consequently, 'reducing the demand for truth, hence for the autonomous dignity of theory, removed all obstacles from the development of the syndrome of science and technicity, theory and human self assertion' (Blumenberg 1974: 236–7, 239). Thus Blumenberg himself reinforces 'history as everything' from another 'post-historical' angle – as a purely human sphere of heterogeneous values, where nothing 'really matters' any more, that is void of redemption, an 'end-time', perpetuating always the 'same old thing' (Schmidt-Biggemann 1991: 125).

(c.) Organizational competence. The post-metaphysical situation requires human beings to assert their own meaning, to manage for themselves their human-all-too-human biosphere. History confirms

that *homo sapiens* is by nature programmed to learn – to secure through reflecting on social customs, institutions, beliefs, and cognitive structures both the conditions for its survival and the values that make survival worthwhile (cf. Dux 1982: 248). But history as a technology has a cognitive advantage of its own: it has persuasiveness built in, irrespective of content. It has to be: the technical knowledge of mankind encompasses 'less knowledge' than the divine optimum. Human truth is, as Baumgarten argued, an 'aestheticological truth'. But how much less is 'less'? How much 'more' could yet be discovered? How could it even be quantified? Here, at least, history comes into its own. This is what the technology is for: to forget nothing and to redeem everything. That is how it works: 'Explanations are "justified" or "supported". Supporting a historical explanation ... consists in telling more of the story. And this requires further specification of the factors involved. ... In this way, the explanation, formerly vague and "open" is given body and weight' (Gardiner 1968: 97). In history – be it for professional scholarship's, be it for comprehensiveness' sake – more is always 'more'.

Furthermore, its aptitude for discovering more sense makes history [*crg*] a crucial technology, because it 'optimizes organizational competence' (Dux 1982: 275). History is the ultimate form of cognitive organization. The more sense it finds, the more sense it has, the more realistic its organization. However, this organizational competence carries a high risk-factor. History confronts human beings with not only the autonomous world they have created, but also with their dependency on, indeed their vulnerability to, the historical-cultural process. Generally, the more successful cognitive structures are, the more complex they become, the more they are driven by their own internal logic, and the longer it takes to assimilate them. This applies particularly to history as a complex *technology of technologies* – which means it may become too complex to learn anything from. The technological argument thus also takes in the vicious circle of apprehension that drives historical understanding and its law of diminishing returns. The more insecure and unpredictable the world, the more difficult it is to discern any sense in it, the more the organizing rationale of history is needed for reassurance, but the less reassurance it really provides (Dux 1982: 274–5).

In the end, history, like other technologies, generates a characteristic ambivalence. It empowers, but also enforces dependency. A technology lasts while it works or until it becomes obsolete. Still it can be preserved for historical reasons – like Cornish tin-mines, Victorian pumping-houses, or steam locomotives, attracting both tourists and industrial archaeologists. As an information technology dealing with the 'same old thing', history surely preserves *itself* for the same old "historical reasons". Tradition tends crucially to shape the routine consensus of knowledge and knowledge production in the 'thought collectives' that academic disciplines represent (cf. Fleck 1983: 53, 170ff.). As 'knowledge already known', history is configured to keep on backing itself up.

Conversely, even when it is working, history certainly causes mankind, the 'prosthesis god', 'quite a lot of trouble from time to time', just like the other prostheses it uses (cf. Freud 1977: 87). History, as a delivery-system, does not always deliver. Like other powerful technological contrivances (e.g. as with planes that crash or nuclear fuel that pollutes), it is potentially catastrophic:

> History is the most dangerous compound the chemistry of the intellect has ever produced. Its properties are well known. It entices the masses with its dreams, intoxicates them, foists false memories onto them, distorts their reflexes, opens up their old wounds, troubles them in their rest, drives them to delusions of grandeur or paranoia, and it makes nations bitter, arrogant, intolerable, and conceited.
>
> (Valéry 1957 / 1960: II, 935)

Moreover, like the car that stalls or the computer that freezes, history is subject to internal interferences that compromise its efficiency. History seems to be set up so that knowledge (about the past) and action (in the present) are out of sync and itself out of control (cf. Bubner 1984: 26–8). The point is that 'mankind makes history, but it does not make the epoch it makes history in'. As Blumenberg explains: human action operates within a horizon of historical possibilities, but it can never follow its intentions through. It gets caught up in a force-field where synchronous and asynchronous elements, integrating and destructive tendencies interact. Hence his conclusion: 'The epoch is the essence of everything that interferes with actions and their outcomes. Since actions and results cannot be matched up, history apparently "makes itself". In the patterns it makes we see more its results than its factors' (Blumenberg 1976: 31). History, like other technologies, is taken for granted while it works and becomes a liability when it malfunctions. When it does crash, humanity is left with its self-induced misery.

Neither art nor science: history as *techne*

Reconceptualizing history as a technology focusses on what history does, not on what it is. Saying what it is leads nowhere – as in the claim that 'the varied nature of the historian's equipment serves to reiterate ... that history is essentially a *hybrid* discipline, combining the technical and analytical procedures of science with the imaginative and stylistic qualities of an art' (Tosh 1999: 107). But the catachrestical assertion collapses. Nothing is more technical than art; science is a broad term embracing all kinds of knowledge. Relating history to other human sciences is similarly fruitless – as in the notion that, 'on the *boundary* where the concerns of anthropology, biology, the humanities, and psychology *meet* and *blend*, the historian is at last beginning to broaden his definitions of human motivation and of psycho-physical change' (Hughes 1975: 21 (my italics)). The crucial words here produce tautology. Defining history as a technology avoids this impasse. It involves: (a) reviewing history's claim to be a science; (b) exposing its inadequate conception of art; (c) re-defining history as the key instrument of an instrumentalized world; (d) confirming historical expertise as technical know-how. Whether history actually "is" an art or a science is ultimately secondary to whether or not it does what knowledge should do.

(a.) History's claim on science. Historians' talk about history as a discipline and themselves as "professional" historians certainly sounds scientific. This is the "normal view" of history – as in the "history subject benchmark statement" made up by a group of professional historians for the Quality Assurance Agency to define the education provided by the "subject community" in higher education institutions in England and Wales. Its 'guiding assumptions' reflect a familiar ambivalence – a mix of dogma and evasiveness, plus a strong dose of conventionality. Start with: 'We take it as self-evident that knowledge and understanding of the human past is of incalculable value both to the individual and society at large'. Add in: 'we do not recognise a specific body of required knowledge'; 'we accept variation in how the vast body of knowledge which constitutes the subject is tackled at undergraduate degree level.' Finish off with a tautological definition of the 'importance of historical knowledge': 'The historian's skills and qualities of mind are developed through the processes of acquiring, evaluating and discussing historical knowledge in the courses ... that History degree programmes demand. Although we

prescribe no particular diet of historical knowledge, programmes need to impart such knowledge and also to encourage students to acquire more' (QAA 2000: 1,2).

As a science, though, history does have one clear advantage: whatever it studies, has already happened. It is a *factum*: not "what if?" but "what was?" It also has one clear disadvantage: dealing with the "same old thing" restricts its scientific scope. It can draw inferences from primary data and verify them through replication or falsifiability. But other methods – immediate observation, experimentation, counter-induction, hypothesis, probability, predictability – are not directly useful.

Scientifically, the central issue is how to relate fact and explanation. No fact is in itself meaningful. Meaning comes from the explanatory context framing the data and from how it is constructed (cf. Cassirer 1994: 325–7; cf. Fleck 1983: 68). What makes knowledge reliable are 'functional forms' of conceptual relationship between rational and empirical knowledge (i.e. neither "incontrovertible" metaphysical principle nor body of fact). As a rule-based activity, scientific thinking relies 'on an ideal structure that is independent of any localized, temporal act of thinking, yet pertains to it uniquely and for all time'. This 'realm of objectively necessary relationships, the validity of which remains stable and constant', orientates the human mind. Knowledge originates in the interpenetration of any given act of thought and this ideal structure of objectively necessary relationships that sustains it (Cassirer 1994: 411, 418). Its logical intention depends on this 'basic resource of ideal relationships' being both 'true to itself' and unaffected by the arbitrary and the temporally variable circumstances cognition happens in (Cassirer 1994: 428).

Facts, however, can never be adequately explained. Scientifically speaking, 'there is not a single theory that agrees with all the known facts in its domain' and '*all methodologies ... have their limits*' (Feyerabend 1988: 21–3). In any case, the very idea of a comprehensive system is '*the great scientific lie*' (Neurath 1994: 376; cf. Weber 1988: 92; Fleck 1983: 128; Popper 1974: 77). This goes particularly for historical knowledge since its historical horizons constantly change and it changes with them (Gadamer 1975: 505–6). Knowledge develops, therefore, either by (theoretical) reconception or by (factual) "re-cognition".

Following Cassirer's definition, new knowledge comes only from theoretical reconception. It means finding ever deeper explanations: 'a satisfactory explanation ... can hardly be understood ... without the *idea* that there is something for us to discover' (Popper 1979: 202–3 (my italics)). Facts both check and motivate the theoretical effort to explain them (Cassirer 1994: 429; cf. Popper 2002: 79–82). Still this quest for a-temporal validity always takes priority. As Einstein remarked to Heisenberg about his work that actually transformed space and time, it is wrong to assume that theory has to be based on observable quantities, since in reality the converse obtains: theory first defines what the senses observe (Heisenberg 1971: 92ff.).[1] Certainly, like the scientist, the historian could find by empathetic study (i.e. not by logical inference) a new conception of a historical period (cf. von Mises 1990: 134). This, however, is less a reconception than a re-arrangement or recoding of the 'same old thing', because historical concepts are not theoretical concepts. A mix of received classifications, behavioural norms, explanatory commonplaces, or heuristic 'ideal-types', they never exactly denominate the usually one-off events they refer to. They are, therefore, always in some way 'false'. If similar sorts of events (e.g. wars, revolutions, heresy, dictatorship) seem to recur, that is due to 'the play of illusions [*jeu d'illusions*] the classificatory concepts produce' (Veyne 1996: 185).

Conversely, factual knowledge develops through "re-cognition". Re-cognition too presupposes a stable world-structure that gives human intentions meaning (cf. Schlick 1986: 161). Knowledge now centres on explaining its objects in terms of common properties, of 'finding similarities with things that appear to have nothing to do with each other'. The identitary procedure works with primary cognitive processes: new experiences are matched with earlier ones. If there were no similarity, reason would be confounded: making sense and constructing identities go together (Schlick 1986: 147, 149). But facts can never be explained by more facts. The additive process does not of itself generate insight: it can lead to historical causality being overdetermined and so make historical explanation inherently imprecise (cf. Weber 1988: 271).

Historical accounts are inherently provisional. But this does not stop history being a science. Far from it: being provisional gives it the science look. Theoretical reconceptions of knowledge are provisional, because they reveal further interesting problems. By contrast, history is provisional because it always needs to know more about how things once really were. Its problems arise from deficits in the knowledge already known; and only knowledge already known benefits from

---

[1] This refutes the absurd notion that 'facts precede theory and general rules rather than the other way around' (Davies 2003a: 4).

resolving them. The difference is rather: as theoretical reconception, science is the process; as affirmative recognition, history is the result. This makes it a dubious science. Scientifically speaking, Clio is, therefore, in a quandary: if one detail eludes her the whole edifice crumbles. But the available evidence is always unmanageable, either too much or too little, history is always unsure what it is scientifically basing itself on. Clio cannot even 'begin the beginning of her own beginning', and so she is 'no longer anything at all' (Péguy 1961: 243).

History's scientific practice never matches its aspirations. In any case, its irrationalism still causes apprehension. Deep down oneiric nostalgias keep stirring, most conspicuously in the student study-guide: 'The past is our heritage; although it is gone, we *feel* we are part of it' (Black & MacRaild 2000: 5 (my italics)). Historical interest goes, as usual, with musty sentimentality: 'Memories of the past are the lodestars of our thoughts, collective and individual. We cannot leave the past: our own present will be someone else's past, our past was once the present. The passage of time, and its important effects, mean that everything will one day be history: that everything has a history' (Black & MacRaild 2000: xii). Historians' science talk hardly seems to convince themselves, let alone anyone else. When disciplinary conviction flags, they reach for "artistic" affectivity. Veyne describes history as an art-form needing artistic talent because, like an artist who draws ancient monuments, it strives for objective fidelity. The point is: 'history is a work of art because, while being objective, it has no method of its own and is not scientific' (Veyne 1996: 303).

(b.) History's inadequate conception of art. So art is history's fall-back position. That shows its idea of art is inadequate. Whatever it may be, art is never a fall-back position. No wonder history causes apprehension. Here it perpetuates a false contrast between science as "recognized cognitive value" (i.e. involving "hard", technical analysis) and aesthetics as "arbitrary, subjective taste" (i.e. based on "soft", affective intuitions). In fact, primary scientific, empirical observations are immediately aesthetic, a 'chaos of feelings' (as Fleck says), dependent on the location of one's body (Fleck 1999: 124; Baumgarten 1983a: 4–5, §§509, 513; Schlick 1986: 19, 288). Art can also involve the acute visual reflexes of the champion baseball player, 'an abstracted and heightened visuality, one in which the eye and its object [make] contact with such amazing rapidity that neither one seemed any longer to be attached to its purely carnal support'

(Krauss 1988: 52).[2] Poetry, catching nuances of human behaviour, anticipates clinical insights – as in Shakespeare's medically accurate depictions of pathological states of mind (cf. Matthews & McQuain 2003). Art's *object*-ivity always needs to be emphasized: 'The intent of fiction is truth. Fiction would speak the world essentially, articulating, mapping point to point as between sign and that which is designated, even its ambiguities. It labours to render words and sentences translucent to being' (Steiner 1997a: 352). *Historics* should reassure historians. History could never ever be an aesthetics: historical and aesthetic interests are essentially divergent; historical description cannot match aesthetic precision.[3]

History and aesthetics diverge: the one depreciates, the other illuminates. History induces apprehension. Professional historians get their students to see themselves as mere adjuncts to the past, their life before them as already past, and life itself as a sequence of illusions. Conversely, art helps life: it 'comes to you proposing frankly to give nothing but the highest quality to your moments as they pass, and simply for those moments' sake' (Pater 1971: 224). So it opposes the powerful historical forces of capital, global corporations, reasons of state, that manufacture history by trashing existing life-patterns. Only art resolves the apprehension that comes with living in a totally

---

[2] Krauss disagrees with this view, but what she goes on to say contributes to the concept of knowledge as *aesthesis*: 'the life of nervous tissue is the life of time, the alternating pulse of stimulation and enervation, the complex feedback relays of retension and protension' (Krauss 1988: 62).

[3] This is why it is erroneous to make the postmodernist claim that 'historiography possesses the same opacity and intentional dimension as art'. Of course 'the literary text has a certain opacity, a capacity to draw attention to itself, instead of drawing attention to a ... reality behind the text'. So does historiography since 'the past presented in a historical work is defined exactly by the language used by the historian in his or her historical work' (Ankersmit 1989: 145). But then all texts draw attention to themselves: how else would they be read? The central issue is what they thus achieve. As an academic text, the historical text builds the illusion of a common language, stabilizes contexts and meanings, submerges the present in truisms, prevents its readers' nondisengagement from itself, binds them into already historicized traditions and continuities, neutralizes their critically reflective capacity, and enforces in them an attitude of nihilistic passivity (cf. Cohen 1988: 1, 15–16, 60–1, 73, 84–6, 93, 104, 134–5, 200, 295). By contrast, as an aesthetic text, the literary text works not for what it represents, but through its very presence, its language, that here speaks for itself. Hence, it exists 'beyond the reach of institutionalized interests and historical projects'; its 'symbolic visions ... compensate for the impoverishing hindsight of history' (cf. Davies 1987: 195, 197, 201). As, e.g. in the poetry of Rilke, Trakl, or Celan, texts of unparalleled opacity, it sustains human survival in the teeth of historical nihilism.

historicized, totally instrumentalized world: 'What is happening to the world lies, at the moment, just outside the realm of common human understanding. It is the writers, the poets, the artists, the singers, the film-makers who can make the connections, who can find ways of bringing it into the realm of common understanding.' Because art is not taken in by the technologically generated illusions of economic-historical rationality, artists 'can translate cash-flow charts and scintillating board-room speeches into real stories about real people with real lives. Stories about what it's like to lose your home, your land, your job, your dignity, your past, and your future to an invisible force' (Roy 2002: 190–1).

No wonder history is not precise enough to be an art-form. Aesthetics is an autonomous mode of cognition. That is to say: 'the cognitive ... does not exclude the sensory or the emotive', since 'what we know through art is felt in our bones and nerves and muscles as well as grasped by our minds' (Goodman 1988b: 259). The structure of any sculpture or the paint-texture of any painting, the sinuous syntax of any poem, will reveal plenty of "hard" technical-analytical competence. Historians' talk of 'imagination pursuing the fact and fastening upon it', 'poetry and imagination that are disciplined by fact', of 'imagination and literary flair', of a 'leap of imagination', is a mystification (Trevelyan 1941: 196; Evans 1997: 251; Fulbrook 2002: 188, 193). But actually in poetry 'the lexical, phonetic, syntactic and indeed, visual components of the literary text aim to embody the sensual and intelligible entirety of that to which they point' (Steiner 1997a: 352). For an artist what "disciplines" imagination is imagination. The work has to look right. It has to come about "objectively" as it is imagined. Imagination operates always in the primary perception, trying to make sense of it: 'on the level of the mental image, the real and the imaginary are one and the same' (Morin 1986: 110).

History, therefore, stays indeterminate and relative. It's too partial, too provisional, to be truly aestheticized. It's too arbitary to achieve the *object*-ivity integral to the work of art. Observing Renée Vautier at work on his bust, Paul Valéry, the aesthetic theorist, reflects on what it is actually to be an object of art. The work is created by a constant dialogue between the sculptor and her work. She is constantly calculating and recalculating the effects of the elements involved: the light, the material, the model, her energy, her intention, her intellect [*esprit*]. The intellectual process of art is a work, a drama in its own right. And the purpose of all this intellectual effort? It recognizes the specific *object*-ivity which pertains to sculpture. It is the need to satisfy the infinite number of perspectives and contexts in which it, as a three-dimensional object, can be viewed [*aesthesis*]. Resemblance [*illusio*] is not, therefore, an end in itself, but the outcome of these combined effects [*aesthesis*]. Hence the artist knows her work is going well when she can achieve more precision without changing either her standpoint or her points of reference (Valéry 1957 / 1960: II, 1360–1, 1363). So, being neither artistic nor scientific, history is left being technical.

(c.) **History, the key instrument of an instrumentalized world.** Technology is instrumentalized knowledge, 'a recipe for procuring certain advantages' (Sorel 1981: 173; cf. Davies 2002b: 53). It is always adaptable, heterogeneously useful – as history, the technology of technologies, demonstrates. But then *techne* itself is a hybrid, indeterminate concept: its meaning has shifted, even if its Classical implications remain. Once designating a fundamentally human, hence fundamentally aesthetic practice for producing truth, *techne* now stands for instrumental or causal thinking. *Techne* [art] originally facilitates *poiesis* [production]. It brings into being 'something that is capable either of being or of not being, and the cause of which is in the producer and not in the product'. That is why Aristotle calls art 'a productive state that is truly reasoned' (Aristotle 1983: 208 (Bk. 6: 1140a1–23)). With its decisive truth-disclosing function, *techne* could operate in both science [*episteme*] and creative production [*poiesis*] (Heidegger 1967a: 13). Now, however, technology constitutes a 'mega-machine' [*Ge-stell*] of self-perpetuating human activity that treats the earth as a vast information-system, a quantifiable and manageable resource [*Bestand*]. *Techne*'s facilitating function has become an end in itself, as instrumentalized science that instrumentalizes the world (Heidegger 1967a: 22–3). Instead of symbiosis with nature, it sets itself up as an apparatus [*Ge-stell*] to exploit the earth's resources.

In the end, the rapaciousness of this 'mega-apparatus' endangers what it was meant to foster: human existence rooted in the truth of Being. Here is the ontological basis of the postmodern 'risk society'. Only because 'the essence of technology is nothing technical', does reflection reveal how instrumentalized human existence has become, how alienated it is from its essential interests (Heidegger 1967a: 5, 27, 32–3, 35). The mega-apparatus requires merely 'resources adminis-trators' [*Besteller des Bestandes*], functionaries to keep the technology functioning. The incongruity between human fate [*Geschick*], as the vocation for the truth of Being and the technological 'mega-machine'

[*Ge-stell*], as its facilitating apparatus, transforms history [*Geschichte*] as the objective production of human truth into a self-estranging fatality. Humanity is taken in, because, to cover itself, technology offers it not the truth of Being, but its simulacrum, 'one last treacherous illusion': absolute identity (i.e. A = A; e.g.: 'how things got to be' = 'the way they are'). The result is: 'it seems that mankind encounters everywhere only itself' (Heidegger 1967a: 24–7; cf. Arendt 1993: 89).

History is, therefore, the universal instrument. That comes out in its indeterminacy (i.e. being 'everything', it can be anything). Depending on its context and history, it can claim to be both scientific and artistic only because *techne* assists both science [*episteme*] and artistic production [*poiesis*] in revealing truth (Heidegger 1967a: 12–13). As a form of *techne*, it need not discriminate between them: its technical essence embraces both. Similarly historians tend to see themselves as both 'practitioners' exercising a 'craft', (cf. *technites* ['artificer', 'craftsman']) and specialist experts (i.e. technicians in the modern sense). No wonder, then, history is an indispensable information-management technology. Programmed not just to make sense, but to make more sense, treating a heterogeneous subject-matter, it proves to be highly adaptable. It must be whatever it needs to be. The scope of historical analysis depends on the concrete purpose of the investigation [*Erkenntniszweck*]. The relevant factors it identifies will be only 'relatively comprehensive' because the rules it follows have only 'a relative degree of precision'. Historical analysis catches at best only 'enclaves' of meaning in the constant flux of everyday experience (Weber 1988: 113–14).

History's scope, therefore, varies. Its technical nature makes it seem most comprehensive, most persuasive. Comparing the work of Acton and Ranke, Butterfield defines 'technical history' as 'a disciplined use of tangible evidence', as 'a science which asserts only what the evidence compels one to assert . . . as the laying-out of a story on which all men and all parties can form what judgements they like when they have read it'. Its rationale is that 'greater degrees of certainty, more practicable forms of communicability and a wider range of unanimity can be achieved when the enquirer performs this act of self-limitation' (Butterfield 1969: 94, 139, 141). However, narrowly specialized as it is, 'technical history' by definition lacks existential veracity, hence, aesthetic credibility. Technical history, says Butterfield, 'is a limited and mundane realm of description and explanation': 'having determined to restrict himself to certain kinds of tangible data, the technical historian can only expect to produce limited results'.

'What must often escape the technical historian's net', is people's 'hopes and fears', 'the spiritual life of man'. The abstracted, virtual world [*illusio*] generated by the technics of history must ultimately be brought to its senses [*aesthesis*]: 'In reality, the poet, the prophet, the novelist and the playwright command sublimer realms than those of technical history because they reconstitute life in its wholeness' (Butterfield 1969: 137, 139, 141).

Conversely, (as, e.g. Dilthey, Ortega y Gasset, Aron, Blumenberg, and Foucault argue), history is a resource [*Bestand*] comprehending all the truths and realities humanity has made for itself. This is what makes it possible to talk about a 'historical ontology' in terms of 'the possibilities for choice, and for being [that] arise in history' (Hacking 2002: 23). That's how history becomes human nature, claims comprehensively, but also organically, irrationally, to be 'everything'. That's what makes it a self-perpetuating 'mega-machine' turning everything into historical values and identities, enclosing humanity in a hall of mirrors reflecting *ad infinitum* its own reflection.

(d.) Professional historical expertise as technical know-how. If civilization and technics evolve together, the evolutionary process itself produces a new social type – the technician. 'Who is it that exercises social power today? Who imposes the forms of his own mind on the period?', asks Ortega y Gasset. 'Without a doubt, the technician: engineer, doctor, financier, teacher and so on,' is the answer. The technician is represented 'at its best and purest' by 'the man of science': 'the actual scientific man is the prototype of the mass-man ... because science itself – the root of our civilisation – automatically converts him into mass-man, makes of him a primitive, a modern barbarian' (Ortega y Gasset 1964: 108–9). By analogy, historicization both transforms the world into a massive information-resource [*Bestand*] and produces the 'professional historian' as the exemplary academic type. History, the technology of technologies, makes historians exemplary technicians, as, e.g. with Ranke, the founder of modern scientific history, 'a lifelong technician in its [i.e. history's] laboratory' (Gay 1988: 72). Versed in the practicalities of knowledge, they are *de facto* intellectual and cultural 'resource managers' [*Besteller des Bestandes*], 'engineers or architects, recon-structors of a past, gardeners of history' (Heidegger 1967a: 22–3, 26; cf. Sartre 1972: 25ff.; Cohen 1988: 67). Being academic means being studious, but studiousness includes the intellectual, managerial, and technocratic expertise historians use to manage the information at

their disposal – e.g. by assessing its significance, promoting its value, administering access to it, helping to disseminate it.

Forget then the alleged humanizing benefits of historical study: technical historians have no need to be "cultured", as Cicero or Goethe were. In a historicized world, historical expertise is the dominant culture. Historians need be only a function of the specialized historical component they identify with. What counts is their own technical efficiency, since historical knowledge compares directly with technological knowledge (as required, e.g. for making bridges, televisions, and bombs) that, as 'essential knowledge', has to be 'as sound as we can make it'. It comes about 'through large numbers of historians *doing* history in strict accordance with the long established, though constantly developing, canons of the historical profession'. Its reliability is guaranteed by 'the careful observance of the methods and principles of professional history' (Marwick 2001: 2–3). But professionalism has its own persuasive force, exerts its own identitary pressures. It produces knowledge through normative, conventional methodologies: 'I am *professionally* correct, not out of a sense of moral obligation or choice of values ... but out of a sense that the structure of a fully articulated profession ... is such that those who enter its precincts will find that the basic decisions, about where to look, what to do, and how to do it, have already been made'. But then professionalization is 'a form of organization in which membership is acquired by a course of special training whose end is the production of persons who recognize one another ... because they perform the same moves in the same game'. That's what sustains historical thinking. Each specialized disciplinary effort 'only makes sense in relation to the traditions, goals, obligatory routines, and normative procedures that comprise its history and are the content of its distinctiveness' (Fish 1999: 32, 44, 82).

Still, professional knowledge does not do what knowledge should do. It creates a knowledge deficit between the knowledge academics saddle society with and the knowledge society needs. Knowledge should alleviate apprehension. It should encourage society *not* to be the way it is. By contrast, an 'increasing technical formalism' loses sight of the 'raw effort of constructing ... knowledge' views knowledge 'in terms of impersonal theories and methodologies', and becomes 'tame and accepting of whatever so-called leaders in the field will allow'. It presents itself as expertise, i.e. as 'certified by the proper authorities', which means 'speaking the right language, citing the right authorities, holding down the right territory' but which 'in the end has rather little, strictly speaking, to do with knowledge'. It necessitates identifying with the way things are: it inevitably drifts 'towards the requirements and prerogatives of power, and towards being directly employed by it' (Said 1994: 55, 57–60). Professional, academic knowledge thus perpetuates itself – and, produced by the 'dominated elements amongst those who dominate', it perpetuates itself as a form of domination (Bourdieu 1984: 70; cf. Davies 2002b: 69).

Professional knowledge thrives because there is a social knowledge deficit. It is designed to be ineffective: 'the style of social organization in which disciplinary work is done,' ensures that. 'The organization of late twentieth century universities has encouraged a narrowness of preoccupations that has ended by rewarding participants who remain closest to the middle of their chosen road,' Toulmin argues. And he concludes: 'by the end of the twentieth century professional activities have developed a highly disciplinary character, which has distorted their fulfilment' (Toulmin 2001: 151, 154). Essentially Toulmin repudiates the 'Myth of Stability' that since the time of Leibniz and Descartes has guaranteed knowledge. As a totalizing form of rationalism, accounting for everything, it institutes knowledge as reliable, certain, and objective. It brought forth the key modern type of knowledge producer, what Toulmin calls 'information engineers', professionals with technical skills (Toulmin 1992: 104). But this technical form of knowledge is questionable and not inevitable. Certainly, it cannot handle the social and economic problems jeopardizing human survival that it itself causes (Toulmin 2001: 102ff.). Toulmin would reconnect with an earlier pragmatic 'reasonableness', associated with Erasmus, Montaigne, or Pascal, or with its modern counterparts, in Kierkegaard, Emerson or Nietzsche (Toulmin 2001:156, 170, 186, 196–7, 214). His view of methodology is radically sceptical: 'Need the pursuit of human enterprises involve us in recognizing, or conforming to, any systematic set of rules *at all*?' 'The idea of a pursuit that requires one to conform to a specific set of procedures is a ... narrowing of the concept', and, in any case, 'imaginative conception of new lines of investigation can take us beyond the realm of rules' (Toulmin 2001: 84–5).

Clearly, history exacerbates the social knowledge deficit. As the technology of technologies, it complicates a complex present in which people live the only life they have to live – their own: 'An attitude of nostalgia implies few expectations, aside from the hope of preserving the *status quo*: the task of defining realistic "futuribles" [i.e. possible types of future still available] is open only to those who ... recognize that the future will reward those who anticipate the institutions and procedures we shall need' (Toulmin 1992: 203).

Historical discourse: the technics of self-authentication

No technology is 'value-neutral': 'embedded in every tool is an ideological bias, a predisposition to construct the world as one thing rather than another, to value one thing over another' (Postman 1993:13). History, being 'everything', will value its own interests first. With its origins and developments, causes and processes, traditions and precedents, legacies and beneficiaries, periods and contexts, history keeps on keeping itself going. But, in perpetuating itself, it perpetuates the 'same old things' themselves. Fixated on what used to exist, it endorses what actually still exists; its cognitive conventions affirm social conventions. Hence – *formally, functionally, structurally* – history *is* the ideology (cf. Davies 2002a: 32–4).

What legitimates a technology is utility. After all, technology develops by offering the latest thing as a 'better' way of doing the same old thing. That goes for history too. But in one respect history is different. Its social utility is automatically self-validating. Because history covers both the past and the study of the past, it is its own object: it always arbitrates in its own interest. But this is not all. All other sciences study specific phenomena, but the object underlying them can be studied in other ways. Social behaviour is approached differently by sociology, psychology, economics, geography and criminology. Physics, biology, geology, zoology, genetics, chemistry each have a particular perspective on the natural world. History, containing 'everything' that ever happened, absorbs all other perspectives: hence its claim to be the knowledge of knowledge, the technology of technologies. Lack of discrimination is its cardinal virtue: to find out about anything, you have to use it. Further, whenever other human and natural sciences reflect on their own development, they too take a historical approach. That makes history a uniquely 'clever' technology: it programmes other disciplines, as they validate themselves, to validate it as well.

History thus emerges 'as the transcendence of its own cultural contradictions, an ingenious and typically historical solution' (Cohen 1988: 65). It works to authenticate itself: that's its purpose, its ideological core. That makes history's "objective truth" simply a product of its self-authenticating techniques, of its disciplinary rules and procedures. The technology is designed to induce belief in itself: history produces what is objective and true because that is what history does (cf. Jordanova 2000: 197). To reveal what makes history useful means dismantling the elements that make it persuasive: its self-affirming tautologies, its comprehensive intention, its knowledge practices.

This focusses on what history does rather than on what historians say it is. And what history does is authenticate itself – (I) in the way the history is instituted; and (II) in the way historical knowledge is constituted. This makes history a supremely powerful, but essentially indeterminate social agent, fully justifying the apprehensiveness it generates.

First, history works as a social institution – (a) by maintaining historical representations already existing in the social imagination as a means of maintaining itself; (b) by producing social meaning through the 'functional connections' it establishes between society's heterogeneous interests and values, past and present; (c) by embedding itself, like any technology, "naturally" in the structure of social reality (cf. Postman 1993: 131); (d) by offering a postmodern society intent on total, technological self-management a technology for managing its total self-knowledge.

(a.) **History maintains historical representations already existing in society as a means of maintaining itself.** 'Representations are social facts' (Rabinow 1996: 34ff., 47ff.). The representations a social group shares are group facts. Their collective status constitutes their independent objectivity, as the obligations the shared representations impose on any individual group member confirm. The central question is how representations are disseminated. History also is nothing but representation [*illusio*]; but because these representations are also widely shared social representations, *illusio* becomes fact.

The past (that history studies) does not exist as an acquaintance: it is not another country or a 'mysterious world' of its own (cf. Gardiner 1968: 38). What actually – materially – exists, are various kinds of remnants (documents, artefacts, buildings, etc.) to which the epithet 'historical' can be applied (e.g. the Bayeux Tapestry). In a thoroughly historicized world these remnants support and are supported by the accounts historians repeatedly give of them (e.g. the Norman Conquest). If history thus claims to be the "default" knowledge of society, it's because of this social basis. Families' memory runs back in most cases probably three generations, if not more. Commemorative ceremonies give communities, peoples, and nations a sense of identity: they are instituted to enable them to realize who they are (cf. Connerton 1992: 41ff.). Memory itself 'however personal it may be ... exists in relationship with a whole ensemble of notions which many others possess: with persons, places, dates, words, forms of language, that is to say with the whole material and moral life of the societies of which we are part or of which we have been part' (Connerton 1992: 36; cf. Halbwachs 1994: 59). Though social memory and historical knowledge are never congruent, the concepts of 'identity' or 'heritage' create common ground. They assimilate personal and local memories to more comprehensive, historically verified, regional, national, and cultural structures of meaning (as Samuel's *Theatres of Memory* shows). The media similarly integrate macro-history, produced by professional historians, into the private sphere (e.g. Simon Schama's TV series, *History of Britain*); or endow authentically re-created versions of ordinary life in the past with macro-historical significance (e.g. the TV series, the *1940's House*). The advisory panel for the popular *BBC History Magazine* involves a score of professional academic historians.

Objectivity and truth, as cognitive standards for the discipline, are vindicated socially by the criterion of relevance that links social memory and historical knowledge. Relevance 'provides the motivation both for storing and transmitting ... information'. If the information concerned is relatively independent of an immediate context, then 'that relevance will be maintained in spite of changes in local circumstances – that is, it will be maintained on a social scale' (Sperber 1966:140). Relevance as a motive for storing and transmitting information governs the dissemination of historical representations. That's because, being comprehensive, linking how things were with how they are, historical knowledge is relevant to any context. As a technical academic resource, it's independent of any immediate context, hence always potentially socially relevant, always compatible with knowledge already known. As a result, historical representations are so socially accessible that it would be a typically scholastic delusion if historians did feel they monopolized them. Still, the ubiquitous social interest thus legitimates both their rôle as technicians [*Besteller des Bestandes*] and their task of maintaining the history 'mega-machine'.

The social transmission of historical knowledge and the technics of academic practice sustain each other. Take the recent UK government sponsored reports *Power of Place* and *The Historic Environment: A Force for Our Future* they reveal a nation mesmerized by historical *illusio*. According to the MORI poll conducted by English Heritage for their *Power of Place* (2000) report, 98% of the population think that the historical heritage is important for what it teaches about the past, 87% think there should be public funding to support it (English Heritage 2000: 1, 25). The same report also states that the Historic Houses Association, representing the owners of 1,200 houses, 270 of which are regularly open to the public, attracts ten million visitors a year (English Heritage 2000: 13). Furthermore, the National Trust has three million members, which means that 'there are more members of the National Trust than of all the national political parties put together' – that historical interests are more immediately "political" than politics itself (Brooks: 2003: 33; English Heritage 2000: 30, 33). So socially significant is the historic environment, that it forms the 'backbone' of the UK tourist industry. In 2000 this totalled some £75 billion in expenditure and in terms of value added 'represented 5% of GDP – larger than the car, steel and coal industries put together' (DCMS 2001: 46).

Statistics such as these reflect an educated society with mass cultural interests. Far more significant is what they reveal about social cognitive practice. It should be stressed: 'beliefs, which are stable across a population, are those which play a central role in the modular organization and processing of knowledge'. In other words, 'information that either enriches or contradicts basic modular beliefs stands a greater chance of cultural success' (Sperber 1996: 140). Being so heterogeneous, history represents one such extremely broad and stable 'belief module'. Even if it were not already comprehensive, if did not already operate with identitary logic, its social presence alone would compel it to – not least because these statistics must include all those who are professionally engaged in history and whose task it is to ensure that historical representations are socially disseminated. Also, since history is stored and transmitted on a social level, historical knowledge can be objective and true only if it is also comprehensive and identificatory – as these implications of the statistical evidence suggest: 'England's historic environment ... embodies the history of all the communities who have made their home in this country. It is part of the wider public realm in which we can all participate'; 'the past is all around us. ... the historical environment ... is central to how we see ourselves and to our *identity* as individuals, communities and as a nation. It is a physical record of *what our country is, how it came to be* ... ' 'it is a collective memory, containing an infinity of stories ... ' (DCMS 2001: 4, 7 (my italics to stress the affirmative, identitary thinking)).

The wide social dissemination of historical representations also explains why historical knowledge inevitably perpetuates, hence authenticates, itself – i.e. why it is persuasive. According to the *Power of Place* and *The Historic Environment*, the chief inducements for socially perpetuating historical representations are economic (e.g. promoting tourism) and educational. Take the educational reasons, given that, apparently, the National Trust 'welcomes 600,000 children to its properties every year' (DCMS 2001: 19). History's educational value motivates UK government policy to widen access to the historic environment. Here too history's identitary thinking, its comprehensivity, its heterogeneity, are conducive to social self-authentication. As these reports point out: historical interests allegedly 'can bring communities together in a shared sense of belonging' (DCMS 2001: 4); 'the fabric of the past constitutes a vast reservoir of knowledge and learning opportunities. This is as true of the oldest archeological remains as it is of buildings of the last fifty years'; 'the educational significance of the historic environment ... is also relevant to subject areas as diverse as economics, geography, aesthetics, science, technology and design' (DCMS 2001: 4, 17). In recognizing the educational value of history, society would thus set up a recurrent process of self-authentication, operating in a typically identitary way: a public, educated to appreciate the historical environment, 'a uniquely rich and precious inheritance', helps ensure its future survival (DCMS 2001: 4); and its future survival will ensure the existence of an educated public to appreciate it.

Lastly, the social management of historical knowledge (particularly of the historical environment) ensures history authenticates itself as socially affirmative knowledge and its objectivity and truth inevitably identify with what already is. That's because it most conspicuously enforces "normal" academic history. The historic environment is a source, a document, or an archive like any others historians work with. As the reports insist, the historic environment 'is the most accessible of historical texts' (English Heritage 2000: 4). Its heterogeneity, hence its accessibility, makes it a national, cultural and economic resource. In engaging with it, society itself is 'doing history': the social process both replicates and validates academic practice. And the Chairman of the Historic Environment Review Steering Group confirms this when he insists that professional historical knowledge is indispensable for maintaining public historical resources: 'Everything rests on sound knowledge and understanding. Good history is history that is based on thorough research and is tested and refined through open debate. It accommodates multiple narratives and takes account of the values people place on their surroundings' (English Heritage 2000: 1). But statements of this sort are deceptive. They enlist history for the benefit of cultural policy; but actually they are an effect of history's own, inherent capacity for self-perpetuation. What makes an institution self-perpetuating, is that it is 'the distribution of a set of representations which is governed by representations belonging to the set itself' (Sperber 1996: 76). If history institutes itself as the definitive, comprehensive, social identity, the comprehensive social identity it establishes will determine how historical representations are distributed. History is bound to be 'good' if it is thorough (i.e. comprehensive): but only because it will be affirming the social values it has already set up. With its identitary logic, this social reflex ensures that historical comprehension affirms itself. History is thus always the affirmative ideology.

(b.) History provides 'functional connectivity' for society's heterogeneous interests and values. 'Functional connectivity' underpins historical comprehension with simple, formal devices to make its heterogeneous arrangements look objective (cf. Simmel 1999: 165). They produce persuasiveness irrespective of content. They come from methodology as a social practice, both from the rules historians work by and from the way historians work. These devices ensure connectivity in physical (temporality), social (order) and psychological (reassurance) terms.

(b.i) Temporal connectivity. History is a prosthetic extension to social time-consciousness. Temporality is essential to cognition. Nothing can be known without presupposing that it is already located in time (and in space). The concept of time (like that of space) is an *a priori* synthetic judgement, 'a necessary conception [*Vorstellung*]', the 'basis of all perception [*Anschauung*]', a 'pure form of sense-perception' (Kant 1971: 74ff., A 31ff.; B 46ff.). History claims priority because time is an *a priori* reality. But the fact that everything happens in time does not make history an *a priori* reality. Historical time is an *a priori* dimension of historical phenomena. It is not an *a priori* dimension of human experience, because immediate experience (as *aesthesis*) precedes any intellectual construction placed on it.[4] In any case, even as it seems to light up ordinary experience, history diminishes it, assimilating it to the "same old thing" or sequestrating it by *force majeure* into its larger, transcendent designs.

---

[4] According to phenomenology, subjective existence is necessarily historical because it is temporal: human "being" is inevitably "being in time". This argument makes historical thinking central to the theory of knowledge (cf. Gadamer 1975: 499–500). *Historics* differentiates between temporality and historicity. It argues that "history" places with hindsight a construction on temporality for various purposes, from structuring time-consciousness to managing social reality.

Temporality also structures social reality. As Mumford points out, 'the clock has been the foremost machine in modern technics'. It is not just the technology controlling the world 'mega-machine', but also 'it marks a perfection to which other machines aspire' and serves 'as a model for many other kinds of mechanical works'. The clock ensures 'the even flow of energy throughout the works ... to make possible regular production and standardized product'. It effects a distinctive social transformation: it was the means of 'synchronizing the actions of men', but only because it was inorganic, only because it 'dissociated time from human events and helped create belief in an independent world of mathematically measurable sequences' (Mumford 1963: 15, 16–17). Historical objectivity derives from this experience of time as an independent, quantifiable, and impersonal means of social regulation. With abstract time 'the new medium of existence', a 'generalized time-consciousness accompanied the wider use of clocks'. As a result, 'it became easier ... to indulge the fantasy of reviving the ... past ... : the cult of history ... finally abstracted itself as a special discipline' (Mumford 1963: 17). Hence, 'to place a thing and to time it became essential to one's understanding of it' (Mumford 1963: 20–1).

The *a priori* cognitive and social concepts of time go together. Both come from a technological conception of nature and society. History extends it to the management of human affairs in general. History is a time-management device, because, as a technological product, historical time is empty: 'Just because of its promise of unlimited possibilities technology is an empty form like the most formalistic logic and is unable to determine the content of life. That is why our time, being the most intensely technical, is also the emptiest in all human history' (Ortega y Gasset 1962: 151). Stripped of its transcendental-religious, personal-organic, or existential qualities, historical time is abstract and quantitative. It can hold everything and anything, hence be inevitably heterogeneous. Historical comprehension will, therefore, result from an 'additive' process (more is always more): history amasses piles of facts to fill out its homogenous but vacant temporal expanse (Benjamin 1977: 260, §XVII); being a descriptive rather than an exact science, history in any case needs factual substance of all kinds to cover its lack of logical coherence (Schlick 1986: 99). Otherwise historical time, as a dominant management technology, defaults to whatever management technology dominates: the instrumental, consumerist values that drive the global mega-machine; the ideology of the free market that sees historical time as 'savings-bank time' and history itself as a universal human investment scheme – a mega-mirror reflecting the mega-machine of late capitalism (cf. Péguy 1961: 128–9; cf. Mumford 1963: 26, 42).

Technology is definitely not 'value-neutral'. The 'technology of technologies', history instrumentalizes time. (With the "time-line", a deceptively simple technology, it pretends that time is a neutral, self-evident basis everybody works with, while – in fact – linearity as such insists on its prevailing economic, technological and ideological values (cf. Neustadt & May 1988: 106, 133, 274; Derrida 1967: 128–9).) Time becomes a historical agent in its own right. The 'prosthetic god', modern *homo sapiens*, makes time work faster – for various reasons: e.g. economic competition; social-policy planning; globalized communications, all compressing time and space (Nowotny 1995: 48–55; Harvey 1990: 284ff.). The 'mega-machine' that is the technologized world has its own momentum (cf. Mumford 1963: 59).

History mirrors this. Braudel claims that 'historical time is measure, like that of the economists' (Braudel 1984: 118). Further, history activates itself as various forms of historicism, such as the liberal-humanist, the Neo-Hegelian *Annales*, or the organicist. It invests time itself with the power to disclose the truth of human agency. Braudel bases history on 'the imperious time of the world', a time that works 'mathematically but also with the power of a demiurge', a time 'external to humans that drives them on, restrains them, and carries their own private, motley time away with it' (Braudel 1984: 117). History constructs meaning in the way it frames itself, e.g. *The Population History of England, 1541–1871*; *English Society, 1688–1832*; *The Long Nineteenth Century: A History of Germany, 1780–1918*. Evidently history expands or contracts time, enhances or diminishes it at will. How it defines its periods and traditions, and where it sets its "milestone-dates", seems arbitrary. Which kind of time-scale is "objectively" appropriate, it cannot say. According to the identitary logic behind it, that depends on the history the historian writes.

In regulating the social experience of time, history is the dominant practice of social domination (cf. Neustadt & May 1988). Time-management, deriving from the monastery and early finance capitalism, is a disciplinary technique. But, taking eighteenth-century concepts of progress and of the genesis of individuality as examples, Foucault radicalizes Mumford's thesis. He argues that making time useful by segmentation, seriation, synthesis and totalization, correlates with the technics of power. This macro- and microphysics of power ensures that a unitary, continuous, and cumulative temporal dimension is integral to the exercise of control and the practices of domination in society. Constituted in this way, historicity is an instrument of the prevailing social power structures, a 'machine of subjugation' (Foucault 1975: 162; Cohen 1988: 185). Objectivity is social coercion in an idealized form; history the affirmative ideology.

(b.ii) Connectivity as classification. History is a system for keeping things in order. It imposes its order as the order of things: the way things were, the way things are, the way things got to be the way they are. History is "objective" because its veracity reinforces social reality. History will always thus be 'didactic and magisterial': it 'teaches its audience where it stands by reorganizing symbolic reference points in the space around it' (Certeau 1975: 103). History imposes order, because it 'is one of those concepts that claim to have a monopoly on explanation'. Being absolute, the concept of history makes everything else relative to it. Moreover, an absolute concept requires absolute obedience. Once historical concepts are used, they become inescapable: they make one's identity dependent on them. As an absolute concept, history thus preserves its own absolute nature (cf. Schmidt-Biggemann 1991: 9ff.).

History 'is always discovering the present in its object [i.e. the past] and the past in its [present] practices' (Certeau 1975: 48). Historical identifications "naturally" impose themselves. They have one clear cognitive advantage: they deal with what has already happened, with what is somehow, somewhere already known. Converging absolutely with its objects, history intends to be comprehensive, to become the "real reality" of things. In this intention it authenticates itself by creating the 'value-ideas' that underpin the "objective" patterns of intelligibility it finds in the 'vast, chaotic stream of events that surges on through time' (Weber 1988: 213–14). What makes behaviour and events already historical are these 'value-ideas', the heterogeneous concepts (e.g. 'Antiquity', *'ancien régime'*, 'festivals', 'heritage'), time-structures (e.g. 'traditions', 'precedents', 'legacies'), and agencies (e.g. 'state', 'nation', 'people'), it reads into its material (cf. Certeau 1975: 115; Veyne 1996: 174ff.). These concepts are simply forms of classification: they are nominalistic. But they impose themselves as real historical factors, as essential principles of order in the historical analysis. A "state" may designate the common identity of many historical and political forms (e.g. from empire, to dictatorship, to democracy): the "state" as civic organization endures even if its type of organization changes historically. What permits the durability of the concept as always the same old thing, is this essentialist aspect.

As Popper remarks: 'Though hardly any describable features have remained the same, the *essential* identity of the institution is preserved, permitting us to regard one institution as a changed form of the other.' According to the metaphysical stance of essentialism, all knowledge 'presupposes something that does not change but remains identical with itself'. But the case of history is uniquely ambivalent: 'History, i.e. the description of change, and essence, i.e. that which remains unchanged during change, appear here as correlative concepts.' The fact that the very idea of essence 'presupposes change, and thereby history', but, conversely, that essence itself 'can be known only through its changes', establishes history's claim to absolute priority (Popper 1974: 31–3).

Essentialism permits history to claim that the allegedly universal, even anachronistic classifications historians invent to explain history really exist in history. It makes history objective and persuasive. If everything is essentially historical, history is the essence of everything. No form of knowledge could come with a better guarantee. And yet this kind of identitary thinking is illusory. Take as a paradigm the period-concept "The Thirties" (as illustrated by the catalogue of an exhibition of pre-war British art and design at the Hayward Gallery in London (1979/1980)). The art, architecture, painting, and design illustrating the period are, by definition, typical. The catalogue also comprises a chronology of incidents that occurred during the decade and a historical reflection on it (by A.J.P. Taylor). This particularly demonstrates historical discourse as structured to colligate the most heterogeneous issues. It presents *inter alia* the rise of fascism, the rise of a mass-market, the disappearance of the cottage piano, the rise in car-ownership, the decline of the birth-rate, and international crises, as being essentially interconnected. In fact the only connection is 'The Thirties' – 'a decade worthy of remembrance' – as though this period-concept had an essential property that made it all happen (Taylor 1979: 8). The knowledge-effect is, therefore, minimal: with the asynchronous aspects arbitrarily excluded, what actually happened in the 1930s and the "'The Thirties'-concept" simply mirror each other. They represent the tautology of the typical: a scholastic abstraction masquerading as past reality.

(b.iii) Connectivity as reassurance. In managing society's time, in keeping things in order, history has a socially stabilizing effect (cf. Cohen 1988: 16–17, 73–5). Its ability to make connections between anything and everything makes it the absolute arbiter of sense and meaning. It charts the parameters of the possible;

it records how the social reality principle fluctuates. This ability naturally to discern meaning – albeit *post festum* – even in the moments of greatest turmoil, is reassuring. It means that, eventually, to future historians even the present, confusing though it may seem, will make sense. Therefore, it must have sense now, which, even if it is not yet clear, is some sort of consolation. History is thus always a 'guide to life' [*magistra vitae*], a dependable source of topics – commonplace arguments – that could be used now to negotiate a treacherous present (Cicero 2001: 224–5, II.ix.36; cf. Schmidt-Biggemann 1991: 16). Furthermore, history's ability to create a sense of stability through its conceptual connections vindicates its claim to objectivity. Still, it needs to be stressed that the stability and objectivity history achieves are technological "media" effects: not past reality.

Regularity, standardization, and objectivity were the earliest advantages of the technological management of time. They structured the generalized time-consciousness technology had created. Both technological progress and the remorseless development of capitalism generated historical consciousness. These modernizing forces make history by constantly making their own achievements, let alone the world in which they operate, obsolete. Conversely, resistance to these forces also produces history. The commotion of the present makes the need for fixed points of social orientation imperative. Recourse to "the" past, to history, to things as they used to be, provides them. But the constant deference to history has an anaesthetizing effect that directly benefits the technological and financial élites that alone stand to profit from their ruination of the world. After all:

> ... the celebration of recurrence is a compensatory device. Capitalism, in Marx's famous phrase, tears down all social mobility, every ancestral confinement and feudal restriction; and invented rites, however implicated they often are in that very process of modernisation which capitalism drives remorselessly on, are palliative measures, façades erected to screen off the full implications of this vast worldwide clearing operation.
>
> (Connerton 1992: 63–64)

If history shows social, economic or political change to be essentially the same old thing, then change itself – the effects of drastic political shifts, ideological agendas – need not cause apprehension.

History offers the ideal "cover" for the powers that be. No wonder history is the ideology.

History operates with objectivity and truth as technical norms to provide 'functional connectivity'. Far from offering a perspective on society, history projects prevailing social conditions. The knowledge it claims for itself as a discipline identifies social practices that ensure its existence. The functional connections history makes, function best for history itself. They sustain the conceit that the order it keeps, is the only valid order possible.

(c.) ***History is a technology naturally embedded in social reality.*** It reassures, but its comforts are false. They are attractive because they apparently offset the strain maintaining modern 'abstract societies' involves. They apparently compensate for the loss of the unchanging world of a primitive 'closed society' (Popper 1974: 160; cf. Popper 2003: I,186–8). Popper is actually criticizing historicism, not history – the idea of "natural laws" of history, not history as human second-nature. But the distinction is not sustainable: all history [*crg*] tends towards historicism. Retrospective inevitability is implicit in anything that shows 'how our world got to be the way it is' (Cannadine 1999: 8). All historical judgements rely on such self-authenticating, paralogical patterns – as this example, a classic instance of *illusio*, shows:

> The old past is dying ... and so it should ... for it was compounded of bigotry, of national vanity, of class domination. ... May history step into its shoes, help to sustain man's confidence in his destiny, and create for us a new past as true, as exact, as we can make it, that will help us achieve our identity, not as ... black or white, rich or poor, but as men.
>
> (Plumb 1973: 115)

Here the historicist abuse of the past is rejected by academic history [*crg*], but only for a different, more "natural" determinism, liberal humanism, to justify its own identitary practice that glosses over precisely those social-pathological conflicts that drive history [*rg*] itself (cf. Cohen 1988: 110–11).

Historicism is most familiar in its "strong", neo-Hegelian forms (e.g. Spengler's *Decline of the West* (1918); Seidenberg's *Posthistoric Man* (1950); Huntington's *The Clash of Civilizations and the Remaking of World Order* (1996)). But, both in "normal" historical judgements and in the nicely theorized "new historicism", the apparently "weak" form is more prevalent. Operating routinely, unobtrusively, as an always affirmative management technology, it is inevitably more persuasive. History authorizes itself to make sense by guaranteeing that all things ultimately interconnect. That is to say, the human environment is so comprehensively, so naturally historicized, that the idea that it could be different – i.e. anything but historical – recedes from consciousness (cf. Postman 1993: 18, 131). So the ubiquitous dissemination of historical representations, the ordinary usage of "history" and "historical" reveal 'weak' historicism to be a "natural" social experience. The history technology insinuates between experience and its objects its *illusio*-tinted filter to produce 'a second-hand world, a ghost world, in which everyone lives a second-hand and derivative life' (cf. Mumford 2000: 97–8). It suggests a present-day public hooked on an 'artificial hallucination of the past' [*illusio*] (Nora 1984: XXXII). It cannot think of how things have got to be the way they are except through "retrospective inevitability". The 'tide of "vulgar-psychological" everyday experience' does after all come shrink-wrapped in causal and conceptual patterns, bundled with assorted traditions and heritages (cf. Weber 1988: 114).

"Weak" historicism as a technology "naturally" embedded in social reality is typically affirmed by the constructivist social theory of knowledge. This theory rejects natural scientific method as a final standard of truth. Instead, it stresses that all forms of knowledge are produced by their social environment which is reflected in their discourses and values, and in the way disciplines now flourish, now decline. It alleges, therefore, a new 'final standard', the "historical process" itself.[5]

Take, e.g., Hacking's concept of 'historical ontology'. 'Historical ontology,' he says, 'is ... about the space of possibilities for character formation that surround a person'. It is 'about the ways in which the possibilities for choice, and for being, arise in history. It is not to be practiced in terms of grand abstractions, but in terms of the explicit formations in which we can constitute ourselves'. These formations have 'trajectories [that] can be plotted as clearly as those of trauma

---

[5] Ironically, in *Technopoly* Postman recommends the teaching of history as an antidote to the ecological influence of technology. Because it alone concerns itself with the 'roots' of knowledge, history is allegedly immune to the technological transformation of the world it operates in (Postman 1993: 138, 188ff.). Here too the history technology imposes itself naturally, organically (cf. "roots").

or child development, or, at one remove, that can be traced more obscurely by larger organizing concepts such as objectivity or even the facts themselves' (Hacking 2002: 23). 'Historical ontology' requires a 'historical meta-epistemology'. This claims 'that present ideas have memories; that is, a correct analysis of an idea requires an account of its previous trajectory and uses'. 'These concepts,' says Hacking 'are ours, and ... are essential to the very functioning of our society, our laws, our sciences, our argumentation, our reasoning ..., which is not to say that we cannot change them, or that they are not changing ...' (Hacking 2002: 8–9). What Hacking calls the 'historical *a priori*' backs this theory up. It designates 'conditions on the possibilities of knowledge within a "discursive framework"', conditions whose dominion is as inexorable, there and then, as Kant's synthetic *a priori*'. These conditions are 'conditioned and formed in history', but they can be 'uprooted by later, radical, historical transformations' (Hacking 2002: 5).

But this argument fails for two reasons – to do with (i) the 'historical *a priori*; (ii) the 'factization of the world'. 'Historical *a priori*' is here used metaphorically not logically. But the Kantian *a priori*, with its systemic logical force, yields not to contingent history, only to a different logical system.[6] Philosophical concepts, like Kant's *a priori*, 'hover above' lived experience. They may have a history and a destiny, but time cannot invalidate them. They are in themselves 'pure events distinct from the conditions in which they formed'. They are not 'discursive formations', therefore, because they have no intentional meanings or external references. Being 'real without being actual, ideal without being abstract', they are defined by their inherent consistency, their 'auto-referentiality' (Deleuze & Guattari 1991: 27, 36–7). The synthetic *a priori* makes temporality essential to cognition: perception logically presupposes the existence of time and space. The temporal structure of the world is granted by the *a priori*. If temporality could change it, it would not be *a priori*. Being contingent on temporality, history must also be contingent on the synthetic *a priori* (as Kant's *Critique of Judgement* confirms). The term 'historical ontology' itself blurs all distinctions: catachresis always confuses. If it means that everything has a history, then it just means "history". If it means that all things come into being solely through history, it contradicts itself: history only exists because, 'Being *qua* Being' must exist first. Being is

---

[6] – as Nietzsche realized. See *Beyond Good and Evil*, §11: why was it even necessary to believe in *a priori* judgements?

'that which is *always* or *usually* so': it sustains the existence of everything else and makes it what it is (Aristotle 1996: 135, 147, 305, III.iv.29, IV.i.1, VI.ii.12). This includes history as a social construct placed on temporality. 'By nature primary', Being and Unity 'might best be supposed to embrace all existing things'. Conversely, if Being and Unity are destroyed, 'everything else is destroyed with them, since everything exists and is one' (Aristotle 1997: 57, XI.i.7–12).

'The factization of the world is a human activity', says Hacking, because 'the unthought world doesn't come in facts'. This means: 'the *kinds* in terms of which the world is described ... are not kinds with which the world is ready-equipped, and which we elicit by probing'. 'They too are constructed,' and their construction involves 'a somewhat novel historicist nominalism' (Hacking 2002: 65). Factization thus differentiates the social from the natural sciences. In natural science, 'our invention of categories does not "really" change the way the world works'. Conversely, 'in social phenomena we may generate new kinds of people and new kinds of action as we devise new classifications and categories'. Consequently 'we "make up people" in a stronger sense than we "make up" the world'. This difference comes back to nominalism and to history 'because the objects of the social sciences ... are constituted by a historical process, while the objects of the natural sciences ... are created in time, but, in some sense, they are not constituted historically' (Hacking 2002: 40). The distinction drawn between 'time' and 'history' glosses over the crucial issue: how history itself is 'made up' to mean more than 'created in time'. If knowledge comes from historically variable social practices (as it does), then historical knowledge itself (as a *type* of knowledge) must also come from these same practices. Hacking invites what he calls 'philosophical technology: a study of the ways in which styles of reasoning provide stable knowledge and become not the uncoverers of objective truth but rather the standards of objectivity' (Hacking 2002: 198). He does not see that history is just another 'style of reasoning', not a value-concept naturally embedded in social evolution. This transcendent stance is typically academic [*illusio*]: the historical ontology that constructs all knowledge as historical discounts itself as a historical construct.

All a historical ontology does is nicely theorize the ordinary use of history (cf. Hacking 2002: 9). The 'historical *a priori*' and the 'factization' process originate in history's self-authenticating self-conception as humanity's 'default setting'. They just affirm the usual, 'weak' historicism – what Hacking calls 'local historicism', for it 'discourages grand unified accounts, but ... does demand taking a look at a lot of little facts'. The postmodernist posture notwithstanding, this is the same old historicist thing, as when Hacking uses 'trajectory' as a euphemism for "retrospective inevitability" and affirms that 'social and cultural phenomena are historically determined, and ... each period in history has its own values that are not applicable to other epochs. In philosophy that implies that philosophical issues find their place, importance, and definition in a specific cultural milieu' (Hacking 2002: 52–3). Historicizing attitudes always embed philosophical discrimination in heterogeneity. That's how they keep thinking affirmative.

(d.) As a total technological management-system, society needs history as a technology for managing its total self-knowledge. As a social product, history then 'remains configured by the system in which it is elaborated' (Certeau 1975: 79). Society uses history for its own affirmative, identitary purposes (e.g. Neustadt & May 1988). History is a system for managing a society's information resources [*Bestand*], the sum total of what it already knows about itself, what it identifies itself as being. History, like all academic writing, is 'a mode of bureaucratic-ideological organization' (Cohen 1988: 8). As a knowledge enterprise, it does come organized like any manufacturing or financial enterprise with many different but cognate businesses or branches with numerous diversified products, interests, and income streams. Historians are the technicians keeping it working. They have a predominantly technical-managerial function defined by all kinds of productivity targets (e.g. students admitted, grant income generated, conferences organized, books produced) in their particular department and area of specialized academic expertise.

A mass society involves technologies of mass organization – e.g. a globalized economy, global communications networks, but also the bureaucracies that manage them. They could be seen as the latest phase of 10,000 years of historical development, as though the principle of comprehensive organization were naturally inherent in the historical process. It seems to reflect 'a comprehensive determinism behind the whole panorama of historic events': it suggests 'a general direction in the historic process from organic to organizational forms and patterns, qualities and attributes' (Seidenberg 1950: 47–8). History would then mark 'a change of direction in the social structure of man, which may be subsumed as the transmutation of society as an organism into an organization of society'. It would be building consciousness, intelligence, knowledge, science, laws, civilization, etc.

into strategies for human survival (as the liberal-humanist and the organic conceptions of history maintain); facilitating 'a movement from innate, preconscious responses to acquired, explicitly defined, conscious reactions'; and tending towards a condition in which 'our instinctual ends are preceded by an ever increasing procession of contrived means' (Seidenberg 1950: 46–7).

So much for historicist hypotheses: Seidenberg's 'posthistoric' world surely culminates in Huxley's or Orwell's dystopias (e.g. *Brave New World*; *1984*). Still, one insight here is worth saving: organization 'is the dominant *modus operandi* of contemporary civilization; an inherent and inescapable process spreading out into ever wider areas and reaching down into ever deeper recesses of contemporary life' (Seidenberg 1950: 4). A complex mass-society and technical-managerial governance go together (Allott 2002: 162ff., 172, 218). Inevitably, the managerial ethos dominates the social ethos: 'the world tends to become the stuff of total administration, which absorbs even the administrators' (Marcuse 1986: 169). To be universally applicable, social organization must encompass mass heterogeneity. The only way it embraces 'the farthest reaches and most diverse aspects of life' is by becoming totally natural, by operating 'beneath the plane of opposition'. Thus 'it unites ... the endless range and diversity of the social scene under one compelling principle' (Seidenberg 1950: 4).

What applies to organization applies *ipso facto* to history. Behind the diversity of culture lies the history 'mega-machine' as its management-system. The technology pushes for ever more extensive organization: 'the machine is accelerating the emergence of organization in every phase and turn of life' (Seidenberg 1950: 29). As control for control's sake, bureaucratic social management is irrational. But, as a technology designed to make sense, history supports it with its own rationale. Thus 'the objective order of things' is increasingly constituted by organizational and technical rationality (Marcuse 1986: 144). In accounting for this order, history will be objective, rational, and verifiable: it's simply mapping the structures underpinning its own design. (It is not fortuitous that, e.g. *Annales* historians and their ilk with their Neo-Hegelian conviction of long-term rational trends in history focus on long-term economic and demographic tendencies.) Here, too, history authenticates itself: as a means of organizing the world, it identifies with the way the world is organized. 'The global triumph of the rhythm of mechanical production and reproduction promises that nothing changes and that nothing comes out that would not conform'

(Horkheimer & Adorno 1973: 120–1). The freedom the citizen-consumer enjoys is purely apparent [*illusio*] since it veils the 'integral power and inevitability' of society's organizational structures. It comes permeated with all kinds of ideological distractions the comprehensive social technology of power produces to conceal itself (Adorno 1976: 26). Be it by managerial-technical or historical-technical means, comprehensive bureaucratic control turns the world into an 'open prison': it ensures 'everything in it always comes back to one and the same thing' [... *so sehr ist alles eins*] (Adorno 1976: 30).

What naturalizes history's social management technology, what keeps it beneath the plane of opposition, is that its products and other mass-produced commodities share similar qualities. The claim of any particular historical account (e.g. monograph, article, TV documentary) to be objective guarantees its reliability. In essence history's technical dependability replicates the reliability required of any other commodity produced for a mass-market by a mass-market producer. Both types of commodity result from the bureaucratic quality-control norms operative in their production-process and required by their use-function (e.g. the safety standards for a car, an electric kettle, a gas-supply). The production-process and the envisaged market impose their own technical criteria – in history's case the personal attributes and professional skills historians claim for themselves. The historian's or the institution's reputation, like the brand name, backs up the limited warranty the commodity (e.g. the monograph) comes with.

Commodities are reified forms not only of labour but also of social-technical knowledge. Reification turns knowledge into things. The mass-media in the postmodern, virtually real world particularly need historical representations: they anchor it in the tried and tested 'same old thing'. That's why 'what is new about a mass culture, is that it excludes anything new' (Horkheimer & Adorno 1973: 120). As popular, socially extensive forms of expression, the media need representations with an already wide circulation to work with formats designed to meet public expectations. Historical representations fit this category, so the media confine themselves to the 'reproduction of the same old thing' [*Reproduktion des Immergleichen*]. The latest thing in media technology and history's same old thing make paradoxically for a seductive combination: the shock of the new enhances recognition of what is essentially still the same. Further, the general prevalence of historical representations in the media confirms their own affirmative tendencies: 'The same old thing governs their relationship to the past' [*Immergleichheit regelt auch das Verhältnis zum Vergangenem*] (Horkheimer & Adorno 1973: 120). The latest media technologies (e.g. computer-generated images in *The Gladiator*, or in BBC 2's historical war-game series, *Time Commander*) do lend veracity to the virtual historical image. But the overall effect ensures the same old thing still dominates [*die Gewalt des Hergebrachten*]. That is to say: it imposes itself most decisively by embracing technical innovations that would otherwise invalidate it (cf. Horkheimer & Adorno 1973: 115). And the historian concurs: 'The influence of video-games and science fiction would be ... pertinent in trying to explain why the idea of chronological reversal, or time travelling, has become a normal way of engaging with the past' (cf. Samuel 1994: 443–4).

Second, history authenticates itself through practices that constitute knowledge as 'historical'. The issue is: what makes historical knowledge persuasive? It invokes standards of objectivity and truth to make the past a supreme social value. History itself produces them through: (e) psychologistic types of interpretation; (f) disciplinary consensus on the key issues and accepted thought-styles; (g) typically academic paralogisms; and (h) the symbolic authority of its self-affirming structure. These procedures replicate society's "natural" attitudes.

(e.) Psychologistic interpretation. 'One of the key features of historical enquiry ... is that whenever the contemporary world develops a fault [*sic*!], historians look at the past to seek its origins' (Black & MacRaild 2000: 51). Historical thinking always takes point of origin as guaranteeing truth and sense absolutely. Sources are the cornerstone of objectivity, the touchstone of certainty. It's a theological reflex (cf. Halbwachs 1994: 200–201). Knowledge comes from not just the origin, but – apprehensively enough – the Originator of all things: 'The fear of the Lord is the beginning of wisdom' (*Psalms*, 111, v.10). By definition, sources anchor cognitive value in point of origin. They come with the aura of authenticity, of divinity. Within a broadly theocentric conception of the world, history [*crg*] always returned to original sources for reliable and unchanging principles of knowledge and morality that actual history [*rg*] had obscured since the Fall (Schmidt-Biggemann 1991: 20). That's how – as Ranke demonstrates – history's scientific claims can support historicist convictions (cf. Gay 1988: 84–5). That history goes back to sources, makes it a privileged form of knowledge. As the storehouse of rhetorical topics (i.e. the precepts, teachings and commonplaces human behaviour illustrates), its contents sustained the various knowledge disciplines. Deriving from Aristotelian logic and Christian theology, this theistic conception of

history also performed a crucial metaphysical function. Its sources gave it access to divinely revealed knowledge about history and nature that was 'timeless and true'. In ordering the topics it comprises, it produced an intellectual practice based on criteria of homogeneity, generality, and deduction, concepts that – significantly enough – neither derive from, nor are dependent on, historical experience itself (Schmidt-Biggemann 1991: 20–5). This conception of history is exemplified by Vico's *New Science*: the history of human society, as made by mankind, stems from its divine origins in the poetic wisdom of Greek and Hebrew antiquity (cf. Vico 1984: 110ff., 281ff.).

The theological framework has gone. History's knowledge practice, a technology naturalized by habit, remains. It alone must fulfil the theological desire for total explanations. "Homogeneity", "generality", and "deduction" all persist as "specialization", "comprehensiveness", and "paralogical hindsight", the usual tropes of academic thinking, technical strategies for managing society's self-knowledge. "Timeless truth", as disclosed by historical sources, now operates ideologically, as identitary thinking, always affirming that the way things are is how they always were. That's what makes it psychologistic, as the principles sustaining Vico's philosophy of history show. The psychological dimension of human reality provides the logical sense of history: 'This queen of the sciences ... took its start when the first men began to think humanly.' Social institutions and the common sense that directs them presuppose a comprehensive, chronological framework that affirms their particular identities, their particular way of thinking and behaving: 'Our science ... comes to describe ... an ideal eternal history traversed in time by the history of every nation in its rise, development, maturity, decline and fall.' Thus identitary thinking provides the logical sense of history: 'this world of thinking has certainly been made by men, and its guise must therefore be found within the modifications of our own human mind.' It also explains why psychologism excludes the hermeneutic scruples that (as Dilthey and others show) make historical comprehension problematic. Working within identitary structures that enforce identitary thinking (e.g. period-concepts, institutions, gender, nationality) with which he or she also identifies, the historian cannot but reach the ultimate condition of objective truth – tautology. As an aspect of human agency in history, the historian also makes history, so that 'history cannot be more certain than when he who creates the things also narrates them' (Vico 1984: 104).

Psychologism is a deceptive attitude, because it assumes the past is identifiable because it originates in psychological agency (e.g. a personality, a 'world'): 'Historians find more than dust in archives and libraries: the records there offer a glimpse of a world that has disappeared' (Appleby et al. 1995: 251). Naturally, the world has disappeared; things do disappear, as personal experience shows. But that's why we can identify with that past. It is "like" us, as Cannadine, citing Trevelyan, confirms: 'The dead . . . were once as real as we, and we shall tomorrow be shadows like them' (Cannadine 1999: 28). Its effects are also regressive: identifying with the vanished object, yearning for origins, induces spasms of nostalgia. Still, the ultimate spiritual reality psychologism represents is a crucial element of historical truth. It responds to an ingrained 'quasi-theological certainty of bourgeois thinking in general' (Jameson 1988: 35). It is so natural, a natural truth, the way people naturally behave.

In fact, psychologism reduces history to a human interest story. Its realism is 'spontaneously presumed by historical intentionality itself': it simply presupposes 'that history has for its subject people like you and me, who act and suffer within circumstances they did not create' (Ricoeur 1994: 21–2). Take Sheehan's description of the Habsburg Leopold II. It reads like a soap-opera synopsis:

> Although Leopold was not *afflicted* by his brother's *pathological insensitivity*, he was also rather an *unlovable character*. . . . Nevertheless, in Tuscany he had earned a reputation as an . . . *enlightened* ruler. . . . He was *prepared* to acknowledge that all authority had to be limited by the dictates of reason . . . Considering these *convictions*, it is not *surprising* that . . . he began at once to defuse the *anger* building throughout his realm.
>
> (Sheehan 1994: 275 (my italics))

The account relies on a stereotypical set of psychological reflexes. They seem objective only because they enjoin readers to presume that they can identify them from their own experience (cf. Gardiner 1968: 86). The psychologistic procedure is actually circular, tautological: biographical details construct a psychological profile 'which . . . is then used to interpret the details' (Menand 2003: x). The text assumes that the current usage of the italicized words identifies nineteenth-century behaviour, even though a U.S. academic historian and a Habsburg Emperor result from different socialization processes. It's, therefore, unclear whether the text represents an "objective" description of a past situation or a series of inferences the historian himself has drawn from it.

Second, psychologism clouds the already murky issue of historical causality. Causal explanations also derive their certainty from origins, but also from generalizations about the regularity with which the phenomena to be explained recur (cf. Popper 1974: 40, 144; Gardiner 1968: 85ff.). Given that 'history provides us with no system of precise correlations', recourse to the *Zeitgeist*, the *mentalité*, or interesting personality offers a plausible substitute finality (cf. Gardiner 1968: 93). Hence, 'historians ... seek to understand the internal dispositions of historical actors .... Such understandings depend on convincing ... interpretations that link internally generated meanings to external behaviour' (Appleby et al. 1995: 259).

This "natural" attitude is, though, quite fallacious. Objective identification such as this is completely unfounded and unproven, as Simmel argues. Certainly, understanding the past is like understanding another person. But the other (i.e. "you") is as much a primal phenomenon [*Urphänomen*] as the self (i.e. "I"). So the idea of the other is not "out there", but an aspect of personal self-consciousness. That, after all, makes human beings social creatures. All the self ever knows of the other are sequences of external physical utterances, gestures, or actions. Afterwards it infers from them an autonomous psychological structure of inwardness that "explains" them by analogy to our own self-understanding. The other can thus appear both very familiar (i.e. like our self) but also very foreign, because the other ("you") is by definition not the self (not "me") (Simmel 1999: 159–62).

According to Simmel, psychologism makes historical sequence incidental. We make inferences about historical figures within a historical time-span just as we do about acquaintances' personality on the basis of long-term personal experience. We now understand the anger Hanoverians felt towards Bismarck for Prussian hegemony in 1866 supra-historically as a psychological reflex by identifying it with our own experiences of anger. History, then, is not the discontinuous past but a set of forms the synthesizing mind uses to organize knowledge already known. History merely offers 'functional connectivity' [*eine funktionelle Verbindungsart*] between the past issues that happen to be under consideration. Only by being organized by the understanding into a coherent unified structure in themselves, can events become historical – dissolve into a dynamic sequence. The historical object is not something ready-found the historical account subsequently mechanically replicates, but a deferred, always vital, always current cognitive structure [*geistiges Gebilde*] that makes the past intelligible (Simmel 1999: 165, 179).

Finally, rejecting psychologism does not mean removing humane values from the humanities. From the humanities, as they actually function in corporate universities, they've long since gone (Davies 2003: 21ff.). Psychologism certainly offers nothing humane. As Simmel argues, it fronts a purely mechanical strategy of manufacturing identities from what it already understands about how things actually were (cf. Simmel 1999: 178–9). Rather, the link between technics and psychologism is 'a central paradox of historical study'. This requires 'the exploration of *human feeling* in all its magnificence ... to be done by scholarly moles and meticulous mice who ... must professionally be bureaucratic *managers of information*' (Vincent 1996: 15–16). Thus historians' reflections on the discipline inevitably stress the ("soft") personality factors the ("hard") technics of history entail. '*Historians' skills* ... are developed and refined over a lifetime, becoming part of the *person*' (Jordanova 1999: 172); 'to test *ideas* in the light of *theoretical developments* is to show *humility* and *insight*: this is the sign of a good historian' (Black & MacRaild 2000: 168); 'history is a human activity carried out by an organized corps of *fallible human beings* acting, however, in accordance with *strict methods and principles*' (Marwick 2001: 28); 'when adhering to certain rather general tenets – to do with *honesty, openness and willingness* to revise conceptual, interpretive and explanatory *frameworks* in the light of new *evidence* – it is possible to say that historical *knowledge* is of a different order from that of fiction, myth and ideology' (Fulbrook 2002: 196). Here, expressed through the figure of catachresis, psychologism backs up identitary thinking. Both the form of historical enquiry and the contents of historical knowledge come from the same stereotypical set of personal reflexes.[7]

Psychologism thus principally creates deficits in the knowledge society needs, as opposed to the knowledge history has saddled society with. "Naturally" familiar it may be, psychologistic explanation works against the interests of knowledge. Valuing ideas and intentions on the basis of origins and identities rather than in relation to actual, objective conditions, cancels the idea of truth in favour of reproducing things as they are, i.e. the same old thing, knowledge already known (cf. Adorno 1975: 131).

---

[7] My italics to highlight the respective convergences of personal attitude and technical demand.

(f.) Disciplinary consensus and accepted thought-styles. Historians recognize that 'the writing of history ... like history itself, changes with the passage of time'. They also add that, though new orthodoxies emerge, continuities persist (Black & MacRaild 2000: 83). Such statements just reaffirm history's heterogeneity. They make the key concepts, 'change' and 'continuity', interchangeable, and historical truth tautological: history [*crg*] mirrors history [*rg*]: history is whatever history is. Consequently, the discipline, as the books about it show, rests on contradictions. How can a subject always changing, seize *the* truth about *the* past? How is it that 'a multiplicity of interpretations (or stories) can be constructed out of the "same" past'? What are its 'implications' (Fulbrook 2002: 186)?

(f.i) Historical knowledge involves a naïve view of cognition. It comes from the psychologistic relationship between the enquiring subject and the object it enquires into. It takes arbitrary, divergent forms. Compare, e.g. 'The past ... existed entirely independently of the activities of historians. No doubt human and personal factors come into play when historians begin to engage with the past ...' (Marwick 2001: 25); and: 'questioning of the ideal of objectivity ... undermines the belief that people can get outside of themselves in order to get at the truth' (Appleby et al. 1995: 7). The cognitive process involves three main factors: the historian (subjective, partial, situated historically and socially); the past ('as it was': objective, real; as a material residue); and its representation (its accuracy, coherence, plausibility; its generic, discursive rules, etc.). Hence, where academic orthodoxy sees an objective past, its postmodernist critic sees a subjective representation: both positions lock into the same *illusio*. Seeing knowledge in terms of a subject–object antithesis automatically defines objectivity and truth in terms of perception and representation. Conversely, making objectivity and truth properties of perception and representation makes them questionable and refractive (cf. Jenkins 2003: 68). Either way, they remain defined by representation [*illusio*], relative to other representations, through historians' own 'self-referencing' through the 'constant machinery of the so-called secondary elaborations' (Cohen 1988: 67–8).

The subject–object relationship (i.e. subject = object) could be the ideal condition of knowledge: e.g. 'history = everything'. In reality, it isn't. Cognitive theory since Descartes stresses that mental structures produce the objects they perceive: exteroception and proprioception work together (cf. Dissanayake 1995: 150). Hermeneutic theory, as in Dilthey or Gadamer, develops strategies to enable the mind to grasp objects from the past other minds have created. The predominant 'thought-style' of the academic discipline, however, generally excludes these "philosophical" issues from the same old history it produces and disseminates. They are seen as subversive equivocations. In fact, the subversive equivocations come from the presumed congruity between subject and object, between history [*crg*] and history [*rg*], that supposedly constitutes objectivity and truth. But what if history really were "everything" (i.e. subject = object)? How then would "everything" be represented? The result must be heterogeneous, hence contradictory, because the concept of "everything" necessarily implies heterogeneity and contradiction. Inevitably, representing "everything" embraces both "proliferating sub-disciplines" and "general history"; both "art" and "science"; both "specialization" and "comprehensiveness"; both "puzzles" and "narratives"; both constant self-revision and constant self-identity – all the same old terms of the same old discussion.

History, therefore, operates on the brink of unfeasibility. What stops historians seeing it are the academic conventions and social habits keeping it going. Still, its inherent contradictions produce a characteristic stress, exemplified by Ranke's description of history as 'this hard but splendid profession' (Gay 1988: 83, 92). In the books historians write about history it comes out typically in a shift in emphasis – from the information historians manage towards the technical virtuosity they manage it with. It displaces the (objective) truth of the representation into the (subjective) strenuousness historical scholarship apparently demands. It happens when the subject–object connection seems to be at breaking-point: when the (objective) material is so vast that coping with it strains the historian's (subjective) resources. Compare: (i) 'It is one of the principles of historical research ... that a *genuine training and mastery* obtained by systematic work on a restricted body of material will show themselves in producing *instinctive rightness* when bodies of material too enormous to be fully worked through are tackled in a more superficial ... way' (Elton 1969: 95); and (ii) 'imperial history, *properly conducted*, is an *extraordinarily demanding* discipline. It is ... *hard enough* to keep up with the latest scholarly work in regard to one ... country's past. To evolve a *workmanlike knowledge* of the histories ... of a wide range of conflicting states ... is *hideously difficult*, and yet *it must be attempted* ...' (Colley 2002: 144–5). Similarly, the comprehensive truth the historian seeks, is displaced into a comprehensive "awareness" of the situation she seeks it in. Compare: (iii) 'the goal of *completeness* is simply impractical, especially since, as the world of *scholarship* expands, there is more and more to read. ... The only ways forward are through *careful* selection, through being *thoughtful and open* about the criteria of selection ...' (Jordanova 2000: 102–3); and: (iv) 'I hope that ... [this book] will have served to raise a *heightened awareness* of the key issues all historians face .... It is ... important that we are *aware of the parameters* of what we are doing, rather than blindly conforming to ... the varied contemporary pressures ...' (Fulbrook 2002: 196). These professions of moral earnestness and heightened awareness all collapse. As typically psychologistic reflexes, they just show that the academic habits they come from are the one thing academics don't see.[8]

The binary, subject–object model of cognition leaves its imprint on the texts historians write about history. They always rely on catachresis, the deliberate use of misapplied terms: e.g. 'qualified objectivity' (Appleby et al. 1995: 259); 'moderately comprehensive' (McCullagh 1998: 3); 'hybrid discipline' (Tosh 1999: 131); 'eclectic discipline' (Jordanova 2000: 198); 'perspectival paradigms', 'partial histories' (Fulbrook 2002: 37ff.,185ff.). This trope organizes the discourse of academic self-reflection. In *In Defence of History* Richard Evans simply elides the heterogeneous elements that allegedly make professional history "objective". Lacking any necessary causal or logical structure, the argument careers through a sequence of catachrestically related propositions:

(*a*) 'Everyone ... concedes in practice that there is extra-textual reality.'

(*b*) 'History is an empirical science ... concerned with the content of knowledge rather than its nature.'

(*c*) 'Through ... sources ... and ... methods ... we can ... approach a reconstruction of the past that may be partial and provisional, and certainly will not be objective, but is nevertheless true.'

(*d*) '... we will be guided in selecting materials for the stories we tell, and in the way we ... interpret them, ... by literary models, by social science theories, by moral and political beliefs, by an aesthetic sense, even by our own unconscious assumptions and desires.'

---

[8] My italics.

(e) '... the stories we tell will be true stories, even if the truth they tell is our own, and even if other people can and will tell them differently.'

(f) *Proof (1) by* ad lectorem *remonstration*:
'Anyone who thinks that the truth about the past does not matter has not, perhaps, lived under a regime like that of the Soviet or Eastern bloc Communists where it is systematically distorted and suppressed.'

(g) *Proof (2) by recourse to authority*:
'For, as G. M. Trevelyan once wrote: "The appeal of history ... is in the last analysis poetic. But the poetry of history does not consist of imagination roaming at large, but of imagination pursuing the fact and fastening upon it."'

(h) *Summation*:
'For a long time, Trevelyan's views have seemed ... out of date. One consequence of the postmodernist incursion into history is to make their emphasis on poetry and imagination seem contemporary once more; but poetry and imagination that are disciplined by fact.'

(Evans 1997: 249–51)

History apparently comprises both "extra-textual reality" and "imagination"; both "empirical science" and "poetry"; both "knowledge" and "beliefs" / "unconscious desires"; both "partiality" and "truth"; both "fact" and "imagination". These terms contradict each other, which confirms the underlying trope of catachresis. Hence the conceptual slippage from "true stories", to the more qualified "the truth is our own", thence to "*the* [now absolute] truth about *the* [now definitive] past". Hence the euphemistic use of metaphor – in the idea that fact "disciplines" imagination. (In fact, the existence of extra-textual referents is conveyed most convincingly by the literature of the fantastic (e.g. Kafka). Representing the 'guilty conscience of the positivistic nineteenth century' and 'far from being a celebration of the world of the imagination', it explicitly 'posits the largest part of the text as belonging to the real world, or more exactly provoked by it, in the manner of a name given to something that already exists' (Todorov 1970: 176, 180).) Catachresis thus proves useless for definitions. Rather it is a disarming strategy: 'The unification of opposites ... is one of the many ways in which discourse and communication make themselves immune against the expression of protest and refusal' (Marcuse 1986: 90).

Catachresis hardly makes academic discourse convincing. Here it signifies an intellectual practice that cannot define itself: historians cannot say what they do. But they never need to: parapraxis is typically academic. The strenuous studiousness, the psychologistic earnestness that explicate the discipline exempt the disciplinary *illusio*. This depends not on professed ideals, but automatic habits – on what historians actually do and the same old way they do it in. These fundamentals cannot be examined without them radically questioning, not just their discipline, but themselves (cf. Bourdieu 1997: 122–3). When they are examined, a different, more plausible account of objectivity emerges.

(f.ii) The societal basis of objectivity. 'The process of knowledge represents the human activity that is most distinctively conditioned by society and knowledge is a social formation in the most literal sense' (Fleck 1999: 58). Objectivity and truth are societal as much as cognitive standards. They are functions of the social institution that is historical knowledge. Since history is a technology designed to produce human meaning, society takes it as the "natural" way to understand itself. History establishes 'functional connections' between all its various interests; it offers a total management-system for its total self-knowledge. Historical representations are, therefore, a widespread, multifarious social currency. They connect with the social memory that frames personal life; they are the staple diet of education; through the mass-media, the heritage, and tourist industries, they generate economic value. These representations are social facts. But representations are always transformed by being communicated. The parameters within which they can be transformed yet retain social recognition always need redefining. Professional historians identify with these social tendencies, not least because history's identitary logic predisposes them to. They correct, extend, reinforce, or re-hash this socially recognized knowledge, the knowledge that is already more or less well known. They use various social media, including specialized monographs or articles, to do so. Their standards of historical objectivity and truth are thus social criteria by which society regulates the production and distribution of its self-knowledge. They necessarily hinge on consensus in the academic community on the issues the discipline itself recognizes and the thought-styles this recognition adopts.

Knowledge is objective if it is reliable, stable – impersonal. ("Impersonal" implies both "beyond the person" (e.g. "society", "community", "professional organization", "institution"), and "disconnected from one's person" (e.g. "circumstances beyond one's control")). Underpinning history, like any discipline, is what the QAA History Benchmark Statement calls 'a vast body of knowledge that constitutes the subject'. The history technology runs on 'a very large body of agreed historical knowledge on which no dispute is possible, and though this body of knowledge may not by itself provide a very sophisticated interpretation of the past it is entirely indispensable to any study of it ' (Elton 1969: 80). This involves 'thousands of basic facts for which there is so much reliable evidence that no one doubts their truth for a moment' (McCullagh 1998: 13, 22). 'Knowledge-seeking' in history is based on 'stable bodies of knowledge that can be communicated, built upon, and subjected to testing' (Appleby et al. 1995: 254). This corpus constitutes a reality-principle in its own right – a stable, impersonal point of reference: 'the "public" history that "everybody knows"' (Neustadt & May 1988: 166). It reflects the existence of widely shared historical representations in society as a whole. It projects the existence of a stable past. It enables it to be inferred as an *a priori* 'extra-textual referent' from whatever the discipline defines as historical sources. That is to say, the past is stable not because it has gone irrevocably. If that were the case, it would have eluded history [*crg*] completely. Rather, what fixes the past as an impersonal object for the present to study is this *ever-present* body of historical knowledge already known (cf. Halbwachs 1994: 290). It affirms the impersonal past as a social obligation on both professional historians and the wider public. That is because (as Durkheim argues) society is experienced as the paramount obligation. As an impersonal force beyond the individual, society is 'the source of all our other obligations'. Consequently, the idea of an impersonal (i.e. objective) past is always an actual social experience because 'it is not anything anyone was able to give their consent to' (cf. Durkheim 1997: 104). So, in talking about 'the ideal of objectivity', about 'trying to say something true about the past', about being 'accurate' or 'unbiased' about a past event, historians are meeting an obligation that is purely social – not primarily historical (cf. Appleby et al. 1995: 7; Fulbrook 2002: ix, 9).

Like any technological apparatus, the social body of knowledge needs to be regularly maintained so that it stays reliable: so that it can keep on projecting the past as impersonal (i.e. as "real", "objective" and "true"). History [*crg*], therefore, has a social obligation to authenticate itself by perpetuating itself. The identity of the discipline, the impersonality of the past, hence the objectivity and truthfulness of its knowledge all depend, therefore, on the academic reiteration of the same old thing. Replication is a type of verification. More precisely: objectivity and truth derive from a relatively stable social consensus about the bodies of knowledge actually worth replicating. Major history publishers' catalogues (e.g. Cambridge U.P., Hodder & Stoughton, Longman, Oxford U.P., Palgrave, Routledge) show that new books re-work the same old topics within broadly similar categories and series. And, e.g., a British Library catalogue search shows that the same old topics, for being replicated, acquire their own, impersonal existence: e.g. "French Revolution" produces 2150 items, "Enlightenment European" 39; "National Socialism" produces 2325 items, "German federalism" 11.[9] Each topic has its own, collective weight and volume of objective truth. But the actual amount still depends on its recognition, as much in society as in the discipline's 'thought style' (cf. Hacking 2002: 191–2).

Needless to say, history's self-replication results from academic specialization. Disciplinary habit forces the historian, as an academic, to keep on putting out knowledge on the same old thing. The familiar ways of thinking that form the 'iron foundation' of any science are taken as self-evident because, as the same old thing, they are familiar (Fleck 1983: 46). Replication fabricates objectivity. It turns particular aptitudes into technical expertise, subjective interests into objective knowledge. Academic practice is designed to 'departicularize and universalize' knowledge, to minimize its contingent, personal basis. Through being debated by other academics who could invalidate it, knowledge substantiates itself – becomes objective. This collective verification process does not detract from personal interest; rather, personal interest legitimizes, and is legitimized, by it. Knowledge emerges as objective and true because the 'academic field' imposes its own 'normative requirements' on its individual members' mutually antagonistic interests. The collective knowledge obligation thus conceals its own contingent origins (cf. Bourdieu 2002: 164–5; Fleck 1999: 91; Markus 1987: 44).

Consequently, where postmodernism enhances authorial intention to make meaning arbitrary, academic method eliminates subjectivity to make meaning compelling (cf. Markus 1987: 15). Here again both tendencies converge. Ultimately, objective knowledge comes down to self-authenticating strategies in the academic text. As Fleck points out, the use of technical or specialized terminology has an

---

[9] i.e. on-line search of the British Library public catalogue.

objectivizing effect. It implies that meaning is independent of the person using it or that the author has a purely instrumental function (Fleck 1983: 121; Schlanger 1994: 33–4). Hence, impersonal contexts, the pre-conditions of objectivity and truth, come from technical historical entities (e.g. "long traditions", "processes", or "periods"), or technical structures (e.g. "revolutionary France", "ancien régime", "fin-de-siècle"), let alone the technological type applied (e.g. "political history", "imperial history"). Further, the technics of the discipline impose their own forms of certainty (cf. Fleck 1983: 122). There is always the latest scholarly work 'to keep up with'. That is because the historiography of the topic – the knowledge already known – helps shape the enquiry while fitting it into an ongoing, collective process of comprehension (cf. Markus 1987: 37–8). Moreover, the conventions of the historical monograph or article genres tend to approach a de-personalized scientific norm whereby the '"inscribed author" ... appears as an anonymous performer of methodologically certified, strictly regulated activities and a detached observer of their results – without any further personal identifying marks beyond possession of the required professional competence' (Markus 1987: 13).

Here, then, the subject–object model of cognition proves endlessly adaptable. The relationship is both absolute (subject = object) and absolutely relative: i.e. both sides of the equation are infinitely variable. History can thus be both 'objective' and 'true' and yet totally heterogeneous. Each sub-discipline has its own 'thought-style', forms its own 'thought collective' (cf. Fleck 1983: 81, 87, 109). Each is what it identifies with: social history deals with 'class, oppression, and exploitation' (Cartledge 2002: 29); political history studies 'the practices and institutions of rule' (Pedersen 2002: 53); religious history argues for 'religion as a category of analysis' (Hufton 2002: 77); imperial history is 'vitally about ... the manifold connections that existed over time between different sectors of the world and different peoples' (Colley 2002: 138). Within the social body of historical knowledge already known, each type of history defines its own object, its own objectivity. The subject of each sub-discipline is a different object; hence, objectivity is subjective to the sub-discipline. "Objectivity" and "truth" tend to act more as incentives than as standards. History thus proves to be a highly flexible, highly effective technology. However it comes, its "objectivity" as a social obligation affirms the obligations society imposes. It represents the 'formal institutionalization of obligative-thought' (Cohen 1988: 176).

(g.) Academic paralogisms or 'cognitive assymetries'. Historians belong to the same temporal-historical dimension as the events they study. History [*crg*] is a strategy for pretending they don't.

The binary cognitive model produces objective truth from the identity of (knowing) subject and (known) object: historical knowledge [*crg*] is true description of history [*rg*]. But if the subject is nothing other than the object, if history [*crg*] is just a variant of history [*rg*], the model collapses. It also makes objective truth duplicitous. If all historical knowledge [*crg*] is historical [*rg*], then objective truth, to be objective and true, would have to be external to history and the already historicized world. If historical truth is the recognition of an objectivity that is disinterested and supra-historical, it would need a means for history to access it, to abstract it from history. Hence, objective truth is ambiguous. It results from a subject–object relationship that is simultaneously symmetrical (History [*crg*] objectively replicates History [*rg*]) and a-symmetrical or transcendental (History [*crg*] seeks a greater coherence than History [*rg*] (cf. Oakeshott 1999: 36, 68–9)). History identifies with the lived experience of the past but also wonders how this comprehensive identification works (cf. Certeau 1975: 47). This duplicity makes the scope of historical knowledge arbitrary, its content heterogeneous, and its objectivity problematic. It also reveals the history of historiography as a futile attempt to discover a logical compulsion in the inherent arbitrariness of interpretative trends.

Producing asymmetrical abstractions from the same old thing involves various *strategies of representation*. Working in combination, these strategies typically produce academic know-ledge: but then the sole, "naturally" acceptable form of objective truth is academic, i.e. historical discourse is 'isomorphic with academic discourse' (Cohen 1988: 19). They can be enumerated briefly, thus:

(g.i) Specialization. Academic specialization is a precondition of objective truth. It works by restricting the mind's propensity for eclecticism. Its constraining force comes out in historians' proclamations of methodological rigour and studious effort. Clearly (they feel), truth can't be binding unless it has a smack of masochism about it.

Specialization is also an information-management strategy. Frag-menting an issue into different aspective "fields" or "areas" of exper-tise minimizes dissent and maximizes truth (Markus 1987: 26, 36).

Specialization affirms itself as an ideal form of comprehension while denying the heterogeneity it really generates. That also makes it essential to history's self-perpetuation. It's a technique of self-authentification, always backing itself up. As with scientific texts, academic articles and monographs have obsolescence built in; they are temporally 'shallow' (Markus 1987: 29–30). Their evidence and conclusions are constantly subject to revision and refinement, the latest thing succeeding the same old thing. Conversely, the very concept of the 'specialist' or 'expert' implies an authorial posture of objective disinterest. Paradoxically, like scientific texts, academic historical texts present themselves as being objective and depersonalized, while circulating under the personal name of their author for reasons of professional status and "brand" recognition (cf. Markus 1987: 11ff.). Lastly, specialization constructs objectivity through standardization: history's subject-matter may well be heterogeneous but it comes expressed in very few genres. Predictability and familiarity, as essential aspects of the natural objectivity of academic historical truth, are also aspects of discursive constraints (Markus 1987: 11, 35ff.; Fleck 1983: 94–6).

(g.ii) Recourse to imaginary aspects. Imagination generates productive asymmetries. It has always been a means of self-abstraction from prevailing circumstances, hence always preliminary to altering the world (Scarry 1985: 171). This is also why it is used 'at an everyday level ... to apply concepts to things', since 'this is the way we render the world familiar, and therefore manageable' (Warnock 1976: 207). So historians use it to contextualize facts. According to Weber, in attempting to discern historical causality the historian constructs various 'fantasy images' [*Phantasiebilder*] of possible causal connections. These are isolated by a process of abstraction from the past reality; their plausibility is assessed by reference to historians' own wider knowledge and experience. They thus construct 'unreal causal contexts' in order to understand real causal factors (Weber 1988: 275, 277, 285). According to Collingwood, 'the web of imaginative construction ... serves as a touchstone by which we decide whether alleged facts are genuine'. That is to say, 'the historian's picture of the past is ... in every detail an imaginary picture, and its necessity is at every point the necessity of the *a priori* imagination' (Collingwood 1978: 244–5). *Illusio* thus makes "objectivity" possible.

(g.iii) Advocacy. History has always been understood metaphorically in juridical terms – from Cicero's *magistra vitae* to Hegel's 'world

law-court'. But history has also been subject to judicial ruling, as in the trials of Eichmann (1961) and Barbie (1987), and in the Irving libel case (2000) (cf. Arendt 1983; Finkielkraut 1989; Guttenplan 2002). The juridical metaphor describes the historian's stance towards the case in hand. Like the advocate or judge, the historian is both involved in the case, but extraneous to the crime. Like the advocate, the historian assembles arguments based on tested evidence to persuade the reader (his jury) of the truth of the case he or she wishes to make (Ginzburg 1999: 57, 62, 64). But it is a case: it aims to incriminate or to exculpate; or, like the judge in a judicial enquiry, the historian would construct a course of events and attribute responsibility or negligence, success or failure.

History's standard of veracity can, therefore, be defined in terms of rhetorical proof. But this does not mean that all truths, as products of their underlying discourse-system, are relative. On the contrary: as Aristotle shows, outside logic and science, the realm of necessary and eternal truths, everything else (i.e. the transient, confused, heterogeneous human sphere) ultimately does depend on persuasion. The rhetorical effect is 'not an optional alternative to an insight you already possess but rather to the evidence you would not be able to possess, at least not here or now' (Blumenberg 1986b: 111–12). Rhetoric is the cognitive structure that underpins heterogeneity; it is 'the means of persuasion in reference to any given subject' (Aristotle 1994: 15, I.ii.2). In its forensic form, it 'has to do with the past, which is already known' (Aristotle 1994: 455; III.xvii.10). It relies on 'inartificial proofs', what historians call sources, i.e. 'witness, tortures, contracts, and the like'; and on 'artificial proofs ... constructed by system and by our own efforts' (Aristotle 1994: 15, I.ii.2). These are based principally on enthymemes, inferences drawn from 'probabilities, examples, neces- sary signs, and signs' – their premises implied by 'rules written in invisible ink on the fabric of Greek everyday life', rules that 'exist in all societies' and make societies 'work' (Aristotle 1994: 337, II.xxv.8; Ginzburg 1999: 42). Thus, Aristotle defines a still familiar 'basic core' of historiography that comprises reconstructing history 'on the basis of traces', involving 'natural connections' that 'can be regarded as certain' or other connections 'that can be regarded as infinitely likely' (Ginzburg 1999: 46). Rooted in already known social interests and truth-values, this rhetorical structure – far from being the discovery of flash postmodern, historical theory – is an essential "truth-device" in the history technology.

(g.iv) Sequentiality.[10] Sequentiality refers to narrative or emplotment. Just as history is society's 'default knowledge', so narrative supplies its default sense of order. It is 'the form *par excellence*' of traditional knowledge, the knowledge through which, as 'the same old thing', tradition perpetuates itself (Lyotard 1979: 38). As with rhetoric, to which, as *narratio*, it belongs, narration, constructing sequences of sense, is a means of managing heterogeneity. Self-contradiction wrecks rational consistency, but narrative can embrace it without losing credibility (cf. Schmidt-Biggemann 1991: 27). This is also why it can be 'the site where different strategies of explanation operate', why it figures so prominently in a postmodernist theory that itself lends prominence to the ludic – i.e. the imaginative, figurative, metaphorical – character of knowledge construction (Munslow 2003: 147ff., 162). Sequentiality thus provides a minimal cognitive structure to heterogeneous material.

Narrative sequences – as sequences – also replicate the process of historical change. Their credibility comes not from the events they represent, but from their semiotic properties, ideological aspects, and cognitive structure. It also comes from the formal, generic properties of narrative, from the tropes by which it is organized, the implied author or reader, not from its content (cf. White 1985: 133ff.; Iser 1972: 7ff.). The fairly constant set of constructs through which history perpetuates itself (e.g. origins and developments, causes and processes, traditions

---

[10] On this topic (i.e. history as a narrative form) a vast literature has developed. As the Introduction explains, *Historics* never intended to go in for self-referential, academic disputation. Rather, it always meant to explore what the academic mentality, exemplified by academic history, does in and to society. A vast literature there may be, but behind it one obsession: that, post-Deconstruction, thanks to the grammar of narrative, the arbitrariness of the sign, the play of difference, the truth-claims of historical discourse and of literary narrative converge. Hence, 'all histories always have been and always will be aesthetic, figurative discourses' (Jenkins 2003: 70). So history will inevitably be in the imaginary, hypothetical mode of 'as if', since (rather self-evidently, i.e. tautologically) 'the particular functional combination of explanatory strategies (aesthetic, cognitive and moral / ideological) the historian deploys will determine the structure of their historical understanding. The way the historian arranges these functional layers and modes will produce their own historiographical style' (Munslow 2003: 36–9, 178). Still, as pointed out in the Introduction, in this theoretical discourse, "history" still retains transcendental value, even as it's being re-functioned, just because it's evidently *worth* being re-functioned. Theory just gives bourgeois-academic discourse a re-tread now that its metaphysical humanist basis has gone. So the aim of this section is simply to show briefly, within the overall conceptual organization of *Historics*, how sequentiality helps sustain the historical *illusio*.

and precedents, legacies and beneficiaries, periods and contexts), provides narrative patterns that pre-shape factual content. They gear its readers' thought 'to think of temporal processes as transcendent: irretrievable, collective, humane, total, nonnegatable, and so on, when, in fact, there are only temporal arrangements, combinations, inclusion-disjunctions, and so on, of uncommon cultural relations' (Cohen 1988: 18). In particular (as we have seen), the academic historical monograph or article follows many of the discursive conventions of scientific papers in general (cf. Markus 1987). Such formal properties make the case being made persuasive: e.g. 'historians ... place such value on "followability"; it limits the possibility of awkward questions, it leaves less to explain'. They make narrative convincing, i.e. objectively true – after all, 'the advantage of third-person narrative is that it is the mode which best produces the illusion of pure reference. But it *is* an illusion, the effect of a rhetorical device' (Kermode 1980: 113, 117). The whole point of narrative is, therefore, its 'refusal of allowing disengagement from its own narrative form', its preventing the reader from thinking out 'how the told is told'. That's because 'in the same intellectual space the reader cannot both "follow" a "story" and think through every sememic ... connection' (Cohen 1988: 104, 230).

In other words, narrative sequence is persuasive because it replicates the "natural" surface-experience of ordinary consciousness, moving from task to task, moment by moment, day after day, reading and re-reading the world. It ensures that 'the facts run by the eye at the correct speed' (Menand 2003: x). History persuasively creates the illusion of objectivity, because the sequentiality in the historical narrative replicates the natural sequentiality of experience: 'the test of fidelity is deception ... The proposed measure of realism, in other words, is the probability of confusing the representation with the represented' (Goodman 1988b: 34). The reader is predisposed to accept the structure of the historical account because it coincides with the structure of his or her routine consciousness: 'the historian reproduces the competence of making a narrativized "world" overlap with a reader's [world]' (Cohen 1988: 232; cf. Lyotard 1979: 42). This coincidence also occurs as the historian constructs historical knowledge: 'the historian's questions are always ... in narrative forms ... Those provisional narratives provide a set of possibilities ... during the process of research. We can compare those narratives to mediating instances between questions and evidence, instances that deeply ... affect the way historical data are ... interpreted' (Ginzburg 1999: 101). Narrative sequence ensures that a present experiential structure (i.e. the representation in the historian's mind) can be taken for the objective reality of the past (i.e. as suggested by the evidence). In making the historically comprehensive past symmetrical with lived experience, sequentiality reinforces history's [*crg*] psychologistic stance. Replicating the structure of history within the structure of ordinary experience assimilates personal existence to history. Embedded in the asymmetrical (transcendental) abstraction that history [*crg*] is, the individual comes to see his or her own lived experience [*aesthesis*] as historical, hence as part of the abstract, rationalized, instrumentalized social order [*illusio*] history promotes. Lived experience thus comes already historicized. It is always already assimilated into whatever kaleidoscopic patterns of identitary thinking history's heterogenous materials happen to fall. History thus functions as an agent of socialization 'reinforcing prevailing group norms at every stage of personal individuation', 'ensuring through the learning-process that the individual's knowledge-interests conform to the external circumstances it lives in' (Habermas 1973: 162). It is truly 'the alibi of an alignment with obligatory values' (Cohen 1988: 329). Hence, for historians to 'define themselves in relation to the past by overtly writing themselves into it' as 'the only way history [can] *really* function to grasp *the* meaning of the past', is the exemplary socially affirmative, but personally self-alienating act (Munslow 2003: 155). The postmodern academic historian who does this is no different from his or her more traditional academic counterpart: Each is working with a 'rigged schema': each is 'deliriously self encoded as a cultural operator incapable of being transcended / overthrown by other discursive systems' (Cohen 1988: 97–8, 227).

As the conventional form of historical knowledge and its objective truth, sequential order is a technique for self-alienation. That's because, what is not narratable, will go unrecognized, not exist, be condemned to 'cultural death' – given that 'historical discourse presupposes as its material context the academic legitimation of narrative culture as such' (Cohen 1988: 18, 94). The view that, because of history, things are the way they are, the past cannot but take priority, is both absolutely normal and absolutely alienating: either way, it substitutes history's hyper-real reality [*illusio*] for ordinary, contingent experience [*aesthesis*]. That this subterfuge is never even noticed, assumed to be culturally legitimate, and even expressly advocated by postmodern history theory, shows how completely alienating it is.

(h.) The symbolic authority of self-affirming structure. Ultimately, history's objective truth comes down to the symbolic authority that underpins its basic assumptions, practices, and habits, that make historical knowledge seem "natural", i.e. normal, incontrovertible.

History's truthfulness is reinforced by its status as the dominant discipline in the humanities. History, a vast surveillance machine, has already claimed the pan-optical focal-point of truth whence it scrutinizes all things without scrutinizing, or being scrutinizable, itself (cf. Foucault 1975: 203ff.). After all, it is 'located in a place that one can do nothing about' (Cohen 1988: 28). This is the transcendental place of God the Father Himself, of paternal authority: 'History supposes that the place in which it produces itself has the capacity to constitute sense. ... The discourse of history supposes the rationale of place. It legitimates the place in which it produces itself, by comprehending everything else as affiliated or external to it' (Certeau 1975: 354; Braudel 1994: 15). From this transcendent, self-vindicating vantage-point history [*crg*] derives its symbolic authority to categorize and organize the past.

The asymmetrical, transcendental perspective permits history to be 'everything', to guarantee social reality. It creates identities, burdens, and constraints (cf. Certeau 1975: 41; Neustadt & May 1988: 232ff.). It demonstrates authority and competence in its entitlement and ability to construct narratives (Lyotard 1979: 40; Foucault 1975: 162–4; Marin 1978: 9, 88). Its strategies endorse affirmative social interests, 'devices' of political governance and managerial decision-making – after all 'seeing time as a stream has an enormous value ... to government decision-makers' (Neustadt & May 1988: 235ff., 246). It reinforces the same old thing, in recognizing that (i) 'the future has no place to come from but the past, hence the past has predictive value'; (ii) 'what matters for the future in the present is departures from the past ... which ... divert familiar flows from accustomed channels'; and operating through (iii) 'an almost constant oscillation from present to future to past and back, heedful of prospective change, concerned to expedite, limit, guide, counter, or accept it as the fruits of such comparison suggest' (Neustadt & May 1988: 251). In these ways, history as a self-affirming structure symbolically affirms the prevailing social structure.

Ultimately, though, its symbolic power is a fabrication. Ironically, the authoritative place that permits history to discern the real reality of all things is the last place for it to discern itself. It discourages self-reflection: if history always already holds the truth-position, why bother examining how it got there and what it does there? Hence, historians can never practice for history [*crg*] the objectivity they adopt for the past [*rg*]: to discount themselves and see what it objectively does. But that's the drawback of depending solely on history's affirmative and identitary practices. To objectivize history, historians would have to see it as something they couldn't *a priori* identify or affirm.

Phantom experiences

There is something uncanny about history. For Nietzsche (an unrespectable historian) history is a mix of intuition and curiosity, a 'sixth sense', a 'divinatory instinct'. Duby (a most respectable historian) concurs: 'the quest for sense is a captivating game whose charms resemble those of exploration, perquisition, even divination' (Duby 1991: 69). It goes with history's essential psychologism: the technics of information management responds to murky oneiric longings and nostalgic fantasies. History is synonymous with traumatic loss: the "mega-bulk" of historical knowledge symbolically substitutes for the real, precious life that time, circumstance, and human ingenuity eradicate.

The painstakingly faithful, technically accurate reconstruction of the past is a deeply melancholic activity: 'few people will guess how much sadness it takes to bring Carthage back to life', remarked Flaubert about his novel, *Salammbô*, that aimed to 'hold fast a mirage' of the ancient world (Flaubert 1961: iv; cf. Benjamin 1977: 254, §VII). Nowadays, however, there is something more. The dead, ever more of them, are being 'brought back to life' – routinely, daily, technologically, on television and radio, in films and videos, at heritage sites and in living museums, through computerized images and virtual realities, let alone in the usual articles, monographs, and text-books. It evokes the grim spectre of a traumatized culture versed in the practice of sadness, mesmerized by its own melancholy. And it would, reflecting as it does a political and economic world dominated by the death-drive – its way of bringing dead things that affirm it alive, reinforcing its way of making live things that threaten it dead (cf. Davies 2004:14). It is beyond doubt that, as a sublimated form of necrophilia, the practice of history affirms the dominion of death in contemporary culture. Its indelible achievements include the architecture of mass death, both the technological destruction of human beings, and the ecological devastation of their planetary home. Like the 'lord of time',

Krishna, 'come to bring death to the world', history materializes in its own mega-appliance, the atom bomb.[11] The mega-machine [*Makrogerät*; *Ge-stell*] that is the technologically managed world automatically manufactures '*megadeaths*' (Brzezinski 1995: 7).

An objective, empirical historical method is, therefore, anything but objective and empirical. Empiricism relies on a concept of sense-data intended to exclude the entire range of sensory experiences that actually goes into making history. Historical knowledge is never produced *ab initio* in a conceptually "clean" environment, as it claims. It is always governed by the rules of the relevant 'interpretive community', the historian's reputed place in the overall 'field' of the discipline, let alone by extraneous social representations that shape his or her outlook (cf. Rabinow 1996: 47–51). Empiricism also forgets that history deprives the world of both senses and sense, in the way it traumatizes individuals, communities, societies and nations by inflicting pain, mutilation, loss, death, genocide, extermination. In fact, in the purely academic discourse of historical knowledge history's death-drive hardly comes out except through uncanny, oneiric nostalgia. Otherwise its mortiferous potential, categorized as "myth", is banished. Still this suffices for history to release its phantoms into a world long since become phantasmic. With this mega-prosthesis inevitably comes phantom pain – but also, in the form of compensating illusions with their own hypnotic power, a temporary anaesthetic.

(a.) The phantasmic world. That history must be objective to capture the reality that was the past holds true only if reality is really real. It assumes that objectivity can be sealed off from agony, trauma, apprehension, hypothesis, wish-fulfilment, imagination, or dreaming. But the assumption is wrong. Private inhibitions and fantasies come out in repetitive-compulsive, obsessional behaviour (cf. Freud 1987); in extreme pain and deprivation and 'beyond the ground of naturally occurring objects', imagining offers the last and only remedy, 'the narrow extra ground of imagined objects' beyond which 'there is no other' (Scarry 1985: 166); the latest thing – the atom bomb – triggers mythical associations.

---

[11] This analogy occurred to Robert Oppenheimer, the Director of the Manhattan Project, when the first atom bomb was tested at Los Alamos on 16 July 1945. He is referring to the *Bhagavadgita*, XI. (cf. http://www.pbs.org/wgbh/amex/bomb/peopleevents/pandeAMEX65.html (8 November 2003)).

The assumption is indeed wrong: technology comes from a dream of total empowerment, hence, with the promise of a total problem-solving capacity (Sloterdijk 1983: 811). It is there to make wishes come true. The prostheses human science and technology create, could almost all have come from fairy-tales (Freud 1977: 87). Wish-fulfilment falls no longer to the imaginative poet but to the commercial entrepreneur 'investing in phantasms and speculating on the ruination of common-sense' (Valéry 1957 / 1960: II, 1024). As 'the means and capacity to make phantasms into reality and reality a phantasm [*Vorstellung*]', money has a 'transformative power' (Marx 1981: I, 635). Capital and technology, these historicizing forces, turn out to be truly magical: history can be whatever their managers wish it to be. The magic works primarily on the level of representation. Where technology makes fantasies real, reality becomes fantastic: the world itself becomes a phantom (Anders 1985: 129ff., 172). The mega-machine of information technology mutates reality into its mediatized representation absorbed by millions of isolated 'mass-hermits' through their main world-optic, the TV set. It suffuses subjective experience, bereft of its traditional reference points, with virtual reality (Anders 1985: 102; Virilio 1984: 108–9). The time delay between reality and its representation collapses into the synchronous production of the virtual; temporal sequence (e.g. the *longue durée*) dissolves with each blink of the eye into ever present, ever elapsing 'real time': 'actuality is what has always just happened' (Anders 1985: 131ff., 159ff.; Virilio 1984: 105). Consequently, the world is immediately experienced as nothing but a constant process of historicization (i.e. *aesthesis* absorbed into *illusio*). The flood of news and comment 'institutes in the name of reality a symbolizing language that both enforces the credibility of what it communicates and forms the spider's-web of our history' (Certeau 1987: 74). At the same time, because the mediatized images consumed are a heterogeneous mix of fact and fiction, document and fabrication, reality coalesces for each individual viewer into a solipsistic phantasm [*Vorstellung*]. That TV history flourishes at the same time as reality TV is symptomatic: the past made real goes with a present made unreal. Their common 'ontological ambivalence' makes them both phantasmic (cf. Anders 1985: 112ff., 131).

Furthermore, the history technology engenders its own oneirism. It serves an archaic desire. History dreams of supernatural omniscience – be it in the regressive longing to be rooted in the origin of all things through knowing their sources; be it in its comprehensive aspiration, as a knowledge-system, to embrace everything. Its reality principle is flexible. History is where absurdity happens: grown men jumping about on the moon, others flying aircraft into skyscrapers, others building transcontinental walls and fences, others still growing a human ear into the back of a mouse ... And history creates its own phantasms. The post-modern compression of space and time, with its acceleration of history, diminishes personal memory for the sake of historical hyper-consciousness (Nora 1984: xviii; cf. Harvey 1990: 62, 240ff.). It makes generating archive-material 'the imperative of our time'. Things change so fast: 'the archive is no longer the more or less intentional residue of memory that has been lived, but the voluntary and organized secretion of memory that has been lost'. It functions as a 'prosthesis memory' [*mémoire prothèse*], 'replicating lived experience, itself often unfolding as a function of the way it has been recorded' (e.g. as with news information in the media). The ever-accumulating archive is thus the 'clearest form of the terrorism inflicted by historicized memory'. It haunts the present, bereft as it is of clear explanatory principles: 'No-one knows what will ultimately constitute the past; an apprehensive uncertainty [*une inquiète incertitude*] transforms everything into a trace, a possible clue, a *soupçon* of history with which we contaminate the innocence of things'. The 'present regime of permanent discontinuity' is what makes this 'artificial hallucination with the past conceivable' (Nora 1984: xxviii–xxxii). Compulsive historicization already implies the "de-realization" of reality.

Lastly, technological process itself de-realizes. Technocratic expertise requires abstraction: it pursues its self-defined aims in its own methodologically hygienic world (Bloch 1985a: 603). It creates historical-conceptual value by sequestrating the naturally experienced object and sterilizing it to seal it off from its uncanny associations. The 'conceptually netted' object is thus assimilated in its 'object-ivity' [*Gegenständigkeit*] to the overall conceptual system of the discipline. It's allocated a place amongst other recognized values as part of "knowledge that is already known" (cf. Heidegger 1967b: 48; Aron 1986: 146). The object thus vanishes from experiential immediacy to be replaced by a sign of itself. In this abstract form it's soon instrumentalized or commodified.

(b.) Phantom pain. 'Phantom pain refers to a patient's experience of pain in a part of the body that has been removed surgically or traumatically' (Dijkstra et al. 2002: 578). Phantom limb experience

does not always involve pain. It can produce 'illusory movements, both voluntary and involuntary': e.g. 'the patient can "wave good-bye" or "reach out and grab" a telephone with the phantom' (Ramachandran & Hirstein 1998: 1619, 1624). But the pain it does cause, is excruciating and enduring ('up to 70% of phantoms remain painful even 25 years after loss of limb' (Ramachandran & Hirstein 1998: 1604)). After amputation of the leg or arm, the (phantom) toes feel 'as though they are being held in a tight vice', a 'slicing, cutting pain' occurs in the sole of the (phantom) foot and 'a chiselling pain' in the (phantom) ankle, the (phantom) fingernails can be felt digging deep into the palm of the clenched (phantom) hand (Oakley et al. 2002: 369; Ramachandran & Hirstein 1998: 1607). Phantom experiences can be attributed to various factors, certainly to stump neuromas, the remapping process in the cortex, and the corollary discharge from motor commands from the brain to the limb. Some are particularly intriguing. Those born without limbs still experience phantoms: this suggests the brain contains 'a primordial, genetically determined internal "image" of one's body' that survives intact for many years, if not the entire life-span. Those who lose a limb due to trauma find not only 'somatic memories of painful sensations . . . of the original limb being "carried over" into the phantom', but 'long lost memories' from that limb re-emerging as well (Ramachandran & Hirstein 1998: 1605–7, 1624).

The phantom limb experience [*aesthesis*] shows something different going on behind history. If history is a mega-prosthesis extending human power, it also compensates for damage to the body-tissue of the community, state, or nation, for a mutilated humanity, or simply for transience and death. If humanity were not traumatized and mutilated, transient and mortal, the prosthesis would be unnecessary. The history mega-prosthesis, therefore, needs to be always reliable, to perpetuate itself, to come up again and again with meaning, objectivity, and truth. It lets humanity pretend not that it is undamaged, but that it can adapt to, hence overcome, *any* damage. (History always has lessons that have to be learned.) However, in the light of genocide and the threat from "weapons of mass destruction", that conviction may be just one more exorbitant wish [*illusio*] the history-technology will have to make come true. Phantom pain hurts most where the trauma is keenest. There are its chronic manifestations: in Kossowo Serb-Albanian rivalry nags on through six centuries since the Serbs lost the territory after a humiliating defeat by the Ottoman Empire in 1389; in Northern Ireland Catholic-Protestant conflicts needle still more than four centuries after Henry VIII's establishment of a Church of Ireland in 1537. There are its acute forms: e.g. the First World War, both mass butchery and interminable work of mourning; or the Holocaust, both industrial efficiency and unrelenting agony of commemoration. Bound up with such phantom pain are deep somatic memories – mythical impulses, uncanny feelings, oneiric nostalgias – that do not make the history prosthesis comfortable to wear, however accurately it fits. The prosthesis itself, rubbing the abused stumps, surely exacerbates the pain.

But why should history not follow the cognitive model of phantom limb experience? The conventionally academic subject–object model is anyway redundant. Take the question of objectivity and truth. The patient does realize that the sensations are 'not veridical', that 'what he/she experiences is an illusion, not a delusion' (Ramachandran & Hirstein 1998: 1604). Conversely, the clear clinical message is that 'the phantom limb should be treated as "real" and the same pain management strategies applied as with a physically present limb' (Oakley et al. 2002: 371, 374). As phantom limb pain shows, illusion and reality are not mutually exclusive. Moreover, both life-impeding for the long-suffering patient and empirically demonstrable in clinical tests, this "illusory reality" is definitely objective. Crucially, it suggests that 'the real world does not actually constitute the world we perceive' (Merleau-Ponty 1990: 97). The brain does not "know" that the limb has gone: 'when motor commands are sent from the premotor and motor cortex to clench the hand, they are normally damped by error feedback from proprioception. If the limb is missing ... such damping is not possible, so that the motor output is amplified even further, and this overflow or sense of effort itself may be experienced as pain' (Ramachandran & Hirstein 1998: 1607). The limb was once there in the past – so too was the past. All pain and re-emergent somatic memory, it persuades the patient (the historian) it is still real – objective. And objective the phantom pain of history certainly is: here and now it is actually, objectively crippling. Lacking any damping feedback from the past, since the eradicated millions watch them in utter silence, having given them more than enough rope: historians (on their own admission) go in for strenuous effort "overflow" to compensate, to find out more, since more is always more. In this respect, the body of historical knowledge is no different from any other corpus of scientific knowledge. It situates itself 'in a "complete" and real world without noticing that this world is constituted by perceptual experience'. Behind this body of knowledge, i.e. 'anterior to number, measure, space, causality', is the 'field of lived perception' [*champ de perception vécue*], although it emerges only as a 'perspective on an objective world, on objects already endowed with stable properties' (Merleau-Ponty 1990: 235).

Referring to religion as the oldest form of historical recollection, Nietzsche remarks: 'only what never ceases to hurt remains in the memory. ... When man thought it necessary to create a memory for himself, he could not do so without blood, torture, and victims' (Nietzsche 1988: V, 295, II, §3) The process of civilization is necessarily cruel: the historically articulated memory of each creative spasm is nothing other than the prolonged aftermath of phantom pain. Historical reality, objectivity, and truth would not be real, objective, and true, if they were not a pathological illusion.

(c.) History as anaesthetic. Since the process of civilization is traumatic, the capacity to feel pain is endemic to survival. The fact is, 'humans with Congenital Insensitivity to Pain Syndrome continually suffer from a variety of traumatic tissue and bone damage and rarely live beyond the third decade of life' (Sufka 2000: 155). The causes of severe distress, projected into imaginative sublimations, have the potential to create divinities and their attendant laws and institutions, or world-historical conjectures and their substantiating theory and data (see Scarry in *The Body in Pain* on Judaism and Marxism, or Nietzsche in *The Birth of Tragedy* on Classical Greek culture (Scarry 1985: 181ff.; Nietzsche 1988: I, 36, §3)). Culture, be it in the form of systematic knowledge [*illusio*], be it in the form of art [*aesthesis*], is thus a form of pain management: pain produces ways of alleviating itself.

The 'virtual reality box' is a simple, but ingenious, prosthetic device. It consists of a vertical mirror placed inside a cardboard box with the lid of the box removed: 'the front of the box has two holes in it, through which the patient inserts his good arm and his phantom arm. The patient is then asked to view the reflection of his normal hand in the mirror, thus creating the illusion of two hands, when in fact the patient is only seeing the mirror reflection of his intact hand.' The patient then 'sends motor commands to both arms to make mirror-symmetric movements.' Consequently, he has 'the illusion of seeing his phantom hand resurrected and obeying his commands, i.e. he receives positive visual feedback informing his brain that his phantom arm is moving correctly.' As long as they kept looking in the mirror, patients could thus, e.g. "unclench" their phantom hand, hence diminish the phantom pain there, even enjoy the feeling of older movements "coming back". One patient who had lost a finger 30 years previously and not experienced a phantom for 28 years, found that using the box restored the phantom. This experiment implies 'that a dormant representation of the faded phantom must exist somewhere in his brain. The representation is ordinarily inhibited, but can be revived instantly with visual feedback' (Ramachandran & Hirstein 1998: 1621–2). A similar therapeutic effect occurs through hypnosis. It helps the patient to re-imagine the causes of the phantom pain, which provides virtual proprioception, which in turn feeds back to the somatosensory cortex. However, the therapy can go a stage further, even if the pain-relief may be only temporary. Phantom limb pain can also be eliminated 'using a hypnotically suggested hallucination of a mirror in a patient with previous experience of [Ramachandran's] mirror apparatus.' This 'hypnotically produced mirror' has 'a major potential advantage': it enables patients to 'recreate the imagery themselves and use it on a continuous basis for pain relief' (Oakley et al. 2002: 374–5).

These cognitive phenomena suggest some general inferences. Clearly, virtual reality, standing in for the lost body-part, 'resurrects' or 'revives' it as it once really was. The *illusio*, like the mesmerizing hallucination, has an objective, analgesic effect, precisely because it is illusory and hypnotic. Similarly, the socially received "body" of historical knowledge stands in for the past and "brings it back to life" – by operating as virtual reality (in the media), as *illusio* (in academic works). The phantom pain history [*rg*] inflicts, gets alleviated by history [*crg*] accurately representing the trauma-site. The image has to match the reality, the *illusio* be truly identical with its object, otherwise its objective, analgesic effect is diminished. (Phantom pain therapy is never completely effective for every patient, anyway.)

That history cannot be an art, this cognitive re-conception of history confirms once more. The aesthetic dimension lifts the sad weight of the world, sensitizes, enhances life. History anaesthetizes, de-sensitizes, broadens the scope of death. History is a socially dominant form of knowledge in the postmodern world of rapid, unprecedented, material change, because it alone both recognizes and soothes the trauma postmodernity inflicts. History's rationale rules because it is the ruling rationale. So the animosity between "traditional" history and its postmodern critique is both predictable and unexceptional. The powers that make history [*rg*] have always been both a threat to history [*crg*] and its necessary precondition.

What makes the postmodern dynamic different, is its key agencies' total power. They truly are 'engineers of world history' [*Ingenieure der*

Weltgeschichte] (Horkheimer & Adorno 1973: 37). Global finance, global technology, global political and cultural interests routinely make not just history, but the history they want. But this mega-capacity does leave them vulnerable, powerless to control the apprehension their power induces. They may keep their machinations secret, but not their consequences: e.g. terrorism, organized crime, technological catastrophe, environmental disaster (cf. Beck 1986, 2002; Benford 2000). So to manage for society the trauma its dominant forces inflict on it, hence to affirm both themselves and society, they resort to history. Thus virtual historical realities that are comprehensively manageable mirror present traumas that are increasingly unmanageable; a society mesmerized into seeing 'everything' as the same old historical thing soon accepts phantasmic catastrophe as normal occurrence: that is what history does. The splendid prosthesis god, with his glittering mega-machine, hides a crippled, traumatized creature, both haunted and hallucinating.

Variation 4
Symbolic Formations of Historical Sense

It's not just such fictions as "historical periods", "historical contexts", or "long traditions" that historicize the world. These explanations work only because the world is already historicized. What historicizes the world, is a historicizing reflex in human cognition. To look for sense and meaning means looking historically. Historicizing is the default setting of human self-reflection – as postmodernist theory particularly shows. It assumes history to be a 'narrative meaning production process', since 'creating moral meaning for the conduct of our lives today' is 'one of the most important' reasons for historians doing history (Munslow 2003: 174, 177). Mind, personal behaviour, and social practice are tuned in to history because they themselves have adapted to a historicized world. However, far from being illuminating, history is actually occluding. Apprehensively enough, it shows there never was anything except what there was: there never will be anything except what there will have been.

The following essays indicate history's occlusive effects in the symbolic sense formations it constructs – in (a) its understanding of itself, (b) its capacity to make human existence unviable, and as (c) the rationalizing, commodifying instrument of a totally instrumentalized, commodified society, and (d) the compulsive, symbolic perpetuation of traumatic experience.

History as a sense-management system

As a technical sense-management device, history would constitute the comprehensive sense of the world – if it were clear how much sense makes sense. History hedges its bets. It can always make more sense; it can always use more sense – more of the same. That's how it backs itself up.

History causes apprehension in the way it makes sense. When it comes to self-reflection, historians chant the mantra: those who forget the past are condemned to repeat it. In their eyes, doubting the veracity of history is like being morally defective – as though no-one (e.g. a historian) with a knowledge of the past (i.e. his or her own past) had ever repeated past mistakes. Suffice it to say, knowledge is vulnerable to abuse, the more vulnerable the less its practitioners reflect on what it does. Fraudulent views (e.g. Holocaust denial) circulate because history is heterogeneous and its plausibility imitable. As the technology of technologies, history is the key instrument of the social reality principle. Designed to be used by social interests, it gets abused by them. That makes the critique of its methodology more, not less, necessary.

History also causes apprehension in the way it unmakes sense – unmakes the very concept of sense. History is nothing if not revisionist: one historian's truth is another's "myth", to be debunked at all costs – and so it goes. The result, for sense, is totally corrosive: meaning does 'drown in a stream of becoming: the senseless and over-documented rhythm of advent and supersession' (Sontag 1991: 75). Historicizing does offer the human mind 'almost as second nature, a perspective on its own achievements that fatally undermines their value and their claim to truth'. 'The historicizing perspective' does reduce existence to 'no more than the precarious attainment of relevance in an intensely mobile flux of past, present, and future.' The result is indeed that 'even the most relevant events carry within them the form of their obsolescence' (Sontag 1991: 74–5).[1]

The more sense history acquires, therefore, the more it qualifies the sense it already has. The more it backs itself up, the more it needs to back itself up. History as a comprehensive form of cognitive organization can, therefore, never know if it is congruent with history as sense-production (i.e. as action). No one event contains within it a specific quantum of meaning. But that's what makes history so useful, so adaptable, so affirmative – be it for political legitimation, for constructing national identities, for justifying financial investment in

---

[1] Sontag realizes that 'there is no outflanking the demon of historical consciousness by turning the corrosive historicizing eye on *it*' (Sontag 1991: 75). Instead, to resist history's perpetuation of the 'same old thing', she affirms the intellectual stance of aphorists such as La Rochefoucauld, Lichtenberg, Novalis, Nietzsche, Rilke, Kafka, and Cioran: thinking as a means of knowing, as an 'extreme act' – even if it should go against oneself (Sontag 1991: 75).

the culture and tourist industry or in academic research. In any case, history's social utility will ensure that history [*crg*] and history [*rg*] remain incongruent. As the management-system of social sense, history [*crg*] operates for other than historical reasons. It must always meet the heteronomous demands on the social production of knowledge – from shifts in disciplinary conventions and variations in the focus of research to intellectual fashions and dominant cultural-political ideologies. Predicated on the identitary reflexes operative in academic (i.e. technocratic) thinking, history can't help identifying with how things are the way they are – particularly since history sees itself as instrumental in things being as they are.

Though history [*crg*] and history [*rg*] are essentially incongruent, it is possible to construct 'ideal-typical' patterns of relationship between them that manage the sense history makes. These respectively involve: (a) historical reflexivity; (b) the over-production of sense; (c) postmodernist interferences; (d) the concept of the 'end of history'; and (e) the idea of the 'antiquatedness of man'. But this profusion of historical "sense-types" produces confusion of existential meaning. How should anyone know which sense-structure to trust? History, being everything, amounts *practically* to nothing.

(a.) **Historical reflexivity:** *cognitive organization and the logistics of sense-production tend to obstruct each other.* The modern world is inherently technological. The problems of the world are essentially problems of the technology that manages it: 'In a world where everything has become available, as a product of the human hand, the age of making excuses is over. There are no constraints any more, unless we ourselves permit or force them to prevail' (Beck 1986: 372). Technology does go wrong, and where it does, as in cases of environmental disaster (Chernobyl, Bhopal), it makes living impossible. But even when it functions as intended, technology creates risks and causes apprehension. Propelled by its own technological dynamic, knowledge generates its own irrationalism, its own taboos: 'internally it becomes a matter devoid of truth, externally an issue devoid of enlightenment' (Beck 1986: 278).

So too with history. What defines the historicized world is its historical reflexivity: a constantly self-authenticating historical consciousness constantly shapes historical action. The historical problems of a historicized world are, therefore, essentially technical problems of the historical disciplines that manage it. Where the history technology catastrophically malfunctions (e.g. Auschwitz, Hiroshima, the former Yugoslavia, the West Bank & Gaza), it makes living impossible. But even when it functions normally, it causes apprehension. History, like any other branch of knowledge, requires professional specialization and this follows disciplinary convention rather than social reality (cf. Beck 1986: 271ff.). Conversely, the broad, popular interest in history, recognizing the way things used to be, endorses the way things still are. With its perpetual recourse to the 'same old thing', its identitary thinking, the discipline leaves changeable circumstances unchanged (cf. Beck 1986: 280).

Clearly the old adage about needing history to avoid past mistakes is obsolete. It's a component of the history-machine that needs scrapping. Anyway, it was always giving trouble: 'many of those who can remember the past are condemned to repeat it anyway. Plenty of people who remembered the past were sent to die in the extermination camps. Their knowledge availed them nothing, because events were out of their control' (James 1992: 32). Future action doesn't tie up with past memory. History evinces mostly patterns of repetition-compulsion, both physical [*rg*] and symbolic [*crg*]. After roughly ten thousand years of it, it's time to ask how much more must happen before anyone remembers not to repeat it. Because in history "more" is always regarded as "more truth", historians continue to insist on more fact, more objectivity, more analysis – lest anyone forget. But the whole, catastrophic, world situation is based on nothing other than more – more fact, more objectivity, more analysis. The problem is: what real sense does all this "more" really make?

Just as with, e.g., the space station programme, the globalized economy, the internet, mankind has in history, *with history*, produced history as a technological contrivance that far outstrips its own "natural" powers. Historical realities as a whole exceed anything human senses alone can comprehend: '**Individual, actual society, history** are, however, as such no concrete component parts **of the work-processes of experience**; as horizons they are incommensurable quantities' (Negt & Kluge 1993: 782, 784 (emphasis in the original)). The fantastic, world-changing, technological imagination, backed by massive commercial investments, 'speculates on the ruination of common-sense' (Valéry 1957/1960: II, 1024). Moreover, 'the history of modern (post-classical) politics has hitherto been the history of format-errors', the failure to find the appropriate size of human community that avoids both totalitarianism and the isolation of minority groups (Sloterdijk 1995: 70). In any case, history's supreme technological capacity to divulge the 'real reality', the total explanation, induces in the empirical individual an inferiority complex, a 'Promethean embarrassment' (Anders 1985: 32ff.). The technology is so perfect, it exposes how fallible the technicians maintaining it, how blinkered the clients using it, really are. History may well be the memory of humanity; it really ought to prevent it from repeating past mistakes. But it's not the memory of particular social individuals faced with real-life choices. That's because knowledge [*Wissenschaft*] itself has been refunctioned. As personal culture [*Bildung*], it no longer strengthens the individual's capacity for reflective judgement. Instead it reinforces the organizational efficiency and economic productivity of society. Consequently, individual scope for reflective action diminishes as the social management systems impose their own technological solutions (cf. Habermas 1973: 106, 111–12). In any case, history's sophisticated technology always underperforms in the short term. Come to that, it proves unreliable in the long term too (Benford 2000: 4–6)! No wonder that, when it looks into the mirror of history, mankind still sees nothing new – only, somewhat apprehensively, itself, as it always has been.

(b.) **Over-production of sense:** *cognitive organization overcompensates for deficiencies in sense-production (i.e. history [rg]).* The crucial question is: how much sense makes sense? History's answer is: more sense always makes more sense. But this "more sense" is not consistently available. Ironically enough, its absence might not even matter. It could even be advantageous. After all, 'if there were no problems with discovering what happened in the past, there would be no need for historians ... and thus no history – just "what happened" without dispute or question' (Arnold 2000: 77). Consequently, 'if it were possible completely to determine lived experience, writing history would be both impossible and insipid' (Veyne 1996: 228). This argument shows how indeterminate history is: total recall makes it redundant, total amnesia impossible. It oscillates apparently between the barely adequate and the not too much. It leaves historical comprehension with two options: 'either to explain a lot, but badly, or to explain a little, but well' (Veyne 1996: 228).

The question should rather be: how do the surviving records represent historical reality? This has not to do with "bias", but with the conventional relationship between the signifier (i.e. the archival record) and the signified (i.e. the past "itself"). This issue is not just (i) *quantitative* and (ii) *qualitative*; but also (iii) *structural* and (iv) *deterministic*.

(b.i) The *quantitative* aspect derives from history as 'the actualization of the potential', since, as Gay explains, 'compared to the mass of possibilities inherent in any situation, the number of possibilities realized is small.' Like Blumenberg, he sees history in terms of conflicting tendencies in a force-field: 'Most events are vectors of competing irreconcilable forces which might well have issued in other, often far different consequences, or in no consequences at all.' The result is the uneven texture of the historical record: 'Modern historians like to complain that they are overwhelmed by the crowding of clamorous events; yet when one reflects on how much might have happened, the texture of what did happen proves remarkably thin.' How much of the historical record – consequently, how much sense – survives depends on history [*rg*] itself: 'While the modern historian selects among the surviving evidences of the past, history itself ... has already done much of his work for him.' Hence, his conclusion: 'history is an implacable Darwinian battle, in which few aspirants succeed in fighting their way into the permanent record' (Gay 1979: 9). What the historical record fails to recognize, inevitably remains unknown.

(b.ii) The *qualitative* aspect is outlined in Charles Péguy's essay, *Clio: A Dialogue between History and the Pagan Soul* (1909). Clio first stresses that history is not about reality, certainly not a 'reality substitute'. What would happen in reality (she asks) if you were to put reality into history? It would take a day to write the history of a second, a year to write the history of a minute, a life-time to write the history of an hour, and an eternity to write the history of a day. You can do anything (she says) except write the history of what you are doing. You cannot construct a historical narrative in its entirety: you can find neither where it begins because there are no pre-set limits to history, nor where it ends because each history is part of an infinite texture (Péguy 1961: 242). Clio also stresses that, though history relies on sources, it also gets written despite them. There are, she says, two kinds of history, Classical and Modern. Where Classical times are concerned, she lacks documents (she says); but, in respect of Modern times, she lacks a lack of documents. Thus she deplores the inherent inadequacies of record-keeping as such. For this reason she doubts that history, as single, integrated cognitive form, can provide any overarching, quasi-metaphysical sense (Péguy 1961: 244).

(b.iii) *Structurally*, material evidence functions as a metonym for the past, not as the past as it "really" was. Given the quantitative and qualitative variations in record-keeping, history's relation to the material supporting its versions of the past will be figurative.

Describing a piece of evidence as a "source", historical practice glosses over this obvious point. In the police archives of Revolutionary Paris Arlette Farge claims to be 'apprehending what is real', 'touching what is real' (Farge 1997: 14, 18). But the documents and artefacts she encounters are samples, swatches of reality, invested with a symbolic value derived from the knowledge she already knows. Like a swatch of material, in itself it indicates the whole reality it belonged to and now must stand in for. The real *properties* of the sample make it a micro-cosmic *version* of the total historical past it comes from.[2] The sense of the document, let alone of the archive, is supplied by metonymy.

History is an effective technology for synthesizing information *because* of its indeterminacy and inadequacy. On the large scale, it works as a metaphysical prosthetic: it finds an autochthonous reason in what human beings do. On the small scale, it is a technique for managing what remains from the past: it enables historians to make inferences from the surviving material and organize them coherently. But history also co-ordinates its macro- and micro-technologies so that the resulting total sense exceeds the sum of all its particular, verifiable truths. Deep down historicism still rules. Professional historians might not explicitly endorse the determinism typified (e.g.) by Herder, Hegel, Marx, or Spengler. Instead, they go in for micro-studies based on academic expertise and disciplinary specialization. But contingent, small-scale constructions of historical sense are no more valid than these epic hypotheses. They need, and they still imply, a wider context for their technical interests to make sense. What makes specialized micro-studies make sense, is a "weak form" of historicism.

(b.iv) This *determinism* now shows up typically in the text-book or monograph series. These enable historical knowledge to be more persuasive, more meaningful. When a particular study joins a series of particular studies, 'more sense' always accrues to it. The series, elaborating a general, regulative, historical idea, always implies more than the sum of its constituent elements. Conversely, the particular study can disclaim any historicism of its own, while being enhanced by the historicist rationale of the series-structure.

---

[2] 'A [fair] sample ... is one that may be rightly projected to the pattern ... or other relevant feature of the whole or of further samples. Such fairness or projectibility, rather than requiring or guaranteeing agreement between the projection made and an actual feature of the whole or of further samples, depends upon conformity to good practice in interpreting samples' (Goodman 1988a: 135–6). Elicited through this figurative, hermeneutic procedure, historical evidence is more than just a 'source' (cf. Arnold 2000: 61) or a semiotic 'trace' (cf. Farge 1997: 41).

From the University Library shelf take *The Origins of the Wars of German Unification* from the series 'The Origins of Modern Wars' (edited by Harry Hearder), well used by student readers – to judge from the volumes' battered appearance. The series-title, exemplifying a comprehensive, nominalist view of historical problems, comes from identitary thinking. The series works chronologically, beginning with *The Origins of the French Revolutionary Wars*, and including, e.g. *The Origins of the Italian Wars of Independence*, *The Origins of the Russo-Japanese War*, *The Origins of the Second World War in the Pacific*, *The Origins of the Korean War*, up to *The Origins of the Arab-Israeli Wars*. Its historical scope imputes an underlying rationale to modern history. Here historicist perspective and commercial interest promote each other: knowledge already known converts easily into commodified information. The series editor merely provides the historicist gloss, thus: 'like the previous volumes in the series,' this volume on the wars of German unification 'is valuable ... as *a further illustration* of the complexity of *the general question* as to why governments have resorted to the murderous method of warfare in attempts to solve their problems ... (Carr 1999: ix (my italics)). He stresses in the specific German case general *technical* issues concerning warfare evinced by the series as a whole, e.g. the responsibility of apparently neutral great powers, the primacy of domestic over foreign policy, strategic miscalculation, and the financing of it. He doesn't exactly formulate general laws of history: they would need to be predictive. He does do the next best thing – propose the elements of such laws: e.g. 'what is the responsibility of the Great Powers who are ... neutral, to stop the war from starting?'; or: 'governments *usually* go to war only if they can afford to do so, unless they are blatantly attacked by an aggressive neighbour' (Carr 1999: ix–x (my italics)). They are formulated like regulative principles or determining factors: e.g. 'The danger points in the history of humanity have *usually* been when a single issue has brought a direct confrontation between Great Powers or superpowers, and there has appeared no room for manoeuvre' (Ovendale 1992: x (my italics)); 'Ian Nish shows very clearly that holding a significant post by a certain individual at a particular moment in a crisis *may well* affect the way the negotiations develop. ... Someone – some people – were responsible for wars, and *more often than not* those people were not all on the same side' (Nish 1985: viii (my italics)).[3] The series-editor

---

[3] The General Editor's preface has gone from *The Origins of the Arab-Israeli Wars*, 3rd edition (1999).

clearly believes in the 'lessons of history' as a weak form of historicism. 'We can learn only from the past,' he says, 'since the past is all we have'. Rejecting 'slick analogies between past and present situations', he insists that 'certain general points ... can and must be learnt from history' (Joll 1994: vii). But, as these examples show, these must-learn general points are merely banalities of informed hindsight. Moreover, they are ethically myopic: they naturalize war (cf. 'origins') as an endemic human condition, rather than deplore it as a pathological symptom of a contingent international order, as a crime against humanity 'that breeds amorality throughout the world' (Allott 2001: 266).

Because it overcompensates, history's a technology that's always giving trouble. The problem is, it has to meet an excessive demand for meaningfulness. It would actually make most sense to 'stop the nonsense' of always making human existence make more sense (cf. Marquard 1986: 40–1). Historical sense, oscillating between the barely adequate and the not-too-much, appeals because it offers a quick fix, a neat, synthetic blend of meaning-substitute [*illusio*]. However, there are no short-cuts (Marquard argues): the human *sense* of things here and now [*aesthesis*] emerges indirectly, laboriously, through the individual's personal and social commitments (Marquard 1986: 44). Doubting that there might ever be enough sense, could prove more reassuring. Particularly for the purposes of ordinary life, less is always more (and history a distraction). 'In its unprincipled, modest, contingent and unsensational way', life is meaningful: 'It makes sense – it is worthwhile – admittedly not because it can be shown to be meaningful, but ... because it cannot be shown to be devoid of meaning' (Marquard 1986: 52).

(c.) Postmodern interferences: *sense-production jeopardizes cognitive organization.* Besides history, language could claim to be a technology of technologies. A conventional system of signs to order the world, a grammatical system to generate its meaning: language makes the world meaningful. It enables its inhabitants to talk about it to one another, to make sense of it, themselves, and their place in it (cf. Arendt 1974: 4).

Language is the last defence against absurdity. Mere literary form, tragedy, redeems humanity's senseless suffering, as Nietzsche observes (Nietzsche 1988: I, 35ff., 38ff., §§3, 4). Nothing but rhetoric disputes the ultimate triumph of death, as Bossuet's *Funeral Orations* confirm. Language, therefore, makes a world for history to happen in, let alone a means of representing it. The earliest cave drawings, the patterns carved on the megaliths of the Armorican peninsula, indicate that sign-systems were required to fix the information society needed to remember. The technics of remembrance have to depend on the technicalities of the linguistic means employed: 'Style is form and content, woven into the texture of every art and every craft – including history' (Gay 1988: 3).

As a technology of technologies, language has its own highly developed logistics of sense-production. History is produced by politics and society as types of human *agency*; language, in all kinds of textual and semiotic forms, presents itself as a type of symbolic *action* (cf. Burke 1966: 5ff.). History offers causal *analysis*; language offers a 'grammar' or a 'rhetoric' of *motives* (Burke 1969a; Burke 1969b). History recycles old news; 'literature is news that STAYS news' (Pound 1968: 29). Clearly their functions diverge. History is a metaphysical prosthesis, language the servo-system it operates with. It is configured to have its own 'autochthonous reason', as a cultural purpose in itself. It compensates in situations where how much sense makes sense is unclear. Language, as a medium (like the sculptor's stone, wood, or bronze), is in itself a cognitive, symbolic resource. It offers more, and qualitatively different, sense than historical categories can deal with. However, language is a technology that gives even more trouble than history itself – not to mention that, like human sentience, it has its own natural history: it too mutates. Even where it works well as *poiesis* in the creative arts, it needs philologists, grammarians, semioticians, narratologists, critics, to maintain it. When it breaks down, spewing out cliché, euphemism, technical jargon, bureaucratese, as it usually does, it needs them even more to correct it.

History and language operate in conjunction with each other (e.g. like the electrical and fuel systems in an internal combustion engine). On the cultural level, language is conventionally assimilated to historical entities (e.g. a people, a nation), which establishes history's absolute claim on all human phenomena (Schmidt-Biggemann 1991: 33). On the historiographical level, discursive practice ensures that the 'historical text prevents disengagement from its own sentence forms', so that 'the reader cannot think out the text's organization' (Cohen 1988: 104, 105). How far this artifice has receded from consciousness, how very 'natural' it now seems, only emerges when the language-system defaults to its own concerns, such as grammar, semantics, semiotics, or rhetoric (cf. Cohen 1988). Then the systems' incompatibility emerges. The conventions of linguistic sense-production – e.g. the tropes underlying historical discourse – inevitably challenge history's own conception of its organizational competence (cf. White 1982). On top of this, the constant surges and shorts in the linguistic system cause feedback that further corrupts the already faulty technics of historical comprehension. However dismantled, history's own persuasiveness proves spurious.

Postmodernism is the quintessence of these vicissitudes of the linguistic system and its representational function. It intensifies the metaphysical doubt about how much sense makes sense. It suggests we get even 'less truth' than we realized. It implies that history is no genuine replacement part, but a dodgy, reconditioned spare – a source of apprehension. It alleges that history, as a technology, might always have been compromised, so that by now no-one could tell if it ever had worked properly. Seeing history jeopardized, historians take against postmodernism. However, dogmatic insistence on disciplinary convention is no effective response.

No response is effective. The fallible technology of linguistic representation may well let history down, but it's hardly a reliable replacement. Where sense is at stake, replacing one faulty device with another makes no sense. Postmodernism comes to a standstill anyway, if history fails. On the one hand, as the debate over "postmodern history" shows, the discipline has attempted to reconfigure its organizational competence, particularly its truth-claims and narrative methodologies, to accommodate reservations voiced by philosophical pragmatism, structuralism, semiotics, and deconstruction (Jenkins 1997; Munslow 1997, 2003). Historical practitioners may just concede that history is essentially a form of *écriture*, a discourse primarily loyal to its own constitutive rules. They can still insist that this reflexive insight does not compromise the way history operates – but only by pretending that a discipline and its methodology are unrelated.

On the other hand, postmodernism, specifically the deconstructionist critique, would replace historical understanding with a vision of the temporal immanence of humanity. Why is history necessary now (Jenkins 1999)? But this idea is even more problematic. It just reaffirms history as the *same old thing* – as the last thing, as the *ultimate consideration*. History is not so much invalidated by philosophical analysis, as merely superseded by a different philosophical analysis. To assume that the world has moved beyond historical understanding, only affirms the 'essentially historicist conception' postmodernism perpetuates (cf. Zagorin 1990: 264). Postmodernism becomes just another symptom of a deeply historicized reality: 'the post-modern condition of plural and provisional perspectives, lacking any rational or transcendental ground or unifying world-view, is our own, given to us as a *historical fate*, and it is idle to pretend otherwise' (Gray 1995: 153 (my italics)). In any case, the deconstructionist critique succumbs to its own fallibility, since 'a form of criticism that cannot come up with any other principles than those it deconstructs, condemns itself to remaining within the circle defined by the objects it criticizes' (Castoriadis 1996: 77). All arguments must make a claim to sense and truth within recognized parameters of meaning (cf. Apel 1996: 26–7). Deconstructionism must presume history to be meaningful: its critique would otherwise be meaningless. But in making history fallible, it makes itself redundant. It closes on a utopian prospect, human existence which would still be temporal but not historical. But this idea seems attractive, only because, illogically, it doesn't deconstruct itself. Conversely, if the postmodernist critique of history is valid, it cannot be entirely a postmodern critique. That history may have once been legitimate but is not now in postmodernist terms, is a fallacious inference. Postmodernism reveals only conceptual or methodological inconsistencies (e.g. the inherently discursive construction of reality) that always already existed but hitherto remained inconspicuous.[4]

To promote a critique because it claims to be actual (as with postmodernism) doesn't guarantee its validity. How that critique relates to actuality, is what matters. The "culture war" between

---

[4] Ironically enough, this conclusion is confirmed by Southgate's – somewhat embarrassed – historical legitimation of historical postmodernism. As he says, 'to make any sense of where we are, we seem still to need to know where it is (or was) that we have come from' – 'surely a paradox that postmodernists ... with their readiness to accept inconsistencies ... might ... accept with equanimity' (Southgate 2003: 89). Consequently we are told, e.g., that 'to Copernicus ... can be ascribed the first move towards that decentring that we have seen to characterise postmodernism' (Southgate 2003: 97). Here, then, postmodernist theory falls in on itself: the latest thing is still the same as the same old thing. As usual, we still need history's identitary thinking to reveal how things have got to be the way they are. The same catachrestical blurring of explanatory categories occurs: since when could "inconsistency" be puffed up into "paradox"? Even so, this line of argument has an excellect precedent: Derrida himself, the symbolic cornerstone of postmodern history theory. What did he lately propose for defending the university's unconditional commitment to critical thinking? History – and lots of it. The humanities, he insists, 'should study their history, the history of the concepts which, in constructing them, instituted the disciplines and were co-extensive with them' (Derrida 2001: 67–8). Thus, in this politically naïve essay (in respect of universities' real delapidated state), the latest deconstructive whizz fizzles out in the same old psychologistic-genetic approach.

postmodernist academic history and traditional academic history is far less important than the fact that both currently exist, even flourish, *together*, in the academic environment. That's what defines contemporary culture. That's what needs analyzing. The prevailing cultural heterogeneity, the relativity of all values, might originate in nineteenth-century historical consciousness. The self-conscious attention to disciplinary boundaries, questions of logocentrism, the management of cultural constructs, the retreat of meaning from the 'big picture' or the 'grand narrative' to highly localized problems, i.e. everything associated with postmodernism, result from historical consciousness turning on history itself. Postmodernism would thus be the historical *hyper*-consciousness of the historicized world, a self-conscious product of historical understanding, the ludic, 'unruly' proliferation of 'disobedient', hybrid forms of historical *illusio*, so many illusions of illusions – modernity reflecting on its own historical logistics 'with scepticism and contempt' for their lack of performativity (cf. Jenkins 2003: 68; Beck 1986: 261). But the recourse to micro-historical issues, as a reaction to large scale logistical failure, does not generate any more sense. The outcome is the collective redundancy of multiple divergent, highly specialized interests, as any bibliography of current historical research or any major conference programme in the United States and Europe shows. It just turns all historical practitioners, each locked into their particular expertise, whatever it happens to be, into nothing if not postmodernists by another name. They themselves largely constitute what Jencks calls 'the first para-class to have it all ways' – a diagnosis close to Nietzsche's critique of the heterogeneity of historical interests. Their situation – i.e. their familiarity with different historical periods and cultures – uniquely 'allows itself to be a compound of previous ones, a palimpsest'. It 'can not only include previous ones, but benefit by their existence'. Meticulous historical scholarship provides them, as true postmodernists, with 'the luxury of inhabiting successive worlds as [they] tire of each one's qualities' (Jencks 1989: 56). The postmodernist critique simply highlights this ultimate, overall *senselessness* of historical sense-production.

(d.) 'The end of history': *cognitive organization gets disconnected from sense-production.* How much sense *in* history does it take to make history make sense? More is needed, but how much more? Perhaps too much is produced: the technology overcompensates. Perhaps too much is expected: it is designed to overcompensate.

But perhaps too much is required: but surely the postmodernist reduction is too severe? Let's cut through this. Let's just say: there's already quite enough sense in history as it is and it supports just the right amount of meaning. This stops future events affecting it. Stabilizing historical meaning endorses the already established power structures and their institutions (cf. Schmidt-Biggemann 1991: 73ff.). This is history as 'knowledge already known', 'the same old thing', the absolute identity of 'how our world got to be' with 'the way it is' – in short, history as identitary thinking taken to its ultimate, ideological conclusion. It disconnects history's capacity for organizing the world from the sense it produces in it. This strategy might seem to compromise historical comprehension. But in this historicized world where historical knowledge influences historical events, it helps ensure historical facts support the sense made of them – as Fukuyama demonstrates: 'If events continue to unfold as they have done over the past few decades', i.e. in the direction of liberal democratic states, 'the idea of a universal and directional history leading up to liberal democracy', i.e. the idea he inferred from history in the first place, 'may become more plausible' (Fukuyama 1992: 338). Fukuyama's 'end of history' thesis exemplifies this strategy: the circularity of the argument is deliberate, if not inevitable.

History [*crg*] here overcompensates because it has to meet a demand for total sense. But what makes this demand, is a claim for total power. Behind Fukuyama's assertion is a cultural psychological reflex inherent in all hegemonies: a need to stop history, to deny change, to invalidate future opposition. He thus represents a version of Popper's conclusion that historicists try to 'compensate themselves for the loss of an unchanging world by clinging to the faith that change can be foreseen because it is ruled by an unchanging law' (Popper 1974: 161). Befitting both this apology for domination and its inevitable pessimism, Fukuyama's new thing is the same as the same old thing. He associates his idea for a 'coherent and directional history of mankind' with the 'most important attempts to write secular versions of a Universal History ... undertaken in conjunction with the establishment of the scientific method in the sixteenth century', not to mention the conceptions of history elaborated by Kant, Nietzsche, and – most importantly – Hegel (Fukuyama 1992: xii, 58).

The basic elements of Fukuyama's argument are conventional. There is the conception of history as an organic, 'evolutionary' process, endorsed by the conviction that this process articulates and responds to human nature: 'we can argue that history has come to an end,' he says, 'if the present form of social and political organization is *completely satisfying* to human beings in their most essential characteristics' (Fukuyama 1992: xii, 136). With its Hegelian pedigree Fukuyama's position resembles that adopted by Aron or Ortega y Gasset: like all historians, 'he already knows the "plot"' (cf. Cohen 1988: 223). It also endorses the conception of history as a technology of technologies. Fukuyama selects 'modern natural science as a possible underlying "mechanism" of directional historical change, because it is the only large-scale social activity that is by consensus cumulative and therefore directional.' These same technologies also drive the economy to produce new consumer goods and so create wealth (Fukuyama 1992: 80–1). There is also the idea of history as a specific realm of human responsibility and self-assertion, here evincing not theodicy, but the drive for social recognition, as embodied in the Platonic concept of *thymos*. This 'desire for recognition,' says Fukuyama, 'remains a form of self-assertion, a projection of one's own values on the outside world'; it can, therefore, also lead to conflict between individuals as well as between peoples or states (Fukuyama 1992: 172). Recognition, being central to Fukuyama's theory since it provides the driving force of history beyond economic interest, thus ensures an autochthonous reason operates in history.

But what, in the end, makes this neo-liberal view of history persuasive? Like all other types of social and philosophical attitude, it's manufactured by the historian himself (cf. Marquard 1982: 112ff.). Fukuyama employs a strategy that has both an affirmative and a negative aspect. In affirmative terms, Fukuyama's theory of history simply vindicates what already happens in the Western world. It exemplifies identitary thinking: equating 'how our world got to be' with 'the way it is' (cf. Cannadine 1999: 8). In a historicized world what happens now is only the *latest* thing, the most recent edition of everything that has already happened (cf. Davies 1999: 250–1). Given that it entails a capitalist society with a high standard of living and of education and freedom of consumer choice, how could economic liberalism fail to affirm itself historically (Fukuyama 1992: 204ff.)? In negative terms, Fukuyama's theory cancels aesthetic reservation. In sharp contrast to the Romantic context of Hegelian thinking, Fukuyama declares imagination redundant. He is, instead, closest to the complacency of Leibnizian theodicy that tends, in some form or other, to underpin political or social hegemony: 'Today,' he alleges, '*we have trouble imagining* a world that is radically better than our own, or a future that is not essentially democratic or capitalist.' Certainly, he concedes that a host of minor ameliorations could be made to it, but he still affirms that 'we cannot *picture* to ourselves a world ... different from the present one, and at the same time better' (Fukuyama 1992: 46 (my italics)). He thus confirms Popper's observation that 'the poverty of historicism ... is a poverty of the imagination'. As Popper explains: 'The historicist continuously upbraids those who cannot imagine a change in their little worlds; yet it seems that the historicist is himself deficient in imagination, for he cannot imagine change in the conditions of change' (Popper 1974: 130).

Fukuyama's position is diametrically opposed to *Historics*'. He makes the aesthetic dimension redundant: 'Other, less reflective ages also thought of themselves as the best, but we arrive at this conclusion exhausted, as it were, from the pursuit of alternatives we felt *had* to be better than liberal democracy' (Fukuyama 1992: 46). Even so, this denial of the aesthetic is not the most negative feature of the theory. That is rather its denial of hope, its terminal pessimism. Less developed states will flounder in the torment of history (old-style) even as they struggle to attain its economic liberal end. What awaits them when they arrive is the predicament already confronting the prosperous western world: either the fate of those Nietzsche called 'the last men', slow moral and physical degeneration in the midst of private comforts; or the prospect of gratuitous violence in pursuit of recognition as 'we return to being first men engaged in bloody pointless prestige battles, only this time with modern weapons' (Fukuyama 1992: 276; 328).

Lastly, the most persuasive feature of Fukuyama's thesis is that, for all the demands it makes on history, it itself is undemanding. With its scientistic pretensions, historicism in any case requires 'that we simply have to submit to the existing laws of development'. It further implies that 'the most reasonable attitude to adopt is *so to adjust one's system of values as to make it conform with the impending changes*' the particular historicist vision envisages (Popper 1974: 53–4). Fukuyama's 'end of history' thesis offers the ultimate refinement of this position, which is the ultimate affirmation of identitary thinking. Of adherents and non-adherents alike: it requires them just to do what they already do. The theory must be successful: it's already in practice.

(e.) **'The antiquatedness of man':** *sense-production disconnects itself from cognitive organization.* Historical comprehension collapses under the pressure of events: too much happens to make sense of it. This syndrome sounds like postmodernist *chic*. In fact, it's the stark conclusion those at the centres of power come to. Still, it suggests that postmodernism coincides with, if not actively endorses, the post

Cold-War neo-liberal melancholy, brought on by the crumbling of the political structures that have organized the world since 1945 – as Zbigniew Brzezinski seems to suggest. 'History has not ended but has become compressed,' he insists (Brzezinski 1995: ix). He starts from the premise of 'the notable acceleration in the velocity of our history and the uncertainty of its trajectory', and goes on to outline its implications. One is the dissolution of the idea of historical epochs. In the past, epochs 'stood out in sharp relief, and one could thus have a defined sense of historical progression'; but today 'history ... entails sharp discontinuities, that collide with each other, condense our sense of perspective, and confuse our historical perceptions'. Another is the asynchronicity between living and understanding that also involves coping with the sense-deficits it produces. On the one hand, 'we live in a world that is already in fact very different from the one which we have begun to comprehend'; on the other, 'by the time our comprehension has caught up with the new reality, the world is likely to be even more drastically different.' The result: 'discontinuity is the central reality of our contemporary history', which in turn 'demands an intensified debate regarding the meaning of our era.' For Fukuyama imagination may be redundant; for Brzezinski it is once more critical. One further implication is the uncertainty of cultural and ethical orientation, given 'the massive collapse, especially in the advanced parts of the world, of almost all established *values*'. Ironically, the exponential expansion of 'humanity's capacity to control itself and its environment', along with the even faster growth of its material expectations, coincides with the increasing vagueness of 'our societal criteria of moral discernment and of self-control'. 'Ethical perplexity,' he concludes, 'does not enhance historical comprehension' (Brzezinski 1995: ix–x).

Not just the pressure of events disconnects historical action from historical meaning. Their qualitative nature, their metaphysical, let alone meta-historical significance, does too. In *The Antiquatedness of Man* Günther Anders also observes that 'the epoch of the succession of epochs has been over since 1945'. He is referring to the beginning of the nuclear age with the dropping of atomic bombs on Hiroshima and Nagasaki. He takes it as axiomatic that in this third industrial age, which is also the age of the totally historicized world, humanity is 'incessantly producing its own decline' (Anders 1986: 20). This age so drastically invalidates what has preceded it, that, whatever happens next, it will be the last age. This is no postmodernist, neo-liberal pessimism; rather historical apprehension sharpened by a sense of metaphysical scandal.

Anders produces a list of hitherto life-orientating concepts that have now become obsolete. Two of them are particularly significant. First, there is the antiquatedness of the concept of an 'organic history' of humanity, of history as the unfolding of human nature. The historicized world produced by history as the 'technology of technologies' has by its own logic produced other 'technologies of technologies', radically inimical to human nature. Anders targets genetic engineering. This is a technology of technologies since it technologically modifies humanity itself. However, as *homo faber*, humanity already has the technological capacity for creating itself and its biosphere. Now genetic engineering would turn human beings into 'raw material' for manufacturing other human beings. In holding out the prospect of producing mutant forms to order, it destroys the very idea of a 'species'. In other words, genetic engineering takes the idea of the identity of history and human nature to its logical conclusion: society assimilates nature totally to its historical demands (Anders 1986: 22–5).

Second, as a counterpart to the threat to the survival of the human species genetic engineering represents, there is the nuclear threat to the survival of all living creatures (Anders 1986: 24). Nuclear technology may be seen as a technology of technologies because of its destructive power that nothing withstands. But that isn't the prime source of the anxiety its induces. After all, humanity has always been exposed to overwhelming, elemental forces as in volcanic eruptions, earthquakes, or tidal waves. Rather his apprehension stems from what he calls 'the theology of the atomic situation' (Anders 1986: 404). In other words, nuclear technology takes the idea of humanity's metaphysical responsibility for the world to its logical conclusion. With history, humanity relieved God of the task of redemption. Now, with the idea of nuclear destruction, it also relieves Him of the need to deliver a Final, *apocalyptic* Judgement (Anders 1986: 407–8). This is what it ultimately means for humanity to be a 'prosthesis god'. The 'present apocalyptic danger', says Anders, has become 'immeasurably more serious than earlier apocalyptic dangers for hardly ever being clothed in religious language'. This is because the science of delivering over-kill is gathering pace. History still continues but only on account of humanity's 'apocalyptic blindness'. Conversely, it may be that in a historicized world, this last, late 'culture of the death-drive', humanity's self-incrimination in history, through history, with history, is so blatant that it does not require divine judgement to determine humanity's guilt. In any case, what history has produced, has paralyzed human comprehension. Certainly, 'the fact that it [i.e. nuclear apocalypse] has not yet happened, does not disprove the fact that our age is a, if not *the*, last one' (Anders 1986: 408).

These anomalies between history (as action: sense-production) and history (as comprehension: as cognitive organization) confirm history as an indeterminate discipline – truly 'the realm of the inexact' (Ricœur 1964: 80). Given its claim to articulate the sense of the world and govern human affairs, that should be a source of apprehension, not just 'embarrassment'. How much sense makes sense? What kind of sense (organic, metaphysical and technological) makes what kind of sense? No one knows. It makes sense because it always makes some sort of sense, because humanity *needs* sense. Still, history's inherent indeterminacy endorses postmodernist allegations that history hardly makes sense: e.g. because of the unreliability of established reference-points that compromises coherent, traditional structures of meaning (cf. Lyotard 1979: 63ff.; Virilio 1984: 27). And historians blame outsiders for subverting their discipline. How perverse! The sense of history subverts itself.

The faith of fallen Jews: on the reliability of history

'History is always a lie' (Lessing 1985: 106; cf. 1984: 193). Lessing's visceral mistrust is an antidote to the 'senseless' [*sinnlos*] historicization of the world and its 'more is always more' syndrome (cf. Lessing 1983). As a catalogue of barbarity and promoting a sterile, technical intellectuality, Western civilization and its cultural heritage are decadent (Lessing 1981: 24, 52–3). This radical disillusionment is symptomatic of the collapse of the high expectations of social self-fulfilment for Jews raised by the prospect of Jewish emancipation – a protest against the rootless abstraction of Jewish existence in its eventual, assimilated, historicized form.

Jewish conceptions of history evince a problematic historical consciousness. European-Jewish philosophers are exercised by a *hyper*-consciousness of history, by the awareness that what has been done to the Jews has been done not just in history, but by history. Their historical thinking agonizes over not just coming to terms with a traumatic history, but also how to confront an already historicized existence and the historical hyper-consciousness that goes with it. It connects with the central themes of *Historics*, i.e. (a) the impossibility of living in history (history as *apprehension*); (b) the questionable validity of history as a means of organizing reality and reflecting on the human condition (history as *illusio*, as an-*aesthesis*); (c) the need to get behind history so as to get on terms with it and its fatality.

(a.) The impossibility of living in history. The Jewish predicament tests history's reliability as a basis for existence. When the modern, political constitution of German Jews was being elaborated, history offered an inviting prospect. Its meta-historical meaning, as conjectured, e.g., by Gotthold Ephraim Lessing's *Education of the Human Race* (1777), Herder's *Ideas for a Philosophy of the History of Mankind* (1784–1791), or Kant's 'Ideas for a World-History with a Cosmopolitan Purpose' (1784), promised the realization of human autonomy. Certainly Judaism had its own history, was its own history – as scripture, in the *Torah*, in the *Talmud*; as religious ritual, in the recurrent holy days (cf. Rosenzweig 1996: 351ff., 410). Still, these historical conjectures enticed German Jews to relinquish the history they had and they were. The modernisation of Judaism appeared to involve assimilation to the stronger, more persuasive dynamic of world history. History, the always latest thing, could only vindicate Judaism's same old thing. As Heinrich Graetz argued in 1846, by emerging provisionally from their narrow confines and getting involved in the manifold variety of the life of the world, Jews could only gain in self-knowledge and self-confidence (cf. Graetz 2000: 45). In other words, Jews gained admission to a world that was already historicized. But the historical world they joined had an essentially Christian eschatalogical structure. It had already marginalized Judaism (cf. Graetz 2000: 42). Judaism entered a historicized world that had already historicized it.

Ambivalence towards history, at least, was the consequence of this move. In modern Jewish experience, 'history becomes what it had never been before – the faith of fallen Jews', so that 'for the first time history, not a sacred text, becomes the arbiter of Judaism' (Yerushalmi 1996: 86). Judaism would figure merely as a transient phase in the development of a rational "universal history". In Germany, where emancipation involved not just assimilation to the dominant society, but also identification with its dominant historical aims and values, it produced the 'double ruination' of Judaism (Scholem 1995: 28). Emancipation did raise the public profile of Jews. But the historicization of Jewish life, the perception that Jewish orthodox observance now belonged to the past, occluded the social situation of assimilated Jews, anaesthetized their sense of reality. Between 1830 and 1930 Jews did make an unprecedented historical contribution to European culture and society in this 'golden age' of secular Jewish culture (Steiner 1979: 125ff.). However, in rendering the perceived "Jewish threat" invisible, assimilation confirmed the anti-Semitism of those who, advocating an *organic* conception of Germanic, if not Aryan, history, repudiated Jewish emancipation in principle.

What, then, does history do? What history does: it makes Jewish existence vulnerable. It becomes vulnerable, not just because of age-old religious prejudice, nor even because of social or economic resentments, but because – after the Holocaust particularly – it has no other refuge than history itself. The European-Jewish situation exemplifies what happens when only history is left and when a people is left to history. With its distinctive historical hyper-consciousness, European-Jewish culture generates an impossible psychopathology that comes out in typical, reflex responses to history – as the following examples suggest.

(a.i) 'New specimens of humanity'. The late eighteenth-century philosophy of history (just mentioned) regarded liberal humanism as the ultimate sense of history. It established an abstract historical framework for an ideal, human solidarity. In removing prejudice and discrimination, it would sanction Jewish social emancipation. Emancipated Jews were to become representatives of this new, humanist ideal, 'new specimens of humanity', a prospect fleetingly manifest in a momentary configuration of political and social circumstances (Arendt 1986: 57). But Jewish emancipation reveals the disjunction between history and the ordinary world of everyday life, between the abstract idealism it projects and the contingent, material location of human existence. In practice, it produced the paradoxical predicament of assimilated Jews in the eighteenth and nineteenth centuries. Caught between pariah and parvenu status, they were 'educated enough not to behave like ordinary Jews, but ... on the other hand accepted only because they were Jews, because of their foreign and exotic appeal' (Arendt 1986: 57). In thus endorsing the dominant historicized values of bourgeois social domination, they came to symbolize everything those 'frustrated and resentful elements' advocating a different, i.e. an organic, racist historicization opposed (cf. Arendt 1986: 53, 170). The suicide of Stefan Zweig in 1942, in Brazil, his refuge from Nazi-occupied Austria, shows how 'spurious' this ideal world-citizenship would become, once the dominant historical circumstances turned vicious (cf. Arendt 1986: 53). Zweig's novellas and essays are amongst the last flowerings of nineteenth-century liberal humanism. They were also amongst the books burned by the Nazis in Berlin in 1933. His autobiography, *The World of Yesterday* (1944),

reads like a *Who's Who* of early twentieth-century European culture, so assimilated was he to the cultural élite. It also describes the emergence of fascism in the 1920s, the Nazis seizing power, the practical effects of their anti-semitic policies, historicizing this cosmopolitan world, consigning it remorselessly to oblivion. It conveys Zweig's growing *apprehension* for the security of his own life as it became increasingly vulnerable as the world he knew vanished (cf. Davies 1981: 108).

(a.ii) 'A process of glaciation'. Far from bringing emancipation, participating in the already historicized world threatened self-destruction. What made non-religious Jews vulnerable, were histor-ical-political events and the opportunities for assimilation they offered. 'This is the only real danger for our people,' Lessing asserts: 'our talents are our danger' (Lessing 1984: 219). Assimilation could be self-destructive, because it could lead to social isolation, illness, even suicide. In *Jewish Self-Hatred* (1930), Lessing castigates figures symbolic of German-Jewish assimilation (i.e. Paul Reé, Otto Weinin-ger, Arthur Trebitsch, Max Steiner, Walter Calé, and Maximilian Harden) who, unobservant of Jewish law and adrift from their communities, helped create a culture as intellectually abstract as the historicized world in which they lived. That's why they represent 'the universal-human, the unpersonal, a cold apotheosis' (Lessing 1984: 76). Living 'as though on telegraph wires, in between nationalities, their tap-roots drawing ethereal sustenance from *Geist*', they typify the Western-European Jewish contribution to 'international culture'. Like Ahasuerus, the Wandering Jew, who lives for all time, they personify heterogeneous historicized culture that contains 'everything', yet still needs always more. Like the face of Ahasuerus, their faces too reveal a person who 'does everything, is good at everything, fingers everything, grasps everything but still lives *apprehensive* [*in der Angst*] of having missed something important, of having overlooked something significant'. Whatever they felt society required of them, they complied with and promoted it – even (as in the case of Maximilian Harden and Arthur Trebitsch) anti-Semitism. Hence, these German-Jewish intel-lectuals represent 'the tragic spectacle of a centrifugal life that is directed against itself' (Lessing 1984: 38–9 (my italics)). That's when, too late, they discovered that assimilation could mean unbearable self-estrangement. Replacing observance of Judaic tradition with devotion to an abstract, historicized culture led assimilated Jews to regard intellectual progress as a surrogate for both the forsaken community and belief in Biblical miracle. Lessing calls this 'a process of glaciation', since, far from promising a fortunate destiny, it makes the insistent

consciousness of being Jewish more a motivating irritant, if not, in the end, a life-diminishing obsession (Lessing 1984: 68–9). Ironically enough, Lessing's immediate experience told him this. That's what makes *Jewish Self-Hatred* a penetrating criticism of historicization and its effects.

(a.iii) Eternity invaded by historicity. If history proves treacherous, one remedy is to de-legitimize it. In *The Star of Redemption* (1921) Franz Rosenzweig offers both a way out of history and a heightened, metaphysical consciousness of the human predicament. The book systematically explores the epistemological and ethical implications of the divine creation of the world, God's self-revelation to humanity, and the ultimate certainty of redemption. It exults in a sense of existential urgency. It would articulate life-affirming values in the immediate aftermath of the First World War and the catastrophic collapse of civilization it represents. It resists a historical situation that otherwise vindicates the nihilism and cultural pessimism associated with Nietzsche and Spengler. But the book also reasserts Judaism as humanistic and future-orientated, to counter the histor-icized humanism [*Bildung*] supporting the 'cultural system' of assimilated, 'confessionalized' Jews in Germany (cf. Volkov 2001: 123ff.; 192).

In *The Star of Redemption* history has no significance in itself. The past is obsolete and reified because it is past; the future, understood as the progress of the world, is simply a projection of the past, of the same old thing: 'every moment has the guaranteed certainty that its turn will come and may be as sure of coming to be as a past moment is of having already been' (Rosenzweig 1996: 253). History completes a triadic scheme of relationships between God, humanity, and the world. The world (as divine creation) and humanity (ethically transfigured by divine revelation) need history – not for its own sake, but for redemption to happen in. History is a means to the philosophical end that Rosenzweig's reaffirmation of Judaism discloses: the unfaltering contemplation of divine truth as it is revealed in the geometry of the countenance of fellow human beings (Rosenzweig 1996: 469–71). What Rosenzweig provides here is a version of the Augustinian idea that, through history, humanity finishes what God began. But Christian eschatology leaves Redemp-tion to the last moment, to the end of history. This Christian concept collapses with mankind in desperation, assuming the guilt for the evil it has committed. Judaism is imbued with the hope that at any moment the Messiah could come and install the kingdom of God on the ruins of history. *The Star of Redemption* is a-historical not least because it urges humanity to hasten the coming of the Messiah. Eternity could break into history at any given moment: 'even today the whole of the future is within reach' (Rosenzweig 1996: 365). Rosenzweig's idealism failed to protect Jewish existence: that's self-evident. This failure is heavy with consequences. Recourse to philosophical idealism a decade before Hitler seized power seems – with hindsight – a colossal political misjudgement. As Emil Fackenheim points out, 'the price for [Rosenzweig's] return to Judaism can no longer be paid'. His 'postmodern return to the premodern Jewish faith' involved 'making *all* Jewish existence ahistorical' – which actually meant 'sacralizing it' (Fackenheim 1994: 33). Rosenzweig certainly intended to reaffirm Judaism: Fackenheim insists that he actually left it mortally exposed. What the future held, was not the expected inception of messianic days, with historicity invaded by eternity. Instead, with the Nazis' intention to eradicate Jews, hence Judaism itself, it meant the very opposite: 'eternity itself ... invaded by historicity', an even more decisive 'plunge into history' (Fackenheim 1994: 95,100).

(a.iv) The search for a historical home. Ultimately, the quest for security in history meant Jewish existence had to reaffirm its own historical-political agency. In Theodor Herzl's *The Jewish State* (1896), the Zionist agenda evinces both historical hyper-consciousness and history as a management technology. That history in itself has made the Jews suffer, compels Herzl to propose the idea of an autonomous, internationally recognized Jewish state. The long years of persecution have already 'hyper-sensitized [*überreizt*] the Jewish nervous-system' (Herzl 1996: 102). He has (he says) 'no need to invent the conditions of Jewish existence that history has brought about', nor even to defend the Jews, since 'everything rational or even sentimental that needs to be said on that subject has already been said'; the Jews have become oppressed and discouraged by their 'historical sufferings' (Herzl 1996: 9, 14, 79). All the more reason then to search for a historical home, for a home in history, a historical home that can be historicized – as the state of Israel has been since its foundation in 1948. A Jewish state would finally dispel the scourge of anti-Semitism. This is where history as a management technology comes in. Herzl's historical hyper-consciousness turns the tables on the Jews' oppressors and historicizes them. In the post-Enlightenment world (he insists), the desperate plight of the Jews is an 'anachronism', the 'Jewish question' a 'hangover from the Middle Ages that, with the best will in the world, the civilized nations cannot sort out' (Herzl 1996: 14–15). The modern world has provided the Jews, in

their bid to found their own state, with technical resources and financial institutions that 'hitherto did not historically exist' (Herzl 1996: 35).

The Jewish State seems utopian. Its pragmatic orientation presupposes a European-wide, Jewish "ethnic solidarity" or political-cultural consensus that did not exist at the time it was written or in the subsequent formation of the Israeli state (cf. Volkov 2001: 43ff.). What makes the project sound plausible (as the choice of metaphor shows), is its underlying, *organic* conception of history. (What other conception of history could offset the idealistic humanism that supported a treacherous, abstract assimilation?) Herzl justifies his plan by asserting that he aims to ensure the survival of the 'ethnic personality' of the Jews: 'Whole branches of Judaism may die and fall away; the tree lives on' (Herzl 1996: 19). For this reason the Jewish state would have to be set up in Palestine. Herzl envisages the 'transplanta-tion' of whole communities to their 'unforgettable historical homeland', even if this means the loss of customs and memories. But they would not be 'torn brutally from their patch of earth'; rather 'lifted carefully, along with their roots, and transferred to better soil' (Herzl 1996: 37, 67). Nevertheless, with its political idealism, Herzl's project is as illusory as Rosenzweig's: it's just a different historical illusion. The existence of Israel has not dispelled anti-Semitism. Besides, in becoming a historical agent, the Israeli state hardly guarantees its own security. Instead, it finds in history only what other historical agents found: further occasions for self-incrimination, further reasons for being *apprehensive*.

(b.) 'An irreplaceable function in the economy of being'. The Jewish predicament exposes the inadequacy of history as a social management technology. It constantly comes up against the impossibility of living in history, faced as it is with the 'grimness of the present', 'too much history', and the 'longest shadow', Auschwitz.

(b.i) 'The grimness of the present'. Most palpable is the sense of historical disillusionment. It comes from being historically hyper-conscious in a totally historicized world. There is no obvious remedy: 'all efforts to escape from the grimness of the present into nostalgia for a still intact past, or into the anticipated oblivion of a better future, are vain.' Arendt thus sees through history's affirmative function: 'We can no longer afford to take that which was good in the past and simply call it our heritage, to discard the bad and simply think of it as a dead load which by itself time will bury in oblivion.' The 'reality in which

we live', is utterly conditioned by history. As the emergence of totalitarianism has shown, 'the subterranean stream of Western history has finally come to the surface and usurped the dignity of our tradition' (Arendt 1986: ix).

This hyperconsciousness of history exposes the mechanisms of its reality management. Jewish existence thus acquires a privileged position. It can stand up to history: after all, 'it exists in the world for as long as there has been a world'. It has survived whatever historical vicissitudes it has faced, so it is entitled to refuse whatever verdict history pronounces on it. Hence, Judaism has an 'irreplaceable function in the economy of being': it alone 'has the power to pass judgement on the visible and organized forces of history, to resist them if necessary, with its head held high or bowed, but always with a stiff neck' (Levinas 1984: 232–3).

(b.ii) 'Too much history'. Conversely, history cannot reassure Jewish existence. Let's momentarily suppose that its claim to be the explanation of 'everything' were justifiable. Let's provisionally suppose, you had to know a people's history to see how they got to be the way they are. What history would reveal how Jewish existence came to be the way it is? In the attempt, its heterogeneity reveals its inevitable arbitrariness, its "comprehensivity" betrays its illusory coherence.[5] The reason is: what determines Jewish history is its indeterminate character. Even in historical-technological terms it is not clear what history is meant by Jewish history: Jewish history in Biblical times, pre-exilic or post-exilic? Jewish history of the Diaspora, but of which communities in which countries and continents, and in which of those countries' and continents' epochs? Contemporary history but of the Diaspora (again) or of the state of Israel? The subject, "Jewish history", breaks up. These histories could be also written from any number of standpoints: Judaic (orthodox, liberal, reform), Zionist, assimilationist, contemporary political. These standpoints themselves would reflect the generation the historian belongs to as well as the variety of historical methodology he or she adopts. As a result, any overall sense of history disappears. Noting the lack of consensus about

---

[5] Explaining his 'selective' approach to Jewish history, David Vital affirms the identitary logic behind historical reconstructions: 'coherence depended on setting a limit to the questions to be dealt with and on being as clear as possible ... about the terms on which answers were to be ... formulated. Above all, both questions and answers had to be *geared* to ... the final determinants of the Jews' situation' (Vital 1999: viii–ix (my italics)). Here too the tautology driving the history technology (cf. *geared*) shows how things 'got to be the way they were'.

how history should manage its meaning, one Jewish historian wonders (like *Historics* itself) if there is not simply 'too much history' (Weiss 2002: 229ff.). The obvious, illustrative case is the Holocaust and its remembrance, coloured by many conflicting claims made on it and the particular historical-political interests driving them (cf. Zimmermann 2000). Certainly the historiography of Jewish history seems increasingly problematic for Jewish historians. It excuses its helpless heterogeneity feebly, in the same old way, in terms of 'scientific norms that shift over time' (Myers 2002: 74). Lessing's scepticism seems vindicated.

History as a social management-system, a technological ancillary to state power, had, therefore, little hold on Jewish existence, vindicated by Judaism. Rather the social management-systems, the state powers history operated with, marginalized or excluded it. 'Lacking for long periods of time any territory or any state of their own, the Jews traversed history as a "people of memory"': a chain of tradition, both spiritual and genealogical, gave Jewish existence its meta-historical meaning (cf. Nora 1986: 656). Designed to weld territory, state, society, customs, beliefs together into tradition, heritage, and identity, history could, in any case, never offer anything more to the Jews than they already had. Toleration, civic rights, human respect, what Jews for long periods did want, are not historical, but ethical values, implicit in the very fact that human beings do not just exist, but need to co-exist, that the world-order is essentially an 'inter-human order' (cf. Levinas 1972: 82–3; 1991: 118–19).

If unable to offer Jewish existence anything it did not already have, history could jeopardize what it did already have. The historical illusion of Jewish emancipation was the conviction that history could afford the ethical recognition that was never actually in history's power to give. In a historicized world everything becomes historicized, even ethical values that transcend the historical process. Accordingly, the everyday, existential situation the self encounters the other in, that creates mutual ethical responsibility, could also be historicized, managed by a historical process that happened to operate through citizenship and equal rights as institutionalized norms. However, what can be historicized, can be historicized more and the apparently "new thing" prove to be the same old thing. Jewish assimilation exacerbated Jewish historical vulnerability. The Jewish predicament in history thus confirms that history always reinforces and authenticates itself. Historicization generates its own momentum: the Nazis' historicization of historicized Jewish existence proved catastrophic.

(b.iii) 'Remembering after Auschwitz'. A paradox apparently lies at the heart of the Jewish historical predicament. History is ineluctable. The only way out is the 'organized oblivion' of the Nazi concentration camps, making death anonymous, depriving the individual's life of meaning, 'as though he had never really existed' (Arendt 1986: 452). But history is also deceptive. As self-incriminating fatality, history is in no place to judge. Rather, it is always susceptible to being judged, which opens up the possibility of human freedom from history. Confident of eternal life lived out through genealogical links to its ancestors and descendants, the community of Jews, being rooted in itself, is estranged from history. Whatever else it needs for its existence (e.g. a state, laws, territory), is purely external (Levinas 1984: 41–2; 270–1). Resolving this paradox comes down practically to 'the choice ... not whether or not to have a past, but rather – what kind of a past shall one have' (Yerushalmi 1996: 99).

The paradox of the Jewish historical predicament is thus the paradox of historicized existence as such. It requires reflecting on Judaism and Jewish existence to see this, because history as a social management technology, fails to. It plays up the ineluctability and plays down the ethical reservation. In revealing how things have got to be the way they are, it automatically precludes radical difference. In postmodern culture, all values, particularly ethical values, are heterogeneous and already historicized. But philosophical reflection on Jewish existence does puncture this seamless veil of the ever-same. Its own conflict between historical ineluctability and personal freedom replicates the fundamental split between *illusio* and *aesthesis* in historical experience in general.

The historicization of the Holocaust is an illustrative case. There is the view that the Holocaust needs historians, that the Holocaust needs to be assimilated to the knowledge already known, to the 'historical culture' of the same old thing. Michael Marrus is resigned to relying 'increasingly upon historians to transmit what is known about the massacre of European Jewry', since 'no-one else is likely to do so in a way which commands credibility and standing in our culture'. He sees the need 'to integrate the history of the Holocaust into the general stream of historical consciousness and to apply to it the modes of discourse, the scholarly techniques, and the kinds of analyses used for all other historical issues'. He intends that the Holocaust 'be acknowledged as an important part of the modern historical experience and not just an episode in the history of the Jewish people'. He expects Holocaust history 'to be in as sound a state as the general historical culture of our society' (Marrus 1993: xiii, 202).

But there's also the view that history, as a total management technology, affirms the same abstract culture, the same instrumental thinking, the same social reification, that motivates totalitarian politics. Referring to historical discussions of the Holocaust, Yehuda Bauer observes: 'There are hardly any easier ways to dehumanize the dead after their murder than by unconsciously imitating the Nazis and turning them into objects once again – this time objects of historical, sociological, or other research. ... the combination between *Techne* and Clio can indeed be deadly' (Bauer 1980: 47 (my italics)).[6]

Integrating the Holocaust into the ineluctable dynamic of history [*illusio*] is incompatible with the immediately ethical and emotional attachment to its victims [*aesthesis*]. Certainly, the need to wrest some meaning from the egregious crime Auschwitz symbolizes does really require both history and memory, both a dispassionate audit of all the evidence and deep sympathy for the victims' suffering. But the history technology is not value-neutral, i.e. its technical neutrality automatically attenuates ethical response. In his discussion of the historicization of the Holocaust with the German historian, Martin Broszat, Saul Friedländer brings this out. He starts from the premise, he says, 'that the transition from an area of knowledge invested with considerable personal commitment to a "purely academic" form of history represents both a psychological and epistemological *illusion*' (Broszat & Friedländer 1988: 367 (my italics)). Historicization, constructing the wider social context of Nazism, placing it in a more comprehensive, historical narrative, takes the focus off its criminal intent. Moreover, the claim that a distance of some fifty years is adequate to establish a historical perspective, unaffected by the Nazi era is problematic. The passing of time seems more to magnify this era, complicating the process of historicization. (This is the classic issue of historical indeterminacy: after what time period does a historical period of time make most sense?) Apart from just documenting what happened, Friedländer concludes, what the Holocaust requires is a new, as yet undiscovered form of historical description (Broszat & Friedländer 1988: 354–5, 368, 371).

Jewish experience places enormous strain on the history technology: the Holocaust is disastrous overload. As a result, the technology is irretrievably compromised. There will never again be a

---

[6] With 'Techne' and 'Clio', Bauer is alluding to Franklin H. Littell (1975), *The Crucifixion of the Jews*, New York: Harper & Row.

"general stream of historical consciousness" nor a "sound state of historical culture", given that the Holocaust is a 'rupture in history', that it represents an unprecedented 'paralysis of the metaphysical capacity', and that in any Post-Holocaust hermeneutic the principle that fails is 'the assertion of an unbroken historical continuity from past to present' (Fackenheim 1994: 193, 201, 231, 260). Once the illusion of comprehension shatters, the sense of history, the way history is sensed, inevitably changes. Clearly: ' ... to remember after Auschwitz is different from remembering before Auschwitz. Something has changed: we cannot "do history" as usual' (Hartman 1996: 136).

In this light, and following the impact of Nora's influential *Sites of Memory*, it is not surprising that a substantial part of Holocaust scholarship has become aestheticized, dealing with the construction and evolution of Holocaust memories, the representation of the Holocaust in a wide variety of media and contexts (e.g. Hödl & Lappin 2000). That has become a disciplinary technology in itself, due to Jewish memory being not a 'closed repertoire', but 'a field of forces constantly generating and reshaping themselves' (Nora 1994: III, 1010–11).

Ultimately, the historical catastrophe Auschwitz confronts each and every one with their own, essentially apprehensive reaction to being implicated in history. That becomes clear intuitively, in moments of reflection, when, e.g., one contemplates the names, legions of them, of the deportees inscribed so painstakingly over the entire surface-area of the interior walls of the Pinkas Synagogue in Prague. These do not testify to a 'modern historical experience': how can annihilation be an "experience" for the living? Nor will they ever be assimilated to the conventionalities of historical explanation. What's left is the rhetoric of tragedy, since possibly only 'a modern Aeschylus and Sophocles could cope with this theme: but they would do so on a level different from that of historical interpretation and explanation' (Deutscher 1981: 164).

(c.) 'Exploding the continuum of history'. The process of Jewish emancipation looks like a 150-year-long experiment in historicization. It shows what history does. Coming both from the near elimination of the Jews from history and from the "eternal contemporaneity of the past" in Judaism itself, European-Jewish attitudes challenge history's knowledge conventions (cf. Yerushalmi 1996: 96). If history really is a

process of progress and catastrophe, a 'machine from hell', it's imperative to see what's behind it (Benjamin 1977: 255, §IX; Adorno 1978: 315, §149).

(c.i) 'Knowing the sense of history before the event'. As chosen by God, the Jews are co-terminous with the world and its history, even if Jewish life had to be lived against it. For the same reason the Jews are co-terminous with humanity. Rejecting the compromise of a local, assimilated identity, Rosenzweig insists: 'the Jew, as a Jew is a human being; the Jew, as a human being, is a Jew' (Rosenzweig 2001: 32). A combination of universality and particularity, of tradition and actuality, Judaism perceives that the "objective" order of history never is the ethical order of justice. It already 'knows the sense of history before the event' (Levinas 1984: 133). It knows the whole set-up is compromised. The way to redemption cannot, therefore, lie through history, least of all through human progress in history. As a way of getting there, history has proved catastrophic (Scholem 1992: 66–7).

History, therefore, cannot be a segment of eternity, a murky prelude to the Last Judgement. With its "inside knowledge" on the sense of history, Judaism knows viscerally what it does. History's same old thing is, therefore, not to be passively, endlessly re-enacted. It cannot be accepted as an ethically and cognitively binding, objective order. That would postpone the inauguration of a humanly just world indefinitely. Hence, for Judaism 'eternity is not a very long time, but a tomorrow that could just as well be today' (Rosenzweig 1996: 250). Judaism, therefore, establishes an imperative for justice, in history, but 'against the grain': 'purity occurs within the impurity of the world' (Benjamin 1977: 254, §VII; Levinas 1984: 200). It is a 'non-coincidence with its time', bolstered by its messianic conviction that at any moment 'a new Logos, a new humanity … would untie the tragic knot of world history ' (Levinas 1984: 99, 297). Thus Judaism exemplifies the attitude to adopt against history and an already historicized world – a combination of vigilance and commitment.

Judaism is a heightened form of consciousness, because ethics, establishing a realm of inter-human responsibility, is an 'optic of divinity': divinity is revealed uniquely in inter-human solidarity. To be conscious, says Levinas, is 'to have time to reflect', 'to refuse neutral and impersonal principles, Hegelian and political totalities, the seductive rhythms of artistic illusions' and 'to take time to judge history as opposed to being judged by history' (Levinas 1984: 223, 408). This vigilant consciousness is focussed on the present time, what Benjamin calls the 'now-time' [*Jetztzeit*], to assess each moment for its messianic potential before it gets irrevocably historicized. The past still has its own 'now-time'. What it was for itself appears fleetingly as it's refunctioned by history [*crg*] into the same old thing. So too does its particular moment of happiness, its own messianic expectation, before the drift of historical events sets in. To get back to the everlasting "now" of the past, to uncover the secret index of messianic promise it contains, means exploding the abstract continuum of historical time and its perpetual reiteration of the ever same (Benjamin 1977: 251–2, §II; 253, §V; 258–59, §§XIV–XV). With vigilance comes commitment, active resistance to history and its identitary thinking. The messianic moment brings history to a standstill: in 1830 in Paris revolutionaries shot at the clocks to stop time itself (Benjamin 1977: 259, §XV). The ethical moment, the inauguration of a world for the human species, will represent something different.

And it really is time to dishabituate oneself from thinking that history bears unique testimony to humanity, to dispel the illusion of an essentially historical, necessarily historicized, human nature – to see that history and historical thinking are actually nothing human, but its negation, a form of 'connivance with mortality' [*complaisance pour la mortalité*] (Levinas 1984: 293]. What makes us human is something much more primordial, language, speech: 'the evolution ... of subjunctives, optatives, counter-factual conditionals and of the futurities of the verb ... has defined and safeguarded humanity,' Steiner observes. 'It is because we can ... conceptualize the Monday morning after our cremation; it is because "if"-sentences ... can ... deny, reconstruct, alter past, present and future, mapping *otherwise* the determinants of pragmatic reality, that existence continues to be worth experiencing' (Steiner 1997b: 85).

Always to speak one's vigilant insights and reservations, is the commitment of ethical action. And for this life-affirming reason: 'If left to themselves, human affairs can only follow the law of mortality, which is the most certain and the only reliable law of a life spent between birth and death.' What interrupts this law and the conditions of human life, is the 'faculty of action'. Action is 'the one miracle-working faculty of man,' as Jesus, the Messiah, knew. Action is the only means humans have of beginning something new. It is a reminder that 'men, though they must die, are not born to die but to begin'. Accordingly, 'the miracle that saves the world, the realm of human affairs, from its normal, "natural" ruin is ultimately the fact of natality, in which the faculty of action is ontologically rooted. It is, in other words, the birth of new men and the new beginning, the action they are capable of by virtue of being born' (Arendt 1974: 246–7).

Hope, as the anticipation of redemption, is eternally present. Rejecting the same old thing, it has nothing to do with history: 'Hope is grammar' (Steiner 1997b: 85).

(c.ii) 'The great non-conformist in history'. 'Laws maintain their credibility, not because they are just, but because they are laws' (Montaigne 1964: 361; Bk.III, xiii). Montaigne stresses a fundamental diremption in Western culture between law and ethics, between the prevailing (i.e. historically legitmized) political order and a morally just dispensation. What, in fact, this 'very opposition between morality and legality – between inner, autonomous "conscience", and outer, heteronomous institutions' comes down to, is a personally compromising depravity. The reason is: 'simultaneous possession of inner freedom and outer unfreedom means that the border where cognitive activity and normative passivity become cognitive passivity and normative activity is changeable and obscure' (Rose 1994: 35).

Here, what history actually does, is crucial. History relies on law, as an instrument of continuity, to establish society's historical coherence and identity (Allott 2002: 56ff., 84ff.). Further, as a social management technology, history implements heteronomy, rather than fosters personal autonomy. In revealing how things got to be the way they are, how the world is the way it is, it blurs the distinction between personal reality and social norm by proposing itself as their common temporal denominator, their transcendent purpose. Its identitary logic ensures that the 'cognitive activity' that produces historical knowledge will be socially normative – as the *History Subject Benchmark Statement* shows (QAA 2000). History develops behavioural norms for human action, given that 'experiences of the past without normative intentions towards the future are blind; [and] normative intentions towards the future without experience of the past are historically empty' (Rüsen 1990: 229). The outcome is: as society's 'default knowledge', history *de facto* enforces cognitive passivity, a 'reactive' thoughtlessness (cf. Cohen 1988: 1, 134–5, 190–2). In learning from it how things have got to be the way they are, we ourselves need only keep on doing what we already do, which is what we have always done.

In becoming historicized, Jewish existence establishes itself on this ethical fault-line. Total absorption into history proves to be destructive. Now historical security, and with it inter-marriage and assimilation, undermines the coherence of Jewish existence (Rubinstein et al. 2002: 439–40). But total introverted withdrawal is also impossible. In a historicized world, everything is historicized, even Judaism after the Holocaust. Even so, where history affirms identities,

Jewish identity still affirms itself against history: 'Jews insist on existing *contra* the norm and logic of history' (Steiner 1997b: 49). But ineluctable fate becomes an ethical mandate, a vocation to resolve the conflict between historical heteronomy and human autonomy, to protest against both cognitive passivity and normative activity. In a historicized world, Judaism testifies to the 'primordial anachronism of the human' (Levinas 1984: 297). To put it bluntly, 'the Jew is the great non-conformist in history, its great dissenter. That is why he exists' (Baeck 1995: 292).

Homo studiosus: *homo oeconomicus*

'Making history', 'the making of the modern world', 'history makes the world what it is': the unselfconscious, 'manufacturing' metaphor is the clue. History is embedded in the things human beings make, and in what they make of things.

Human beings are makers [*homo faber*]: amongst the things they make, is history. History is one product of the human manufacturing capacity: 'The work of our hands ... fabricates the sheer unending variety of things whose sum total constitutes the human artifice.' Human artifice gives the world its 'durability'. Things do get used up, but it ensures that 'all single things can be constantly replaced with the change of generations which come and inhabit the man-made world and go away.' This durability 'gives the things of the world their relative independence from men who produced and use them, their "objectivity" which makes them ... "stand against" and endure ... the voracious needs ... of their living makers and users'. It also has the 'function of stabilizing human life': 'their objectivity lies in the fact that ... men ... can retrieve their sameness, that is, their identity, by being related to the same chair, the same table'. Thus 'against the subjectivity of men stands the objectivity of the man-made world rather than the sublime indifference of untouched nature' (Arendt 1974: 136–7).

Thus the essential features of the concept of history – the apparently conflicting issues of heterogeneity (cf. 'variety of things') and objectivity, the restless fabrication of new things (as the 'durable' same old things) and stabilized identity – only cohere in terms of the manufacturing conception of human activity. History [*rg*] manufactures objective heterogeneity by producing the latest things as the same old things.

This model is powerful, but limits human potential. Stressing manufacturing as the paradigmatic human activity downgrades other socializing activities such as theoretical reflection and aesthetic creation (cf. Arendt 1974: 284ff., 294ff.). Further, if manufacture is the basis of history, its development can only enlarge it. The shift from product to process, from the thing produced to exactly how things are produced, is a historicizing move. Making process 'the principle for doing in the realm of human affairs', historicizes everything (Arendt 1974: 296ff., 299, 300). The process producing the same old thing, is history: history itself becomes the production process of every thing. The historicized world is, therefore, a world in which 'the ... fabricator [is elevated] to the highest range of human possibilities' (Arendt 1974: 305). It is a world characterized by the 'hegemony of the economic', 'a form of general social development which has led to the conceptual and practical dominance of economic phenomena over all other social phenomena' (Allott 2002: 311). A world in which the production process and all it entails – its corporate governance, its instrumentalizing mentality, its conception of nature and humanity as "resources", its managerial technology, its reliance on organizational systems and mechanisms, its reduction of all values to the values of commerce – cannot be anything other than irretrievably historicized. As the intellectual form of these dominant social forces, history is the dominant social idea.

The historicized world is much more than this, though. History doesn't just affirm the durability of the world humanity has made. Postmodern society harnesses the history technology to the already historical production process: 'Entrepreneurs [are] in touch with a certain form of history-making that has been with the culture of the West since the classical Greeks and Ancient heroes'. Now what happens: the more the world can be historicized, the more things the production process produces. In this already historicized world, 'entrepreneurs are in the business of changing history. They give their cultures or industries new styles for dealing with people and things' (Spinosa et al. 1997: 55, 57). The postmodern economy can't wait for things to wear out. So it deals in disposable commodities (e.g. cars, computers), knowledge and skills, services and subscriptions, designs and styles, images and looks (e.g. films, CDs, DVDs, videos, fashions) (cf. Harvey 1990: 284ff.). With obsolescence built-in, needing always to be renewed or updated, representing the ever "latest thing", these products are, by their very nature, already historicized objects (cf. Davies 1999: 250).

But the historicized world is more than this still. Once the history technology drives the production process, the durability of the world and the stability of identity are transfigured

(Sennett 1999: 31, 133, 147). The world is always in the process of self-fabrication: what continues is change, what lasts is flux. Experience now comprises virtually everything humans have produced. Consequently, anything virtual humans produce, also counts as experience: that is the illusory nature of society at its latest – an abstract, theoretical, technical culture, a transparently oneiric society (cf. Nietzsche 1988: I, 115ff., 145ff., §§18, 23; Vattimo 1990: 17). Hence, the illusory nature of history and historical knowledge [*illusio*]. When only history is left, everything is left to history. Everyone functions as an adjunct to the remorseless production process historicized society has become. The historicized world itself is a commodified reality: its objective reality is a reality in which only objects (products of human artifice) are real.

Because history is 'everything', it does still include the belief that identity is organically rooted in history. But identity is actually just another historical product. The historicized production process, applied to history itself, turns it out in so many heterogeneous forms and combinations (e.g. local, regional, national, gender, ethnic, social, political, cultural, etc., etc.), that the identities deriving from them are also heterogeneous. They too are turned out by a manufacturing system that produces as the latest things heterogeneous objects that are still the same as the same old things. As with the standardized, serial production of Yale locks, each identity, each with its fractionally different profile, remains ... identical (cf. Horkheimer & Adorno 1973: 139). Identity is the ideal, historical product, the quintessential commodity.

History [*crg*] and the historian are instrumental in this commodity producing process. As a studious person [*homo studiosus*], as a technocratic 'resources-manager', the historian is also an economic person [*homo oeconomicus*]. He or she operates within a social institution (i.e. the school, college, university, museum, gallery, the communications media), that is similarly instrumental in socializing young people into accepting fabrication (and everything that goes with it) as the ultimate principle of social life. Historians do still establish historical objectivity and assess historical veracity in their teaching and publications. That's because objectivity and veracity are anchored in and defined by the historicized fabrication process that sustains their institution and them in their socially affirmative, history-teaching function.

History [*crg*] is, then, just a surface phenomenon of society, a commodified product of its production process, not a form of reflective knowledge – as two defining features of historians' historicized

mentality confirm: (a) the rejection of myth and myth-making; and
(b) the automatic recourse to commodity thinking.

(a.) Historicized world = de-mythologized world. As is known, the
female praying-mantis, after copulating, devours the male. The
behavioural reflex in the insect world evokes, via anthropomorphism,
an archaic *apprehension* in the human sphere. Disclosing a mortal
vulnerability at the moment of intimate submission, its effect is
disturbing. Always beyond the pleasure principle lurks a sinister
chthonic presence – the more so currently, in the current risk-society,
e.g. as AIDS threatens a global pandemic. Common to both insect
behaviour-pattern and human apprehension is a fatal inevitability
rooted in the procreation of life. In the insect-species it comes out as
natural reflex; in *homo sapiens* as recurrent, mythical paradigm, the
femme fatale – an Eve, a Delilah, a Salome, a Pandora, a Clytemnestra
(cf. Caillois 1987: 33, 70–2, 82–5).

As in the disobedience of Adam and Eve or in the fate of
Prometheus, human life is rooted in primordial transgression. Myth
signals 'the havoc in the very essence of things', the tragic, innate
'error' in human arrangements, the archaic, yet ever-present trigger of
human apprehension (Nietzsche 1988: I, 69, §9; Aristotle 1965: 48).
But myth also suggests a remedy for the havoc it demonstrates, by the
way it demonstrates it. It needs to be stressed: 'mankind escapes from
its animality only through mythology. Man is nothing but a
mythological animal' (Tournier 1979: 191). As one of the experientially constant, central motifs of art, music, literature, film – as in
Sophocles' *Oedipus* dramas or in Picasso's *The Tragedy* (1903) – myth
offers exclusively in the aesthetic dimension an optic for contemplating
the essential enigma of human Being. The function of art [*aesthesis*]
is to tap into this archetypal stratum of Being that conditions
experience: to bring us to our senses.

History reacts to myth as anathema, unless – since everything is
historicized – it comes up with a history of mythology or of the
'imaginary' (cf. Patlagean 1988: 310–11). This comes out in its
attitudes towards it. History sees itself as superseding mythology: the
origins of history are "lost" in myth, so that it takes up where myths
leave off (cf. Vico 1984: 29ff.). It would be more scientific than
myth: it relies on source documents, verifiable testimony, done deeds
[*res gestae*], facts [*factum*: 'what has been made']. Myths are just
fables: '"myth" suggests an invented story … devised to achieve
certain ends that are usually assumed to have a strong emotional

component' (Jordanova 2000: 112). It claims to be ethically more reliable than myth: it gets at the truth, the real reality, what actually happened. Being imaginary, myth is inherently deceitful, 'a version of the past which usually has some element of truth in it, but which distorts what actually happened in support of some vested interest' (Marwick 2001: 292). History is so opposed to myth that it repudiates anything "mythic" within itself. Accordingly, it applies it to historical accounts and interpretations that 'resist debate and modification' (Jordanova 2000: 112). The very credibility of history is staked on its myth-busting intent. Historians uniquely 'equip society with a truly historical perspective ... to save it from the damaging effects of exposure to historical myth'. If they, being 'professionally trained', don't defend it, 'others who are less well informed and more prejudiced will produce ill-founded interpretations' (Tosh 1999: 32–3; cf. Warren 1999: 146).

This self-deception [*illusio*] is astonishing. Myth is nothing irrational. Rather, because it taps straight into an archaic matrix of Being and its ever-present apprehensions, it bypasses the instrumentalized rationality that governs historicized existence. For this reason it can be exploited for irrational purposes and induce phobias – but so too can history. What historians characterize as "myths", with their 'distortions' and 'prejudices' (e.g. 'myths held by Serbs or by Northern Ireland Protestants about ethnic superiority, about ... persecutions in the past' (Marwick 2001: 33)), are in reality *historically* triggered, socio-pathological delusions.

But what's gained by treating archetypal "myth" as social delusion? Everything: the whole historicized world as both 'durable' product and instrument of its instrumental reason. Resisting myth (whatever it may be) is the foundational act of a world fabricated by human artifice. It's exemplified by Odysseus, Homeric hero and archetypal 'economic man' [*homo oeconomicus*], who, by means of calculated deception and self-renunciation, asserts himself and his self-identity throughout his epic journey from Troy back to Ithaca. His encounter with the Sirens, the most fatal of *femmes fatales*, whose seductive song lures sailors to their death, is typical. Knowing how irresistible their song is, Odysseus resorts to technology to escape the fatal threat they pose, by having himself *chained* to the mast of his ship. Since he has his oarsmen block their ears with wax, they row past oblivious to both the sirens' song and his ravings (Horkheimer & Adorno 1973: 55, 57). What the Enlightenment has come down to, instrumental reason, calculation, deception, as resources of human artifice, produces a technological, utilitarian, normatized society. In its totalitarian organization and rationalized efficiency it is made to fulfil human ends by human means, such that humans become the means to serve social ends. Human subjects become assimilated to the manufacturing technology, itself the basis of a totally rationalized society (cf. Nietzsche 1988: I, 145–6, §23; Horkheimer & Adorno 1973: 30, 36–7; Allott 2002: 174). As accountable for 'everything', as the possibility of total explanation, history is the ideal affirmation of rationalized society, the ideal product of human fabrication, their ideal management technology.

Fabricated by human technologies, the historical world human beings make for themselves is disenchanted: it neutralizes the archaic appeal of myth. Humanity must resort to its own devices. Its exemplary type is the "studious man" [*homo studiosus*], the 'theoretical man' who prefers the unending search for truth to the actual possession of it: the ideal-type of the academic technocrat, the 'resources manager' (cf. Nietzsche 1988: I, 98–9, §15). Partly, he or she is motivated by the ethical concern to lead a 'good life' in the Aristotelian sense (cf. Blumenberg 1973: 130). Partly, too, he or she is driven by curiosity. After the Fall mankind had to recuperate intellectually the knowledge of God it had enjoyed immediately. However, the human knowledge capacity is limited since final causes remain concealed and nature is accessible only through instruments of human fabrication (cf. Arendt 1974: 137). In compensation, knowledge of the world still proves valuable to human interests and goods. There is so much of the world to know about, that this knowledge need not be traced back to God as its final cause (Blumenberg 1973: 132). Moreover, within this world, there is the world humanity has made for itself, a historical world, that is an adequate object of knowledge for the purely human cognitive aptitude (Vico 1984: 104; Arendt 1974: 298).

This inquisitiveness about the world defines curiosity. It produces the heterogeneity of historical knowledge: 'Curiosity involves dwelling superficially on the object, on the perspective view of phenomena, being diffused into objective, arbitrary selections from a broad spectrum, the downplaying of knowledge expectations that are content with truths while renouncing *the* truth' (Blumenberg 1973: 132).[7] It thus generates the 'more is more' syndrome behind historical comprehension; it backs up its claim to comprise 'everything'. It's also

---

[7] Blumenberg is commenting on the concepts of studiousness and curiosity in Aquinas, *Summa Theologica*, II, ii, QQ.166–7.

symptomatic of the melancholy that haunts the historicized world with its realization that its truths will always remain 'partial', that some issues may never be fully explained, that reality will never fully disclose itself. Hence, conscious of its inherent inadequacy, curiosity is always liable to being 'dominated by the powers within whose force-fields it operates', even to entering into Faustian pacts with the devil – to letting itself be instrumentalized, in order to satisfy itself (Blumenberg 1973: 134, 135–6). Nietzsche's rejection of the sense of history for its vulgar curiosity and of historical consciousness for being so studious [*studirt*], is, therefore, vindicated (cf. Nietzsche 1988: V, 157, 159, §§223, 224). Curiosity is a debased, compromised form of knowledge. It's neither the vigilant reservation that watches out for the deceptiveness of the historicized world, nor the theoretical reflection that dwells on the essences of things.

A world fabricated and managed by mankind for its own ends is meant to be more secure than the archaic world dominated by the fatal inevitability of myth. In sealing itself off from nature's numinous forces, the historicized world would liberate itself from the primordial apprehension inherent in human existence. History drives the technological apparatus [*Gestell*] that keeps it running with clockwork regularity. It becomes the essential instrument [*techne*] of the commerce in manufactures. As Thomas Henry wrote in 1791, 'a knowledge of history is an indispensable accomplishment to the opulent tradesman': outside business 'will not the time he can spare ... be ... usefully employed in the study of history ... ; or at an air pump, an electrical machine, or a microscope ... ?' After all, 'the philosophical historian does not content himself with the mere relation of facts; he endeavours to trace their causes, to shew the principles by which commerce should be actuated' (Henry 1972: 7, 9, 10).

Still, in defining itself as technological efficiency in opposite relation to inscrutable mythical forces, the historically fabricated world only exposes itself to their fatal influence in a more insidious form. Its symptoms are the nostalgias that deep-down motivate objective historical analysis; the social dissemination of occlusive oneiric images generated from the past (e.g. in the mass-media and heritage industries); the unconscious rational-technological replication of archaic paradigms (e.g. skyscrapers in the form of megaliths or tombstones).

Myths are never banished, only repressed – and the repressed always returns, to hold us spellbound but incapacitated. Then, as in a Rorschach test, suddenly an unsuspected configuration emerges: the historical enterprise shows up as the ultimate identity-trip. Humanity lost in contemplation of itself and its fabrications as admirable objects in their object-ivity: that really is an archaic, mythical posture – the fatal self-infatuation of Narcissus (cf. Davies 1989). History has actually become the new mythology.

(b.) 'Commodity thinking'. History is a 'totalitarian-monological scheme of manufacturing' (cf. Schnädelbach 2000: 142). It's the process for producing social reality, the production of 'durable things' in idealized form. This conception sustains history both as the story of human progress, as the intensification and expansion of human productivity, and as heritage, as the accumulated output of historical product. That's why Bacon saw the seventeenth century as 'a more advanced age of the world, ... *stored* and *stocked* with infinite experiments and observations', and Hume observed that 'a man acquainted with history may ... be said to have lived from the beginning of the world, and to have been making continual additions to his *stock* of knowledge in every century' (Bacon 1960: 81; Hume 1971: 561 (my italics)). That's also why Anders dismisses history today as a 'never-ending succession of production models' and historical time as simply 'a form of production, alternate types of production, and consumption' (Anders 1986: 300–1).

Furthermore, commercial production apparently benefits historical knowledge. It engenders a historicized consciousness, since 'at every instant the present moment transforms itself ... into relatively ... comprehensive, historical accounts, and no important business of public life occurs any more without it being vividly conscious of the historical context it enters into ... At every instant ... there now occurs the turnover of business into history and the evaluation of history for business' (Droysen 1977: 70). Conversely, historians confidently demonstrate that a historicized consciousness benefits social reproduction. As a recent survey shows, the 'skills of historians' are evidently highly marketable commodities, given that 'the subject turns out more directors of top companies than any other' and that 'significant numbers of cabinet ministers ... and vice-chancellors are historians' (Utley 2002: 1, 12). History apparently needs to keep affirming itself, to keep conforming to an affirmative concept of society. This survey only confirms similar, earlier findings: as always in history, for history, 'more is always more'. The 1994 survey, 'British University History Now', found that 'students can study *more* history

– in *more* varied ways – than ever before. Along the way not only can they pick up valuable "transferable" skills that they will need in the increasingly competitive and crowded job market, but they can also develop a *more* rounded understanding of their chosen field' (Fitzgerald & Hodgkinson 1994: 53 (my italics)). Commenting on this survey, the editor of *History Today* remarks that it is 'testament to the fact that history has adapted very well to the market condition' (*THES* 1994: 2). Even so, the 'market condition' does itself make history. A system of research output geared to university funding mechanisms has ended up 'producing more and more goods [i.e. history monographs, articles, etc.], on which a diminishing value is placed'. As a result, the manufacturing metaphor turns sour: 'late twentieth-century historians are increasingly coming to resemble another sad, demoralized and proletarianized fraternity: the handloom weavers of the early nineteenth century' (Cannadine 1999: 13).

The fabrication-production model of history is widely applicable. It brings out in the synergy between society's managers (who make history what it is) and history's managers (who show how history has made society what it is) the identitary logic that governs the socio-historical totality. It crystallizes in its symptomatic, exemplary form, the historical facsimile [*illusio*] as found in museum, gallery, and theatre shops, and marketed by retail outlets such as *Past Times* or by mail-order repro-antique companies such as *Ancestral Collections* and *Manners*. Here historical associations, the synthetic historical patina, make the commodity desirable, create the commodity fetishism.

The point is: history sells. So, 'to boost its finances', V&A Enterprises, the 'commercial arm' of London's Victoria and Albert Museum, set up a licensing programme 'authorising companies at home and abroad to use some of the designs in its collections on a range of products'. Explaining this move, the managing director pointed out that it took the Museum 'back to its origins, since it was known in the nineteenth century as the Museum of Manufactures'. 'Working with manufacturers,' he adds, 'raises money and raises consciousness about the museum' (Trapp 1995: 14). The new manufacturing enterprise turns out to be the same as the same old manufacturing enterprise: the latest commodities "go back to" the original sources. The commercial structure replicates the identitary logic of historical reconstruction. Moreover, history pays: 'It's hardly surprising museums and galleries are turning themselves into department stores when you consider the amount of money to be made.

Last year more than £97m worth of V&A brand tableware, furnishings and fashion pieces were sold worldwide.' Apparently 'the licence fees have boosted V&A's fortunes and made it a formidable business partner', with profits up 45 per cent and sales 47 per cent: 'And with more than five million objects in the collection to inspire designers, the opportunities appear limitless' (Russell 1998: 12).

History is for anyone and everyone to buy into. History [crg] affirms, here too, social and material values it itself sets up in the first place. The *Ancestral Collections*, Winter 2002 catalogue (p.43) offers a 'Book of Hours bell pull' (price: £73) as 'a lovely accent piece for your wall and a nice reminder of days gone by'. The days concerned are 'those days long gone when you could ring for tea' and bell pulls were 'essential in the rooms of huge country houses where up to a quarter of a mile separated you from your kettle and where an army of people were employed to keep such houses running smoothly'. Thus the thing itself goes back to a communications technology and the instrumentalized human servants on the end of it. Feudalism may well be dead, but its idea, objectivized into a commodity and its design, is still marketable. The *Past Times* shop offers bars of "Ration Chocolate" for sale (140g bar @ £3.50): the days of the week are imprinted on each section to indicate the war-time daily ration. That and its retro packaging-design supply the crucial historical associations, plus a brief 'History of Food Rationing'. It produces a historicized mode of consumption: a present self-indulgence made sweeter still by the nostalgic evocation of austerity. The historicized consciousness is adept at passing social atavism off as personal refinement.

The historical facsimile, the reproduction antique, are exemplary historicized objects. The new thing is the same as the same old thing, it identifies itself in relation to its 'durable', historical original. In the same thing, the consumer buys a decorative object and indulges a subjective nostalgia. It's also historical thinking in its reified form, the synthetic product of objective historical knowledge and historical veracity. The new thing replicating the same old thing, deriving from a historical source, physically demonstrates that historical objectivity and veracity are reified – and reifying – values. The facsimile is, in fact, a concretization of historical consciousness: the structure of history, the structure of production, the structure of mind. It's all the same thing.

With their concern for objectivity – apparently, a stock of five million-plus objects in the case of the V&A – historical methods reveal their reliance on commodity thinking. It goes with the studious curiosity that drives them. The act of thinking as such is based, anthropologically speaking, on 'making prices, assessing values, elaborating and exchanging equivalences', on commerce in commodities (Nietzsche 1988: V, 306; II, 8). Commodity thinking thus derives from a materialistic social theory of mental processes. It involves 'the values of linearity, continuity, career, and accumulation – strategic exchange values of social reproduction ... the sign forms of both academic culture and capitalist economy' (Cohen 1988: 326). It reveals that forms of consciousness, what are called rational forms of 'knowledge', emerge from the objectification (reification) that occurs in commodity transactions (Sohn-Rethel 1978: 37). The direct link between objectivity and thinking comes through money, since it's integral to the exchange process. Money produces an identical, abstract, rational system of exchange-values that sustains a market in heterogeneous commodities (cf. Simmel 1989: 64; Sohn-Rethel 1978: 81). Consequently, 'the identification of the money-owner with the money-function on the sole basis of what money is, is the original act of theoretical subjectivity': i.e. the social legitimation of the money-function permits each particular subject to identify with a transcendent, uniform concept of subjectivity. The money-owner reproduces in his own mind the closed system of objectifications he would turn to his own account. The material context of things he mentally replicates is the commodity production process sustained by the social laws of appropriation driven by money. This material basis, comprehended intellectually, in its ideal form, is the protoype of what counts socially, culturally, as valid knowledge. As a result, a transcendent, evaluating, knowing "subject" comes to confront a world of objects, of object-ive relationships (cf. Sohn-Rethel 1978: 80, 81, 83, 87). That's why '"money" is a good sign, a stable signifier, appropriate, in its very form, for academic denotations, its ever-presence a true use-value for discourse' (Cohen 1988: 304). That's essentially why 'raising money raises consciousness' – why, for academic historians in the corporate university, making money '*is* ... the most interesting *thing* to do' (Steiner 1997a: 288 (my italics)).

Thinking arises from managing commerce in commodities in an abstract system of exchange. This same system of equivalences decides the value of the fabricated object. It becomes a mental abstraction through the social form in which the exchange system operates. The value of the commodity takes its form from this system that turns the commodity into an abstraction, while its content is abstracted from the labour that produced it – i.e. from its origins, its past.[8] The notion of abstraction involved in this kind of objective assessment is synonymous with the formal abstraction that governs thinking in general. Further, the commercial transaction itself remains non-empirical, abstract: it discounts empirical issues of practical use – how a given, private consumer actually will, after all, use that particular item. It's left to him or her to imagine, purely in thought, in abstract terms, what he or she will make of it (Sohn-Rethel 1989: 16–20).

In a historicized world produced by the fabrication of the same old durable things, reality consists of how these things relate to each other, of how objects relate to other objects, objectively. Made by history to be objectively the way it is, all reality consists of made-objects, commodities in a market-system of equivalent exchange-values. Individuals, as subjects being confronted by these objects, seek to infer from them the comprehensive system of objective relationships that governs the way they are arranged, that constitutes reality. But to do so, the subject itself becomes an object for itself, alienated from what it produces by the conditions in which it operates, reduced in its own reified situation to contemplating and rationally ordering its knowledge-objects (cf. Lukács 1976: 183ff., 187, 190–4). In the historicized world cultures and industries are interchangeable, as are people and things – and the new style (as in the entrepreneurialism of the V&A) is the same old style (cf. Spinosa et al. 1997: 55, 57).

The convergence between history and the market, the museum and the department store, enacts the convergence between the process of commodification operative in historical comprehension and the manufacture of durable things. Like the commodity-market, history is an abstract arrangement for the evaluation of human acting and making. Historical comprehension reproduces this acting and making in an object-ive, commodified form. The objectively true historical facsimile in the museumshop is as much a reification of the past as the nominalist conceptions (e.g. "monarchy", "feudalism", "religious

---

[8] A concrete analogy would be a consumer comparing two or three similar products, e.g. chairs, for quality of manufacture, and value for money. Crucial elements would be: quality of materials used; place of purchase (e.g. an antiques shop, a department store); the brand, the style statement; the consumer's own anticipated need. Underpinning the comparisons would be a conceptual 'ideal-type' of the commodity and its quality, value, and status.

non-conformity") that fabricate the objectively true historical monograph in the academic department. Determined to be objective and, therefore, true, history makes them both: 'the past, seized in isolation and held fast, is merely a category of commodity, a reified fact [*Factum* – 'what was made'] unconscious of its being made and of its still ongoing process' (Bloch 1979: 7). In a world made by history, knowledge is defined essentially in relation to the past, because the past can be contemplated objectively by the similarly self-object-ivizing historian (i.e. the historian as technocratic, "dispassionate observer"). Conceptually, this knowledge cannot accommodate anything really new: the present as the front-line of the unprecedented, is a source of embarrassment. Hence, 'thinking in commodity terms only heightens its impotence. In making people and things into commodities, capitalism not only alienates them. It also reveals that thinking in commodity form is a heightened form of thinking in terms of things-having-got-to-be-the-way-they-are [*Gewordenheit*], in terms of fact' (Bloch 1979: 329).

In a risky, historicized present, what else offers tangible, material consolation than a past constructed from simulacra, cleaned up, adapted, antiqued – a past consumers can relate to, on a diminished scale for the modern home, dishwasher and microwave proof, a tasteful, sanitized past, free from self-incrimination? One can be at home 'in days gone by', i.e. in the 'remoteness of the preterite tense' (as Bloch puts it), engrossed in how things used to be: 'the more remote the objects lie back in time, the more their isolation makes them suitable for quiet contemplation. According to the nexus linking knowledge and the past, the Crusades afford more studious scholarship than the last two World Wars, whereas Egypt, being even more remote, affords more than the Middle Ages' (Bloch 1979: 330).

In the historicized, totally fabricated world, no section of reality can be left unproductive. The past is a particularly fruitful resource, safer than investing in what is new and unprecedented, if anything can be in a historicized world. It's readily available to be 'confiscated retroactively' by the present (cf. White 1985: 363). Its designs are tried and tested, they have an already recognized status and value. Thus the dead are still borne along in the triumphal march that the victors hold to humiliate those they have always defeated (cf. Benjamin 1977: 254, §VII). And then they're put to work, harnessed to the profit motive through the commodities they 'inspire', the catalogues' euphemism for "copied" or "appropriated". That's why the culture industry is an 'imperialistic, colonial enterprise': 'its Congo is called "history"', and this Congo remains even today largely undiscovered'. It has vast resources to exploit, but 'because its [now dead] artisans go unpaid, while the industry still profits from their work, they have become posthumously its slaves' (Anders 1993: 71). It's tempting to say with Nietzsche, commenting on the way the past is valued for the nostalgia it stimulates, that too much energy is wasted on raising the dead and bringing the past back to life (Nietzsche 1988: III, 145, §159). In fact, the investment in restoration, in the reproduction of historical artefacts, is more than repaid by the 'heritage dividend' that through business and commerce revitalizes areas of urban neglect (English Heritage 2002). In thus extending and exploiting the influence of the dead, the market acts just like the historian who explains contemporary institutions through the "long traditions" that allegedly made them what they are. As the commerce in facsimiles and repro-antiques shows, it's accurate history, objective historical information that sells the product and legitimates the market. History's marketing of traditional values reflects the commodified knowledge it deals in. The resulting chaotic bazaar of historical periods and tastes, the cult of the simulacrum, the sheer heterogeneity of historicized product one encounters in the museum shop, the mail-order catalogue, or a publisher's history list, may well epitomize the postmodern phantasmagoria of all cultural and social values. But that's totally historicized culture, a culture in which all its past returns to haunt it.

The prevalence of historical consciousness, the over-production of historical meanings, does not augment reality. It diminishes it twice over: the loss of the past, of what the dead wanted for themselves, but also the loss of the present, what it would want, if history had not made what it is, if it were not itself a historical reproduction, an 'invisible machine' for reproducing historical reproductions (cf. Negt & Kluge 1993: 296). It's worth remembering instead that, in order to make, one has to live. A commodified, objective world, a historicized world, is impossible to live in, since it reproduces an alienating, commodified, objectivized, facsimile of a life. Living, being alive, is something different: it means 'being present, not only before or after, initial tasting or after-taste. It means seizing the day in the simplest, basic sense; it means adopting a concrete attitude to the now' (Bloch 1979: 341).

History as symbolic re-enactment

History claims to be 'everything'. However, in an already historicized world, 'everything' is not enough. An already historicized world also includes the process of historicization, not only the history still ongoing, but the history that is always still being written. 'Everything', therefore, can't be quite enough, since there's always more history for history to grasp. History is always having to catch itself up: if only it were not always late.

The recorded, analyzed, and evaluated history we do have, is a monument to lateness. It represents knowledge that can be, even needs to be, deferred. The more remote the past moment, the more late, delayed, the knowledge now known about it. That's why those who can't or won't wait – e.g. politicians desperately seeking self-vindication – anticipate history's otherwise deferred verdict. That's why historicism comes in handy: it seeks a deeper meaning in what history we already have. Still the economics of historical sense never work out. It's never clear how much historical sense makes sense (in historicist terms), which means that it can be both utterly unreliable (as in the case of Jewish history) and infinitely exploitable (as a commodity, a 'durable thing'). History thus traps and baffles us in our own immediate situation. If history is the real reality, this knowledge, endlessly deferrable, comes too late for us now, when it's really needed. History, capable of revealing how the world 'got to be the way it is', comes too late to tell us how the way it now is will get to be. The present moment is always obscured, 'all but inaccessible' (Bloch 1985a: 74; Cohen 1988: 326). *Though* we live in an already historicized world, we shall never ever know our own historical meaning. Conversely, in an already historicized world, history infiltrates the 'semiosphere', the system of signs and symbols that enables consciousness to know both itself and its environment (cf. Lotman 2001: 123ff.). It thus historicizes everything in the world, inevitably occluding our own immediate situation too (cf. Cohen 1988: 93, 95). Consequently, *because* we live in an already historicized world, we never know our situation here and now in its actual immediacy. In a world always historicizing itself, history has all exits blocked.

And yet ... Immediacy is the overriding imperative – ethically, the overriding human interest. It flashes out in the apprehensive response the present, inhuman, historical situation provokes.[9] Immediacy will always (a) subvert the history reference-system to reclaim the means of expression it immediately needs. By definition, it cannot wait.

---

[9] As the photos of American forces mistreating Iraqi prisoners that surfaced publicly in May 2004 show, it takes an immediate aesthetic effect to shatter the historical, ideological illusions that were said to motivate the Iraq War in the first place.

Still, the conflict between one's immediate situation and the historicized semiosphere produces (b) the current, distinctive psychopathology of historicized life. To recover from it, means (c) dispelling the shrouds of historical meanings that occlude immediate reality and its attendant ethical obligations.

(a.) History and the symbolic structure of reality. History [*crg*] appears as a total reference-system, as the ultimate symbolic structure of meaning, only when it too suffers historical damage. That happens because, according to the hallucinatory logic of a historicized world, there is only history for history to impact on.

(a.i) '*The past is all around us*'. Consider, e.g., the response to the office of Lord Chancellor being abolished in Prime Minister Tony Blair's government re-shuffle in June 2003. In the press there was dismay over this allegedly hasty constitutional reorganization. But it was easily matched by the furious reaction to scrapping the '1400 years of history' the office "represented". 'Blair sweeps away 1400 years of tradition' runs the sub-title of *The Guardian* leader column. 'The Lord Chancellor of England, an office almost as old as that of the monarch, has existed in one form or another since 605,' it explains. It continues: 'Yesterday, just in time to catch the six o'clock news, and after 1,398 years, Mr Blair abolished the post altogether'. It evokes a unique, momentary conjunction. The structure of the immediate life-world and the transcendental *longue durée* briefly intersect. Socially coercive clock-time hits the juggernaut of imperious tradition. But no sooner has the symbolic order of history been damaged, than it repairs itself. In an already historicized world, if one tradition ends, another always takes over. Whatever happens, a past precedent will justify it. The past always has precedence. Blair's 'revolution by reshuffle' could easily be reconfigured 'as the biggest single step towards the separation of powers since the Glorious Revolution more than 300 years ago'. By invoking history's deferred verdict, this historical scandal can be already historicized, configured in terms of the past, as 'something that may eventually be remembered as the largest single legacy of his premiership' (*The Guardian*, June 13 2003: 29). Historical sense in an already historicized world is inevitably both gratuitous and self-authenticating. On one and the same day one historical act, sweeping away fourteen centuries of tradition, vindicated by a 300-year-old precedent, is already imagined being remembered as a legacy.

By contrast, *The Daily Telegraph* sees 'Blair's coup d'état' as jeopardizing the nation's historical fabric. In an article explaining the 'quaint' but 'crucial constitutional function' the Lord Chancellor performs, it points out that the last Lord Chancellor's 257 predecessors 'included saints, cardinals, archbishops, earls and even a queen' (Johnston 2003: 4). Similarly its leader column invokes traditional legitimation: 'by phasing out ... the oldest secular office of state, Mr Blair proposes to remove one of the keystones of our unwritten constitution'. The Lord Chancellorship 'is woven into the seamless robe of constitutional custom and practice, which may easily unravel unless change is accomplished gradually and by common consent'. It links British national integrity to the nation's history and traditions: 'our system has served us better than any other nation's. Mr Blair presumes to tear its delicate membrane apart'. The Government now wears 'the ugly face of arbitrary authority and contempt for tradition' since 'Mr Blair shows his contempt for the rule of law, as it has evolved over the last thousand years and more' (*The Daily Telegraph* 2003: 27).

Both newspapers evince different ideological positions; both resort to history to defend what is by 'validating what has always been' (Weber 1988: 580). In an already historicized world, the historicizing reflex ensures legitimation of current practice through tradition and legacy. History is affirmative ideology, because society projects a historicized, if not historicist, structure of symbolic values that already takes precedence. History [*crg*] automatically configures continuity as determined evolution. It ensures that, over any time-period, time itself gains value and so means qualitatively "more" than just the quantity of time elapsed. '1400 years' still has no immediate meaning for mortals who live for just a few score. So the immediate situation has to be made historical – harnessed into history's symbolic structure, to reinforce its ghostly, authoritarian precedents (Lessing 1983: 35). Hence the use of the perfect ('has existed ... since 605') or the present tense (as in the expression 'goes back to ...'): both position the present as a dimension of the past. Hence, too, the recourse to mystifying figures of speech – technological ('*keystone* of our unwritten con-stitution' and '*woven* into the seamless robe of constitutional custom') as well as organic ('*evolution*' of law and 'delicate *membrane*' of governance) – to give spurious substance to affirmative abstractions (my italics).

In a historicized world, there's nothing that can't become a historical symbol. There's nothing that isn't already a historical text: 'The past is all around us. ... the historic environment ... is a collective memory, containing ... stories written in stone, brick, wood, glass, steel; stories inscribed in the field patterns, hedgerows, designed landscapes and other features of the countryside' (DCMS 2001: 7). Whatever existed, makes itself known only through some kind of existing historical text within the historicized semiotic system. So there really can't be an extra-textual referent for the historical text, a knowable, objective reality unless the semiotic-system describes it (cf. Evans 1997:110ff., 249). The illusion of an extra-textual referent – e.g. a 1400-year-old membrane of governance – boils down to a purely self-referential, textual coherence (cf. Oakeshott 1999: 124).

(a.ii) 'The language-net cast backward'. There is no independent world "out there" to be known: that's the premise of the philosophy of symbolic forms. *Homo sapiens* is a 'language animal', a 'symbol using animal' (Steiner 1975: 66ff.; Burke 1966: 3). For that reason 'language forms quite literally underlie and perpetuate human behaviour' (Steiner 1975: 71). The world, or rather versions of worlds, we live in consist of semiotic structures and symbolic arrangements. They are made 'with words, numerals, pictures, sounds, or other symbols of any kind in any medium' (Goodman 1988a: 94). They are constantly being revised and redescribed, not least when historians' research compulsively keeps re-describing and reworking (recoding) historical versions of the world.

Human life is necessarily enacted in the dimension of symbolic forms. Consciousness operates reflexively through systems of representations: 'dissatisfied with merely receiving impressions from the outside, [it] associates and imbues every impression with the gratuitous activity of expression'. A sign-system of its own making confronts what we term "objective reality"; it asserts itself by virtue of its own 'independent plenitude and immanent force'. These signs intervene between ourselves and objects. Far from signifying 'in a negative sense our distance from the object', they create 'the only possible mediation as well as the dimension in which intellectual being of any kind may at all be apprehended and understood by us' (Cassirer 1977: 175–6).

Freudian theory adds its own twist. It regards symbolism as a necessary supplement to an organic inadequacy inherent in human existence as nature. The fascination by the human subject with its mirror-image betrays its sense of inadequacy with its own, inner reality. The very link between the human organism and the world around it cannot be made except through fiction and reflexive illusion, the aesthetic dimension. Consequently, 'the symbolic order may no longer be conceived as constituted by man, but as constituting him': 'the world of words creates the world of things'. Hence, 'the human being speaks but only because the symbol has made him or her human' (Lacan 1966: 46, 96–7, 276).

The past is thinkable and knowable only through the current semiotic or symbolic system. 'Our sense of the past, not as immediately, innately acquired reflexes, but as a shaped selection of remembrance, is ... radically linguistic. History, in the human sense, is a language-net cast backward' (Steiner 1975: 70). The current social stock of historical knowledge in all its heterogeneous forms stands in symbolically for everything that once was, but now eludes immediate experience. What is conventionally received as "naturally objective", is a symbolic projection, a virtual image, generated by disciplinary practice and social thought habits. In an already historicized world, however, the language-net is always cast backward. Nothing can be imagined or expressed except in the preterite and the imperfect. That reinforces the naturalistic illusion of an "objective past" as a substantive extra-textual referent. The past takes extra-textual priority, because the historicizing reflex is already intended in the texture of signs and symbols, in the grammatical structures that make up the language-system: 'At some formative level, we conduct our lives from the cliché of birth to that of death. We vary innumerably, but rarely in essence, on themes pre-set and always restated by the pre-established facticity of language' (Steiner 2001: 128). The grammatical and conceptual schemes already existing in language exert a 'passive force' in thinking (as Nietzsche realized), thus promoting ready-made 'cultural paradigms' that offer new significations 'an organization of "sameness"' (Cohen 1988: 190). Whatever the historical reflex produces is, in some form or another, already known, already there.

That's why, in a historicized world, history has nothing new to teach (even if its lessons could be learned). That's why, conforming always to what was, history remains authoritative. But what it authorizes is the constant reproduction of the already existing, morbid culture of traumatic experience, phantom memories, and petrified objects. It sanctions a mentality that defers automatically to a traditional value-system that puts a selection of dead 'saints, cardinals, archbishops, and earls' before the generations of the living. It thereby sustains a pessimistic, misanthropic ideology that always has seen 'prelates and nobles as the repositories and guardians of conservative truths' (Maistre 1980: II, 108). One day, history's fatal arrogance might provoke opposition: the dissociation of humanity from history, the institution of a new language and a new 'thought-style' for the humanities. The humanities could easily start right now. It just takes something different: 'a new, large custom to be adopted immediately, the custom of thinking anew in each new situation' (Brecht 1966b: 17).

What beckons, therefore, is a new Enlightenment. The ultimate act of human liberation, the fulfilment of an individual, but species-essential obligation, would be human beings releasing themselves from their traumatic, self-incriminating history, from their self-inflicted, historical immaturity (cf. Kant 1977: XI, 53). In an already historicized world, history [*crg*] breeds obscurantism as much as the religious superstitiousness Kant repudiated. The immaturity is historical, because the human cognitive faculty submits to history's tutelage, acquiesces in its conceited verdict that 'the right way of investigating mind is by the methods of history' (Collingwood 1978: 209; cf. Cohen 1988: 154, 170). It conforms to its authoritative precedents as much as it's seduced by its oneiric nostalgias. The way out is for thinking not to defer to tradition or revelation, follow social convention, or be cowed by public attitudes, but to make responsible use of its inherent need and capacity to orientate itself (Kant 1977: V, 268–71, 277, 280–3). This enlightened attitude involves 'imagining the present being other than it is'. It means 'adopting an attitude ... in which the critique of who we are involves both analyzing historically the limits laid down for us and testing the possibility of transgressing them'. That means 'permanently reactivating ... a permanent critique of our historical being' (Foucault 2001: II, 1389, 1390, 1396).

(b.) The psychopathology of historicized life. History [*crg*] is a deferred, symbolic substitution for the traumatic loss the past represents, an imaginary compensation for the temporality of existence, the projection of the desire for a redemptive significance in human behaviour. Consciousness needs this symbolic dimension since it cannot cope adequately, immediately, with the predicaments human behaviour occasions.

The historical predicament is psychopathological. Trauma, obsessive memories, oneiric nostalgias, longings for ideals, redemptive desires testify to an underlying affective disorder with characteristic bi-polar features. In its depressive form, it presents itself in unintended consequences, in the finitude of human effort for the unsolicited, inherited task, the feeling of abandonment in being left to cope with it so late in the day, and, not least, the discomfiting appreciation of the marginal eccentricity of human existence (cf. Foucault 1983: 201–2). In its manic form, it generates the narcissistic identifications, ideal wish-fulfilments that social or political group-interests use to vindicate themselves (Lessing 1983: 118). It turns history into a scene for human self-aggrandizement, where the ego (be it personal or collective), positing itself as 'all reality', becomes a 'quantum that fills up eternity' (Fichte 1970: 191).

The historical predicament is, therefore, delusional – identitary logic, defining it always as 'how it got to be the way it is', its crucial symptom. History is allegedly the enactment of human autonomy – the Kantian concept here supplying the humanist ethos of academic history. Through their participation in state and society, human beings realize the immanent moral purpose of nature (Kant 1968: 301–2, §83). Yet, as the world historicizes itself through 'unsocial sociability', it turns out to be a process of human self-incrimination, the 'perpetual peace' of the graveyard its culmination, should its morbid tendencies prevail (Kant 1977: XI, 37, 195). In a world already historicized, the inherent historical priorities it imposes undermine autonomy. As political idealism morphs into moral culpability, humanity is left looking at itself for having done what it did.

In history [*rg*] people behave as they do, things are the way they are. As history [*crg*] it becomes clear why things turned out as they did, how what is, came to be. In a historicized world, historical priorities reconfigure its underlying moral principle. Projected back onto history [*rg*], the moral idealism vindicating humanity as the highest purpose of creation – e.g. the notion that history is the "story of humanity" – makes up for its absence in any current, contingent predicament. Psychologically, therefore, history [*crg*] offers an affirmative, narcissistic compensation for the ontological destitution of the human species (Kant 1968: 305, §84; cf. Freud 1982: 35). But, the Narcissus complex is treacherous: it just reinforces the bi-polarity of humanity's historicized predicament. After the event, humanity can admire itself as a historical object true to itself; yet it knows this object is just an image (and such a true one!), and that it can never embrace itself in this specular, historical form. History may well be '"for" human self-knowledge' (Collingwood 1978: 10). But the Narcissus myth always did disclose a 'paradoxical conjunction of self-recognition, hopelessness and death'. It reveals that identities, mirror-images, identitary constructions, not least because they exclude difference, solicit a morbid fascination (Davies 1989: 265; cf. Morin 1976: 189; Kristeva 1983: 122). The narcissistic subject, particularly the historical subject in a historicized world, engrossed 'in knowing what it is to be the man *you* are', becomes a 'victim of pure representation' (Collingwood 1978: 10; Davies 1989: 268). It comes to know who it is through what it has done [*res gestae*]. It identifies itself with the signs and gestures its historical reflection makes. Mistaking its historical self-concern with the world itself, it becomes infatuated with the psychic space – the historical knowledge – that sustains the reflected object. Narcissus is drowning when he realizes he has been mesmerized by semiotics, when too late he sees the falsity of his predicament (Davies 1989: 268; Kristeva 1983: 102,113). History [*crg*] that would de-mythologize the world by revealing its real human reality, *is* the new mythology. Unconsciously it perpetuates in the present day a fatal, archaic compulsion.

History, as an essentially identitary construction, therefore, prompts the further question: on what kind of identifications does it rely? Any object we become attached to both provides gratification and solicits emotional investment. What is the libidinal economy operative in historians' attachment to their research subjects? What investment is required, what gratification received, when a historian creates a true image of the historical object she loves, or admires himself in the historical object he has faithfully fashioned? That kind of self-reflection would be a *desideratum* in the humanities! Psychologistic by nature, historical explanation can replicate the past only by the historian, on the basis of personal experience, projecting him- or herself into the mentality he or she aims to understand (Simmel 1997: 264, 266). History is one vast Place de la Morgue (the square in Paris where the corpses of those drowned in the Seine were displayed) 'where everyone comes to search for their nearest and dearest amongst the dead [*die toten Verwandten seines Herzens*]' (Richter 1970: I, 1016).

Any theory of history 'must embrace a theory of neurosis' (Brown 1970: 23). Historical studiousness and curiosity demonstrate behaviour-patterns that come from psychopathological reflexes such as (i) neurotic repetition-compulsion, (ii) hysteria, and (iii) melancholy. *(b.i) Repetition-compulsion.* 'A short time after the patient's death … the work of *reproduction* begins within her, which brings the scenes of illness and death once again before her eyes. Every day she goes through each impression again … She manages to do this while going about her daily business … . The whole experience passes over her mind in chronological sequence': thus Freud's description of an acquaintance who had nursed to the end 'three or four of her nearest and dearest [*ihrer Lieben*]' (Freud & Breuer 1975: 132 (my italics)). Similarly, 'the historian must re-enact the past in his own mind' (Collingwood 1978: 282). Mental re-enactment thus makes historical knowledge 'the knowledge of what the mind has done in the past, and at the same time ... the *redoing of this,* the *perpetuation of past acts in the present.*' The historical object is 'an activity of thought, which can be *known only in so far as the knowing mind re-enacts it* and knows itself as so doing'. What the historian studies, are 'experiences to be *lived through in his own mind;* they are ... known to him, only because they are also ... activities of his own' (Collingwood 1978: 218 (my italics)). Hysteria and history work through repetition-compulsion.

Collingwood's argument, like all idealism, is limited by its schematic character. The present perpetuation of the past (as historical knowledge) cannot be just a cerebral abstraction. It must also be a form of social behaviour. By definition, it operates whenever, wherever the historicizing experience occurs – be it in the National Trust's Calke Abbey on a Bank Holiday or in the scholar's study in the small hours. The re-enactment cannot be other than a deferred symbolic reproduction. Freud's 'slightly neurotic' acquaintance, 'presenting all the symptoms of hysteria' without being indisposed by them, not only repeats all the mourning rituals, but also each year commemorates the anniversaries of her loved ones' deaths (Freud & Breuer 1975: 132). Similarly, historicization as social behaviour needs the semiotics of the public historic environment as much as mental re-enactment requires the historicizing discourse of the academic monograph. In both cases the 'perpetuation of past acts in the present' works symbolically. The symbolic dimension perpetuates the past in the present.

Though idealistically conceived, the mental re-enactment in practice subverts the idealist stance sustaining it. How can all history be 'the history of thought', how can liberty be 'the explicatory principle of the course of history', when history is just the surface effect of unconscious, archaic impulses (Collingwood 1978: 215; Croce 1966: 585)? Whether it ritually reproduces traumatic situations or mentally re-enacts past events (themselves involving trauma such as genocides, wars, battles, revolutions), the very compulsion to repeat is anything but cerebral and conscious. Rather it reveals a psychopathological present arrested and mesmerized by its past. The patient consciously experiences in symbolic form, as a 'reproduction occurring with unwanted precision', only the hurt he or she must keep working through, if not repressing (Freud 1982: 130–1, 134). The compulsive, symbolic reproduction of human action puts paid to meta-historical configurations of history as 'a science of human nature', the guarantor of the 'moral ideal of mankind' (Collingwood 1978: 220; Croce 1966: 585). Instinctively responding to anniversaries, endorsing commemorations, riding the going social-intellectual trends, the historical disciplines sell out on both their conscious self-determination and their professed idealism. Reiterating the same old thing, on the same old topics, in the same old periods, they unconsciously affirm their own 'archaic heritage' (cf. Freud 1973: 67). The already historicized world unconsciously perpetuates and accommodates a pathological relationship to the past – principally since it reinforces a social practice that (as Collingwood says) repeatedly obliges historians to relive past experiences in their own minds. As focal-points for society's pathological tendencies, historians ensure that, at any given time, for any given time, things always stay as they were, the way they actually always were.

(b.ii) Deferred reactions. Historical knowledge is always out of sync with one's actual situation. The temporal continuities and periodicities that appear to "shape" history, the factors that apparently configure a historical event, are products of deferred after-sight. The past re-enacted in one's own mind has no natural link to current temporal location or to the past itself, as it was for itself, however much historical sequentiality pretends otherwise. If some thing – the same old thing – keeps being mentally re-enacted, then it must still have some uncanny, oneiric hold over the self. It won't let itself be let go of. Conversely, what is deferred, tends consciously or unconsciously to have unpleasant associations that have caused it to be put off. Either way, having to keep going over the same old thing, the already historicized world keeps deferring to how it really was, keeps rediscovering 'what it all meant' (Evans 1997: 253).

Here Freud's concept of *Nachträglichkeit* comes in, touching as it does 'upon the fundamental relationship between event and history' and designating 'the transformation and rewriting of experiences, impressions, and memory traces on the basis of later experiences and in the context of a new phase of development' (Nägele 1987: 174). Meaning 'deferred action' or 'belatedness', it signifies the delayed action of a trauma on the psyche, its belated emergence into consciousness. It enables 'those elements of the past that in their own time could not enter into the economy of signification and were therefore excluded, repressed, or marginalized' to be redeemed (Nägele 1987: 2, 4–5). It also generates a cluster of related meanings: the noun, *Nachtrag*, means 'codicil', 'addendum'; the verb *nachtragen* means both 'to rectify an account' and 'to bear a grudge'; the adjectives *nachtragend* or *nachträgerisch* mean 'being unforgiving, vindictive' – each designating a way in which history instrumentalizes the past.

Nachträglichkeit makes the usual apology for history – i.e. that understanding the past is required for understanding the present – redundant. The present constructs its own past through its present psychopathological obsessions. According to the principle of deferred enactment 'the "after" becomes constitutive of the "before"' (Nägele 1987: 2). (So Hindenburg invented himself as mythical 'saviour of the German nation' by arbitrarily claiming his victory over the Russian army in the Masurian region of East Prussia in August 1914 avenged the Polish victory over the Teutonic Knights at Tannenberg in 1410: Ortelsburg and Gilgenburg, towns closer to the battle-area, had much less resonance with the German public than Tannenberg which historically it *already* knew about (cf. Krumreich 1994: 2).) History is, therefore, not just 'what happened', nor primarily the verification of what happened. It's altogether more deceptive, the scene of postponed action, delayed reckonings; the instrument of adjourned comprehension, of belated (self-) vindication, of deferred vindictiveness – done up as verification, as 'the cautious rationality of academic historical scholarship', 'reasoned conclusions', 'best explanations', 'fair interpretations' (cf. Evans 2002: 114, 256, 272; McCullagh 2004: 49, 149).

'Deferred reaction' [*Nachträglichkeit*] decisively determines the structure of the past. That the primal event manifests itself – as primal – only afterwards and in symbolic form, is the psychopatho-logical reflex that drives historicization. The past acquires historical objectivity always afterwards. This comes out particularly in cases of hysteria, the classic symptom of the suffering reminiscence causes. Here 'the process that induces it remains active in some way or other for years, not indirectly through the mediation of a chain of connecting links, but as a *cause that immediately releases it*, just as psychical pain remembered with alert consciousness brings forth the secretion of tears even at a later time' (Freud & Breuer 1975: 10, 178 (my italics)). What's more, it confirms the crucial feature of knowledge in a historicized world: the split between *illusio* and *aesthesis*. The past returns in a vengeful, alien form as a symbolic illusion [*illusio*]. Intruding on the patient's actual immediate situation [*aesthesis*], its mental re-enactment distracts and incapacitates her, even threatening her safety (Freud 1981: 100; Freud & Breuer 1975: 9, 73, 166, 182, 185).

The hysterical subject is split between the shock it suffers and its capacity to cope with it. As a result, it has 'a large complex of representations that are presentable to consciousness lying adjacent to a smaller complex of representations that are not presentable'. In other words, there's more scope for generating representations than consciousness allows. The trauma that's thus repressed returns to incapacitate the patient. How strongly the original event still has her in its grip the intensity of the crisis reveals. The conscious mind loses control over the symbolic representations [*Vorstellungen* [*illusio*]] that come from the unconscious. They take over muscular movement, speech, even ideational activity, producing apparently motiveless fluctuations of mood and feeling, periods of compulsive behaviour or of hallucinatory seizure. The patient can become self-detached, seeing herself object-ively. She becomes a spectator to her own hysterical crisis and looks on with '*curiosity* and astonishment' (Freud & Breuer 1975: 182, 184, 185 (my italics)).

In the deferred mental re-enactment of the past event symbolization plays a central role. The hysterical patient who feels she is 'not making any progress' in her life *will* suffer physically from paralysis. The unavowed trauma – the fear of being left alone and single – undergoes symbolic conversion as a defence mechanism. The temporal delay between the original trauma (e.g. disappointed aspirations) and its subsequent conversion into psychopathological behaviour (e.g. immobility) reflects the figurative relationship between the ideational cause (e.g. 'no progress') and its material effect (e.g. paralysis). Thus hysterical behaviour comes not just from the physical fact (e.g. paralysis) but also from its figurative symbol (e.g. 'no progress'). At various times symbol and sensation both trigger and reinforce each other, so it's never clear which takes precedence (Freud & Breuer 1975: 119, 123–4, 147). The mind normally works through symbols, ordered by a grammar of its own making. But the hysterical subject is mesmerized by the pathological turn this symbolism takes, by hallucinations, illusions – oneiric images and nostalgic longings. What they mean, is discovered only subsequently [*nachträglich*] through a process akin to archaeological excavation (cf. Freud & Breuer 1975: 112). The past, as a "former present", always has to be reconstituted after the event: nothing originary, it lacks any inherent, vital, abundance of sense (cf. Derrida 1979: 314). Its compelling sense of priority is symptomatic of its actual psychopathological grip. As the analogy with hysteria shows, this grip gets tightened not just through the re-constituted original event (i.e. the archival record, the primary source, the 'stories inscribed in ... field patterns, hedgerows, designed landscapes' (DCMS 2001: 7)), but also through the recurring symbolic forms it takes (i.e. the subsequent historical accounts). In a traumatized, historicized world, history [*rg*] feeds on, is fed by, history [*crg*].

History, then, can't help mentally re-enacting itself. It won't relinquish its nearest and dearest and their unfinished business.

That's why it resists psychological, sociological, semiotic, or ontological reconceptions of human experience that might extend the scope of consciousness (cf. LaCapra 1996: 46). As the psychopathology of hysteria shows, historical knowledge as the mental re-enactment of past events is 'a cultural symptom of anxiety and stress' (Showalter 1997: 9). It's an expression of a culture of apprehension generated by an already historicized world, vulnerable because traumatized, repressed because (self-) incriminated. Its whole system – with its "traditions", "legacies", "periods", "continuities", "milestones", "identities" – is symptomatic of something numinous, spooky, that remains repressed yet manifests itself symbolically: an archaic existential apprehension, a radical "dis-ease" [*Unbehagen*] of being in the world. Given that 'mass psychogenic disorders ' – like the sociopathic compulsion to historicize – 'are metasymbols of the deep structures of our culture', it will never be clear how much sense in history makes sense of history (Showalter 1997: 8). Sense arises not from a 'comprehensible' rational process, but from the intensity of symbolic expression projected by an apprehensive, ideational reaction that can last for 'long continuous periods of time'. Without any correlation between the length of its duration and its original cause, the patient, deep in melancholy, stays 'continuously absorbed for a long time *in the same embarrassing representation* that is always alive and actual' (Freud & Breuer 1975: 183; cf. also 8, 73, 191 (my italics)).

(b.iii) Melancholy. Clearly the past makes a lot of work for the present. The angel of history, propelled irresistibly backward by the storm howling out of paradise, leaves catastrophe upon catastrophe behind it (Benjamin 1977: 255, §IX). Sometime afterwards Clio hobbles along to tidy it up, to put a nice finish on it. History [*crg*] is left with the melancholy work of mourning.

Freud's analysis of melancholy also shows how history objectively constructs itself. Its references to the self [*Ich*; ego] and the desolate psychic 'space' occupied by the lost object don't exclude either the historian-function or the vast space the collective social mind allows for deferred historical representations. It confirms the depressive nature of identitary thinking: in finding a mesmerizing object to identify with, this thinking becomes a mesmerizing object for itself. It reinforces history [*crg*] as *illusio*. Historians may well claim to revive the past. In reality the past keeps historians alive: through history death directs present life. If the past really were over and done with, history would be redundant, historians superfluous. Were it not so self-absorbed, present historical consciousness would realize that, to identify with the past at all, it must first have produced itself as a historical object, become petrified in historical form. That is ultimately why historical interests are not existential interests, why history is an anaesthetic [an-*aesthesis*], nothing vital.

As a 'pure culture of the death drive', the already historicized world is a typically melancholic formation (Freud 1982: 203). The historicization process conceals a morbid psychopathology.

Mourning already makes the past seem richer: suffering the loss of someone or something dear induces a state of mind that, by contrast, makes the present seem 'destitute and empty' (Freud 1982: 107). Suddenly removed to the past, the cherished object belongs to personal memory and anecdotal recollection. If it is not to be forsaken and the attachment not to weaken, it must be mentally perpetuated in its now reified object-ivity. The grieving self turns away from present reality and holds its object fast by means of an 'hallucinatory wish psychosis', *illusio* in its psychopathological form. Incapable of dealing with the loss of the old thing it cherished, the grieving subject historicizes itself. What lies at the heart of a historicized society heavily into conserving and replicating all cherished old things, the same old things, is this mournful, now historicized personality.

In melancholy the objectivizing process works differently. Melancholy is a depressive illness that makes the self perceive itself as 'destitute and empty'. The self internalizes the desolation it suffers: the loss of the object triggers a drastic loss of self-esteem. In disparaging itself, the psyche must disparage its own past. It claims 'that it was never any better', that it always was the same old, worthless, melancholic thing as it now is (Freud 1982: 107). Melancholy thus induces the identitary thinking behind historical explanation. The posture is essentially narcissistic. Melancholy produces comprehensive "objectivity", because the personal attachment to the lost object does not transfer to another, present object. Instead, it withdraws into the self to make it identify itself with the object it has lost. Projected onto the social scale, this personal reflex generates historical consciousness. Through the process of history, the past offers social consciousness a host of heterogeneous objects to identify with to compensate it for its ever recurrent losses.

Furthermore, along with melancholy objectivity comes objective truth. The self-disparagement triggered in the melancholic subject by the sense of loss is received as self-knowledge. The deferred revelation of its abject situation permits it at last to describe itself properly, to perceive the truth about itself. Truth gratifyingly confirms the melancholic's abject situation: abjection seems inexplicably to be the necessary pre-condition of truthful self-knowledge (Freud 1982: 108, 109). Faced with the loss of objects it still cherishes, historical consciousness is thus left to rebuild them for itself, objectively, truly – identical to the 'true object' it has now become for itself in its present abjection. That's why history [*crg*] needs facts to fill its gaping emptiness (cf. Benjamin 1977: 260, §XVII; Schlick 1986: 99). This objectification process is, however, fraught with ambivalence. Identification, here as in all intimate relationships, may involve resentment as much as admiration (cf. Freud 1982: 112). It reminds the self that the object that desolated it is actually lost (i.e. dead and past) and can't account for itself any more. Henceforth, this object, reified in its own past, will always have priority over a self that bases its own truth on this object-ively enforced abjection.

Thus the melancholic attitude, taken to its psychological conclusion, is fatally self-defeating. The narcissistic identification can be so complete, the desolate self so absorbed in its lost object, that it is totally overwhelmed by it, suicidally convinced of its own inadequacy (cf. Freud 1982: 113). The present thus loses itself in the past, its self-assertion expressed as self-negation. The disparaged self is narcissistically absorbed into the lost object it has reconstructed as itself (cf. Freud 1982: 110–11). The vital personal interest, 'reconciled with the depradations of time', freezes in its reified form (cf. Sontag 1986: 6). Objectivity, resulting from a self-disparaging identification with a lost object, symbolizes an already historicized world, a structure of reified configurations of petrified identities. It discloses a terrifying prospect: objects existing "out there", beyond the text, beyond anything that can be said about them, *before* anything can be said about them. To make this objectivity the cornerstone of a form of knowledge that claims to be 'every-*thing*' is inhumane. A world filling up with heterogeneous thing-objects, remaining always as they actually were – regardless of human intervention – eventually petrifies life itself.

(c.) The occlusion of experience. Between immediate experience [*aesthesis*] and its subsequent symbolic representation [*illusio*] gapes a metaphysical chasm. It is identified by Charles Péguy after describing the Dreyfus affair (for him a personally formative issue) to a younger researcher. 'What I gave him was reality, what he received was history,' he observes. 'In which mysterious, interpolated chasm did this loss occur, this disappearance take place, this defection happen?', he wonders: 'in which chasm of memory itself; in which chasm did this

most precious of all vessels, this vessel which is destined for only one voyage, go down?' In dismay he reflects that it gapes open everywhere, 'between enquiry and response, between departure and arrival, between every enquiry and every response, between any departure and any arrival.' It's a mysterious chasm: one puts something into it, something real, yet out of it comes something quite different, 'an imitation; a forgery; invariably a parody; a substitution; a surrogate; a replacement; something quite alien: an intellectual procedure; a history' (Péguy 1961: 46). Thus history encodes experience [*aesthesis*] as a 'nonsemiotic entity', as something essentially 'uncoded', to which it subsequently applies a deferred meaning (cf. Cohen 1988: 200).

Experience is sequestrated by the self-same history that would reveal its reality. It happens because of an inevitable 'cognitive asymmetry', a form of astigmatism structurally inherent in the discipline, that necessarily distorts the cognitive relationship between present and past. Involving a 'retroactive re-alignment of the past', it is synonymous with what Freud calls 'belated attribution' [*Nachträglichkeit*]. It designates the radical discontinuity between what the actors in the event knew at the time and what historians know now (on the basis of subsequent knowledge) of that past event. The result is: 'events under narrative descriptions could not have been experienced as such by those who lived through them – unless those people had a knowledge of the future we would very likely impugn as impossible'. It means that 'events are continually being re-described, and their significance re-evaluated in the light of later information'. It means too, therefore, that 'historians can say things that witnesses and contemporaries could not justifiably have said' (Danto 1985: 11, 168, 294).

History thrives on this disjunction. It's the source of its ambivalence, the sanction of an already historicized world. It enables it, as a symbolic reproduction of the past, to claim to be its objective, truthful representation. But it also permits it, as an 'historically understood past' suspended in the asymmetrical, academic dimension, to proliferate through its same old, self-generated patterns of coherence (Oakeshott 1999: 36). History can, therefore, assume the demeanour of a disinterested, objective human science. But as 'a substitution, a surrogate', it can also operate affirmatively, project pathological obsessions, and sustain ideologies. Furthermore, cognitive asymmetry ensures these functions remain identical. According to its own identitary logic, history stays always true to itself, since it always turns out as it does.

But wherever history stands, it stands in the way of experience. The view that history is a 'form of self-knowledge' doesn't wash any more. The idea that 'in history man constantly returns to himself', that 'he attempts to ... actualize the whole of his past experience', in practice produces a historicized, therefore morbid, world (Cassirer 1967: 191). To be engrossed in history, means being engrossed in what is dated, obsolete. It generates apprehension because it occludes the human reality it symbolically simulates. It keeps attempting to take precedence over the one, real, unprecedented issue: each person's own encounter with the world in which all other persons live. In this situation, to defer to history to discover how things have got to be the way they are, is an act of bad faith. That's because history promotes a grand illusion – that the totality of dead humanity means more than its living representatives.

This illusion sanctions all kinds of havoc. Introspective self-knowledge boosted by retrospective world-knowledge, particular interests inflated by cognitive abstractions asymmetrical to lived experience, have proved to be intoxicating but fatal combinations. The result: a self-incriminated humanity and the wasteland that is the historicized world. The reason: introspection and retrospection disregard circumspection. They leave out the now. Instead, self-knowledge must unlearn its identitary habits. That means 'going beyond oneself', seeking what is external to one's self. Knowledge, let alone self-knowledge, arises from being challenged by something different. Encountering differences sustains knowledge along with its essentially ethical stance. It's the defining activity of human consciousness that wouldn't be human, were it not programmed *a priori* for responsibility for others (Levinas 1972: 52–3). Consciousness with its ethical intention thus reveals a matrix of human apprehension prior to historical culture. It always constitutes an opportunity to defy the way things are – to be 'untimely'. The self-transcendence it requires, implies transcendence of the historical epoch in which one lives (Levinas 1972: 46–7, 54–6, 58). Realizing ethical obligations just doesn't go with affirming historical identities.

Still, at every turn ethical vigilance is anaesthetized by history's symbolic reproduction of the same old thing. In the historicized world, history saturates reality with its heterogeneous images. But the fluidity of postmodern reality is deceptive. Slick and heavy with historical meaning, it is more like a supersaturated solution always about to crystallize. History as a technology for managing the historicized world, affirms a mediatized social reality manufactured 'repeatedly to confirm and reinforce merely the ways things are, what the course of world events has made people for'. Energized by history's identitary logic, the social dynamic of an already historicized world perpetually ensures that 'everything always remains the same' [*Immergleichheit des Ganzen*] (Adorno 2003: 514, 633).

Should we then accept that our experience will fall into a metaphysical chasm, only for history to mine and refine it later? It certainly is repugnant to think that, for the purpose of technical comprehension, academic experts sequestrate personal experience, only subsequently to distil from it some synthetic aggregate of sense, to manufacture replicas designed to be more real than the reality we thought we had experienced. The historicized world is indeed deceptive. In 'assuming that cultural subjects live in order to be remembered in their future', and 'presuming history to be present all along as a natural motivation', it deprives us of the inevitably deferred historical significance of our *own* experience, leaving us apprehensive of its unforeseeable, unintended consequences (Cohen 1988: 91). It also insists that present experience never amounts to adequate reality, since it must await validation by a later, deferred historical perspective. The immediate present thus dwindles to a dreary margin of being – a depleted, sub-historical reality.

Coda
'Untimely' Thinking

The reader who left *Historics* with the idea that history was finished would be mistaken. History [*crg*] puts a finish on things, on its objects – *Historics* doesn't. If *Historics* recognizes one thing, it's that history continues. After all history perpetuates and authenticates itself. Society can't help being historical, its managers, directors, technical experts, opinion-formers, can't help their mental reactions defaulting to history. Everyone and everything ends up being historicized. It's this "can't help" syndrome history induces, that *Historics* has tried to get behind and get at. It wanted to find out what kinds of mental and behavioural habits constitute history, what history does – what you have to do to do history, and when you do history, what you end up doing: what intellectual stance you must take, what ideological principles you must swallow, what thought conventions you must observe. And this enquiry is imperative. The world, now, suffers from severe problems of political and social justice, scandalous inequalities of opportunity and the distribution of wealth and resources, alarming and irreversible environmental damage. This is how the world has, in historical terms, turned out: this is the historicized world. Historians, those who are quick to demonstrate how 'our world got to be the way it is' (Cannadine 1999: 8), those who make history by representing the "real reality" of things, what really happened, those who teach others how history is made and how to make history, thus equipping them with marketable, technical-managerial skills – they are uniquely implicated in the way the historicized world is now. By their very function, their formal, social position, historians furnish the intellectual justification for its perpetuation and reproduction, for constantly symbolically re-enacting the historical changes throughout history that always perpetuate the same old thing.

History is tempting. Whenever cultural contradictions emerge, the social fabric gapes, a political crisis breaks, an economic catastrophe erupts, history comes ready with sets of soothing, already recognized values, skeins of traditions and habits, narratives of origins and causes, accounts of precedents and outcomes, successes and failures. History works as the all-purpose "filler" for a heterogeneous, fragmented, historicized reality. But it's deceptive: it's the ultimate reality fix, but only because of its drowsy, an-*aesthetic* side-effects. In reality, it's 'the absence of being, the negation of everything, a rupture of the living amongst the living', something alien to our 'intemporal nature': there's no reason to go along with it. Certainly, it can erase us regardlessly. Still, nothing stops us inverting the normal continuities. Nothing stops us seeing the whole of time 'coming to visit us, one last time, before disappearing'. Certainly this 'eternal present' seems as phantasmic an idea as 'normal continuities' and just as empty. But, Cioran insists, does not this ever-present emptiness dispense a plenitude far more real than all of history put together (Cioran 1987: 146–7)?

At least, it's a reminder, a pang of apprehension. One may not be able to help being historical. One might not be able to help living in a historicized world, confronting daily the demoralizing heterogeneity of all historical things. But one can, however, help what one thinks, how one thinks. One should just think – and not just go along with the readily available historical, historicized concepts, ordering, reordering, and recoding knowledge already known. One should think, because thinking is where it's always at. Only usually, *historically*, thinking defaults to knowledge already known. History de-intellectualizes, prevents alternative thinking, 'encourages a consciousness that is never able to arrive at criticism' (Cohen 1988: 1, 77, 230). One can't help living in historical world: that doesn't mean having to adopt a historical or historicizing thought-style. The melancholy, ruined, historicized world must be confronted daily: that doesn't mean routinely resorting to historical categories to deal with it. In getting behind the history thought-style that sustains the thought-collective not just of historical disciplines in the human sciences, but also of historicizing as an entrenched social practice, *Historics* aims to subvert the compulsion to historicize. It thus endorses the true social-critical function of philosophy: i.e. 'to prevent people succumbing to the ideas and forms of behaviour that society as it is currently organized encourages them to adopt' (Horkheimer 1976: 283). Thinking obeys its own, always interruptive imperatives. It is anachronistic and, in Nietzsche's sense, 'untimely' [*unzeitgemäß*]. It urges reflection on what needs to be thought – not just on how things are, but on what's behind how things are. It makes its own demands, such as the practice of self-distanciation, the observance of its own logical, and grammatological proprieties. It means that, whenever, wherever the historical past, the historicized world are confronted intellectually, the opportunity arises – for reflection, for backing one's own sense of things, for choosing one's own attitude in the given circumstances (cf. Bettelheim 1986: 158).

One should just think and for one good reason: it brings us to our senses. The capacity for reflection that defines the human creature as human is nothing historical. History may well be able to catalogue what has been thought about; but cataloguing is merely a technical procedure, the dull housework, after the party's end. Thinking offers 'a domain where the whole of one's life and its meaning ... where this ungraspable whole can manifest itself as the sheer continuity of the I-am, an enduring presence in the midst of the world's ever-changing transitoriness'. For this reason, 'the primacy of the present, the most transitory of the tenses in the world of appearances' is 'an almost dogmatic tenet of philosophical speculation' (Arendt 1978: 211).

In a heterogeneous, historicized world, the disruptive potential of thinking that brings out the human presence, is underwritten by human creativity in the aesthetic dimension, both in its transfigurative potential and in the practice of discrimination it fosters. Hannah Arendt emphasizes 'the strange survival of great works, their relative permanence throughout thousands of years,' which (she says) 'is due to their having been born in the small, inconspicuous track of non-time which their authors' thought had beaten between an infinite past and an infinite future'. In imposing their own perspective on this past and future, these authors established 'a present for themselves, a kind of timeless time in which men are able to create timeless works with which to transcend their own finiteness' (Arendt 1978: 210–11).

Few may be able to create timeless works – but one can live with them, extract 'good things' from them, and, in so doing, venture into the infinity in one's own finiteness. That's reason enough for not letting oneself be lulled into living an illusory life in history.

Appendix

The following tables present in diagram form an overview of the main structures of the argument.

Table 1   *Historics*: Schematic overview of the basic conceptual framework

HISTORICS: DEFINING THE NATURE OF HISTORY	
History as *illusio*	Knowledge as *aesthesis*
Autochthonous reason in history 　　—religion 　　—state 　　—culture 　　—society 　　—economics	The immediate, human sense of things: 　　—sensation 　　—feeling 　　—remembering 　　—thinking 　　—reflection 　　—judgement
Coercive processes [*Geschichte*]	Self-possession [*Eigensinn*]
Historicism: (a) Rationale: 　　—organic 　　—materialist/economic 　　—metaphysical 　　—cultural morphological 　　—teleological 　　—postmodernist (b) Progress (c) Tradition (d) Heritage	The ordinary world of everyday life [*Lebenswelt*]
Comprehension	Apprehension
Heterogeneity	Discrimination/differentiation
Technology	Art, aesthetic medium: 　　Poetry/drama/music, etc.
	Reflective thinking/symbolic form

Historics aims to isolate the function of history by contrasting its instrumental character with a broadly aesthetic attitude to the world. The conceptualizations in the left-hand column characterize history. They are either unverifiable, hypothetical, provisional, indiscriminate or ultimately unpredictable. They are classed as *illusio*. Those in the right-hand column derive from aesthetics. They represent inferences, forms and concepts achieved through reflection on primary, immediate experience. They are classed as *aesthesis*.

Table 2 *Historics*: Schematic overview of the basic analysis of history

ANALYSIS OF HISTORICAL COGNITION: The Structure of Historical Consciousness		
Action in the past *res gestae* [rg] [*illusio* (i)]		**Understanding (comprehension)** *Cognitio rerum gestarum* [crg] [*illusio* (ii)]
Intention/cause		Horizon of expectation Realization/outcome
Fact: action/material evidence: 'deed'		Interpretation/evaluation
Mentality [*Geist/Esprit*]		Common denominator of all sensibilities Understanding [*Verstehen*]
Sense-production logistics/delivery	memory	Cognitive organization autochthonous reason in history
Technology (i): cultural enhancements/prostheses [*techne*]	Historical	Technology (ii): information retrieval systems [*techne/technasma*]
Production process: artefacts commodities institutions		Management-systems technics of management: historiography/theory of history/philosophy of history/historicism

"History" refers to "action in the past" as well as to "understanding action in the past": both aspects have to be kept in mind. *Historics*, however, also restates them in social terms, since it sees disciplines as functions rather than as substantive entities. Thus it fixes on what history actually does rather than what it is. *Historics* shows how prevailing social forces, facilitated by the discipline itself, direct the "history function" in society. Because of unresolvable disparities between its disciplinary claims and its social function, history appears as *illusio*.

Table 3   *Historics*: Schematic overview of the structure of historical understanding

HISTORICAL UNDERSTANDING Functions/Modes/Properties		
Function/mode	Comprehension (*illusio*)	Apprehension (*aesthesis*)
(a) Intellectual basis:		
acquirement of knowledge	X	X
mental grasp	X	X
conceptualization	X	X
(b) Synthesis:		
inclusivity (heterogeneity)	X	—
summation	X	—
total arrangement	X	—
(c) Analysis:		
sensation/feeling	—	X
discernment/discrimination	—	X
realization/appreciation	—	X
(d) Temporal orientation:		
past: recollection	X	X
present: reaction/response	—	X
future: anticipation	—	X

Historical understanding is initially produced by both comprehension and apprehension working together. However, in the final account the rôle of apprehension is discounted. Historical knowledge is a heterogeneous and abstract management technology. It makes its own synthetic arrangements.

Glossary

aesthesis from the Greek *aisthesis*: 'perception by the senses', a 'sensation, sense of a thing' (cf. Appendix: Table 1).

affirmative behaviour, ideas, that endorse the already prevailing cultural and social circumstances, as, e.g., in 'affirmative culture' (cf. Marcuse 1973).

anthropomorphic describes attitudes or philosophies that attribute human form or personality to things.

a priori designates logically presumed principles or concepts from which an argument is deduced.

catachresis, catachrestical a figure of speech that links inappropriate or contradictory terms, e.g. 'small height', 'long wisdom' (cf. *Rhetorica ad Herennium*, IV. xxxiii. 45 ([Cicero] 1968: 342–3)).

catharsis from the Greek: 'cleansing', 'purification'. For Aristotle it meant the purgation of pity and fear that was the outcome of tragedy (cf. Aristotle 1965: 39 (Chapter 6.)).

cognitio rerum gestarum from the Latin: 'knowledge of things, matter or events enacted', i.e. history as knowledge about past events (cf. Appendix: Table 2).

diachronic to do with the development of a subject or thing over time, i.e. historical development.

Eigensinn means 'stubbornness', 'recalcitrance' (German); literally it means 'having a sense [*Sinn*] that is one's own, that is characteristic of oneself [*eigen*]', hence, self-possession. In the *Phenomenology of Mind* (1807), Hegel defines it as the self-consciousness that persists even in coercive situations of servitude (Hegel 1979: 155 (§IV.A)). Negt & Kluge (1993) explore the social–critical implications of the Hegelian concept.

enthymeme a term in rhetoric for a form of inference or deduction 'drawn from probable premises and ... therefore not a strictly demonstrative proof' (Aristotle 1994: 475).

epistemology   the theory of knowledge, the systematic study of how one knows what one knows.

eschatology, eschatological   refer to the theological doctrine of death, judgement, heaven and hell and to the historical structure derived from it.

essentialism, essentialist   designate the philosophical or moral attitude that people and things have intrinsic, fundamental properties that make them what they are.

ethology, ethological   the science of the formation of character and behaviour, hence of ethnicities and species.

exteroception   covers the activity sensory receptors that are stimulated by changes in the external world (cf. Reber 1987: 260).

Geschichte   'history' (German). In Negt & Kluge (1993), it designates the collective social, economic and technological forces that induce alienation. It's the antithesis of *Eigensinn* (qv).

illusio   from the Latin: 'illusion', 'deceit' (cf. Appendix: Table 1).

induction, inductive   the process of inferring general principles from particular facts and instances.

kinesthesis, kinesthetic   a psychological term for the 'feeling of emotion' that 'covers the sensations originating in muscles, tendons and joints' (cf. Reber 1987: 383).

Lebenswelt   'life-world' (German): in phenomenology the term for the world as it immediately appears to consciousness, the world one ordinarily lives in.

mentalité   from the French: 'mentality' — describes that type of history, developed partly by *Annales* historians, concerned with popular beliefs, social attitudes and the cultural practices they sustain.

metonymy, metonymic   a figure of speech 'which draws from an object closely akin or associated an expression suggesting the object meant, but not called by its own name', a trope of substitution, e.g. 'Britain' for 'British people', 'No. 10' for 'the Prime Minister's Office' (cf. *Rhetorica ad Herennium*, IV. xxxii. 43 ([Cicero] 1968: 335–7)).

oneirism, oneiric   to do with dreams, dream-like (from the Greek *oneiros*).

ontology, ontological   to do with the study of Being, the metaphysics of Being.

paralogism, paralogical   unselfconscious or unintended illogical reasoning, fallacy.

parapraxis   in the Freudian sense [*Fehlleistung*], the term given to slips of the tongue, momentary forgetfulness, phobias, involuntary gestures, symptoms of the psychopathology of everyday life that reveal inhibitions or release unconscious desires, etc. (cf. Freud 1987).

phylogenesis, phylogenetic describe the history of the evolution of animal and plant types, including the evolution of humanity as a species.

preterite grammatical term for the tense that expresses past action or a past state (from the Latin *praeterire*, 'to pass', 'to go before').

proprioception designates the sensory systems that provide information about the location and orientation of one's body (cf. Reber 1987: 584).

prosthesis, prosthetic artificial limbs or surgical extensions to the body, especially as the result of traumatic injury.

psychologism, psychologistic forms of explanation that are based on human personality, character, behaviour and intention as the sole or sufficient cause of an event or situation.

reification, reify, reified to do with the conversion of a person, a concept or an idea into a thing, an instrument or a commodity.

repetition–compulsion, repetitive–compulsive describe the irrational and irresistible desire to repeat patterns of behaviour without any advantage being derived from it (cf. Reber 1987: 639).

res gestae from the Latin, 'things, matters or events enacted', i.e. historical events, what happened in the past (cf. Appendix: Table 2).

sememic, semiotic linguistic terms describing the study of signs and meanings.

solipsism, solipsistic philosophy or mental attitude that remains restricted to the self, that claims that the self is both the limit and totality of knowledge.

syllogism a form of reasoning from two premisses that have a common middle term that generates an inference from which the middle term is absent.

synchronic, synchronous to do with what happens at a given moment in time or what happens at the same time.

teleology a type of construction of history that imputes to it a direction, a purpose or a goal (cf. theodicy).

tempocentric 'time-centred', i.e. in relation to consciousness and conceiving of the human situation in the world.

theodicy the philosophical construction of world history with a view to 'vindicating the ways of God to Man' (Alexander Pope, *Essay on Man* (1733/34), I, l.16).

trope, tropic   by analogy with 'tropism', the turning of a word or expression from its proper to its figurative use; figurative language; the character of a discourse or style that uses figurative language; structures of discourse that shape the way language is used and thinking expressed.

tropism   the development or growth of an organism in response to an external stimulus.

tropological   an organism or entity exhibiting the characteristics of tropism

ultimate situation; *Grenzsituation*   the German term means literally 'frontier situation'. Its particular resonance comes from Karl Jaspers' philosophy where the term represents 'fundamental situations of our existence ... which we cannot evade or change', e.g. death, suffering, struggle, chance, guilt (cf. Jaspers 1967: 19–20).

Wissenschaft, wissenschaftlich   'science', 'scientific' (German); refers to a systematically developed corpus of knowledge (i.e. not just 'science' as in the English usage, 'natural science' or 'science and technology').

Zeitgeist   'spirit of the age' (German), a misty, historicist notion.

Bibliography

Historics draws on a wide range of literature relating to the problem of history. It involves synthesis as much as analysis. Listed below are works cited in the text, plus some of the others that helped formulate the argument. They were used in their original language wherever possible: unless otherwise mentioned, all translations are my own.

The essential strands of the arguments set out in *Historics* can be found in the titles marked*.

Adorno, T.W. (1975) 'Zum Verhältnis von Soziologie und Psychologie', In: *Gesellschaftstheorie und Kritik*, Frankfurt am Main: Edition Suhrkamp.*

— (1976) 'Kulturkritik und Gesellschaft', In: *Prismen. Kulturkritik und Gesellschaft*, Frankfurt am Main: Suhrkamp Taschenbuch Wissenschaft.*

— (1978) *Minima Moralia. Reflexionen aus dem beschädigten Leben*, Bibliothek Suhrkamp, Frankfurt am Main: Suhrkamp Verlag.*

— (1982) *Negative Dialektik*, 3rd ed., Frankfurt am Main: Suhrkamp Taschenbuch Wissenschaft.*

— (2003) *Kulturkritik und Gesellschaft II: Eingriffe, Stichworte*, Frankfurt am Main: Suhrkamp Taschenbuch Wissenschaft.

Allott, P. (2001) *Eunomia. A New Order for a New World* (pb. ed.), Oxford: O.U.P.

— (2002) *The Health of Nations. Society and Law beyond the State* (pb. ed.), Cambridge: C.U.P.*

Anders, G. (1985) *Die Antiquiertheit des Menschen. Erster Band: Über die Seele im Zeitalter der zweiten industriellen Revolution*, 7th ed., Munich: C.H. Beck.*

— (1986) *Die Antiquiertheit des Menschen. Zweiter Band: Über die Zerstörung des Lebens im Zeitalter der dritten industriellen Revolution*, 4th ed., Munich: C.H. Beck.*

— (1993) *Philosophische Stenogramme*, 2nd ed., Munich: C.H. Beck.

Angehrn, E. (1985) *Geschichte und Identität*, Berlin and New York: Walter de Gruyter.

Ankersmit, F.R. (1989) 'Historiography and Postmodernism', *History and Theory*, 28, 2: 137–53.

— (1990) 'Reply to Professor Zagorin', *History and Theory*, 29, 3: 275–96.

— (2001) *Historical Representation*, Stanford, CA: Stanford U.P.

Apel, K.-O. (1996) 'Das Selbsteinholungsprinzip der kritisch-rekonstruktiven Geisteswissenschaften', In: *Sich im Denken orientieren. Für Herbert Schnädelbach*, Eds S. Dietz, H. Hastedt and G. Keil, Frankfurt am Main: Suhrkamp Taschenbuch Wissenschaft.

Appleby, J., Hunt, L. and Jacob, M. (1995) *Telling the Truth about History*, Norton Paperback, New York and London: W.W. Norton & Co.

Arendt, H. (1974) *The Human Condition*, Ninth Impression, Chicago and London, University of Chicago Press.*

— (1978) *The Life of the Mind. Volume One: Thinking*, London: Martin Secker & Warburg Ltd.

— (1982) *Lectures on Kant's Political Philosophy* (Edited with an Interpretive Essay by Ronald Beiner), Brighton: The Harvester Press.

— (1983) *Eichmann in Jerusalem. A Report on the Banality of Evil* (Revised & Enlarged Edition), Harmondsworth: Penguin Books.

— (1986) *The Origins of Totalitarianism*, 6th ed., London: André Deutsch.

— (1993) 'The Concept of History', In: *Between Past and Future. Eight Exercises in Political Thought*, New York: Penguins Books USA Inc.*

Ardrey, R. (1970) *African Genesis. A Personal Investigation into the Animal Origins and Nature of Man*, 6th impression, London: Fontana Books.

Ariès, P. (1986) *Le Temps de l'Histoire*, Préface de Roger Chartier, Paris: Éditions du Seuil.

Aristotle (1965) *On the Art of Poetry*, In: *Classical Literary Criticism* (Translated with an Introduction by T.S. Dorsch), Harmondsworth: Penguin.

— (1983) *The Nicomachean Ethics* (Trans. J.A.K. Thomson. Revised with Notes and Appendices by H. Tredennick. Introduction and Bibliography by J. Barnes), Harmondsworth: Penguin Classics.

— (1994) *The "Art" of Rhetoric* (Trans. J.H. Freese, Loeb Classical Library), Cambridge, MA and London: Harvard U.P.

— (1996) *Metaphysics, I–IX* (Trans. H. Tredennick, Loeb Classical Library), Cambridge, MA and London: Harvard U.P.

— (1997) *Metaphysics, X–XIV* (Trans. H. Tredennick); *Oeconomica. Magna Moralia.* (Trans. G.C. Armstrong, Loeb Classical Library), Cambridge, MA and London: Harvard U.P.

Arnold, J.H. (2000) *History. A Very Short Introduction*, Oxford: O.U.P.

Aron, R. (1986) *Introduction à la philosophie de l'histoire. Essai sur les limites de l'objectivité historique.* Nouvelle édition revue et annotée par Sylvie Mesure, Coll. Tel, Paris: Gallimard.

Bacon, F. (1960) *The New Organon*, Ed. F. H. Anderson, The Library of the Liberal Arts, 3rd Printing, Indianapolis and New York: The Bobbs-Merrill Company, Inc.

Baeck, L. (1995) *Das Wesen des Judentums*, 6ᵗʰ ed., Wiesbaden: Fourier.

Baeumler, A. (1981) *Das Irrationalitätsproblem in der Ästhetik und Logik des 18. Jahrhunderts bis zur Kritik der Urteilskraft* (Reprint of 2ⁿᵈ Revised Edition), Darmstadt: Wissenschaftliche Buchgesellschaft.

Bann, S. (1984) *The Clothing of Clio. A Study of the Representation of History in Nineteenth-Century Britain and France*, Cambridge: C.U.P.

— (1995) *Romanticism and the Rise of History*, New York: Twayne Publishers.*

Barraclough, G. (1974) *An Introduction to Contemporary History*, Harmondsworth: Pelican Books.

Barthes, R. (1984) *Le bruissement de la langue*, Paris: Seuil.

Bateson, G. (2000) *Steps to an Ecology of Mind*, Ed. M. Catherine Bateson, Chicago: University of Chicago Press.*

Baudrillard, J. (1992) *L'illusion de la fin ou La grève des événements*, Paris: Galilée.*

Bauer, Y. (1980) *The Holocaust in Historical Perspective*, 2ⁿᵈ Printing, Seattle: University of Washington Press.

Baumgarten, A.G. (1983a) *Texte zur Grundlegung der Ästhetik*, Ed. H. R. Schweitzer, Philosophische Bibliothek, Hamburg: Felix Meiner.

— (1983b) *Philosophische Betrachtungen über einige Bedingungen des Gedichts* (Trans. H. Paetzold), Philosophische Bibliothek, Hamburg: Felix Meiner.

— (1988) *Theoretische Ästhetik. Die grundlegenden Abschnitte aus der "Aesthetica" (1750/58)*, Ed. H. R. Schweitzer, Philosophische Bibliothek (2ⁿᵈ Revised Edition), Hamburg: Felix Meiner.

Beck, U. (1986) *Risikogesellschaft. Auf dem Weg in eine andere Moderne*, Frankfurt am Main: Edition Suhrkamp.*

Benford, G. (2000) *Deep Time. How Humanity Communicates Across Millennia*, Perennial Edition, New York: HarperCollins.*

Benjamin, W. (1977) *Illuminationen. Ausgewählte Schriften*, Frankfurt am Main: Suhrkamp Taschenbuch.*

Berkhofer, Jr., R.F. (1997) *Beyond the Great Story. History as Text and Discourse* (pb. ed.), 3ʳᵈ Printing, Cambridge, MA and London: Harvard U.P.

Bettelheim, B. (1986) *The Informed Heart*, Harmondsworth: Peregrine Books.

Black, J. and MacRaild, J.M. (2000) *Studying History*, 2ⁿᵈ ed., London: Macmillan.

Blanning, T.W.C. (2002) *The Culture of Power and the Power of Culture. Old Regime Europe 1660–1789*, Oxford: O.U.P.

Bloch, E. (1977) *Erbschaft dieser Zeit*, Frankfurt am Main: Bibliothek Suhrkamp.

— (1979) *Das Prinzip Hoffnung*, 6ᵗʰ ed., Frankfurt am Main: Suhrkamp Taschenbuch Wissenschaft.*

— (1985a) *Philosophische Aufsätze zur objektiven Phantasie*, Frankfurt am Main: Suhrkamp Taschenbuch Wissenschaft.

— (1985b) *Politische Messungen, Pestzeit, Vormärz*, Frankfurt am Main: Suhrkamp Taschenbuch Wissenschaft.

Bloch, M. (1974) *Apologie pour l'histoire ou métier d'historien* (Préface de Georges Duby, Coll. Prisme), Paris: Armand Colin.

Blumenberg, H. (1973) *Der Prozeß der theoretischen Neugierde*, Frankfurt am Main: Suhrkamp Taschenbuch Wissenschaft.

— (1974) *Säkularisierung und Selbstbehauptung*, Frankfurt am Main: Suhrkamp Taschenbuch Wissenschaft.

— (1976) *Aspekte der Epochenschwelle: Cusaner und Nolaner*, Frankfurt am Main: Suhrkamp Taschenbuch Wissenschaft.

— (1986a) *Lebenszeit und Weltzeit*, 3rd ed., Frankfurt am Main: Suhrkamp.*

— (1986b) 'Anthropologische Annäherung an die Aktualität der Rhetorik', In: *Wirklichkeiten in denen wir leben. Aufsätze und eine Rede*, Stuttgart: Reclam.

Bodinat, B. de (1996/1999) *La Vie sur Terre. Réflexions sur le peu d'avenir que contient le temps où nous sommes*, 2 vols, Paris: Éditions de l'Encyclopédie des Nuisances.*

Böhme, H. (1989) *Albrecht Dürer. Melencolia I. Im Labyrinth der Deutung*, Frankfurt am Main: Fischer Taschenbuch.

Bossuet, J.-B. (1961) 'Discours sur l'Histoire Universelle', In: *Œuvres*, Eds L'Abbé Velat and Y. Champailler, Bibliothèque de la Pléiade, Paris: Gallimard.

Bourdieu, P. (1984) *Questions de sociologie*, Paris: Éditions de Minuit.*

— (1993) *La Misère du monde*, Coll. Libre Examen, Paris: Éditions du Seuil.

— (1997) *Méditations Pascaliennes*. Coll. Liber, Paris: Éditions du Seuil.*

— (2002) *Science de la science et réflexivité*, 2nd ed., Coll. Cours et Travaux, Paris: Raisons d'agir.*

Boutang, P. (1999) *Les Abeilles de Delphes. Essais I*, Pref. S. Giocanti, Paris: Éditions des Syrtes.

Braudel, F. (1984) *Écrits sur l'histoire I*, Coll. Champs, Paris: Flammarion.

— (1994) *Écrits sur l'histoire II*, Coll. Champs, Paris: Flammarion.

Brecht, B. (1966a) *Ausgewählte Gedichte*. Nachwort von Walter Jens, Frankfurt am Main: Edition Suhrkamp.

— (1966b) *Der Jasager und der Neinsager*, In: *Lehrstücke* (pb. ed.), Hamburg: Rowohlt Taschenbuch.

Brooks, E. (2003) 'In for the count', *The National Trust* 98: 33.

Broszat, M. and Friedländer, S. (1988) 'Um die "Historisierung des Nationalsozialismus". Ein Briefwechsel', *Vierteljahrshefte für Zeitgeschichte* 36: 339–72.

Brown, N.O. (1970) *Life Against Death. The Psychoanalytic Meaning of History*, London: Sphere Books Ltd.*

Brzezinski, Z. (1995) *Out of Control: Global Turmoil on the Eve of the Twenty-First Century*, Touchstone Books Edition, New York: Simon & Schuster.

Bubner, R. (1984) *Geschichtsprozesse und Handlungsnormen*, Frankfurt am Main: Suhrkamp Taschenbuch Wissenschaft.

Burckhardt, J. (1969) *Weltgeschichtliche Betrachtungen*, Ed. R. Marx, Stuttgart: Kröner.

Burke, K. (1966) *Language as Symbolic Action. Essays on Life, Literature, and Method*, Berkeley, LA and London: University of California Press.

— (1969a), *A Grammar of Motives*, Berkeley, LA and London: University of California Press.

— (1969b), *A Rhetoric of Motives*, Berkeley, LA and London: University of California Press.

Butterfield, H. (1969) *Man on His Past. The Study of the History of Historical Scholarship* (pb. ed.), Cambridge: C.U.P.

Caillois, R. (1987) *Le mythe et l'homme*, coll. folio/essais, Paris: Gallimard.

Campbell, C. (1989) *The Romantic Ethic and the Spirit of Modern Consumerism* (pb. ed.), Oxford: Basil Blackwell.

Cannadine, D. (1999) *Making History Now*, London: University of London Institute of Historical Research.

— (Ed.) (2002) *What is History Now?* London: Palgrave Macmillan.

Carr, E.H. (1968) *What is History?* (pb. reprint), Harmondsworth: Pelican.

Carr, W. (1999) *The Origins of the Wars of German Unification*, 4th impression, London and New York: Longman.

Cartledge, P. (2002) 'What is Social History Now?', In: *What is History Now?*, Ed. D. Cannadine, London: Palgrave Macmillan.

Cassirer, E. (1961) *Freiheit und Form. Studien zur deutschen Geistesgeschichte*, 2nd ed., Darmstadt: Wissenschaftliche Buchgesellschaft.

— (1967) *An Essay on Man. An Introduction to a Philosophy of Human Culture*, 18th Printing, New Haven and London: Yale U.P.

— (1977) *Wesen und Wirkung des Symbolbegriffs*, 6th ed., Darmstadt: Wissenschaftliche Buchgesellschaft.

— (1994) *Substanzbegriff und Funktionsbegriff. Untersuchungen über die Grundfragen der Erkenntniskritik*, 7th ed., Darmstadt: Wissenschaftliche Buchgesellschaft.

Castoriadis, C. (1975) *L'Institution imaginaire de la société*, 5th ed., Paris: Éditions du Seuil.*

— (1984) *Crossroads in the Labyrinth* (Translated from the French by K. Soper and M.H. Ryle), Brighton: The Harvester Press.

— (1990) *Le Monde morcelé*, deuxième édition revue et corrigée, Paris: Éditions du Seuil.*

— (1996) *La Montée de l'insignifiance*, Paris: Éditions du Seuil.*

de Certeau, M. (1975) *L'écriture de l'histoire*, Paris: Gallimard.

— (1987) *Histoire et psychanalyse entre science et fiction*, folio essais, Paris: Gallimard.

[Cicero] (1968) *Ad C. Herennium. De Ratione dicendi (Rhetorica ad Herennium)* (Trans. H. Caplan, The Loeb Classical Library), London: William Heinemann; Cambridge, MA: Harvard U.P.

Cicero (1996) *Tusculan Disputations* (Trans. J.E. King, Loeb Classical Library), Cambridge, MA and London: Harvard U.P.

— (2001) *On the Orator. Books I–II*, (Trans. E.W. Sutton and H. Rackham, Loeb Classical Library), Cambridge, MA and London: Harvard U.P.

Cioran, E.M. (1987) *Histoire et Utopie*, Coll. Folio, Paris: Gallimard.*

Cohen, S. (1988) *Historical Culture. On the Recoding of an Academic Discipline* (pb. ed.), Berkeley, LA and London: California U.P.

Colley, L. (2002) 'What is Imperial History Now?', In: *What is History Now?*, Ed. D. Cannadine, London: Palgrave Macmillan.

Collingwood, R.G. (1978) *The Idea of History* (pb. ed.), Oxford: O.U.P.

Connerton, P. (1992) *How Societies Remember* (Reprint), Cambridge: C.U.P.*

Cornford, F.M. (1970) *Plato's Theory of Knowledge. The "Theaetetus" and the "Sophist" of Plato Translated with a Running Commentary* (pb. ed.), London: Routledge & Kegan Paul.

Croce, B. (1966) 'History as the History of Liberty', In: *Philosophy, Poetry, History* (Translated and Introduced by C. Sprigge), London: O.U.P.

— (1984) *Die Geschichte auf den Allgemeinen Begriff der Kunst Gebracht* (Trans. F. Fellmann, Philosophische Bibliothek), Hamburg: Felix Meiner Vlg.

Danto, A.C. (1985) *Narration and Knowledge*, Morningside Edition, New York: Columbia U.P.

Davies, M.L. (1981) 'Romain Rolland: A French Interpretation of German Liberal Humanism', In: *Gedenkschrift for Viktor Poznanski*, Ed. C.A.M. Noble, Bern: Peter Lang.

— (1987) 'Orpheus or Clio? Reflections on the Use of History', *Journal of European Studies* 17, 3: 179–214.*

— (1989) 'History as Narcissism', *Journal of European Studies* 19, 4: 265–91.*

— (1995) *Identity or History? Marcus Herz and the End of the Enlightenment*, Detroit: Wayne State U.P.*

— (1999) 'The Lateness of the World, or How to Leave the Twentieth Century', In: *Romancing Decay: Ideas of decadence in European culture*, Ed. M. St. John, Aldershot: Ashgate.*

— (2002a) 'Wissenschaft und Ambivalenz: Zur Rezeption der Aufklärung in Großbritannien', *Das achtzehnte Jahrhundert* 26, 1: 18–34.

— (2002b) 'Enlightenment and University', *Higher Education Review* 34, 3: 53–70.

— (2003) 'On the Concept of an Ecology of Knowledge', In: *Breaking the Disciplines: Reconceptions in Knowledge, Art and Culture*, Eds M.L. Davies and M. Meskimmon, London: I.B. Tauris.*

— (2004) 'On Two Types of Knowledge in the Human Sciences', In: *Bejahende Erkenntnis. Festschrift für T.J. Reed zu seiner Emeritierung am 30. September 2004* (Eds. Kevin F. Hilliard, Ray Ockenden, and Nigel F. Palmer with Malte Herwig), Tübingen: Niemeyer.*

Davies, S. (2003a) *Empiricism and History*, Basingstoke: Palgrave Macmillan.

Deleuze, G. and Guattari, F. (1991) *Qu'est-ce que la Philosophie?* Paris: Éditions de Minuit.

Derrida, J. (1967) *De la grammatologie*, Paris: Minuit.

— (1979) *L'écriture et la différence*, Coll. Points, Paris: Éditions du Seuil.

— (2001) *L'Université sans condition*, Paris: Galilée.

Descartes, R. (1966) *Discours de la méthode*. Chronologie et Préface de Geneviève Rodis-Lewis (pb. ed.), Paris: Garnier-Flammarion.

— (1970) *Méditations métaphysiques*, Ed. F. Khodoss, Paris: Presses Universitaires de France.

Deutscher, I. (1981) *The Non-Jewish Jew and other Essays*, Ed. T. Deutscher, London: Merlin Press.

Dijkstra, P.U., Geertzen J.H.B., Stewart, R. and van der Schans, C.P. (2002) 'Phantom Pain and Risk Factors: A Multivariate Analysis', *Journal of Pain and Symptom Management* 24, 6: 578–585.

Dilthey, W. (1959) 'Der Aufbau der Welt in den Geisteswissenschaften', In: *Gesammelte Schriften*, vol. VII, Ed. B. Groethuysen, Stuttgart: B.T. Teubner; Göttingen: Vandenhoeck & Ruprecht.

— (1962) 'Die Typen der Weltanschauung und ihre Ausbildung in den metaphysischen Systemen', In: *Gesammelte Schriften*, vol. VIII, Ed. B. Groethuysen, 3rd ed., Stuttgart: B.T. Teubner; Göttingen: Vandenhoeck & Ruprecht.

Dissanayake, E. (1995) *Homo Aestheticus. Where Art Comes From and Why*, Seattle and London: University of Washington Press.

Droysen, J.G. (1977) *Historik*. Textausgabe von Peter Leyh, Stuttgart-Bad Canstatt: Frommann-Holzboog.

Duby, G. (1991) *L'histoire continue*, Paris: Éditions Odile Jacob.

Durkheim, E. (1996) *Sociologie et philosophie*, Présentation de Bruno Karsenti, Préface de Célestin Bouglé, Coll. Quadrige, Paris: Presses Universitaires de France.

— (1997) *Les règles de la méthode sociologique*, 9th ed., Coll. Quadrige, Paris: Presses Universitaires de France.*

Dux, G. (1982) *Die Logik der Weltbilder. Sinnstrukturen im Wandel der Geschichte*, Frankfurt am Main: Suhrkamp Taschenbuch Wissenschaft.

Eagleton, T. (1990) *The Ideology of the Aesthetic*, Oxford: Basil Blackwell.

Eliade, M. (1968) *Myths, Dreams and Mysteries. The Encounter between Contemporary Faiths and Archaic Reality* (Trans. P. Mairet, Fontana Library of Theology and Philosophy), London: Collins.*

Elias, N. (1992) *Studien über die Deutschen. Machtkämpfe und Habitusentwicklung im 19. und 20. Jahrhundert*, Ed. M. Schröter, Frankfurt am Main: Suhrkamp Taschenbuch Wissenschaft.

Elton, G.R. (1969) *The Practice of History*, The Fontana Library, 2nd Impression, London: Fontana.

Evans, R.J. (1997) *In Defence of History*, London: Granta Books.

— (2002) *Telling Lies About Hitler. The Holocaust, History and the David Irving Trial*, London and New York: Verso.

Fackenheim, E. (1978) 'The 614th Commandment', In: *The Jewish Return to History. Reflections in the Age of Auschwitz and a New Jerusalem*, New York: Schocken Books.

— (1994) *To Mend the World. Foundations of Post-Holocaust Jewish Thought*, Midland Books, Bloomington and Indianapolis: Indiana U.P.*

Farge, A. (1997) *Le goût de l'archive*, Coll. Points, Paris: Seuil.

Fernández-Armesto, F. (2002) 'Epilogue: What is History Now?', In: *What is History Now?*, Ed. D. Cannadine, London: Palgrave Macmillan.

Feyerabend, P. (1988) *Against Method* (Revised Edition), London and New York: Verso.

Fichte, J.G. (1970) *Grundlage der gesamten Wissenschaftslehre als Handschrift für seine Zuhörer (1794)*, Ed. W.G. Jacobs, Philosophische Bibliothek, Hamburg: Felix Meiner.

Finkielkraut, A. (1989) *La mémoire vaine. Du crime contre l'humanité*, Paris: Gallimard/Folio.

Fish, S. (1999) *Professional Correctness. Literary Studies and Political Change*, Cambridge, MA and London.

Fitzgerald, I. and Hodgkinson, S. (1994) 'British University History Now', In: *History Today* 44: 53–7.

Flaubert, G. (1961) *Salammbô*, Ed. É. Maynial, Classiques Garnier, Paris: Garnier Frères.

Fleck, L. (1983) *Erfahrung und Tatsache. Gesammelte Aufsätze*, Eds L. Schäfer and T. Schnelle, Frankfurt am Main: Suhrkamp Taschenbuch Wissenschaft.*

— (1999) *Entstehung und Entwicklung einer wissenschaftlichen Tatsache. Einführung in die Lehre vom Denkstil und Denkkollektiv*, Eds L. Schäfer and T. Schnelle, 4th ed., Frankfurt am Main: Suhrkamp Taschenbuch Wissenschaft.*

Foucault, M. (1975) *Surveiller et punir. Naissance de la prison*, Paris: NRF/Gallimard.

— (1983) *Naissance de la Clinique. Une archéologie du regard médical*, 5th ed., Paris: P.U.F.

— (2001) *Dits et écrits 1954–1988*, Eds D. Defert, F. Ewald, and J. Lagrange, 2 vols, Paris: Gallimard/Quarto.

Frank, T. (1998) *The Conquest of Cool. Business Culture, Counterculture, and the Rise of Hip Consumerism* (pb. ed.), Chicago and London: Chicago U.P.

— (2001) *One Market Under God. Extreme Capitalism, Market Populism, and the End of Economic Democracy*, London: Secker & Warburg.

— (2002) *New Consensus for Old. Cultural Studies from Left to Right*, Chicago: Prickly Paradigm Press.

Freud, S. (1973) *Massenpsychologie und Ich-Analyse*, Frankfurt am Main: Fischer Taschenbuch.

— (1977) *Das Unbehagen in der Kultur*, In: *Abriß der Psychoanalyse/Das Unbehagen in der Kultur*. Mit einem Nachwort von Thomas Mann, Frankfurt am Main: Fischer Taschenbuch.

— (1981) *Der Mann Moses und die monotheistische Religion. Schriften über die Religion*, Frankfurt am Main: Fischer Taschenbuch.

— (1982) *Das Ich und das Es und andere metapsychologische Schriften*, Frankfurt am Main: Fischer Taschenbuch.

— (1986) *Hemmung, Symptom und Angst*, Frankfurt am Main: Fischer Taschenbuch.

— (1987) *Zur Psychopathologie des Alltagslebens. Über Vergessen, Versprechen, Vergreifen, Aberglauben und Irrtum*. Mit einem Vorwort von A. Mitscherlich, Frankfurt am Main: Fischer Taschenbuch.

Freud, S. and Breuer, J. (1975) *Studien über Hysterie*, Frankfurt am Main: Fischer Taschenbuch.

Fukuyama, F. (1992) *The End of History and the Last Man*, London: Hamish Hamilton.

Fulbrook, M. (2002) *Historical Theory*, London: Routledge.

Gadamer, H.-G. (1975) *Wahrheit und Methode. Grundzüge einer Philosophischen Hermeneutik*, 4th ed., Tübingen: J.C.B. Mohr (Paul Siebeck).

Gardiner, P. (1968) *The Nature of Historical Explanation*, Galaxy Book Edition, New York: O.U.P.*

Gasché, R. (1990) 'Of Aesthetic and Historical Determination' in *Post-Structuralism and the Question of History*, Eds D. Attridge, G. Bennington and R. Young (pb. reprint), Cambridge: C.U.P.

Gay, P. (1979) *Freud, Jews and Other Germans. Masters and Victims in Modernist Culture* (pb. ed.), New York: O.U.P.

— (1985) *Freud for Historians*, New York: O.U.P.

— (1988) *Style in History*, New York and London: W.W. Norton.

Ginzburg, C. (1999) *History, Rhetoric and Proof*, Hanover and London: U.P. of New England.

Goodman, N. (1988a) *Ways of Worldmaking*, 5th Printing, Indianapolis: Hackett Publishing Company.*

— (1988b) *Languages of Art. An Approach to Theory of Symbols*, 2nd ed., 6th Printing, Indianapolis: Hackett Publishing Company, Inc.*

Graetz, H. (2000) *Die Konstruktion der jüdischen Geschichte*, Ed. N. Römer, Düsseldorf: Parerga.

Gray, C.H., Figueroa-Sarriera, H.J. and Mentor, S. (Eds) (1995) *The Cyborg Handbook*, New York and London: Routledge.

Gray, J. (1995) *Enlightenment's Wake. Politics and Culture at the Close of the Modern Age*, London: Routledge.

Guttenplan, D.D. (2002) *The Holocaust on Trial. History, Justice and the David Irving Libel Case* (With a New Afterword by the Author), London: Granta.

Habermas, J. (1973) *Technik und Wissenschaft als Ideologie*, 6th ed., Frankfurt am Main: Edition Suhrkamp.

— (1988) *Nachmetaphysisches Denken. Philosophische Aufsätze*, 2nd ed., Frankfurt am Main: Suhrkamp Verlag.

Hacking, I. (2002) *Historical Ontology*, Cambridge, MA and London: Harvard U.P.

Halbwachs, M. (1994) *Les cadres sociaux de la mémoire*, Postface de G. Namer, Paris: Albin Michel.*

Handke, P. (1980) *Die Lehre der Sainte-Victoire*, Frankfurt am Main: Suhrkamp.

Hartman, G. (1996) *The Longest Shadow. In the Aftermath of the Holocaust*, Bloomington and Indianapolis: Indiana U.P.

Harvey, D. (1990) *The Condition of Postmodernity. An Enquiry into the Origins of Cultural Change* (Reprint), Oxford and Cambridge: Basil Blackwell.

Hassan, I. (1984) *Paracriticisms: Seven Speculations of the Times* (Illini Books Edition), Urbana and Chicago: Illinois U.P.

Hegel, G.W.F. (1961) *Vorlesungen über die Philosophie der Geschichte*. Mit einer Einführung von Theodor Litt, Stuttgart: Philipp Reclam Jun.

— (1967) *Grundlinien der Philosophie des Rechts*, Philosophische Bibliothek, 4th ed., Hamburg: Felix Meiner.

— (1979) 'Phänomenologie des Geistes', In: *Werke*, Theorie Werkausgabe, Eds K. Moldenhauer and K. Michel, vol. III, 20 vols, Frankfurt am Main: Suhrkamp.

Heidegger, M. (1967a) 'Die Frage nach der Technik', In: *Vorträge und Aufsätze I*, 3rd ed., Pfullingen: Neske.*

— (1967b) 'Wissenschaft und Besinnung', In: *Vorträge und Aufsätze I*.*

— (1972) *Holzwege*, 5th ed., Frankfurt am Main: Vittorio Klostermann.

Heisenberg, W. (1971) *Der Teil und das Ganze. Gespräche im Umkreis der Atomphysik*, Munich: R. Piper & Co. Vlg.

Heller, A. (1984) *Everyday Life* (Trans. G.L. Campbell), London and New York: Routledge & Kegan Paul.*

— (1987) *Radical Philosophy* (Trans. J. Wickham, pb. ed.), Oxford: Basil Blackwell.*

Henry, T. (1972) 'On the Advantages of Literature and Philosophy in General, and Especially on the Consistency of Literary and Philosophical with Commercial Pursuits', In: *Twenty Essays on Literary and Philosophical Subjects* [1791] (Reprographic Reprint), Eds T. Henry, and others, New York: Garland Publishing, Inc.

Herzl, T. (1996) *Der Judenstaat. Versuch einer modernen Lösung der Judenfrage*. Mit einem Nachwort von H.M. Broder, Augsburg: Ölbaum Vlg.

Hesiod (1995) *Works and Days*, in *Homeric Hymns, Epic Cycle, Homerica* (Trans. H.G. Evelyn-White, Loeb Classical Library), Cambridge, MA, and London: Harvard U.P.

Hessen, S. (1909) *Individuelle Kausalität. Studien zum transzendentalen Empirismus*, "Kantstudien". Ergänzungshefte im Auftrag der Kantgesellschaft, Eds H. Vaihinger and B. Bauch, Berlin: Reuther & Reichard.

Hitchens, C. (1998) 'Goodbye to All that. Why Americans are not Taught History', *Harper's Magazine* 297, 1782: 27–47.

Hobsbawm, E. (1995) *The Age of Extremes. The Short Twentieth Century 1914–1991*, London: Abacus.

Hödl, S. and Lappin, E. (2000) *Erinnerung als Gegenwart. Jüdische Gedenkkulturen*, Berlin and Vienna: Philo Verlag.

Hölderlin, F. (1946) *Sämtliche Werke*, Ed. F. Beissner, 7 vols, Stuttgart: J.G. Cottasche Nachfolger/W. Kohlhammer Verlag.

Horkheimer, M. (1974) *Notizen 1950 bis 1969 und Dämmerung: Notizen in Deutschland*, Eds A. Schmidt and W. Brede, Frankfurt am Main: Fischer.

— (1976) 'Die gesellschaftliche Funktion der Philosophie', In: *Die gesellschaftliche Funktion der Philosophie. Ausgewählte Essays*, 2nd ed., Frankfurt am Main: Bibliothek Suhrkamp.*

Horkheimer, M. and Adorno, T.W. (1973) *Dialektik der Aufklärung. Philosophische Fragmente*, Frankfurt am Main: Fischer Taschenbuch.

Hufton, O. (2002) 'What is Religious History Now?', In: *What is History Now?*, Ed. D. Cannadine, London: Palgrave Macmillan.

Hughes, H.S. (1975) *History as Art and as Science. Twin Vistas on the Past*, Midway Reprint Chicago: University of Chicago Press.

Hume, D. (1971) *Essays Moral, Political and Literary*, The World's Classics, Oxford: O.U.P.

Huntington, S.P. (1998) *The Clash of Civilizations and the Remaking of World Order*, London: Simon & Schuster/Touchstone.

Iser, W. (1972) *Der implizite Leser*, Uni-Taschenbücher, Munich: W. Fink Verlag.

James, C. (1992) *The Dreaming Swimmer. Non-Fiction 1987–1992*, London: Jonathan Cape.

Jameson, F. (1988) *The Ideologies of Theory. Essays 1971–1986. Volume 1: Situations of Theory*, London: Routledge.

Jaspers, K. (1948) *Der philosophische Glaube*, Munich: R. Piper & Co.

— (1958) *Rechenschaft und Ausblick. Reden und Aufsätze*, Munich: R. Piper & Co.

— (1967) *Way to Wisdom. An Introduction to Philosophy* (Trans. R. Mannheim, 9th Printing), New Haven and London: Yale U.P.

Jencks, C. (1989) *What is Post-Modernism?*, 3rd ed., London: Academy Editions; New York: St. Martins Press.

Jenkins, K. (1995) *On 'What is History?' From Carr and Elton to Rorty and White*, London and New York: Routledge.

— (Ed.) (1997) *The Postmodern History Reader*, London and New York: Routledge.

— (1999) *Why History? Ethics and Postmodernity*, London and New York: Routledge.

— (2003) *Refiguring History. New Thoughts on an Old Discipline*, London and New York: Routledge.

Johnson, B.S. (1973) *Aren't You Rather Young to be Writing your Memoirs?* London: Hutchinson.

Johnston, P. (2003) '257 predecessors Going Back 1400 years Include Saints and a Queen', *The Daily Telegraph*, June, 13: 4.

Joll. J. (1994) *The Origins of the First World War*, 2nd ed., 4th Impression, London and New York: Longmans.

Jordanova, L. (2000) *History in Practice*, London: Arnold.

Joyce, P. (1997a) 'History and Postmodernism', In: *The Postmodern History Reader*, Ed. K. Jenkins, London and New York: Routledge.

— (1997b) 'The End of Social History?', In: *The Postmodern History Reader*, Ed. K. Jenkins, London and New York: Routledge.

Kafka, F. (1983) *Sämtliche Erzählungen*, Ed. P. Raabe, Frankfurt am Main: Fischer Taschenbücher.

Kant, I. (1968) *Kritik der Urteilskraft*, Ed. K. Vorländer, Philosophische Bibliothek, Hamburg: Felix Meiner.

— (1971) *Kritik der reinen Vernunft*, Ed. R. Schmidt, Philosophische Bibliothek, Hamburg: Felix Meiner.

— (1977) *Werkausgabe*, Ed. W. Weischedel, 12 vols, Frankfurt am Main: Suhrkamp Taschenbuch Wissenschaft.

Kermode, F. (1980) *The Genesis of Secrecy. On the Interpretation of Narrative*, 3rd Printing, Cambridge, MA and London: Harvard U.P.*

Kierkegaard, S. (1967) *The Concept of Dread* (Translated with Introduction and Notes by Walter Lowrie), 2nd ed., Princeton: Princeton U.P.

Kracauer, S. (1969) *History. The Last Things Before the Last*, New York: O.U.P.*

Krauss, R. (1988) 'The Im/Pulse To See', In: *Vision and Visuality*, Ed. H. Foster, Seattle: Bay Press, 51–75.

Kristeva, J. (1983) *Histoires d'amour*, Paris: Denoël.

Krumreich, G. (1994) 'Tannenberg, la revanche et le mythe', *Le Monde*, No.15394, 26 July.

Lacan, J. (1966) *Écrits*, Paris: Éditions du Seuil.

LaCapra, D. (1996) *History & Criticism*, 4th Printing, Ithaca and London: Cornell U.P.

Laplanche, J. and Pontalis, J.-B.(1990) *Vocabulaire de la Psychanalyse*, 10th ed., Paris: P.U.F.

Leibniz, G.W. (1962) *Essais de Théodicée sur la bonté de Dieu, la liberté de l'homme et l'origine du mal. Suivi de la Monadologie* (Préface et notes de J. Jalabert), Paris: Aubier/Éditions Montaigne.

— (1992) 'Betrachtungen über die Erkenntnis, die Wahrheit und die Ideen', In: *Philosophische Schriften und Briefe 1683–1687*, Ed. U. Goldenbaum, Berlin: Akademie Verlag.

Lemonick, M. and Dorfman, A. (2002) 'Father of Us All?', *Time* 160, 4: 46–53.

Lerner, G. (1997) *Why History Matters. Life and Thought*, New York and Oxford: O.U.P.

Lessing, T. (1981) *Die verfluchte Kultur. Gedanken über den Gegensatz von Leben und Geist* (Mit einem Essay von Elisabeth Lenk), Munich: Matthes & Seitz.

— (1983) *Geschichte als Sinngebung des Sinnlosen* (Mit einem Nachwort von Rita Bischof), Munich: Matthes & Seitz.*

— (1984) *Der jüdische Selbsthass* (Mit einem essay von Boris Groys), Munich: Matthes & Seitz.

— (1985) *Nietzsche* (Mit einem Nachwort von Rita Bischof), Munich: Matthes & Seitz.

Levinas, E. (1972) *Humanisme de l'autre homme*, Paris: Fata Morgana/Livre de Poche: biblio/essais.

— (1984) *Difficile liberté. Essais sur le judaïsme*, 3rd ed., Paris: Albin Michel/ Livre de Poche: biblio/essais.

— (1991) *Entre nous. Essais sur le penser-à-l'autre*, Coll. Figures, Paris: Bernard Grasset.

Lévi-Strauss, C. (1985) *La Pensée sauvage*, Collection Agora, Paris: Plon.

Lotman Y. (2001) *Universe of the Mind. A Semiotic Theory of Culture* (Introduction by Umberto Eco), London and New York: I.B. Tauris.

Lowenthal, D. (1993) *The Past is a Foreign Country*, Cambridge: C.U.P.*

Lukács, G. (1976) *Geschichte und Klassenbewußtsein* (pb. ed.), Darmstadt and Neuwied: Luchterhand.

Lyotard, J.-F. (1979) *La Condition Postmoderne*, Paris: Minuit.

McCullagh, C.B. (1998) *The Truth of History*, London and New York: Routledge.

— (2004) *The Logic of History. Putting Postmodernism in Perspective*, London and New York: Routledge.

MacGregor, N. (2004) 'In the Shadow of Babylon', *The Guardian*, June, 14: 18.

Maistre, J. de (1980) *Les Soirées de Saint-Petersbourg ou entretiens sur le gouvernement temporel de la Providence, suivies De la traduction d'un Traité de Plutarque sur les délais de la justice divine*, 2 vols, Paris: Éditions de la Maisne.

Mann, H. (1976) *Ein Zeitalter wird besichtigt*, Hamburg: Rowohlt Taschenbuch.

Marcuse, H. (1973) 'Über den affirmativen Begriff der Kultur', In: *Kultur und Gesellschaft I*, 11th ed., Frankfurt am Main: Edition Suhrkamp.*

— (1986) *One-Dimensional Man. Studies in the Ideology of Advanced Industrial Society*, London: Ark Paperbacks.*

Marin, L. (1978) *Le Récit est un piège*, Paris: Les Éditions de Minuit.*

Markus, G. (1987) 'Why Is There No Hermeneutics of Natural Sciences? Some Preliminary Theses', *Science in Context* 1, 1: 5–51.

Marquard, O. (1982) *Schwierigkeiten mit der Geschichtsphilosophie*, Frankfurt am Main: Suhrkamp Taschenbuch Wissenschaft.

— (1986), *Apologie des Zufälligen. Philosophische Studien*, Stuttgart: Reclam.

Marrus, M.R. (1993) *The Holocaust in History*, Harmondsworth: Penguin Books.

Marwick, A. (2001) *The New Nature of History. Knowledge, Evidence, Language*, Basingstoke: Palgrave.

Marx, K. (1968) *Die Frühschriften*, Ed. S. Landshut, Stuttgart: Alfred Kröner.

— (1981) *Zur Kritik der Nationalökonomie — Ökonomisch-philosophische Manuskripte*, In: *Werke*. 4 vols., Ed. Joachim Lieber, 4th ed., Darmstadt: Wissenschaftliche Buchgesellschaft.

Matthews, P. and McQuain, J. (2003) *The Bard on the Brain*, London: Dana Press.

Meinecke, F. (1936) *Die Entstehung des Historismus*, 2 vols, Munich and Berlin: R. Oldenbourg.

Menand, L. (2003) 'Foreword', In: E. Wilson, *To the Finland Station. A Study in the Writing and Acting of History*, New York: New York Review of Books.

Merleau-Ponty, M. (1990) *La structure du Comportement* [1942], Coll. Quadrige, Paris: P.U.F.*

— (1995) *Phénomenologie de la Perception*, Coll. Tel Quel, Paris: Gallimard.*

— (1996) *Le primat de la perception et ses conséquences philosophiques*, Paris: Éditions Verdier.

Miller, H. (1962) *The Time of the Assassins. A Study of Rimbaud*, 15th Printing, New York: New Directions Books.

Mills, C.W. (1970) *The Sociological Imagination*, Harmondsworth: Pelican Books.

von Mises, R. (1990) *Kleines Lehrbuch des Positivismus. Einleitung in die empirische Wissenschaftsauffassung*, Ed. F. Stadler, Frankfurt am Main: Suhrkamp Taschenbuch Wissenschaft.

Monbiot, G. 'Out of the Wreckage', *The Guardian*, 25 February 2003: 19.

Morin, E. (1976) *L'homme et la mort*, Coll. Points, Paris: Seuil.

— (1986) *La Méthode: 3. La Connaissance de la Connaissance. Anthropologie de la Connaissance*, Paris: Seuil.*

— (1999) *Introduction à une politique de l'homme*, Coll. Points, Paris: Seuil.

Montaigne, M. de (1964), *Essais*, Eds A. Lheritier and M. Butor, Coll. 10/18, 4 vols, Paris: U.G.E.

Montesquieu (1949) 'Mes Pensées', In: *Œuvres Complètes: I*, Ed. R. Caillois, Paris: Gallimard.

Mumford, L. (1963) *Technics and Civilization* (Harvest Edition), San Diego, New York and London: Harcourt Brace & Company.

— (2000) *Art and Technics* (With a new introduction by C.N. Blake), New York: Columbia U.P.

Munslow, A. (1997) *Deconstructing History*, London and New York: Routledge.

— (2003) *The New History*, Harlow: Pearson Education Ltd.

Myers, D.N. (2002), 'Selbstreflexion im modernen Erinnerungsdiskurs', In: *Jüdische Geschichtsschreibung heute. Themen, Positionen, Kontroversen*, Eds M. Brenner and D.N. Myers, Munich: C.H. Beck, 55–74.

Nägele, R. (1987) *Reading after Freud. Essays on Goethe, Hölderlin, Habermas, Nietzsche, Brecht, Celan, and Freud*, New York: Columbia U.P.

Negt, O. and Kluge, A. (1993) *Geschichte und Eigensinn*, Frankfurt am Main: Edition Suhrkamp.*

Neurath, O. (1994) 'Einheit der Wissenschaft als Aufgabe', In: *Otto Neurath oder die Einheit von Wissenschaft und Gesellschaft*, Eds P. Neurath and E. Nemeth. Vienna, Cologne, Weimar: Böhlau Vlg.

Neustadt, R.E. and May, R.E. (1988) *Thinking in Time. The Uses of History for Decision-Makers*, New York: The Free Press.

Niethammer, L. (1989) *Posthistoire. Ist die Geschichte zu Ende?*, Hamburg: Rowohlt Taschenbuch.

Nietzsche, F. (1956) *Werke*, Ed. K. Schlechta, 3 vols, Munich: Carl Hanser Verlag.*

— (1988) *Kritische Studienausgabe*, Eds G. Colli and M. Montinari, (2nd Revised Edition), 15 vols, Berlin and New York: Walter de Gruyter, Munich: DTV.

Nish, I. (1985) *The Origins of the Russo-Japanese Wars*, London and New York: Longman.

Nora, P. (1984) 'Entre Mémoire et Histoire. La problématique des lieux', In: *Les Lieux de Mémoire I: La République*, Paris: Gallimard.*

— (1986) *Les Lieux de Mémoire II: La Nation*, 3 vols, Paris: Gallimard.

— (1994) *Les Lieux de Mémoire III: Les France*, 3 vols, Paris: Gallimard.

Nowotny, H. (1995) *Eigenzeit: Entstehung und Strukturierung eines Zeitgefühls*, 2nd ed., Frankfurt am Main: Suhrkamp Taschenbuch Wissenschaft.

Oakeshott, M. (1991) 'The Activity of Being an Historian', In: *Rationalism in Politics and Other Essays* (Foreword by T. Fuller), Indianapolis: Liberty Fund, Inc.

— (1999) *On History and Other Essays* (Foreword by T. Fuller), Indianapolis: Liberty Fund, Inc.

Oakley, D.A., Whitman, L.G. and Halligan, P.W. (2002) 'Hypnotic Imagery as a Treatment for Phantom Limb Pain', *Clinical Rehabilitation* 16: 368–77.

Ortega y Gasset, J. (1962) *History as a System and other Essays: Toward a Philosophy of History*, Ed. J. W. Miller, New York and London: W.W. Norton & Company.

— (1964) *The Revolt of the Masses*, New York and London: W.W. Norton & Company.

Orwell, G. (2001) *Inside the Whale and Other Essays*, Harmondsworth: Penguin Classics.

Ovendale, R. (1992) *The Origins of the Arab-Israeli Wars*, 2nd ed., London and New York: Longman.

Pascal, B. (1963) *Œuvres complètes*. Préface d'Henri Gouhier, Présentation de Louis Lafuma, Coll. l'Intégrale, Paris: Seuil.

Pater, W. (1971) *The Renaissance. Studies in Art and Poetry* 3rd Impression, (Introduction and Notes by Kenneth Clark), London: Fontana/Collins.

Patlagean, E. (1988) 'Histoire de l'imaginaire', In: *La Nouvelle Histoire*, Ed. J. Le Goff, Paris: Éditions complexe.

Pedersen, S. (2002) 'What is Political History Now?', In:, *What is History Now?*, Ed. D. Cannadine, London: Palgrave Macmillan.

Péguy, C. (1961) *Œuvres en Prose 1909–1914*, Ed. M. Péguy, Bibliothèque de la Pléiade, Paris: Gallimard.*

Plumb, J.H. (1973) *The Death of the Past*, Harmondsworth: Pelican Books.

Pollard, J. (2003) *The Seven Ages of Britain* (With a foreword by Bettany Hughes), London: Hodder & Stoughton.

Pomian, K. (1999) *Sur l'histoire*, Coll. folio/histoire, Paris: Éditions Gallimard.

Popper, K. (1974) *The Poverty of Historicism* (pb. ed.), London: Routledge & Kegan Paul.*

— (1979) *Objective Knowledge. An Evolutionary Approach* (Revised Edition), Oxford: Clarendon Press.

— (2002) 'Die Logik der Sozialwissenschaften', In: *Auf der Suche nach einer besseren Welt. Vorträge und Aufsätze aus dreißig Jahren*, 11th ed. Munich: Piper Vlg.

— (2003) *The Open Society and its Enemies*, 2 vols, Routledge Classics, London: Routledge.

Postman, N. (1993) *Technopoly. The Surrender of Culture to Technology*, New York: Vintage Books.

Pound, E. (1968) *The ABC of Reading* (Faber Paper Covered Editions), London: Faber & Faber.

Rabinow, P. (1996) 'Representations Are Social Facts: Modernity and Postmodernity in Anthropology', In: *Essays on the Anthropology of Reason*, Princeton, N.J.: Princeton U.P.

Ramachandran, V.S. and Hirstein, W. (1998) 'The Perception of Phantom Limbs', *Brain* 121: 1603–30.

Rathenau, W. (1918) *Zur Kritik der Zeit*, 13–15th ed., Berlin: S. Fischer.

Readings, B. (1997) *The University in Ruins*, 2nd Printing, Cambridge, MA and London: Harvard U.P.

Reber, A.S. (1987) *The Penguin Dictionary of Psychology*, Harmondsworth: Penguin Books.

Richter, J.P.F. (1970) *Hesperus* [1795], In: *Sämtliche Werke*, vol. II, Ed. N. Miller, Munich: Carl Hanser.

Ricœur, P. (1964) *Histoire et vérité*, 3rd ed., Paris: Seuil.

— (1983/1985) *Temps et récit*, 3 vols, Paris: Seuil

— (1994) 'History and Rhetoric', In: *The Social Responsibility of the Historian*, Ed. F. Bédarida, Providence and Oxford: Berghahn Books.

— (2000) *La Mémoire, L'Histoire, L'Oubli*, Paris: Seuil.

Rose, G., (1992) *The Broken Middle. Out of our Ancient Society*, Oxford: Blackwell.

— (1994) *Judaism & Modernity. Philosophical Essays*, Oxford: Basil Blackwell.

Rosenzweig, F. (1996) *Der Stern der Erlösung*, 5th ed., Frankfurt am Main: Bibliothek Suhrkamp.

— (2001) *Zweistromland*, Ed. G. Palmer, Berlin and Vienna: Philo.

Rousseau, J.-J. (1959) *Discours sur l'origine et les fondements de l'inégalité parmi les hommes* (1755), In: *Œuvres complètes*, vol. 3, Eds B. Gagnebin and M. Raymond, Bibliothèque de la Pléiade, Paris: Gallimard.

Roy, A. (2002) *The Algebra of Infinite Justice*, Flamingo Edition: London HarperCollins.

Rubinstein, H.L., Cohn-Sherbok, D., Edelheit, E.J. and Rubinstein, W. (2002) *The Jews in the Modern World. A History since 1750*, London: Arnold.

Rüsen, J. (1990) *Zeit und Sinn. Strategien historischen Denkens*, Frankfurt am Main: Fischer Wissenschaft.

Russell, R. (1998) 'Museums for Mantelpieces', *The Independent: Your Money* Section, March 14: 12.

Said, E. (1994) *Representations of the Intellectual. The 1993 Reith Lectures*, London: Vintage.

Samuel, R. (1994) *Theatres of Memory. Volume 1: Past and Present in Contemporary Culture*, London and New York: Verso.

Sartre, J.-P. (1972) *Plaidoyer pour les intellectuels*, Coll. Idées, Paris: Gallimard.

Scarry, E. (1985) *The Body in Pain. The Making and Unmaking of the World*, New York and Oxford: O.U.P.*

Schlanger, J. (1994) *Gestes de philosophes. Essai*, Paris: Aubier.

Schlegel, F. (1972) 'Athenäums-Fragmente', In: *Schriften zur Literatur*, Ed. W. Rasch, Munich: DTV.

Schlick, M. (1986) *Philosophische Logik*, Ed. B. Philippi, Frankfurt am Main: Suhrkamp Taschenbuch Wissenschaft.

Schmidt-Biggemann, W. (1991) *Geschichte als absoluter Begriff. Der Lauf der neueren deutschen Philosophie*, Frankfurt am Main: Suhrkamp.*

Schnädelbach, H. (2000) '"Sinn" in der Geschichte? — Über Grenzen des Historismus', In: *Philosophie in der Modernen Kultur*, Frankfurt am Main: Suhrkamp Taschenbuch Wissenschaft.

Scholem, G. (1992) *Walter Benjamin und sein Engel*, Frankfurt am Main: Suhrkamp Taschenbuch.

— (1995) *Judaica 2*, Frankfurt am Main: Suhrkamp.

Schorske, C.E. (1999) *Thinking with History. Explorations in the Passage to Modernism* (pb. ed.), Princeton: Princeton U.P.

Sebald, W.G. (2002) *Luftangriff und Literatur*, 2nd ed., Frankfurt am Main: Fischer.

Seidenberg, R. (1950) *Posthistoric Man. An Inquiry*, Chapel Hill: University of North Carolina Press.

Sennett, R. (1999) *The Corrosion of Character. The Personal Consequences of Work in the New Capitalism*, New York and London: W.W. Norton & Company.

Sheehan, J.J. (1994) *German History 1770–1866* (pb. ed.), Oxford: Clarendon Press.

Showalter, E. (1997) *Hystories. Hysterical Epidemics in Modern Culture*, London: Picador.

Simmel, G. (1989) 'Zur Psychologie des Geldes', In: *Aufsätze 1887–1890: Gesamtausgabe Band 2*, Ed. H-J Dahme, Frankfurt am Main: Suhrkamp Taschenbuch Wissenschaft.

— (1997) *Die Probleme der Geschichtsphilosophie. Eine erkenntnistheoretische Studie* [1905/1907], In: *Gesamtausgabe Band 9*, Eds G. Oakes and K. Röttgers, Frankfurt am Main: Suhrkamp Taschenbuch Wissenschaft.

— (1999) 'Vom Wesen des historischen Verstehens', In: *Gesamtausgabe Band 16*, Ed. G. Fitzi and O. Rammstedt, Frankfurt am Main: Suhrkamp Taschenbuch Wissenschaft.*

Sloterdijk, P. (1983) *Kritik der zynischen Vernunft*, 2 vols, Frankfurt am Main: Edition Suhrkamp.

— (1995) *Im selben Boot. Versuch über die Hyperpolitik*, Frankfurt am Main: Suhrkamp Taschenbuch.

— (2000) *Die Verachtung der Massen. Versuch über Kulturkämpfe in der modernen Gesellschaft*, Frankfurt am Main: Edition Suhrkamp.*

Smith, A. (1982) *The Theory of Moral Sentiments*, Eds D.D. Raphael and A.L. Macfie, Indianapolis: Liberty Classics.

Sohn-Rethel, A. (1978) *Warenform und Denkform. Mit zwei Anhängen*, Frankfurt am Main: Edition Suhrkamp.*

— (1985) *Soziologische Theorie der Erkenntnis*. Mit einem Vorwort von J. Hörisch, Frankfurt am Main: Edition Suhrkamp.*

— (1989) *Geistige und körperliche Arbeit. Zur Epistemologie der abendländischen Geschichte* (Revised Edition), Weinheim: VCH, Acta humaniora.

Solso, R. (1994) *Cognition and the Visual Arts*, Cambridge, MA and London: The MIT Press.*

Sontag, S. (1986) 'Fragments of an Aesthetic of Melancholy', In: *Veruschka: Transfigurations*, Eds V. Lehndorff, and H. Trülzsch, London: Thames & Hudson.

— (1991) *Styles of Radical Will*, Anchor Books Edition, New York: Doubleday.*

Sorel, G. (1981) *Réflexions sur la violence*, Paris and Geneva: Slatkine.

Southgate, B. (1996) *History: What & Why? Ancient, Modern and Postmodern Perspectives*, London: Routledge.

— (2000) *Why Bother with History? Ancient, Modern and Postmodern Motivations*, Harlow: Pearson Education Ltd.

— (2003) *Postmodernism in History. Fear or Freedom?* London and New York: Routledge.

Spengler, O. (1977) *Der Untergang des Abendlandes. Umrisse einer Morphologie der Weltgeschichte*, 4th ed., Munich: DTV.

Sperber, D. (1996) *Explaining Culture. A Naturalistic Approach*, Oxford: Blackwell.*

Spinosa, C., Flores, F., and Dreyfus, H.L. (1997) *Disclosing New Worlds. Entrepreneurship, Democratic Action, and the Cultivation of Solidarity*, 3rd Printing, Cambridge, MA and London: MIT Press.

Starobinski, J. (1989) *La mélancolie au miroir. Trois lectures de Baudelaire*, Paris: Julliard.

Steiner, G. (1971) *In Bluebeard's Castle. Some Notes Towards the Re-definition of Culture*, London: Faber & Faber.*

— (1975) *Extraterritorial. Papers on Literature and the Language Revolution*, Harmondsworth: Peregrine Books.

— (1979) *Language and Silence. Essays 1958–1966*, Harmondsworth: Peregrine Books.

— (1989) *Real Presences. Is there Anything in what we say?* London and Boston: Faber & Faber.

— (1997a) *No Passion Spent. Essays 1978–1996* (pb. ed.), London: Faber.

— (1997b) *Errata: An Examined Life*, London: Weidenfeld & Nicholson.

— (2001) *Grammars of Creation*, London: Faber.

Sufka, K.J. (2000) 'Chronic Pain Explained', *Brain and Mind*, 1: 155–79.

Tarde, G. de (1993) *Les Lois de l'Imitation* (Présentation de B. Karsenti), Paris: Éditions Kimé.*

Taylor, A.J.P. (1979) 'The Thirties', In: *Thirties. British Art and Design before the War. Hayward Gallery 25 October 1979–13 January 1980*, London: Arts Council of Great Britain.

Todorov, T. (1970) *Introduction à la littérature fantastique*, Paris: Seuil.

Tosh, J. (1999) *The Pursuit of History*, 3rd ed., The Silver Library, London: Longman.

Toulmin, S. (1992) *Cosmopolis. The Hidden Agenda of Modernity*, Chicago: Chicago U.P.*

— (2001) *Return to Reason*, Cambridge, MA and London: Harvard U.P.*

Tournier, M. (1979) *Le vent Paraclet*, Coll. Folio, Paris: Gallimard.

Trapp, R. (1995) 'Museum Pieces Dusted off for a New Market ...', *The Independent on Sunday: Business* Section, March 19: 14.

Trevelyan, G.M. (1941) 'The Present Position of History', In: *Clio, A Muse. And other Essays*, London: Longmans, Green and Co. Ltd.

Utley, A. (2002) 'Past Opens the Door to Fortune in Future', *The Times Higher Education Supplement*, November 15: 1, 12.

Valéry, P. (1957/1960), *Œuvres*, édition établie et annotée par Jean Hytier, Bibliothèque de la Pléiade, 2 vols, Paris: Gallimard.

Varela, F.J. (1999) *Ethical Know-How. Action, Wisdom, and Cognition*, Stanford, CA: Stanford U.P.*

Vattimo, G. (1990) *La Société Transparente*. (Trad. J.-P. Pisetta), Paris: Desclée de Brouwer.

Veyne, P. (1996) *Comment on écrit l'histoire*, Coll. Points, Paris: Seuil.

Vico, G. (1984) *The New Science of Giambattista Vico* (Unabridged Translation of the Third Edition (1744). Trans. T.G. Bergin and M.H. Frisch), Cornell Paperbacks, Ithaca and London: Cornell U.P.

Vincent, J. (1996) *An Intelligent Person's Guide to History* (Revised and Expanded Edition), London: Duckworth.

Virilio, P.(1984) *L'espace critique*, Paris: Christian Bourgois.

— (1988) *La machine de vision*, Paris: Galilée.

Vital, D. (1999) *A People Apart. The Jews in Europe 1789–1939*, Oxford: O.U.P.

Volkov, S. (2001) *Das jüdische Projekt der Moderne*, Munich: C.H. Beck.

Warnock, M. (1976) *Imagination*, London: Faber.

Warren, J. (1999) *History and the Historians*, London: Hodder & Stoughton.

Weber, M. (1988) *Gesammelte Aufsätze zur Wissenschaftslehre*, Ed. J. Winckelmann, 8th ed., Tübingen: UTB / J.C.B. Mohr (Paul Siebeck).

Weiss, Y. (2002) 'Kann es zu viel Geschichte geben? Zur Diskussion über den Stellenwert des Holocaust in der neueren Geschichte', In: *Jüdische Geschichtsschreibung Heute*, Eds M. Brenner and D.N. Myers, Munich: C.H. Beck.

Wellmer, A. (1985) *Zur Dialektik von Moderne und Postmoderne. Vernunftkritik nach Adorno*, Frankfurt am Main: Suhrkamp Taschenbuch Wissenschaft.*

White, H. (1982) *Tropics of Discourse. Essays in Cultural Criticism*, 2nd Printing, Baltimore and London: Johns Hopkins U.P.

— (1985) *Metahistory. The Historical Imagination in Nineteenth-Century Europe*, 5th Printing, Baltimore and London: Johns Hopkins U.P.

— (1987) 'Droysen's *Historik*: Historical Writing as Bourgeois Science', In: *The Content of the Form. Narrative Discourse and Historical Representation*, Baltimore and London: Johns Hopkins U.P.

Wilkinson, P. (2000) *What the Romans Did For Us*, Ed. A. Hart-Davis, London: Boxtree/Macmillan.

Wilson, N.J. (1999) *History in Crisis? Recent Directions in Historiography*, Upper Saddle River: Prentice Hall.

Wollheim, R. (Ed.) (1966) *Hume on Religion*, The Fontana Library. Theology and Philosophy, London: Collins.

Wood, D. (1996) *Post-Intellectualism and the Decline of Democracy. The Failure of Reason and Responsibility in the Twentieth Century* (Foreword by N. Postman), Westport CT and London, Praeger.

Wrigley, C. (1994) 'Liking Local History', *The Historian*, 42: 2.

Xenophon (1979) *Memorabilia and Oeconomicus*, (Trans E.C. Marchant); *Symposium and Apology* (Trans. O.J. Todd, Loeb Classical Library), Cambridge, MA: Harvard U.P.; London: William Heinemann Ltd.

Yerushalmi, Y.H. (1996) *Zakhor. Jewish History and Jewish Memory* (Foreword by Harold Bloom, pb. ed.), Seattle and London: University of Washington Press.*

Zagorin, P. (1990) 'Historiography and Postmodernism: Reconsiderations', *History and Theory*, 29, 3: 263–74.

Zimmermann, M. (2000) 'Der Wettbewerb um die Erinnerung an die Shoa: Institutionen, Ideologien und Interessen', In: *Erinnerung als Gegenwart*.

Jüdische Gedenkkulturen, Eds S. Hödl and E. Lappin, Berlin and Vienna: Philo Verlag.

(Other Documents:)

AHRB (2004) *The Bright Path. The Strategy for Arts and Humanities Research in the UK 2004–2009*, Bristol: AHRB.
Ancestral Collections (Winter 2002), 22.
Department for Culture, Media and Sport (2001) *The Historic Environment: A Force for Our Future.*
English Heritage (2000) *Power of Place. The Future of the Historic Environment*, London.
— (2002) *The Heritage Dividend. Measuring the Results of Heritage Regeneration 1999–2002*, London.
Guide de Tourisme Alsace et Lorraine. Vosges (1986), Paris: Michelin.
Manners (Spring 2003).
Quality Assurance Agency for Higher Education (2000) *History Subject Benchmark Statement.*
The Daily Telegraph (June 13 2003) '*Blair's coup d'état*': 27.
The Guardian (June 13 2003) '*Revolution by reshuffle. Blair sweeps away 1400 years of tradition*': 29.
The Times Higher Educational Supplement, August 12 1994, '*History adapts to the modern marketplace*': 2.
Web: http://five.tv/factsheets/war/ (April 14 2004).
Web: http://www.aetv.com/global/corporate/index.jsp?NetwCode=AEN (February 16 2004).
Web: http://www.pbs.org/wgbh/amex/bomb/peopleevents/pandeAMEX65.html (November 8 2003).

Index

Printed in the United Kingdom
by Lightning Source UK Ltd.
108223UKS00001B/130-162